**pascALEjandro**

This book is published on the occasion of the eponymous exhibition organized by Galerie Azzedine Alaïa, Paris, between April 28th and July 9th, 2017.

# pascALEjandro

## Alchemical Androgynous

Edited by Donatien Grau

*ASSOCIATION AZZEDINE ALAÏA | ACTES SUD*

# Foreword

**Azzedine Alaïa**

"Yesterday is history; tomorrow is a mystery; today is a gift." This saying comes to mind for Pascale and Alejandro. They live in the present, like forces of nature: they are at home in any climate under the sun, right now.

I am delighted to present their collaborative creation pascALEjandro. The drawings and the colors go hand in hand. You would think they were made by a single person and not by two separate individuals. This shows the depth of Pascale and Alejandro's encounter, their mutual understanding: they are two persons who have fused into one. Their work has a vision, a prescience. They have created this world between themselves, according to their own rhythm. They don't go incessantly looking here and there: they carry on with their work in their own path, and they get where they are going, because they are strong. In their strength, they know what frailty is too. Through these drawings, they go very far in their love: in all its brutality, its modesty, its poetry. These drawings carry you off into a dream: you can't look at them in the same way as other paintings. Between earth and heaven, they show you a different vision.

I invited Pascale and Alejandro to show pascALEjandro in my gallery immediately after I met them. I felt I knew them from the very beginning. They are a part of what we are all doing here: they have become like family. I felt this, and I feel it now, as we share in their dream and their vision.

# Preface

**Edgar Morin**

Like a visitation of Plato's primordial androgyne, behold pascALEjandro: created in common by Pascale Montandon-Jodorowsky and Alejandro Jodorowsky. Alejandro, born in Chile, discovered at a very early age that he was a poet. On his own, he reached the same conclusion as the Surrealists halfway across the world: that poetry must not limit itself to poems, but must take shape in real life. He lived through encounters and experiences in which dreams became real and reality became the stuff of dreams. He put together wild parties. This existential and fanciful element has remained present throughout his work, though in gradually more controlled and seamless forms.

From the very beginning, he sought out the authentic life, the hidden truth, and this search has led him through a succession of initiation experiences: first he discovered Tarot and alchemy, then the astounding powers of a healer in Mexico who could perform life-saving operations on her patients' bodies with her bare hands. He himself became a therapeutic psychologist through psychomagic, treating a wide variety of ills by issuing conflicting commands; as he delved still deeper into the power of the occult forces that govern our lives, he discovered the shamanic sources of knowledge and action. He narrates this experience of life—this life of experience—in his book *The Dance of Reality.*

Jacob wrestled with the angel in a struggle that was at the same time an embrace. Alejandro experienced an extraordinary wrestling with the Great God Pan, which found voice in the word "Panic," the name of the collective he formed with Arrabal and Topor.

After a life of love and break-ups, he was blessed to meet Pascale Montandon, an artist; she, a scenographer who painted in shades of black and white, discovered color through him. And that is when, with her at his side for the work on the colors, he was able to make the cinematic masterpiece, *Poesía sin fin*, an assertion of mastery over his own destiny and a magnificent message to humanity. Now they hold their art and thought in common in these collaborative paintings, signed with the name of pascALEjandro, in which, as in Wagner's *Twilight*, all the overriding themes of a life and body of work return.

This fusion of two names into one—of a man filled with experience and a young woman giving herself entirely to their union, in which each turns out to resemble the other—demonstrates that love, always the rebellious child, is blind to differences of age, origin, ethnicity and nationality. It shows us that the richest and fullest harmony is possible when two beings come to form an indivisible entity.

Each painting bears the mark of one of Alejandro's obsessions or experiences: his major anthropological, oniric and magical themes make their appearances, but they only come into being thanks to Pascale's colors. Pascale appropriates Alejandro who appropriates Pascale: this double appropriation becomes a mutual gift that nurtures, and is nurtured by, pascALEjandro, a third reality. Behold the androgyne: two heads and a single heart.

# Preface

**Adonis**

This is a book of colors: not simply for the eye, but also for the imagination—a book which doesn't merely present a story but creates landscapes and horizons for our inner and outer sight, so that we can travel better, further into the depths of humanity and the hollows of the world.

This exhibition-book opposes itself to what impetuous humans did to the sky when they forced it to reveal answers to everything and anything the earth might ask. In doing so, they transformed the universe into a mere surface, into a set of banal doctrines, and they turned human beings into vessels to contain and preach these, to establish them as divine and definitive words, as ultimate truths.

And so this book transgresses these established doctrines, as if to give the sky a new shape and man a new size, by teaching the former how to vary infinitely and the latter how to greet the sun on the horizon as if he were the first person to lay eyes on it.

This exhibition-book is neither a link in a chain nor a piece of a puzzle. It is singular, rebellious, transgressive. That's why this book doesn't have a meaning behind it: the meaning is out ahead. It doesn't come from history; it comes from experience. The question this book raises, the creative dilemma, is this: How do you give form to a world that changes incessantly?

Infinite change imposes the artistic requirement of an infinite form. The form must not contain its subject, but rather allude to it. The essential thing is to disassemble what you see, to point to the invisible that lies behind it. It takes a kind of creative and lawless game for a man or a woman to be able to see the world.

Through this game, pascALEjandro affirms that reality does not consist in what our physical eye perceives, but rather in what our inner, clairvoyant eye envisions. Reality is thus a state of constant change, because it is a state of constant creation. This makes for a disconcerting aesthetic, based on the perpetual movement of shifting trajectories, discovery and flashes of insight.

In order to reveal and truly understand reality, we must see it not through perceived elements, but rather through all that hides behind, invisible. One might say that pascALEjandro's visual forms allow us to see the world as Alejandro himself once described it: "like a tree growing in the shape outlined by the songs of its birds."[1]

Thus we see how pascALEjandro's visual game goes beyond figuration: figuration is limited because it remains only surfaces, no matter how far it reaches. pascALEjandro's forms have a peculiar alphabet, halfway between the language of words and the language of lines and colors. It embodies the absent, the hidden, the invisible in a structure of lines and colors; it is neither surface, nor painting, nor speech, nor poem; it is rather a movement shuttling between these and elsewhere.

Take the lines and colors of this exhibition-book for as many flashing arrows, circling the heart of the night. One arrow pierces

1. *A l'ombre du Yi jing*, trad. Nelly and Alex Lhermillier, Le Relié, Paris, 2014, p.146.

that heart with a unique kind of game, with an invisible wound, like an incision made in air. Another arrow follows in the wake of the hoopoe that visited Solomon, keen to gaze on the Queen of Sheba now his guest. These lines and colors are poetic creations before they are visual creations: pascALEjandro unites them in a solar and lunar harmony. The meaning sends forth the sun; the imagination, the moon. So these lines and colors take on the seduction of light. They flash in the darkness of matter.

Reality, surreality, East, West, North, and South— all of these find equal place, identical twins at the breast of the universe.

In every work, there's a breath that whispers: Whoever looks on this, let him learn to doubt even his throat and tongue, and let him always attend to the portion recited on the day of his birth: man doesn't exist by what he is, but by what he will be.

Thus, the works of this exhibition-book speak to all of us, saying: "Forget—especially when you come to old age—everything except one thing: childhood. Childhood holds the only gaze that can see the universe beyond the eye." That's also why these works enjoin each artist: "Even in your great weariness, never stop to rest in the chair of memory. Inhale its perfume and always heed how the wind blows, especially when it rests its cheek on a rose's shoulder." Perhaps these works also say to each of us, whose thirst is never satisfied: "Always ask one question of the water: O flowing body, when are you at the height of your pleasure, when you run on a wild rock or when you touch a blade of grass?"

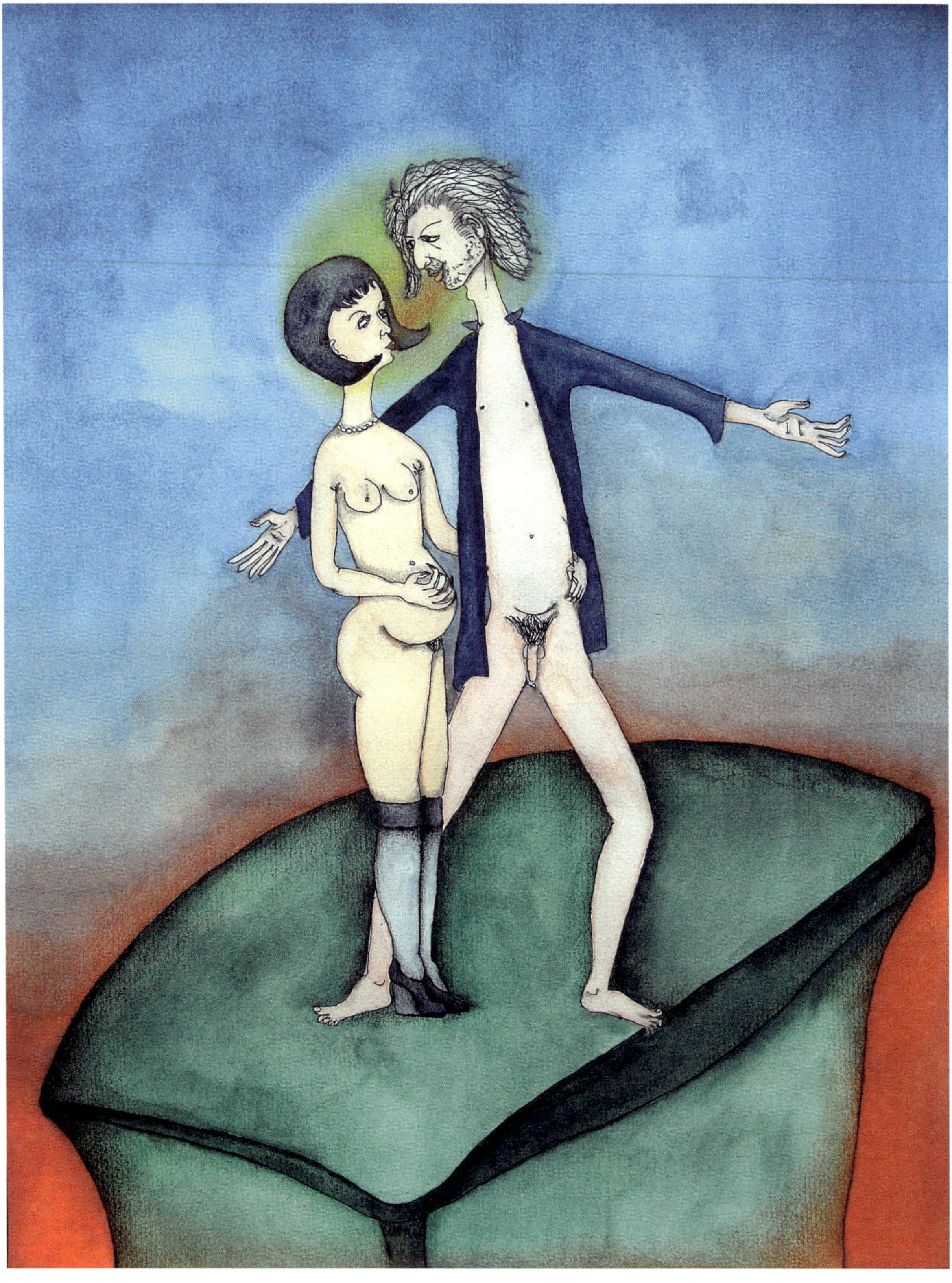

*The Two of Us*, 2009
56 × 42 cm

# Conversation

## pascALEjandro and Klaus Biesenbach

***Klaus Biesenbach:*** *How, when, and where did you figure out pascALEjandro's existence?*
**pasc**ALE**jandro:** When our relationship began, we knew there was a forty-three year gap between us. Alejandro was seventy-seven and Pascale was thirty-three. If we had a child, Alejandro would be old enough to be its grandfather. We considered that a couple exists when it can create something together. And when we saw the similarity of the names—the repetition of ALE—we decided our child would be the union of our two names in a single artist.
We never rejected the possibility of a biological child: it would have been the fruit of love, come what may. We never wanted to force anything or stand in the way of anything: if the child comes, what a wonder; if the child doesn't come, what a wonder, because the most important thing is our love and the fact of being united no matter what. The union is there in our names: plain as day. The child came in another form, but in the same way: it's the fruit of our love, created with the same energy as for a biological child, which is born out of the fusion of two beings and exists on its own. We nurture it, raise it, and it has its own life.
***K. B.:*** *Was it at the first encounter between Pascale and Alejandro?*
**P.:** When a man and a woman find each other at first sight, beyond the shadow of a doubt, for something that might be forever, everything's there from the beginning. You have to know how to unveil it. pascALEjandro existed in an unconscious way.

Alejandro saw Pascale and was enchanted at first sight, without knowing her name, without knowing their names coincided. Pascale immediately recognized Alejandro as the being she had always been waiting for. pascALEjandro is a match made in heaven, a miracle-meeting.

***K. B.:*** *When did you know it was love? Is there a difference between love at first sight and eternal love at first sight?*

**P.:** It happened like a catastrophe: a cataclysmic fact. For us humans, an earthquake is terrible; for the Earth, it's a pleasure. She settles in, makes herself comfortable. A meeting is a happy catastrophe. Any love that can end someday isn't true love. True love is always eternal. It was already there in us, somewhere.

***K. B.:*** *How does eternal love manifest itself on a regular day, in the morning, during the day, during the night?*

**P.:** It doesn't manifest itself at all: things that are present don't manifest themselves. The manifestation occurs once, and then it's here. It's not a question of planning, of a routine. It doesn't manifest itself in a daily ritual. Each instant is new; there isn't the slightest repetition of anything. We don't have any fixed habits. It's a continuous and absolute joy: a filter which makes us see the world in all its fullness. Someone who's bitter and unsatisfied sees everything through the filter of bitterness: when you're full of love, you're constantly carried along. You experience everything with a feeling of strength and permanent joy.

***K. B.:*** *Is your collaborative artmaking now a result of the closeness of your relationship and your devotion to each other?*

**P.:** A painter or a poet says "I." pascALEjandro says "we": it's a different experience. It's not about illustrating a personal quest. Alejandro's drawings depicted individuals at first, then, gradually, couples began to appear: a couple creates a spirit, a balance between life and death, a pair of revolutionaries forging ahead; being kissed by an angel constitutes a union. pascALEjandro's existence is a given: you can't collaborate if there isn't an ideal relationship to begin with. It's a collaboration with no rivalry and no arguments: complete respect, complete trust.

Alejandro wanted, as it were, to inseminate Pascale, and he did it symbolically. Now, Alejandro isn't a painter—Pascale is. Alejandro has worked in every profession, except as a painter: his drawings were stored away somewhere. He never thought of himself as a draftsman: he knew how to draw, but he wasn't interested in expressing himself in that way, and above all he harbored a kind of insecurity about his own talent, even though he was mistaken. With Pascale, his drawing became a means of seduction: she discovered his drawings and told him he draws very well, that his drawings have a special grace. He replied, "You can impregnate me," and that was how he understood he'd be able to seduce her.

pascALEjandro has taught both of them about themselves: drawing was the least appreciated aspect of Alejandro, the skill in which he had the least confidence in himself. Pascale, though already a painter, had the epiphany of a color scale she never otherwise would have used in her personal work. These works could not exist in the absence of one or the other. They are the fusion of two visions: the artists put themselves at the service of this symbolic child. Neither of them is at the service of himself or herself. "I" and "you" have become "we."

***K. B.:*** *How do you avoid creative conflicts and creative tension?*

**P.:** We don't avoid them, because there aren't any. Alejandro draws quietly, and Pascale paints quietly. We allow ourselves to give each other little indications in the midst of the work and we also share these at the end. Alejandro explains what he wanted to say, his intention, and then we share this work we've made. When Pascale goes to color the drawing Alejandro has just finished, sometimes he takes a look, but he doesn't say anything. He knows all is well. Everything takes place in mutual respect and complete trust.

***K. B.:*** *Is pascALEjandro a third or a synthesis of Pascale and Alejandro?*

**P.:** Both: a third person and a synthesis. We're multiple artists: there's pascALEjandro, but Pascale has her own painting, writing, and costume design, and Alejandro makes films and writes poetry and prose.

The synthesis happens for this visual activity, but it isn't a total synthesis: poetry is Alejandro's backbone, and it's a completely personal activity—he can't write poems with anyone else. Just as Pascale's personal painting is an individual creation.

pascALEjandro is an entity created by two individualities. It's precisely because the two individualities exist independently that they can nourish this entity and thus create a symbolic child, nurtured by two persons who also go on with their lives.

***K. B.:*** *How do you avoid any dominance in the double character?*

**P.:** There simply isn't any: there's only complementarity, respect, trust. There's no struggle in this story. That might seem too good to be true, but it wouldn't work otherwise. Nothing negative. We don't struggle against domination: there isn't any.

When you love someone, you love their intellect. You have a pleasurable mental bond. You have a pleasurable emotional bond. You have a pleasurable sexual bond. Your bodies touch in pleasure. When Pascale speaks, sometimes Alejandro loses himself and just listens to the melody of her voice and that's all he could ask for. He knows that what she's saying is perfect for him—he is in complete agreement with what she is thinking.

***K. B.:*** *Years ago, Alejandro and I made an alphabet of words and Alejandro associated what these words meant to him. So perhaps we do a small one, but now pascALEjandro answers these questions.*

*What does love mean to you? What does sex mean to you?*

**P.:** Understanding something is one thing, and knowing it is another. That question is a purely academic question: if love had a meaning for us, it wouldn't be love. When you know something, it forms a single whole; there's no duality between the knower and the thing known. Knowledge isn't intellectual. If someone asks you "What does sex mean to you?" the desire vanishes. You can't explain it. You can't define it: but, for having lived it, you can say it can't be contained, it's something we carried deep inside ourselves and that we recognized in each other. In alchemy, they say the alchemist can't accomplish the *magnum opus* without having known true love.

Our bodies fit perfectly; we fit together perfectly, just as our names fit together, like our thoughts, our feelings, our way of life. We're enraptured; it's like a permanent state of ecstasy. We give everything to each other in this love: we're free to give everything, because we know the other won't take anything secretly. The joy of life: every night, it's a pleasure to go to bed together. For someone who's never experienced the bond of love, sex exists outside of love. In our case, everything is linked: the sex involves the intensity of our love.

In our society, through misperception and fear of true love—which is so rare that it comes along only once in a lifetime, if at all—we think of sex as something independent of love, something unrelated, the search for a kind of pleasure that can only be found by detaching yourself from your emotions and seeking out a multitude of partners, whereas in a true bond of love you give everything to the beloved, you feel everything, you receive everything and there aren't any limits anymore. It's perfection, complete union, the sacred bond. Before, it used to bother Alejandro to speak of love: now it doesn't bother him anymore because he's experienced it.

People who separate the feeling of love from sexual and mental desire think they have to seek out strange practices in bed to sexually fulfill themselves. We're natural: we don't use any toys, no drugs to be out of our heads. It's about staying in something natural, something which industrial society has transformed into a marketplace.

***K. B.:*** *What does death mean to you? What does work mean to you?*

**P.:** It's strange to link those two. When death comes, philosophers are at a loss for words: the intellect falls silent. It's something that's coming; it's better to think about being alive. What's to come will come; if there's nothing, we won't be aware of it. Death's the terror of parting and the hope for eternity.

With a forty-three-year age difference, normally Alejandro's going to go before Pascale: not like Stefan Zweig, who committed suicide with his wife. He wants to protect Pascale completely so that she'll have a peaceful life. Pascale doesn't project herself beyond Alejandro: in her mind, her life expectancy is identical to Alejandro's.

Work isn't work. We've never worked; we're artists; when you work on what you love with those you love, and you love what you do, it's not work, it's ecstasy. In our case, work is our way of being in the world. There's no distinction between work and life, between life and art. It's a wild pleasure to see these works come alive: the drawing's the skeleton; the color's the flesh; for artists, work is ecstasy.

***K. B.:*** *What does art mean to you?*

**P.:** A thing doesn't mean something. It either is or it isn't. Art is a way of being in the world: there's no division between our life and humanity. We love life and human beings: we don't have any negative conceptions, even though every human being has a monstrous side—social, religious, and economic conditions create the monster. Art doesn't concern itself with the result of the work, but only with the work itself.

# Conversation

**pascALEjandro and Hans Ulrich Obrist**

***Hans Ulrich Obrist:*** How did the encounter between Alejandro and Pascale give birth to you, pascALEjandro?

**pascALEjandro**: Tarot brought us together. Before we met, Alejandro had identified himself with The Hermit in the Tarot. On the day we first saw each other, he was giving Tarot readings in a café, just as he would do every week back then, for free, to thousands of people who came from all over the world… He looked up—which he never usually did because he was always so focused—and there was Pascale right in front of him. We both understood at first sight; we recognized each other because in a certain way we had been prepared for this meeting, which was meant to happen. Up until then, Alejandro's connections with women had been very different from this present relationship, but he had always had this ideal of love there in his art and books, just as Pascale had always been expecting to meet this superior being whom she recognized in Alejandro, and whom she could have described feature by feature before even having laid eyes on him… All of Alejandro's children knew the woman of his life would be Asian; all of Pascale's family knew the man of her life would be an older artist.

***H. U. O.:*** What is the creative process leading to those works? Is it divided? How long is it?

**P.:** We're real people who create works because we love each other, and not artificial people who care more about the results of the work than the work itself. We're like an apple tree: we make apples without asking ourselves how. When the time comes, an artist gives birth to a work. The gestation process is completely unconscious.

It has to be a necessity, and like all things born of true necessity it doesn't present itself as a choice but simply as a natural imperative. The questions only come afterward: we can analyze the things we make, but only afterward; at the time, we follow the mystery and necessity of the work. As Lacan says: "I speak before thinking."

***H. U. O:*** Do the colours come quite automatically when you add them to the drawings? Does this relate at all to Pascale's work making sets?

**P.:** The colors arrive in a completely irrational and intuitive way; they appear in a very fluid way. We only understand what they mean once the work is finished. Alejandro's drawing inspires in Pascale these colors which she never used in her personal work, which up until recently was composed of a range of blacks and grays, of very cool colors, rather dark, in very subtle combinations, but pascALEjandro's colors have ended up suffusing her personal work, enriching it: like communicating vessels.

Our working material is the material of our lives: each expressive act contributes to the next, and all of pascALEjandro's creations strengthen our personal work. Scenic design arose out of a desire to escape the two-dimensional limits of painting on canvas, to work more directly in space: but at root it was still painting transferred into space. Everything is absolutely connected.

***H. U. O.:*** How does Pascale's background as an artist have an impact on PascALEjandro?

**P.:** There's no distinction between artistic progression and personal evolution—no separation between life and art. Pascale gives her entire being to pascALEjandro: her skill, her sensibility, her way of seeing and of being in the world, her unlimited love for Alejandro and for creating their work. The artistic practice draws just as much on the materials of her work, with all its tools, as it draws on the materials of her life.

***H. U. O.:*** Do you always use the same materials for the drawing series?

**P.:** To date, yes. Ink on paper for the line drawing; watercolor and pencil for the colors. We don't rule out the possibility that the choice of materials could evolve.

***H. U. O:*** Where does your interest in spirituality and the celestial stem from?

**P.:** It doesn't come from anywhere: it's a part of us. Human beings are cosmic animals—it's as simple as that. People preoccupied only with social problems have their minds locked up in a cage of presuppositions straight out of the darkest depths of history. When you free yourself from the cage, you become a cosmic being. The earth is a ball floating amidst an immensity of suns much bigger than our own: it's an infinite world that exists eternally in infinite space. A person who isn't interested in the celestial world is like a mole.

***H. U. O.:*** What are the main themes in the work? How does this relate to the themes in Pascale's and Alejandro's individual practice?

**P.:** We don't look for themes, but rather an artistic attitude: no critical or destructive art—art isn't an act of demolition; it isn't a confirmation of neurosis. We love life; we can see the sickness of the world, but we have no intention of profiting from fanatical sociopolitical events. There are other venues in which to express that: for our part, we're trying, with great difficulty but also with great pleasure, to arrive at a sublime depiction of the human being. This isn't something that exists as a utopia or an ideal: it's the portion of sublimity that actually exists in human beings and in reality.

Alejandro and Pascale follow different paths, but these bring them finally to a similar vision, in complete balance.

Alejandro has a prolific imagination: full of imagery and very literary, phantasmagoric and dream-like, steeped in his earlier creations, in all he's invented and made, in psychomagic, in the unconscious, in all the wisdom and spirituality of this entire globe which he has studied at length, in all his learning acquired over the course of many years and experiences. Pascal has a very intuitive knowledge— she can't always say exactly why she knows what she knows, and her learning often comes after the fact to confirm this purely intuitive, almost mediumistic knowledge: her artistic practice issues from this principle and comes to her in a very unconscious and abstract way, just as her thoughts are visual and oftentimes abstract. Alejandro, who initiates the image, fills it with all his knowledge, and then Pascale interprets it and develops it through a kind of abstraction.

At first, the starting point of certain drawings was a slightly critical mindset, slightly phantasmagorical, with a kind of metaphysical anxiety; now, we're able to create unity as opposed to duality. pascALEjandro is the union of a couple; it's what a couple composes, like a self-portrait. In one of the latest drawings, there's a set of scales with two skeletons on one side and a couple making love on the other: the tray with the couple making love outweighs the other; it's an emblem of the triumph of love over death. Another drawing depicts a couple on a tiger holding the world between its paws: despite the decadence of the world, we do what we can to look at it differently. In a third drawing, we see the lightest of kisses from an angel, only the touch of a tongue: beyond this world, and close by our side: it's all the mystery of a universe we can never decipher.

In all of this, there's no real theme to speak of, but rather a vital attitude of the love of life. We each take what comes from our souls and try to find a sublime meaning to it, to awaken sublime feelings in the other.

***H. U. O.:*** Pascale and Alejandro collaborated on a performance, *A Spiritual Journey* – how does this performative work tie into pascALEjandro?

**P.:** That was a collaborative performance with the dancer and choreographer Carolyn Carlson, and it wasn't pascALEjandro, but rather Pascale and Alejandro. The show's backbone was Alejandro Jodorowsky's poetry, and Pascale Montandon-Jodorowsky designed the scenery. It was already an act of collaboration, but it was different: there was the pleasure of working together, but not of creating something together; the fusion wasn't there yet. It was a collaboration of a more traditional kind, a meeting of disciplines.

pascALEjandro is more than a collaboration. Each painting is a manifesto. We live in an age in which relationships are in crisis. And here's an experience of the fusion of a couple, which doesn't mean to lose yourself, but truly to fuse, to nurture this new entity. In the case of Delaunay, you can see the parallels that exist between them, but it's always two parallel paths; there's never any fusion. Each of them is at the service of his or her own work. pascALEjandro is a human experience and not simply an artistic one. It shows how a man and a woman can collaborate without being in competition, without those horrible stories Hollywood dwells upon, for example.

To collaborate with a woman, you have to have a true conception of her, without condescension and with true respect; conversely, to collaborate with a man, you can't see him as an enemy or competitor. There needs to be mutual admiration and complete trust. You have to know you can give the other person everything, because there's no chance that he or she will take anything behind your back. But there's no doubt that you have to have this level of a bond to get to this artistic union.

***H. U. O.:*** *Does the healing power of art—psychomagic—have an impact onto pascALEjandro?*

**P.:** The fact of creating something together is an act of psychomagic for the couple, and for us as artists: there are no conflicts of ego; we put ourselves at the service of the work. This act of psychomagic also replaces the biological child we never had: so pascALEjandro is our symbolic child.

***H. U. O.:*** Since pascALEjandro has been described as a symbolic child: how do you nurture the work and develop the series?

**P.:** In the same way as if it were a biological child: with love. Like a child, the work grows up; we do our best to help it develop, all while leaving it free to be what it is, and not what we want it to be.

***H. U. O.:*** *How important are symbols in your practice?*

**P.:** What do you mean by "symbols"? This question brings us back to the revelation that everything is a symbol. Everything becomes important: the least detail becomes a meaningful symbol. A "symbol" doesn't have a specific meaning: the entire meaning of a symbol is that its meaning is enigmatic. It becomes a mirror of the person interpreting it. A symbol has a different meaning for each person. In pascALEjandro, there aren't any specific symbols of anything whatsoever.

In the drawings, Alejandro makes use of his psychological, metaphysical, and esoteric references, both consciously and unconsciously: it's a part of him. Pascale's conception of the colors is at once completely intuitive and purely visual. She has a codification that's mostly unconscious, related to hallucination. It all comes as in a dream. When you dream, each dream is considered a series of elements to interpret: psychoanalysis delves into the interpretation of dreams to understand what they mean. It's the same thing with symbols: their content is infinite. We have to seek out the meaning of a symbol in order to discover a truth within ourselves. A cross might be the symbol of a god's bountiful sacrifice, or it might simply be a "plus" sign in mathematics.

***H. U. O.:*** Do the symbols of Tarot readings and the outcomes of these reading influence your work?

**P. :** That's like asking us—if we were American or English: "Has the English language influenced your work?" We're artists: painting and drawing are a visual language, like the Tarot. Our art was born of a cultivation of intuition and magic, like the Tarot. And we found each other thanks to the Tarot.

***H. U. O.:*** How does the collaborative process of pascALEjandro in film, behind *La danza de la realidad* and *Poesia Sin Fin*, with costumes, sets, colors, differ from your drawings?

**P.:** They're two very different things: pascALEjandro is a body of work created by four hands. The cinematic collaboration is a collaboration on films by Alejandro Jodorowsky. In the world of "pascALEjandro," Pascale and Alejandro vanish to give way to pascALEjandro. In a film by Alejandro, Pascale places her creativity at the service of Alejandro's work: his film.

In the collaboration "pascALEjandro," there's no criticism, but rather an absolute acceptance of what each person does. In films like *La Danza de la realidad* or *Poesia sin fin*, it's very different: since it's Alejandro's work, he can say what's right for him and what isn't, even though he has complete faith in Pascale's creativity, and she herself takes care to respect Alejandro's vision in what he's trying to express, by interpreting it, translating it into images without modifying or distorting it. In auteur cinema, and especially in the cinema of Alejandro Jodorowsky, the film is the realization of a vision, which each person has to serve.

On the other hand, it was indeed pascALEjandro who designed the colors of *La Danza de la realidad* and *Poesia sin fin*, in a direct extension of the graphic works. This artistic fusion goes beyond the frame of any particular body of work or means of expression to become an authentic artistic position, with real emotional, philosophical and spiritual content.

We have an attitude of love towards our work, and it is the work of our hands. pascALEjandro is the manifestation of a romantic relationship in which everything the other makes is sacred. It's like creating a child: the ovule is the ovule and the spermatozoid is the spermatozoid. Each one brings what it is, and this creates a being which is neither the one nor the other but couldn't exist in the absence of either.

***H. U. O.:*** *La danza de la realidad* is the title of Alejandro's book and film, and *La realidad de mi danza* the title of Pascale's book:

what is the importance of truth and authenticity for you?
**P.:** Fundamental, essential: there's no such thing as art without authenticity and absolute honesty; the work has to be a manifesto of artistic liberty and integrity. You can't accept any compromise that would lead you astray from artistic necessity.
***H. U. O.:*** Yin and Yang is often mention when discussing your work; how are feminine and masculine principles present in your work?
**P.:** There's a man and a woman, of course, but it's a soul-to-soul relationship and not a male-female relationship—and yet still we're masculine and feminine… As the Japanese say, the work goes "from my soul to yours." It's a principle of complementarity which becomes a principle of inseparability. The pitfall of collaborative work is to keep an ego, to keep an individuality, and not to make two individualities become one. To make the work we want, the first thing we have to do is eliminate the ego and get rid of any competition in the outcome of the work.
Each of us integrates the other: this requires an absolute trust in each other, which you can't create, but which has to be there. It's a daily miracle: two people find each other and coincide completely in a project without a hint of doubt. Alejandro, in his drawing, makes the first move; the active impulse of the drawing has to integrate the absolute humility of submitting oneself to the other's choice: "I've made this drawing, and if you don't like this drawing, we'll tear it up." That hasn't happened yet.
We leave ourselves the option of working together: it's open. It's not a fanatical decision to collaborate; it's something natural.
***H. U. O.:*** Are the roles in Pascale and Alejandro's relationship also collaborative? Do you think their closeness as a couple is what allows them to work so well in creating artistic work together?
**P.:** Obviously! We've united our drawings, our colors, our feelings, our phallus and vagina. There's a palpable union. The work is a wonder because the union is a wonder. It leads, step by step, to something sublime. It's the end of vengeance, lament and

dissatisfaction with the world, and it's the beginning of wonder in the face of the world—love of life, of collaborating, of each other.

***H. U. O.:*** Have you got any heroes/heroines or other collaborations that you admire?

**P.**: No. This isn't a rejection or a mark of pride: we just haven't followed anyone else's example. Everything is original in this process and so far we aren't aware of anything equivalent. When two people collaborate, it often becomes an act of mirroring: they work together on everything and it becomes a kind of mutual imitation.

That's not how it is for pascALEjandro: one of us works on the drawing, that's active; the other works on the color, receptive. It's not a question of resembling each other, but rather of assembling two principles, each of which is present and remains so.

***H. U. O.:*** Both of Pascale and Alejandro's individual art practices often deal with biographical details and refer back to your childhood. Can you talk about the experiences of Alejandro, growing up in Chile, and Pascale, in France?

**P.:** In all humility, we were two child mutants: launched above and beyond the level at which we were born. Alejandro's family, all Jewish, had lost hold of their tradition of mysticism and intellectual development—which used to be reserved for the men because the women didn't participate in studying sacred texts like Talmud or Torah. This tradition, which survived the immigration, was transmitted to the deepest level of Alejandro's unconscious where he rediscovered this legacy of knowledge, as though he were a mutant straight out of the past. Pascale's family is similar: her two grandparents, French painters, left for Vietnam to found a family; then came the war, exodus, and the family had to emigrate permanently back to their home country, France; when Pascale appeared, the visual arts were deeply embedded in her unconscious; like a mutant, she too was born with all this talent linked to the past. It's at once similar and different.

***H. U. O:*** I know Alejandro had an asteroid — 261690 Jodorowsky — named after him: as the International Astronomical Union named a three-mile-wide chunk of rock orbiting between Mars and Jupiter. With all of your focus on the cosmos and our positions in the universe, can you tell me more?

**P.:** By definition, an artistic creation is about expressing one's relation to the world, to the cosmos, to the sacred in a non-religious sense, to the spiritual, the ungraspable, the infinite—to the mystery of creation and existence. In Greek temples there used to be three sayings, one of which has captured our imagination: "Know thyself," "Nothing to excess," and "Everything is one." Each one of us is a part of the universe. When you're an artist, you end up coming as close as possible to the totality, which you eventually discover within yourself. For that to happen, you have to go beyond time, space and form, which are englobed in the totality.

***H.U.O.:*** Alejandro has tweeted tarot-card readings and "psychomagical" advice to his many followers. I read this quote from his son Adan: 'Look, this is the literature of the future. They answer you, they argue. If they're not interested, they delete you. They steal from you, it's something alive!' " Pascale is also on Instagram: in the post-Internet age where Social media is so prevalent, how do you engage with these platforms and how to they affect your day-to-day? Does it have an impact on pascALEjandro?

**P.:** Social networks are a tool: the important thing is how you use them. If you put them to good use, they can be thrilling—which is what we're trying to do. What happens once you reach enlightenment in Zen Buddhism? The first thing an enlightened person realizes is the sickness of the world; with this realization comes a sense of responsibility: why have I been able to realize this among masses of people who are blind to it? Do I have something they don't have? No. We are all part of the whole and each person is a perfect entity. Each person is caught in a cage of presuppositions based in human history.

Where there's a sense of responsibility, there's a desire to change the world—simply to do away with the cage, the confines of our presuppositions, like a dark cloud blocking the light—the artist says: "With my art, I can't change the world, but I can change myself. I have to get rid of my limitations, to show others what a mind without limitations looks like." When that's your goal, you ask yourself: "Who's listening to me? My reach is limited. My work might take a century to become known, but I have to begin."
You adopt the attitude of the alchemists: all metals are sick metals. The only state of health is gold. Sick metals take centuries to turn into gold—a very slow process in view of my own life span. The artist of the twenty-first century says he or she doesn't have centuries to spare, because we're on the brink of destroying the planet. How can we accelerate the transformation, the growing awareness of our limitations? Twitter, Facebook, all social networks have their good points and bad points, like anything new. Anonymity unleashes all the world's hatred: it spreads and becomes collective. But all the good of the world spreads throughout the world as well: you can work directly with the rest of humanity. Each week, millions of people transmit the message around the world. What you give, you give to yourself; what you don't give, you take away from yourself; we're liberating the collective consciousness, which is what you find here. Social networks are the acceleration of a process which used to take centuries. As for the work of "pascALEjandro," since it isn't at the service of the ego, it shares all the more in this process, in these interactions. Social networks use different languages: visual for Instagram; written for Twitter… we use them all and make them interact; we link them just as we've linked our voices in pascALEjandro who uses a visual language, and not a written one. It's up to him now, and as good parents we have to let him do what he wants.
***H. U. O.:*** Dune *has been described as "the greatest film* never *made" (Richard Stanley, in* Jodorowsky's Dune*)—what unrealized projects does pascALEjandro have?*

**P.:** We don't have any: when we want to realize a project, we realize it. There's no such thing as an unrealized project. *Dune* didn't get made, but it became Alejandro's most famous film: a myth has its own existence, it's a realized object.
There's no such thing as failure: it's just a question of switching paths. When you can't accomplish something in one field, you do it in another. Nothing is impossible. That's the mainspring of our work. Otherwise, we never would have achieved this union. In the beginning, we created pascALEjandro out of a need to work with each other; what an immense delight! And the proof that nothing is impossible is that we started out with one small exhibition, and then another, and then, from one little exhibition to the next, we've been invited to have a big exhibition at Azzedine Alaïa's gallery! The child has grown up.
***H. U. O.:*** *I've seen Alejandro's production drawings for* Dune, *and Mœbius's storyboard: do these drawings have a relation to pascALEjandro? The idea of the storyboard, and of the comic book?*
**P.:** From a practical standpoint, a graphic novel is a script and a series of drawings you can either associate with the script or separate from it. The principle of pascALEjandro is to make drawings that are created by four hands and constitute a single whole. You can edit a screenplay or a graphic-novel script independently of the images. For graphic novels, Alejandro writes, the illustrator draws in ink, and the colorists come afterwards. pascALEjandro can't be separated or defined as "drawings by Jodorowsky, colors by Montandon"; it isn't the coloring of something fixed. Alejandro leaves certain zones untouched so Pascale can create colors that exist on their own and enrich the drawing: it isn't an act of illustration. The two stages are integral to creating the work. The principal thing in a graphic novel is the story you're telling: the drawing serves the story—it illustrates it—and the color serves the drawing. Here, there's no illustration: only pure expression.
***H. U. O.:*** In an interview, Alejandro once said that 'modern artists need to be like modern objects that are polymorphous':

do you think this is how we should deal with the modern world?

**P.:** Absolutely. But it's not "the modern world": it's the world as it is. Before, our world used to be a mental world, governed by ideologies; we've passed into another world, surrounded by a religious, philosophical and human crisis.

People are multifaceted by nature: anything a computer can do, a brain can do a thousand times better. If we knew how to use a brain the way we use a computer, we'd be flying of our own free will. We'll get there eventually, through technology. The problem with technology is that currently it's part and parcel with commerce.

***H. U. O.:*** *Why is it important to you to show your drawings in the museum?*

**P.:** We want what's best for pascALEjandro, our symbolic child. When you have a child, you don't do it for yourself, you do it to perpetuate the human race.

Displaying pascALEjandro in a museum is a way of allowing him to exist in the eyes of the world, to gain a kind of recognition in the art world, and to prove we're not making commercial works, even though museums have been corrupted a little. Every work of art, in so far as it exists at all, is addressed to other people.

***H. U. O.:*** Alejandro said, "In order to do something you need to organize your time." What rituals or structures do you have in place? Is PascALEjandro the ultimate ritual?

P. That isn't how we think of it. The ritual is to wake up, to live calmly. Alejandro, by his experience and his awareness of how much time he has wasted, is teaching Pascale how to waste as little as possible, which means eliminating the superfluous, making choices, being efficient, in order to devote as much time as possible to the most important thing: creating. Life and art are never separate.

"Nothing to excess"—and focus on the essentials so that you can know yourself, and thereby know the universe. It's like polishing a sculpture: eliminate whatever might lead you astray from yourself, which is to say, from your deep inner truth. Pure creation takes place in truth, at the core of something authentic. When you do this work, you step into pure pleasure, into a kind of ecstasy. And so you learn how to put aside the things that take you away from it.

Each day is an empty bottle you fill with a message and cast upon the ocean. It'll arrive where it's supposed to arrive, someday. What does making paintings for an exhibition amount to? It's to create a collection of messages, without knowing just what messages you're creating. As artists, this is what we know how to do, and what we are able do, and what we want to do. We do it without wasting our time on useless actions that would eat away our days and keep us from creating a body of work. Each work is a sacrifice to the divine.

# *La Danza de la Realidad*

Film by Alejandro Jodorowsky
Costumes by Pascale Montandon-Jodorowsky
Colors by pascALEjandro’

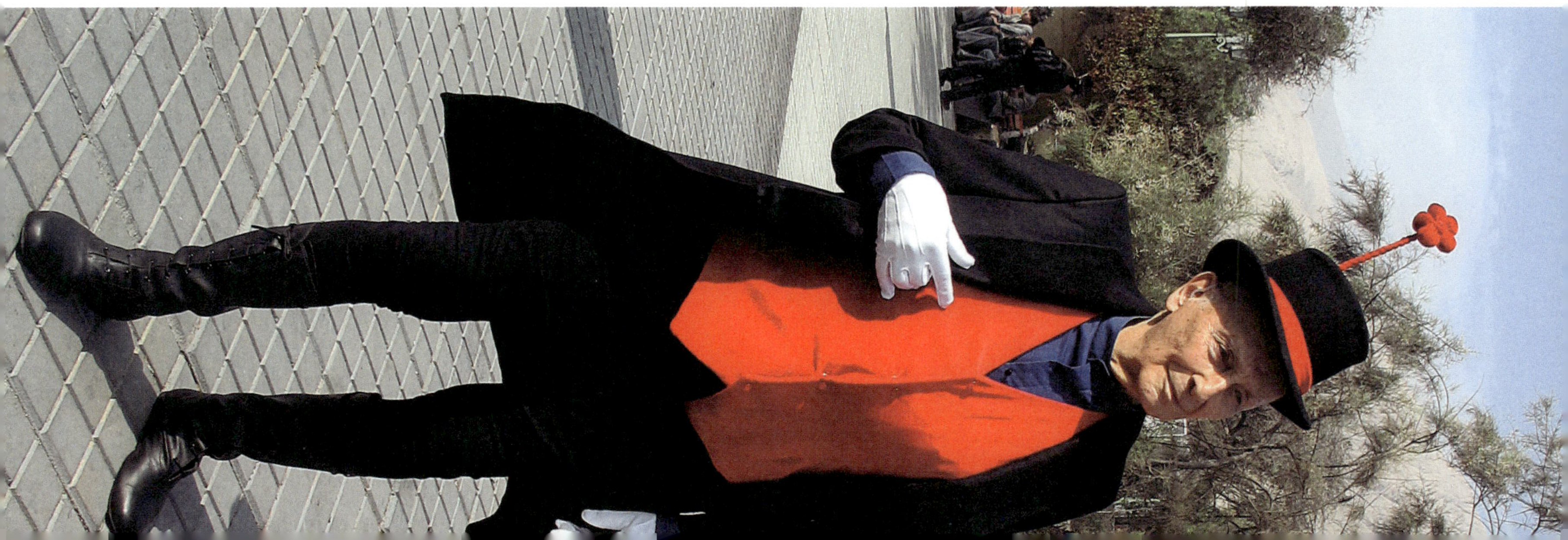

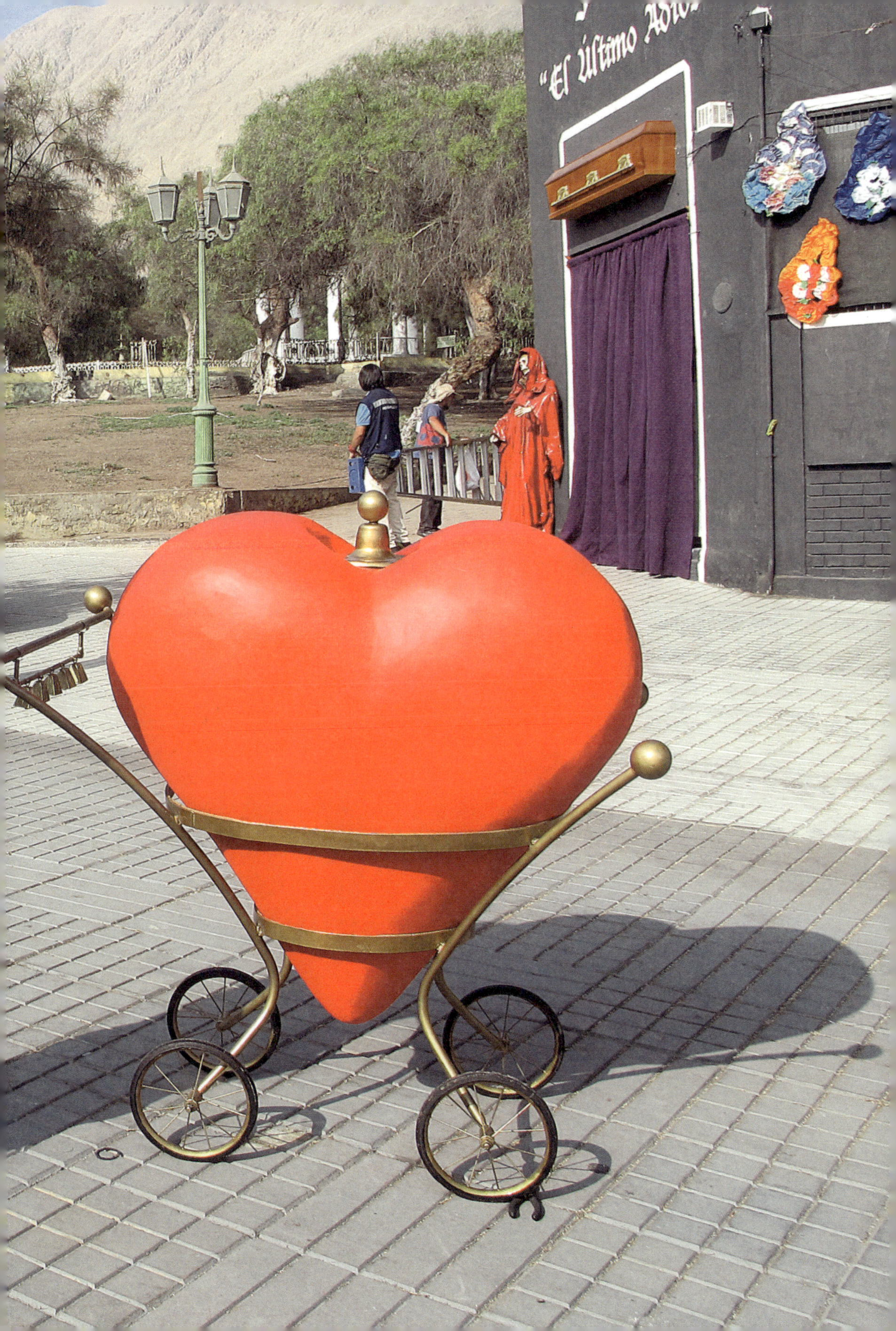
"El Último

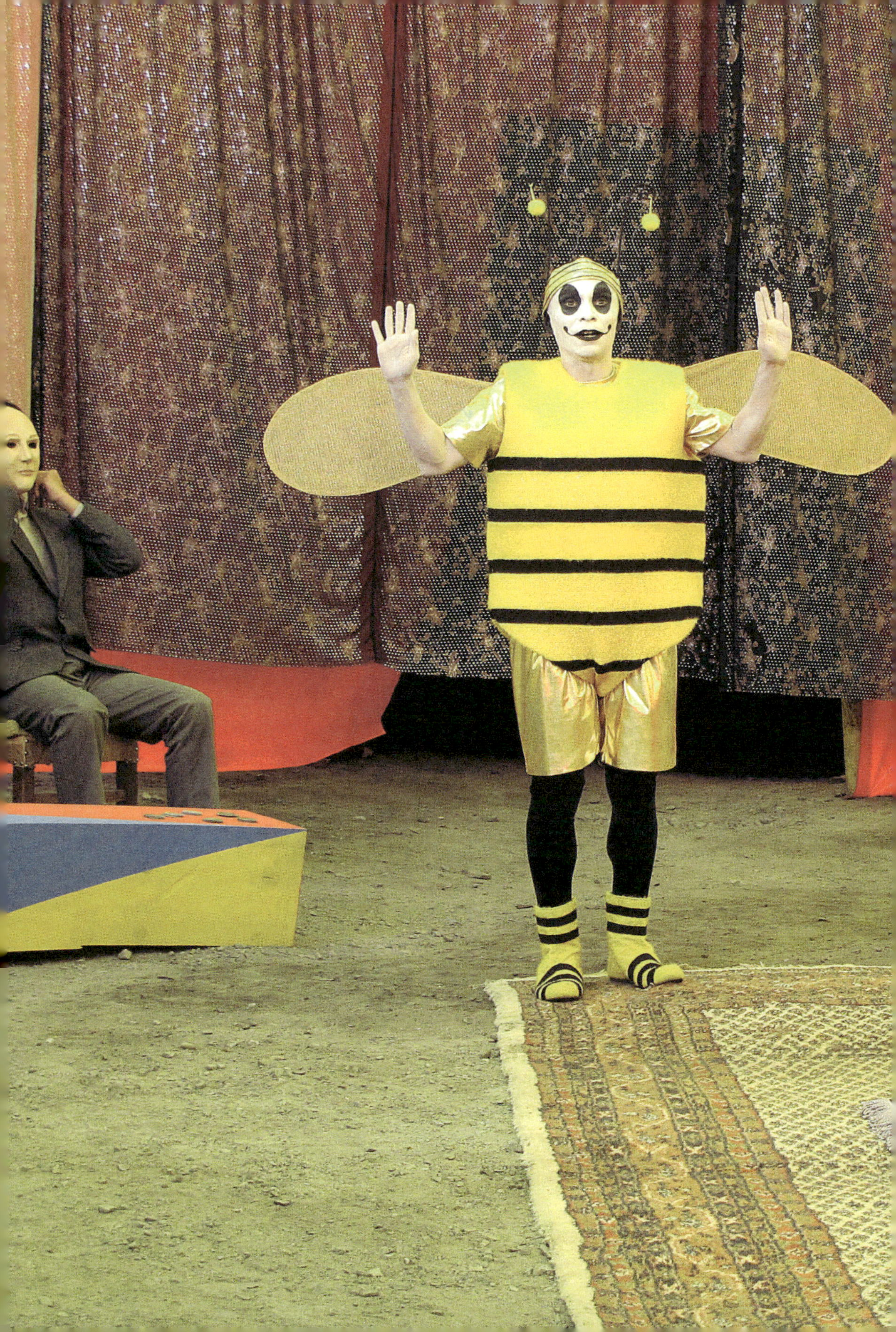

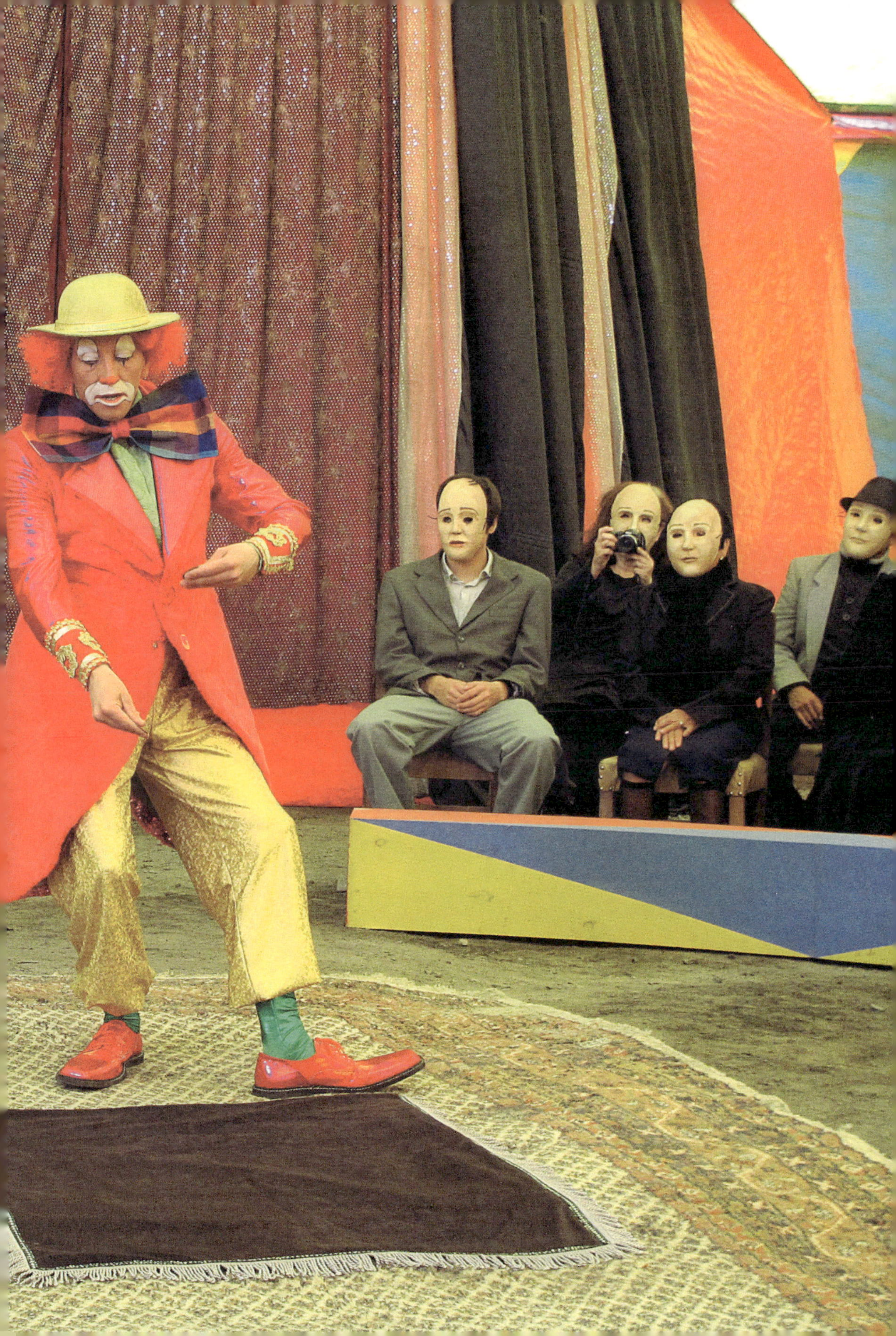

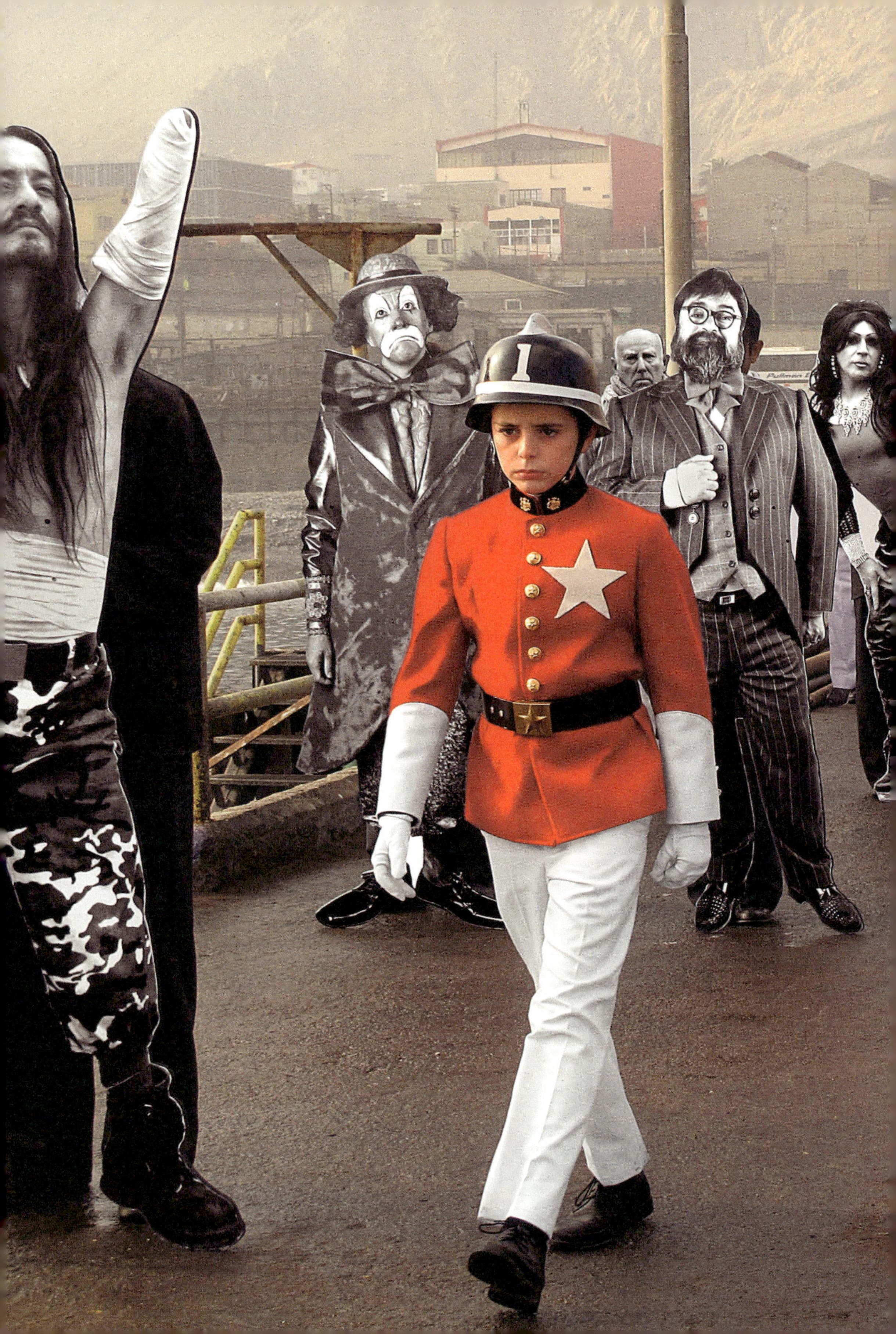
1

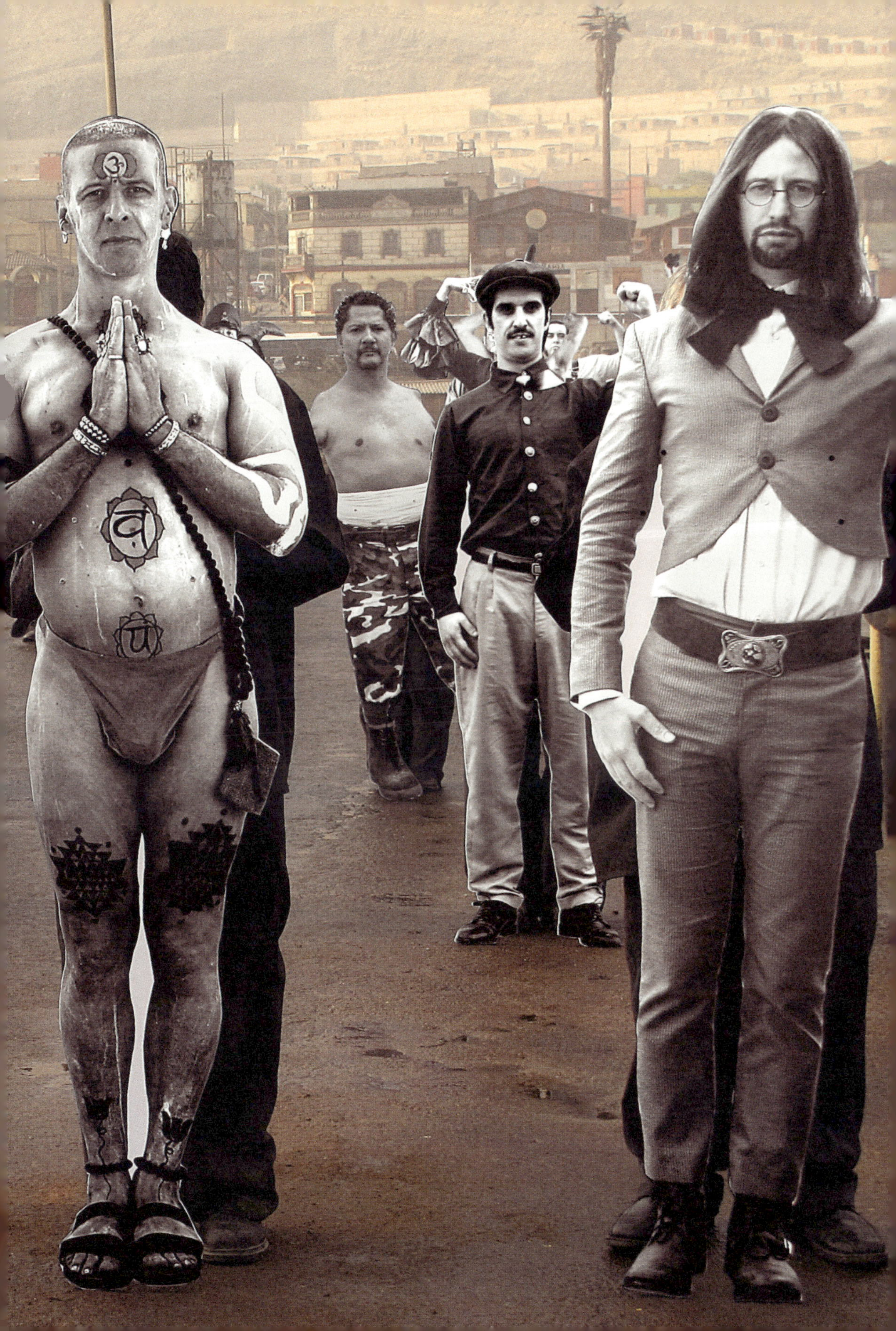

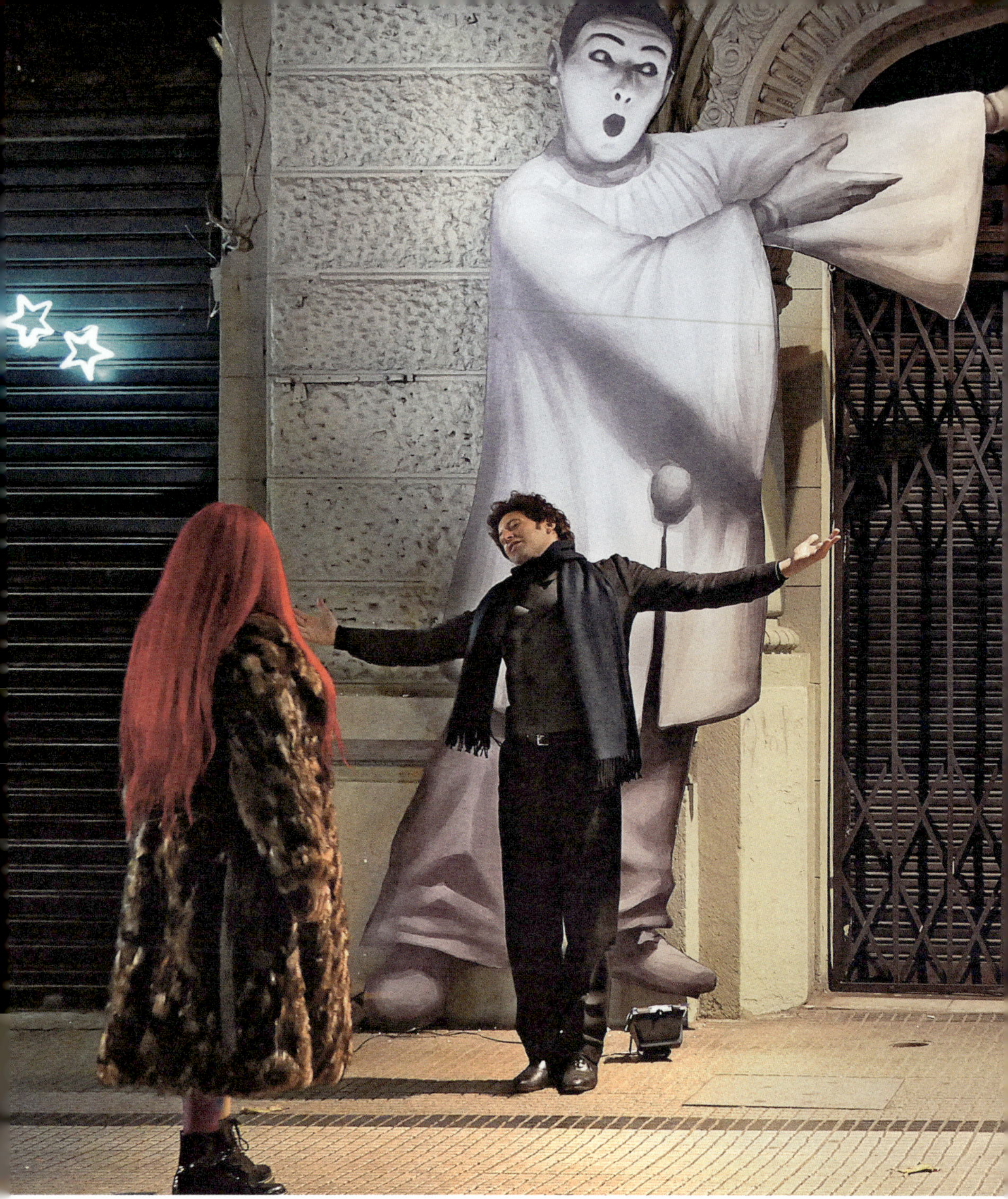

# *Poesia sin fin*

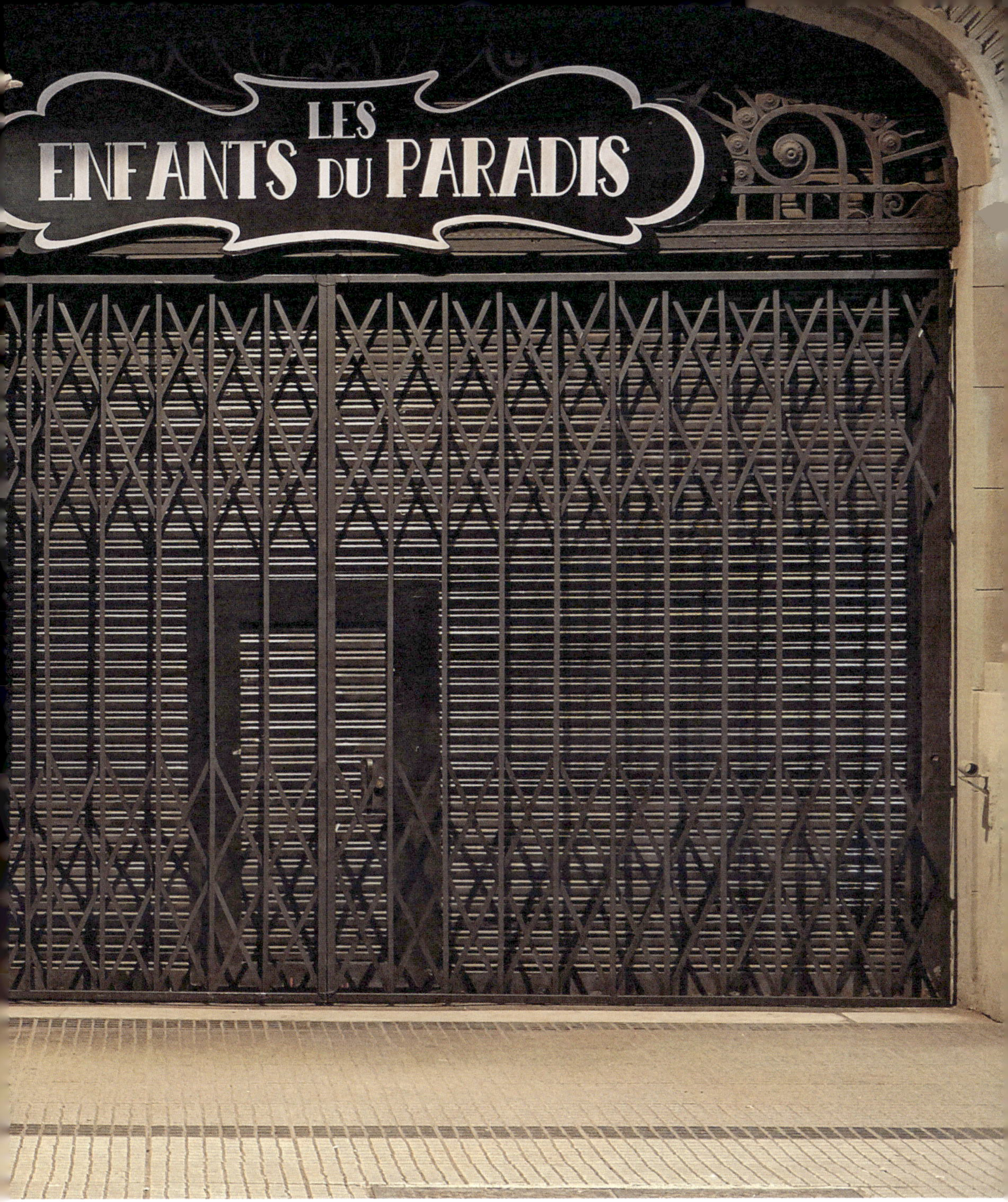


Film by Alejandro Jodorowsky
Costumes by Pascale Montandon-Jodorowsky
Colors by pascALEjandro

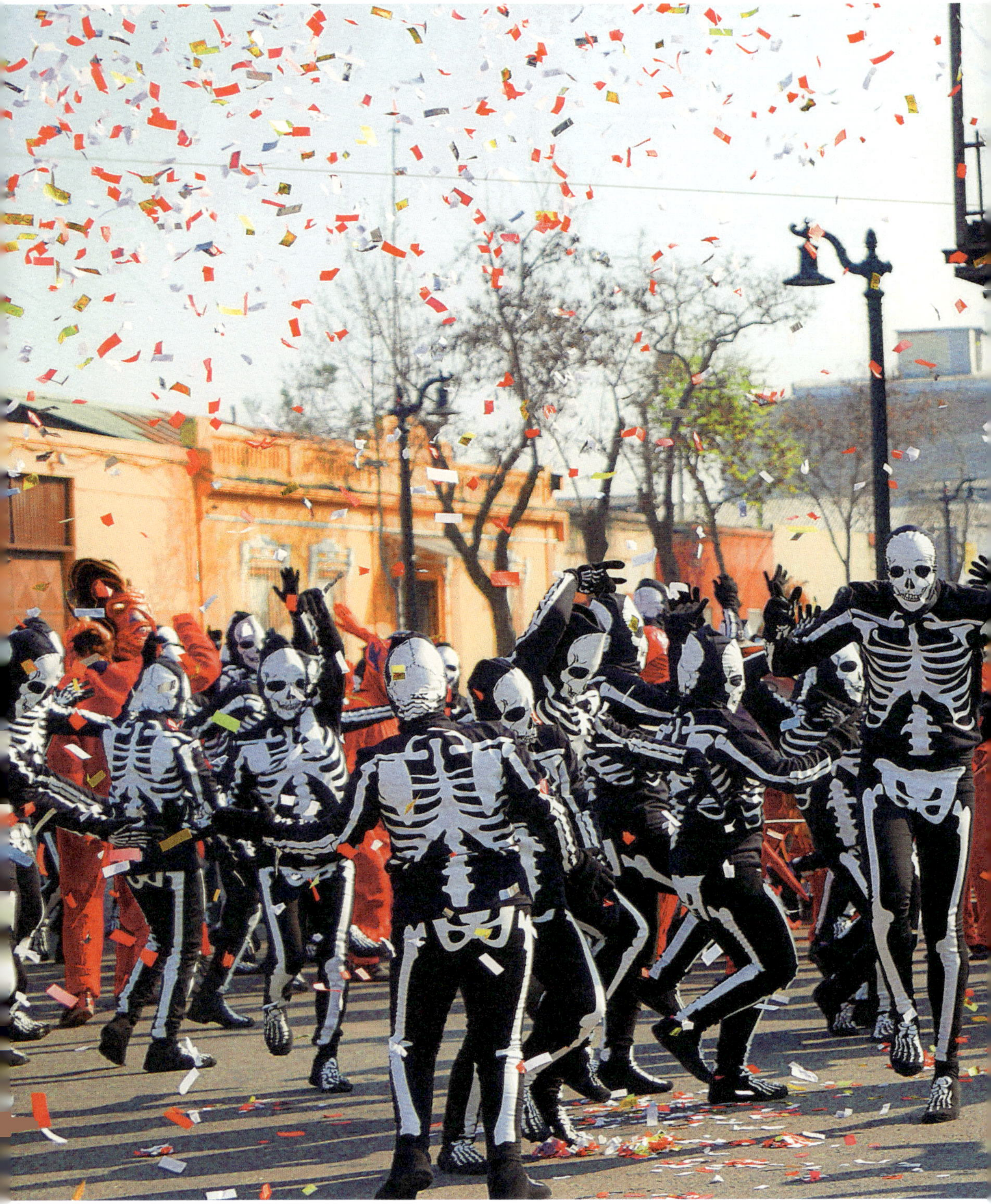

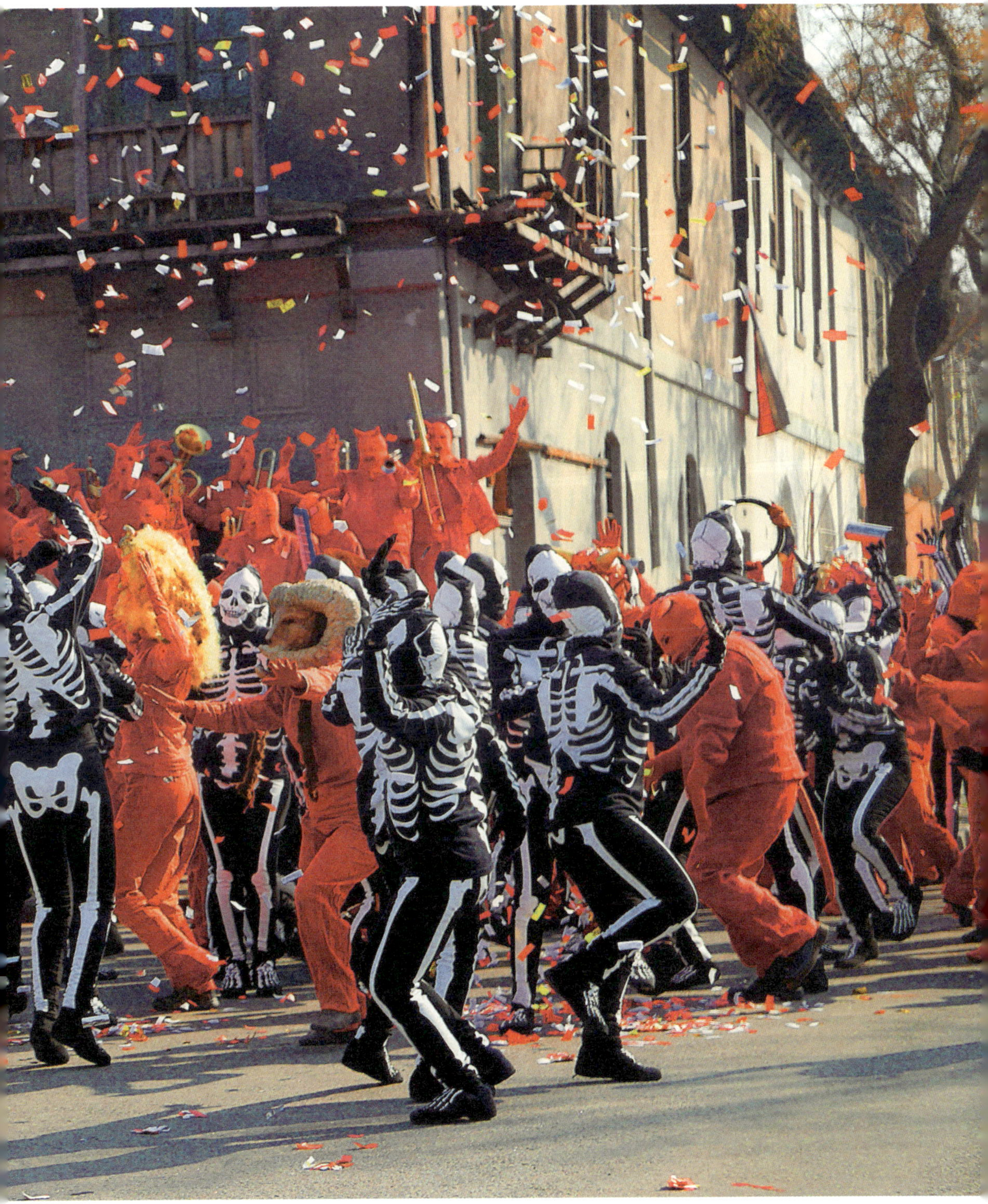

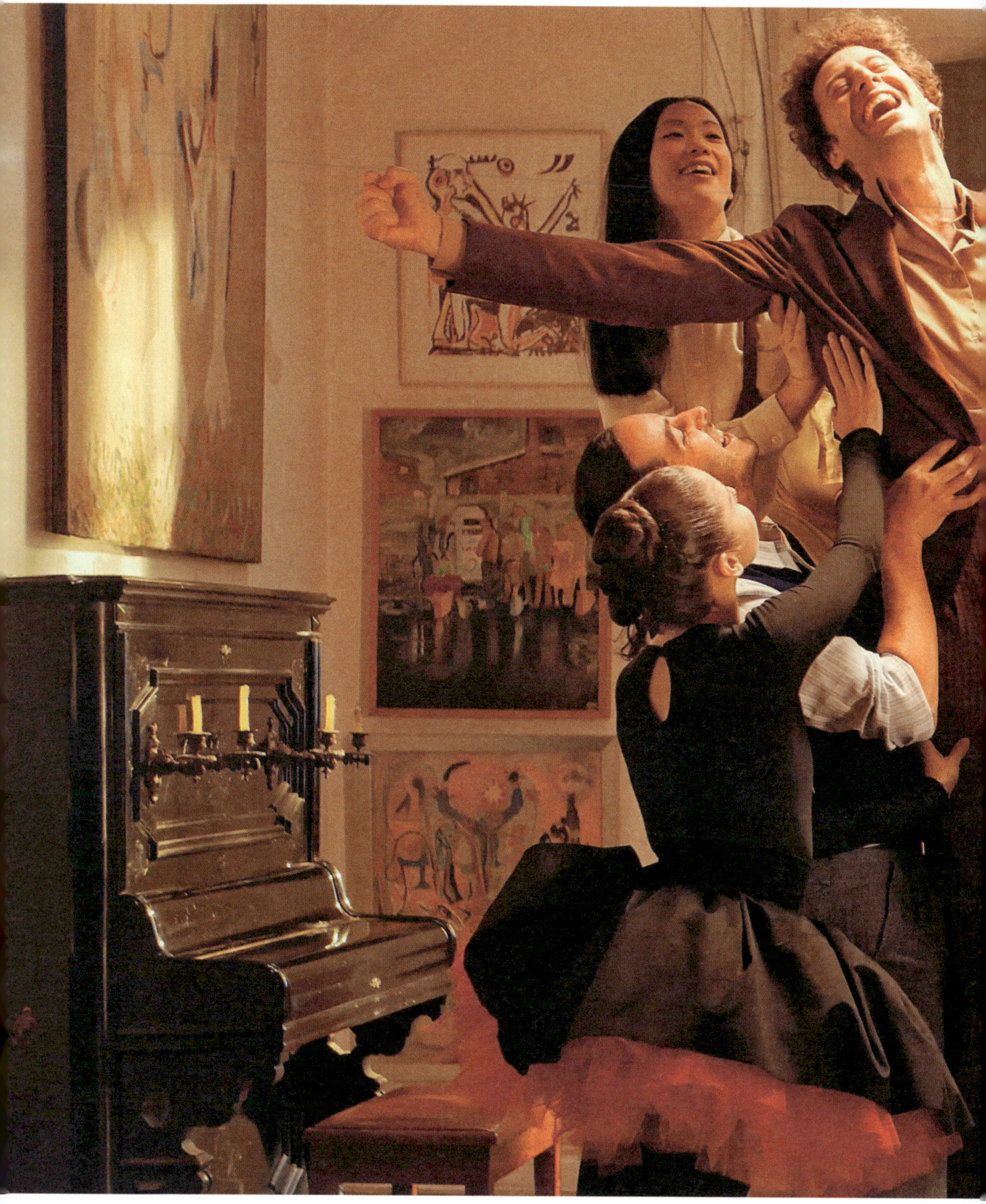

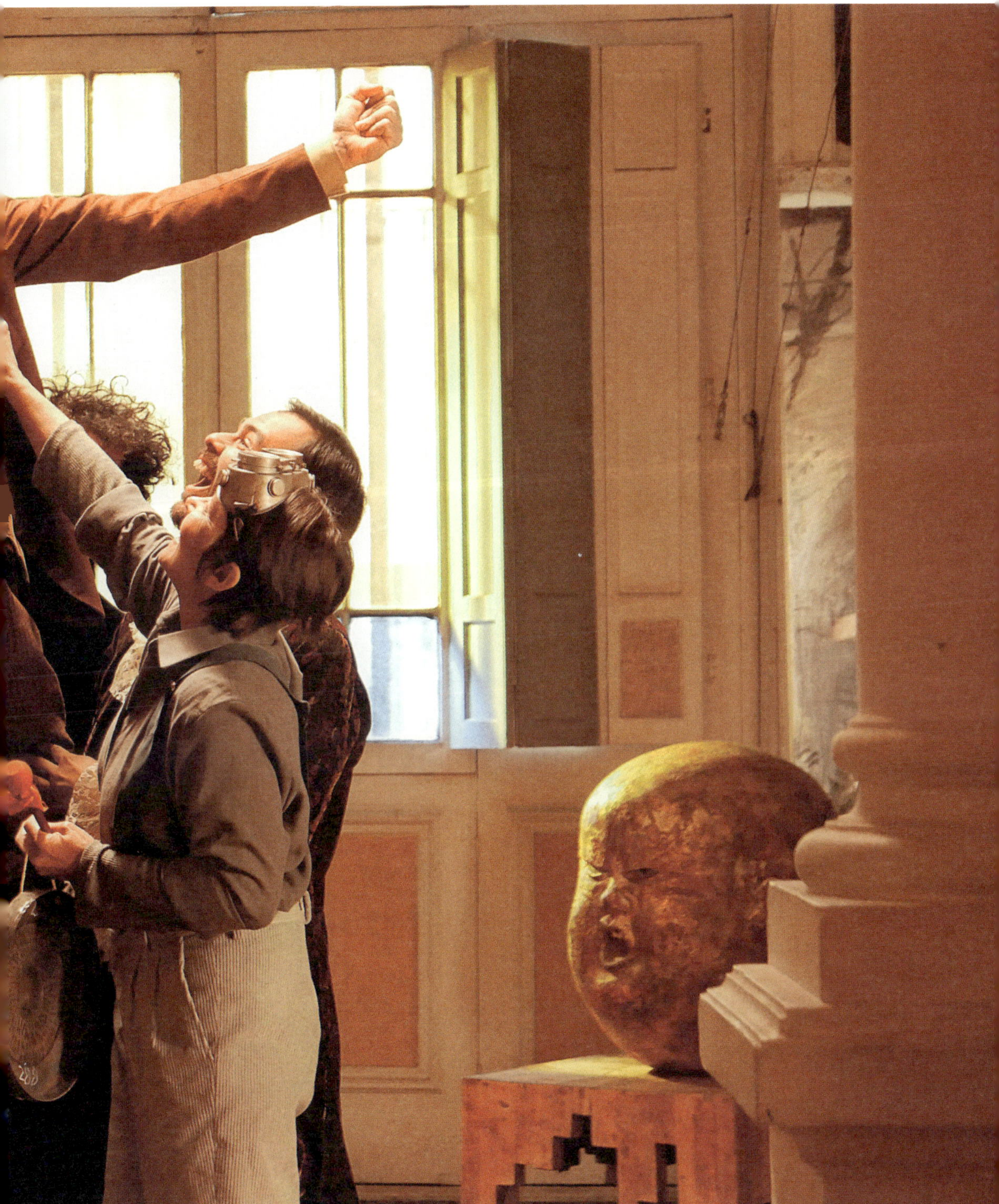

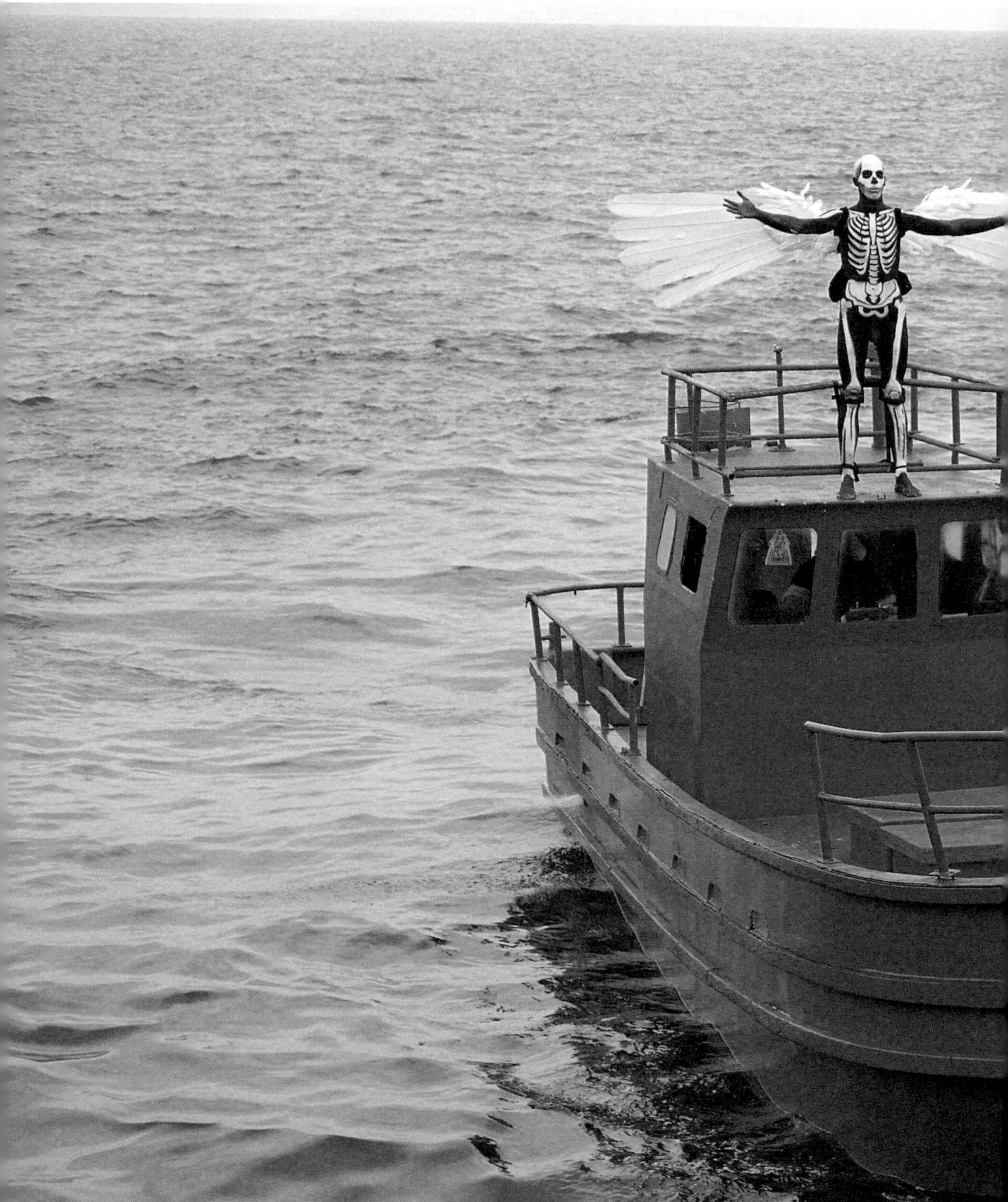

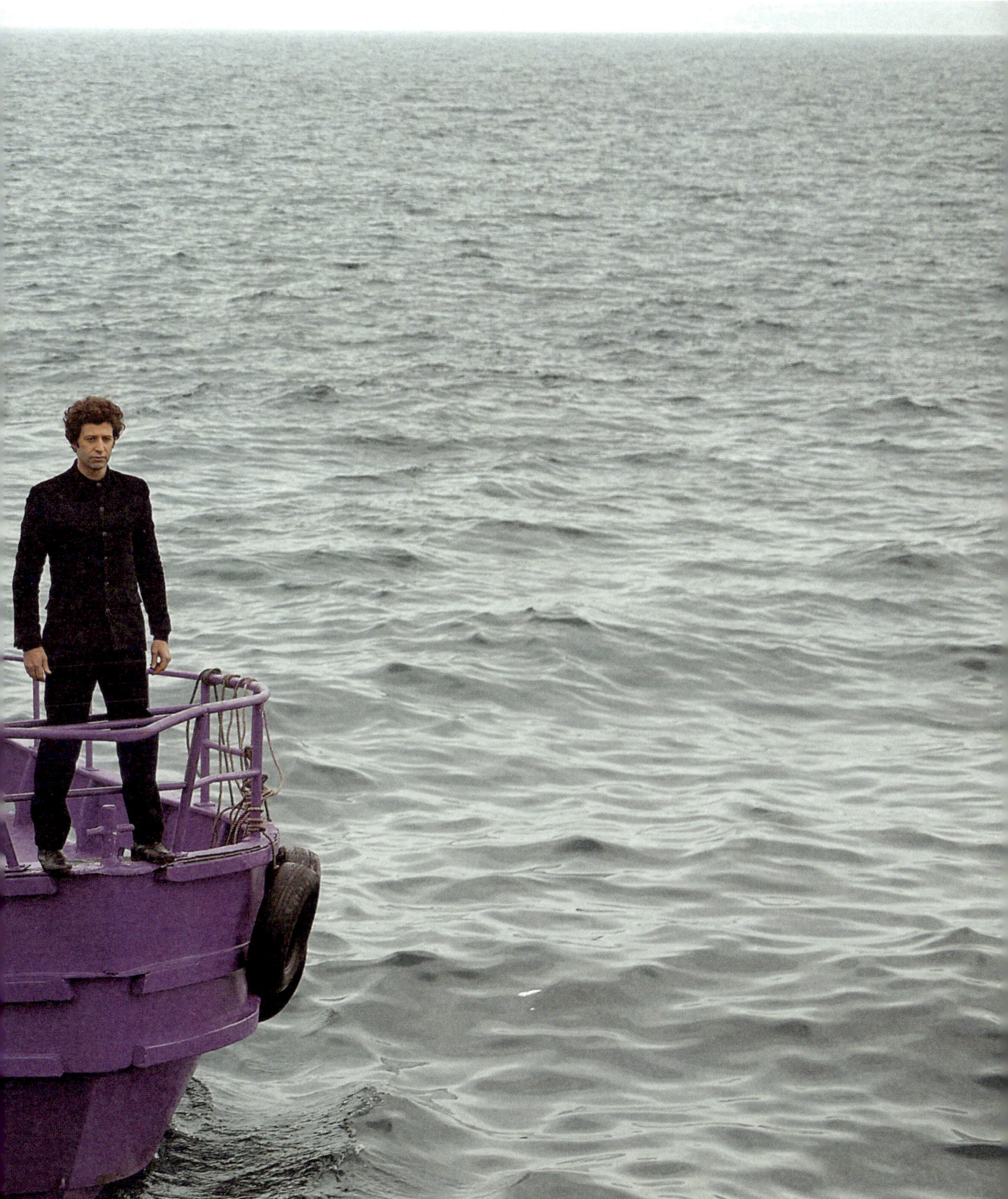

# The Art of PascALEjandro

**Diego Moldes**

What is pascALEjandro? Who is the artist known as pascALEjandro? For Art with a capital A, pascALEjandro is neither two artists united by a common project, nor a married artist couple collaborating one artistic life project, nor two people united in pursuing a common interest. Of course not. In life, they are indeed this and much more. But in Art, pascALEjandro is a single Artist: two people – two souls – united as a single being make one artist, not two. There were many differences between Pascale Montandon and Alejandro Jodorowsky: age, experience, family situations, native language and culture, gender, race, nationality, and religion. But they were united by something much stronger: the desire to live for and through art, to live for original artistic creation. It didn't matter that Pascale was a young Frenchwoman with Cambodian and Vietnamese paternal grandparents, or that Jodorowsky was a French citizen from Chile, of Jewish and Ukrainian heritage. None of that mattered. Ever since I met him in 2006 (over a decade ago, *tempus fugit…*) Jodorowsky, who knows I am a writer, has been telling me the Buddhist proverb, "think of the work and not the profit." Alejandro and Pascale, or Pascale and Alejandro, for it amounts to the same, have tried to create a child of their own. Not a physical child with their genetic material, but rather a spiritual child, a spiritual union that materializes for the viewer – not for the artists themselves, of course, who already *are* – only when they create a work of art, such as a drawing, a painting, or a film.

## Life

*I might well be the child abandoned on the jetty on its way to the*
*high seas, the little farm boy following the lane,*
*its forehead touching the sky.*
*The paths are rough. The hillocks are covered with broom.*
*The air is motionless. How far away are the birds and the springs!*
*It can only be the end of the world ahead.*

Rimbaud, fragment of "Childhood" (Enfance)
(*Les Illuminations*, 1886)

If my memory serves me well, it was Arthur Rimbaud who said it is impossible to know someone without knowing about his or her childhood. I had already known Pascale, through Alejandro of course, since at least 2009 when I learned that she was also an artist. When she returned from Chile after the filming of *The Dance of Reality*, Pascale sent me, from Paris to Madrid, a copy of her book *The Reality of my Dance* (2013), published in a trilingual French, Spanish, and English edition. In that extraordinary hardcover, landscape-oriented book – which will soon be a collector's item, if it isn't already – I enjoyed Pascale's fine artwork, her delicate sketches, drawings, paintings, photographs, and illustrations, often alongside Alejandro's, and I also learned about her origins and her childhood. What was this artist's childhood like? Here's how Pascale remembered it: "Childhood is full of contrasts, it is gentle and harsh at the same time. Unlike what sensed in the outside world, especially at school, at home I felt as if I was in a haven of peace, with no crying or accidents, shielded from any kind of violence or aggression. The transition from one space to the other was sometimes brutal. As the youngest, I was often alone with my mother. She was the filter through which I attempted to understand the world. She would often tell me that to get to the hill, you have to be able to see the mountain. I applied that principle literally." Pascale had a happy childhood, unlike Alejandro, whose childhood was unusual and unfortunate, and who felt neither loved nor understood by his family or the people of Tocopilla. This is perfectly expressed in his film *The Dance of Reality* (2013), and also in his autobiography of the same title, published in Spanish for the first time in 2001.

What unites Pascale and Alejandro, as is often the case, is the search for an identity. As children of immigrants born far from their countries of origin, each was different, and each was aware of this difference. Pascale, a child of Cambodian and Vietnamese grandparents in Paris – "I was born in France, but I am Eurasian, like my parents: I have a Cambodian grandmother, a Vietnamese grandmother, and two French grandfathers" – and Alejandro, born in Chile, with Russian-Ukrainian Jewish grandparents of Sephardic and Ashkenazi heritage. Was it that search for an identity that forged the artist-soul in them as children, or was it the other way around? Chicken or egg? Pascale writes about her childhood in France in the seventies in a way that recalls Jodorowsky's childhood in Chile during the thirties: "I always felt different, out of step. I am the youngest in a family of four children, eleven years younger than my sister and brothers, who are all a year apart. I have always lived among people older than me: nobody ever addressed me as a child, and the language of adults became part of my childhood normality." Her words should be reread. And she adds a reflection that helps understand her personality: "For me, school was a painful limitation. The first time I went, I was shocked to confront other students my age, their cries, tears, complaints, stories... all of that made them different from me and from the serene and loving atmosphere of my home. Their violence and brutality affected me. On top of that, they also branded me as different: being a good student meant I was known as "the smart one," as if it were an insult. And they were the first to make me aware of my Asian origins, since they called me *the Chinese Girl* because of my slanted eyes." Children were quick to point out difference. Alejandro, white-skinned, circumcised, and blond, had to endure the cries of "Jew! Jew!" from his schoolmates. An Asian in Europe, a European Jew in Latin America: two people whose childhood identities were split between two different worlds. Alejandro fled Chile for France in 1953 to escape trauma. In Pascale's case, the split was an asset, since she quickly channeled her dual culture and identity into artistic creativity. She adds, "I have always lived this double culture, French and Vietnamese, not as a duality but as a whole, a complete layering of two worlds that creates one single world, an identity that can be expressed in one word rather than two: Eurasian. I am the only one among my siblings born when my family lived in France rather than Vietnam, and that's why I always felt I came from somewhere else, but the search for personal artistic expression has helped me discover, develop, claim, and ultimately absorb this inheritance inscribed in my genes." We will return to this.

When Maryline Buda interviewed Pascale for the magazine *Ventana Latina*, she asked "How would you define your artistic collaboration with Alejandro?" Here's how Pascale responded: "It began almost by chance. In the early days of our relationship, we had the sense that despite the great love that united us, we came from very distinct universes, and did things very differently. He came from a strong visual universe, very influenced by Latin America; and I was doing something quieter and more austere, influenced by my Asian origins. But when we began living together, we realized the differences were insignificant, and that we were similar in our approach to a work of art. It's all about complementarity. The exhibition "*Yin & Yang/ Yin*" began as a game: Alejandro drew, and suggested I add the colors. Then some friends saw our work and said we had to show it, and we ended up in the Museum of Modern Art in Paris. We think of this work as our symbolic child. In our relationship there are no walls, only bridges. We each know everything about the other, we admire and respect each other, and we also respect what we do as individuals. And every once in a while we have to create something together, but none of it is calculated."[1] The art of both Pascale and Alejandro is an act of love. pascALEjandro is an act of artistic generosity shared with the viewer, and between the artists. Let's examine it.

### Paintings

Like everything worthwhile in life, the collaboration between Alejandro Jodorowsky and Pascale Montandon arose by chance. In 2009 the couple came across some drawings Alejandro had done twenty years earlier, and Alejandro asked Pascale to color them. Pascale spent over three years giving the drawings new life, and creating a new art form. In 2012 the couple agreed to their first joint exhibition, *Resisting the Present*, at the Musée d'Art Moderne de la Ville de Paris, under a symbolic name: pascALEjandro. The three capital letters, ALE, connected the two names, fusing them in a graphic demonstration of how the end of Pascale's name is also the beginning of Alejandro's. There is no beginning or end. There is Everything. Remember the famous *koan* the Japanese monk Ejo Takata formulated for Jodorowsky in Mexico, in around 1966 or 1967: Alejandro said of Takata that he was "the man who has most influenced me in my life." Pascale has explained that pascALEjandro reflects their complementarity, since their "works are based on a fusion of the masculine and the feminine, and the drawing, the stable element, came together with color, the fluid element." She adds, "we are constantly fuelling and developing this four handed work, and we see a broad horizon for it." (Montandon-Jodorowsky, 2013, 126). The artistic horizon is undoubtedly immense.

When I interviewed Jodorowsky for my doctoral dissertation (which later became a book), I asked him about his influences in cinema and literature, and he answered, understandably annoyed:

1. Buda, Marilyne, *Ventana Latina*, January 2014, "http://www.ventanalatina.co.uk/2014/01/la-pintora-pascale-montandon-jodorowsky-un-ideal-de-vida/" (consulted august 28th, 2016).

"why do you keep asking me about my influences? Everything has influenced me in general, and nothing in particular." Jodorowsky's art springs from his unconscious; when he produces a drawing, a book, a script, or a play, he does not rationalize it. Only when it is finished and revealed to the world do we hear any analytical comments on its origin in his fertile imagination. What were Alejandro's drawings like before Pascale colored them? They were sketches, line drawings, but something was missing. When they were given color, a new art form appeared, and pascALEjandro was born. In his *Fábulas Pánicas*, which appeared in *Heraldo de México* between 1967 and 1973, Alejandro drew and colored cartoon strips where he illustrated a syncretic philosophy akin to Zen Buddhism. The content was profound, but the coloring was intuitive and often random, and the drawings irregular and imperfect. Four decades later Alejandro's drawings are richer, more vivid, and better drawn, possessing a greater expressive charge. But the color was missing, and Pascale was missing. The intense greens, reds, blues, lively oranges, pinks, and yellows have a recurring expressive power. This is clear in works like *Oiseaux angevores / Pájaros angelívoros* (*Angel-eating Birds*, 2010), in which horrible green, large-beaked birds with threatening eyes attack an angel with incredibly pale skin, a bluish tail-coat, and a top hat. Or in *L'un vers l'autre / El uno hacia el otro* (*One Facing the Other*, 2009), where an angel in flight – in this case, in a yellow suit and a green top hat – holds and caresses a woman with a red dress, green hair, and a regal green crown. From the woman's mouth emerge orange threads that could be stars, arrows, ribbons, or flowers. Both wear black masks, or perhaps sunglasses. Are they blind? The angel so beloved by Marc Chagall (1887-1985), whose influence on pascALEjandro is notable whether it is conscious or not, reappears in two major works: *La lutte avec l'Ange / La lucha contra el ángel* (*Struggle with Angel*, 2009) y *Le corps, l'âme et l'esprit / El cuerpo, el alma y el espíritu* (*Body, Soul, and Spirit*, 2011), both of which are laden with deep spirituality and a complex metaphysics. The angel reappears in an androgynous and perhaps feminine form in *Amour éternel / Amor eterno* (*Eternal Love*, 2011), represented allegorically as a guardian angel helping an old woman water some plants. These paintings are richly suggestive. In *Cadavres heureux / Cadáveres felices* (*Happy Corpses*, 2009), in a drawing dominated by sky blue and leaf green, we see the decapitated corpses of a man and a woman, their necks bloody, holding smiling heads in their hands. *Trois générations / Tres generaciones* (*Three Generations*, 2009), shows the three ages of woman, whose forms and coloring, along with the figure of an enormous blue mosquito climbing up a girl's chest, remind me vaguely of *Woman in three Stages* (1895) and *The Dance of Life* (1899), both by Edvard Munch (1863-1944). In *Nature vivante / Naturaleza viva* (*Living Nature*, 2009), the vegetation recalls some of the plant forms in the paintings of Hieronymus Bosch (circa 1550-1616), or the exuberant jungle scenes of Henri Rousseau, such as *The Dream* (1910). Symbolism and allegory are constantly present in the paintings' subjects, perhaps showing a search for the ineffable. When I look at works by pascALEjandro like *Amour fou / Amor loco*, (*Crazy Love*, 2009), *Radio folle / Radio loca*, (*Mad Radio*, 2009), *Le duc de la marmelade* (*the Duke of Marmalade*, 2014) – a smoking cat-woman! – my imagination flies free and completely unbound, and the conscious and unconscious sides of my psyche embrace. We have entered the territory of surrealism, combined with the Panic Movement. It is as if Bosch[2] had joined up with Joan

2. As Borges said, "all that is not tradition is plagiarism." There is no such thing as complete originality. Whether artists like it or not, Art is a synthesis of the collective (artistic) unconscious, and all of them are mutually indebted. In the Bosch exhibition at the Prado celebrating the fourth centenary of the artist's death, a number of texts praised the originality of this precursor of surrealism. Bosch is unique, and one of the artists I most admire. However, there are figures in *The Garden of Earthly Delights* and other paintings that appear in other fifteenth century drawings that precede him. Cf. the German-Alsatian Martin Schongauer (c.1445-1491) and his *Heiliger Antonius von Dämonen gepeingt* [*San Antonio Tormented by Demons* (prior to 1481)], to which Pieter van der Heyden (1530-1572) is doubly indebted en *Luxuria* [Lust, 1558], from his series *The Seven Deadly Sins*, which can be seen at the Germanisches Nationalmuseum in Nuremberg.

Miró (1893-1983) and Roland Topor (1938-1997) was their child. The affinity between these three artists, so formally and culturally different, and Jodorowsky, is clear. I am not speaking of influence and much less of appropriation, but rather of an elective affinity, or an artistic kinship. The drawings' lines remind me of the great Jean Cocteau (1889-1963), especially the style of the heads, and the theme of the angel between two (almost orphean) worlds. Just as he did with the short film *La cravate* (Jodorowsky, 1957), I am sure Cocteau, a Renaissance man, would happily have applauded pascALEjandro's works. The much missed Topor would also have praised such Panic-like works as *Pierrot sur mouche / Pierrot sobre mosca* (*Pierrot on Fly*, 2014) (perhaps inspired by his story *The Incredible Human Fly*), *Notre amour / Nuestro amor* (*Our Love*, 2014) or *Le poids du passé* (2014), all imbued with a dynamic and almost painful energy. As in Goya's later phase, in Topor and pascALEjandro, treatment of the human figure always involves caricature; the dreamlike quality is achieved through unusual metamorphoses between animals, people, and plants, occasionally pursued by imaginary beings or monsters appearing in landscapes of the mind, almost like vivid architectures, inspired by biology. In works like *Deuda* (*Debt,* 2012), *Dans la main de Dieu /En la mano de Dios* (*In God's Hands*, 2009) or *La vierge du Grand-père / La Virgen del Gran Padre* (*Virgin of the Great Father*, 2014), as with Topor, the erotic grotesque is sometimes sarcastic. Other works such as *Coito divino* (*Divine Sex*, 2014) suggest an irrepressible erotic impulse, in this case represented by multiple arms – six on the woman and six on the man – recalling the Hindu goddess Kali in her higher form, Mahākālī, who is described in the Sanskrit tradition as having six, eight, or ten arms, and an equal number of legs and even heads. Works such as *Patria* (2012), meanwhile, make fun of flag-waving nationalism.
When the erotic acquires humorous strokes, we might think of the French *fabliaux* of the twelfth to fifteenth centuries, those erotic-burlesque poems that satirized courtly love, the chivalric

romance, and even the clergy. Whatever the subject, the human body, with its movement and variations, is always the drawing's primary image; its recurring omnipresence is like waves crashing against rocks, or sea-foam caressing the sand with its tongue. The corporeal is always attacked, suspended, shot through, or pierced by the spiritual, since all – or almost all – the works express a duality like the yin and yang of Buddhism. When Pascale was asked what she seeks to express in her work, she replied: "There are recurring themes: fragility, impermanence, the balance between what disappears and what remains, between movement and the trace it leaves."[3] In the drawings, one can see how the body is defined through pain, and the spirit through love. Love and pain, past and future, youth and old age, matter and spirit, solid and liquid, the earthly and the ethereal, create a style always in a state of irresolution, with everything obedient to a cosmic play of dualities exemplified in the unity between movement and stability – what is, and what will become. It is almost a metaphysics of space, in which the body appears harassed, mistreated, pursued, punished, wounded, and even mutilated. This apparent disorder, this blended, multiplied, chaotic style nevertheless covers the artist's recurring and irrational obsessions in a coherent way. While symbols may erupt uncontrolledly, they have a purpose. The body-spirit seeks the masculine-feminine duality through art, in order to reach eternity. In another style, there are highly accomplished compositions about motherhood and creation, and the fetus as a symbol of new life, such as *Vases communicants / Vasos comunicantes* (*Communicating Vessels*, 2012) or the extraordinary *Mère Sacrée / Madre sagrada* (*Holy Mother*, 2009), where the nude mother lies face-down on her long black hair which is transformed into a tree-stump. Her hands are large with green fingernails. In her left arm she holds a blue baby, who rests ecstatically across her knees, and in her right hand she holds a pearl. The

3. Buda, Marilyne, *Op. Cit.*

pearl symbolizes a new human soul; for Muslims, it symbolizes heaven, since they believe that the fortunate are hidden within it; for Lao Tzu, the pearl symbolizes the spirit of darkness, since it is the spirit within the body, just as the pearl is inside the oyster; for the ancient Greeks, the pearl was the essential androgynous being. *Mère Sacrée* and *Vases communicants* remind me of the esoteric symbolist Frantisek Kupka (1871-1957) and his suggestive aquatint *The Beginning of Life* (1900-1903), which can be seen at the Centre Georges Pompidou. In this painting, a fetus is suspended in the air and connected to a lotus flower, a symbol of the soul, in an attempt to unite the modern scientific-medical vision with the spiritual tradition. The drawings of pascALEjandro also remind me of other analogous symbolists, like the Belgians Léon Spilliaert (1882-1946), Fernand Khnopff (1858-1921), the occultist Jean Delville (1867-1953) (*Angels of Night*, 1894, *The Treasures of Satan*, 1895), the angels and demons of the Russian Mikhail Vrubel (1856-1910) (*Flying Demon*, 1899, *Fallen Demon*, 1901, *Pearl*, 1904), or Vasiliy Denissov (1862-1921), and also certain oils on canvas by the Swiss painter Carlos Schwabe (1866-1926) (*Pain*, 1893), and the dreamlike mystery of the great Odilon Redon (1840-1916). The feeling of movement, the anthropomorphic figures, the soft, folded plant figures, and the level of accumulation, are also reminiscent of the Dutch painter Jan Toorop (1858-1928) (*The Young Generation*, 1892, *The Three Brides*, 1893), who was born in Java and became an Art Nouveau painter in the Low Countries. The anguish we feel on seeing the *pascalejandrian* drawings *L'Abus* (2014), *La sepáration* (*Separation*, 2014) o *La visite de l'ombre* (*The Shadow's Visit*, 2014), make me think of the style of Alfred Kubin (1877-1959), Goya's (1746-1928) black paintings, Max Klinger (1857-1920) (*Dream*, 1884), of my much-admired Bruno Schulz (1892-1942), and of Richard Nicolaus Roland Holst (1868-1938), the creator of *Ananke* (*Necessity*, 1892). Obviously, this play of connecting vessels, artistic affinities, and correlations of all kinds are not what the artist (in this case one artist who is two) has in mind, at least during the act of creation, but they are present in the mind of the viewer, the recipient of the work, who in this case is me. Art is by nature polysemic, and occasionally involuntarily referential. Lets leave subtle symbolism aside, and think about color.

**Drawing and Color**

At university we took a class called Color Psychology. Anyone who works in communication – be it audiovisual, advertising, design, etc. – knows the importance of color, which, like music, escapes philosophy of language and ontology.

When one looks carefully at works by pascALEjandro such as the stunning *La vengeance de la bête* / *La venganza de la bestia* (*The Beast's Revenge*, 2011), the aforementioned *Vases comunicantes*, or the drawing-manifesto *Re-évolution poétique* / *Re-evolución poética* (*Poetic Re-evolution*, 2011), in which a tense group of protestors carries a giant blue bird with a knife plunged into its bleeding breast, it's impossible to avoid the thought of Fauvist color combined with Panic-surrealism. It is an unthinkable combination, which nonetheless works in an original way.

At the same time, pascALEjandro can be added to an artistic movement concerned with warm colors that includes the Nabis, (*mouvement nabi*, 1888-circa 1918), especially the warm colors of Paul-Élie Ranson (1864-1909) (*Paysage nabique*, 1890), Édouard Vuillard (1868-1940) (*L'Intérieur vert*, 1891 and *Le Corsage rayé*, 1895), and Félix Valloton (1865-1925), whose paintings *La Chambre rouge* (1898), *Femmes nues aux chats* (circa 1898), and *Nuage à Romanel* (1900) are at the Musée cantonal des Beaux-arts in Lausanne. Long live the warmth of color.

Before she met Jodorowsky, Pascale took a minimalist approach in her paintings, expressing as much as possible with the least possible material. This is evident in her portraits of faces resembling funeral shrouds – *Ange double* (2001), *Ange noir* (2002),

*Ange noir au visage clair* (2002), and *Ange tracé* (2002) – in which the expression is diminished and the eyes transformed so that the gaze can reach the immaterial, the soul. In these works I see some correlations with analogous portraits by the aforementioned Odilon Redon, the greatest French symbolist of his time and a clear precursor of Surrealism, such as his lithography *Yeux Clos* (*Closed Eyes*, 1890), with the exception that in this work the model's eyes are closed, as the title indicates. Pascale's abstract works, especially those made during the early period of her relationship with Alejandro, are characterized by the search for an essential beauty, and the attempt to capture the eternity of the sublime with a minimum of elements, eliminating all trace of the hand or line. These works possess a seductive spirituality devoid of any kind of self-satisfaction or artifice: *Naissance du Monde I y II* (2007), *Aurora* (2008), *Éclipse* (2010), and *Tracé Nuageux* (2010). They were finished during the year Pascale and Alejandro married.

**Film and Design**

It could be said that pascALEjandro first appeared as a film artist. The costumes worn by Jaime (Alejandro's father, played by Brontis Jodorowsky), Sara Felicidad (Alejandro's mother, played by the soprano Pamela Flores), the anarchist (played by Adán Jodorowsky), the Theosophist (Axel Cristóbal Jodorowsky) and Alejandro (Jeremías Herskovits) are coherent with the director's descriptions and with the period, and work to define the characters' psychology. Pascale began as a costume designer, and her sketches from the eighties are already very promising. Sara's Parisian-style costume, especially in the final scene, is suggestive and even erotic (the cleavage, and the way the costume emphasizes the feminine form, are reminiscent of the Paleolithic and Mesopotamian Venuses). Pascale's photography in the still also shows details of the filming and of Alejandro's artistic wisdom, immortalized here by his wife and companion.

### *Endless Poetry*

I will discuss this film further since it is the most recent (it premiered in France in October 2016) and because it best shows how the mimesis or symbiosis of pascALEjandro takes shape. In *Endless Poetry*, the religious quest through a persistent mysticism and symbolism – which, along with their religious and cultural syncretism, was what made Jodorowsky's earlier films so original – yields to a vital artistic search that rather than abandoning spirituality gives it a new, more poetic focus. In the contrast between the Jodorowsky of today and the Jodorowsky we remember (since memory is a reconstruction of the past rather than its expression) the artist bears his soul, reveals himself to his audience, asking for nothing in return. "What you give, you give to yourself. What you do not give, you give up," is one of his favorite expressions. Today, in his eighties, Jodorowsky understands the art of film not as an art of conflict that attempts to transform the audience – a task as enormous as it is quixotic – but rather as a therapeutic art for both artist and audience, and an act of spiritual generosity in a world corrupted by consumerism and the absurd and obscene accumulation of material objects.

Jodorowsky and Pascale retouched many of the film's objects, garments, bodies, landscapes, and sets, coloring them scene by scene according to the director's criteria.[4] The digital color matching works as a new expressive tool for the artist, in which the director

4. Clearly, digital cinema is not synonymous with a new cinematic language, despite new digital technologies having coexisted with the older photochemical method for twenty years. But it is equally clear that the replacement of the photochemical method by the digital has allowed for new techniques, and the generation of new emblematic styles and syntaxes of modernity. As Esteve Riambau writes, "when filming in the photochemical method, the camera captures the world and transforms it into an image. This positions it closer to recording than to representation. On the other hand, "digital visual effects provide the art of recording with the expressive power of the visual arts of representation." (McLean, 16)," Riambau, E. *Hollywood en la era digital*, Madrid: Ediciones Cátedra, 2011. p. 15.

or film editor uses digital technology in a method analogous to the way a painter colors or retouches a painting. The result of this new digital color matching is an extraordinary proof of the couple's artistic harmony, and the rapport I have attempted to define, describe, and analyze in this piece: pascALEjandro.

# pascALEjandro goes to the movies
## The paintings of pascALEjandro and the films of Alejandro Jodorowsky

**Philippe Rouyer**

By its very signature, pascALEjandro lays claim to the fusion—and not the mere summing—of two artistic worlds. The name pascALEjandro is a portmanteau of the first names of Pascale Montandon-Jodorowsky and Alejandro Jodorowsky: at the core of this fusion, three upper-case characters, ALE, compose at once the last letters of Pascale and the first of Alejandro. Is this a gift of providence, a visual pun on the part of two artists who juggle words as readily as forms and colors? Surely. But it is also a discourse on method: in pascALEjandro's paintings, created by four hands, the work of each begins where the work of the other leaves off. In interviews, the two artists have often insisted on the fact that pascALEjandro represents the biological child they never had. This union of first names—with its intersecting letters rising separate at the center—belongs to an artistic, playful and even loving communion which Alejandro evokes when he speaks of his desire to present Pascale with drawings that would amaze and seduce her. Hence the impressive number of canvasses dedicated to the coupling of bodies and souls, from the early self-portrait *The Two of Us* (2009), to the more stylized *Our Love* (2014), by way of every permutation of romantic pair: *Adam and Eve, Love at First Sight, Wild Love, All of Love*—even up to the emblematic *Love which is Stronger than Death.*

pascALEjandro is an artist in its own right: its body of work cannot be reduced to that of one or the other of its progenitors. When she isn't working collaboratively on pascALEjandro,

Pascale Montandon-Jodorowsky paints her own pieces independently, just as Alejandro, for his part, carries on with making books, graphic novels, and films. One nevertheless finds pascALEjandro's name linked to the two films Jodorowsky has directed since breaking his twenty-three year long silence as a filmmaker: *La Danza de la realidad* (2013) and *Poesía sin fin* (2016). This should come as no surprise as he also asked his spouse Pascale Montandon-Jodorowsky to work on these films (as a costume designer) and gave the two lead male roles to his sons Adan and Brontis. The question of pascALEjandro's role in the creation of these two films therefore poses itself at once in a factual light (what precisely was its contribution?) and also in a subterranean way: have pascALEjandro's paintings influenced Jodorowsky's mise-en-scène? One might begin by flipping this line of questioning around and attempting to determine the influence of Jodorowsky's early films on the paintings of pascALEjandro.

**pascALEjandro and the early films of Jodorowsky**

We know that Jodorowsky used to draw when he was young. Though he (provisionally) put this aside when he began to collaborate on graphic novels with artists such as Mœbius, he retained from drawing a taste for visual composition and the surge of vivid images we find throughout his films. It is this quasi-pictorial approach to cinema that authorizes a comparison with the paintings of pascALEjandro. This is not to say that Jodorowsky has ever sought to recapture the imagery of his early films in pascALEjandro's drawings. But it is indeed same author expressing himself in each of these two artistic modes, and it is normal to find, from one body of work to the next, a certain number of similar preoccupations, both visual and formal. We might add that, by its art of cultivating the shock-image, Jodorowsky's cinema asserts its pictorial tendency from the outset. In all his early films, the most beautiful scenes appear as a result of static framing, by which he privileges frontal compositions and relegates camera movements to a secondary, functional role. He himself explains this clearly in his anecdote of a street accident (a man hit by a tramway) he once witnessed: "I said to myself that, from the point of view of photography, the scene would work well from any angle. So, as a filmmaker, I decided to cause accidents and only afterwards think of how to film them."[133] Jodorowsky's cinema is even more visual in that he cultivates an opposition to dialogue: he resorts to speech only when there is truly no way of expressing his idea visually. The result is a spectacular series of images which play with symbols and radiate great emotional force.

### *Fando and Lis*

When Alejandro Jodorowsky embarked on his first feature film *Fando and Lis* in 1967, he was already an accomplished artist. Adapted from a play written by his partner Fernando Arrabal—a text which Jodorowsky knew perfectly as he had acted it on stage—the film depicts the world and aspirations of a young filmmaker. One finds here, ensconced in a coming-of-age narrative, an array of figures of perverted, martyred youth and longings for wild love, motifs which run though Jodorowsky's entire body of work and also appear in pascALEjandro's.

A comparison of two frames from this film and two paintings from 2014 (*Abuse* and *All of Love*) sheds much light.

In *Abuse*, the abused young girl carries a doll which recalls the marionette with cut strings in *Fando and Lis*. In both instances, the disjointed doll prefigures the fate reserved for the body of the girl herself, with the difference that, in the film, the puppet also serves as bait for the child: once the little girl has latched onto one of the puppet's arms, the man only has to pull the other to draw the child to him. In the painting, the assault is even more brutal.

1. Interview conducted by Philippe Rouyer and Michel Ciment for the review *Positif* n° 668, October 2016.

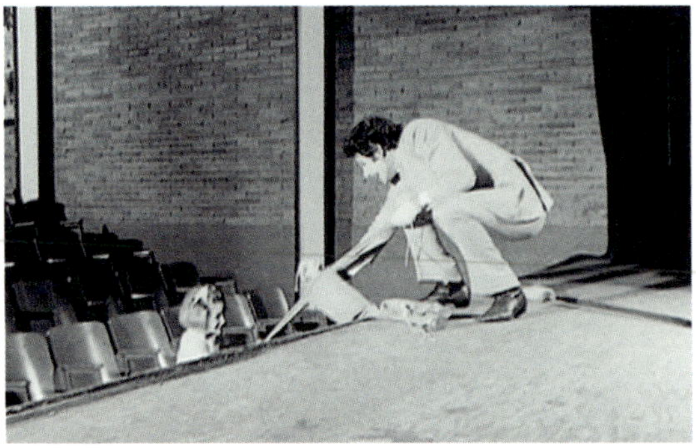

*Fando and Lis.*

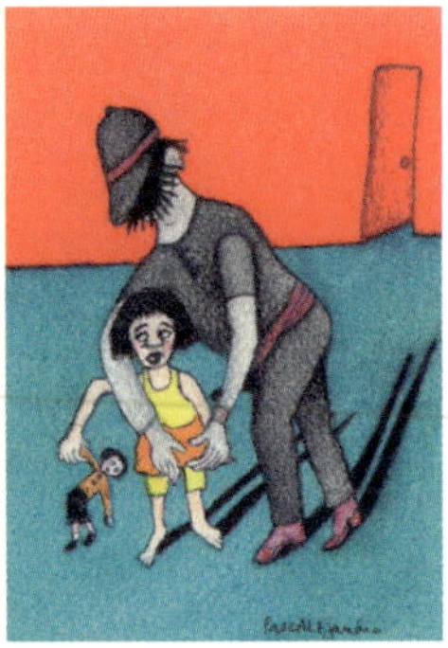

*Abuse* (2014).

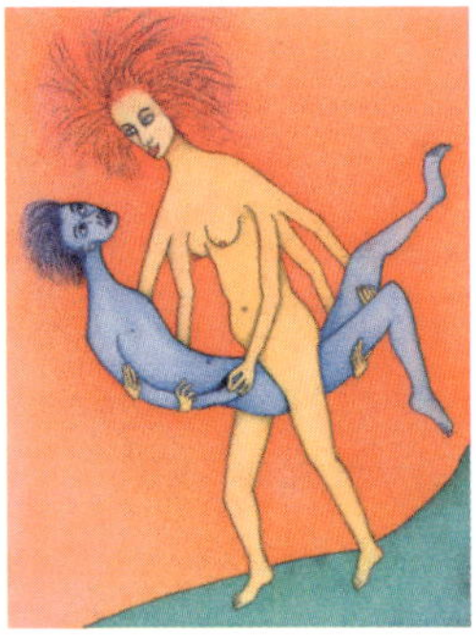

*All of Love* (2014).

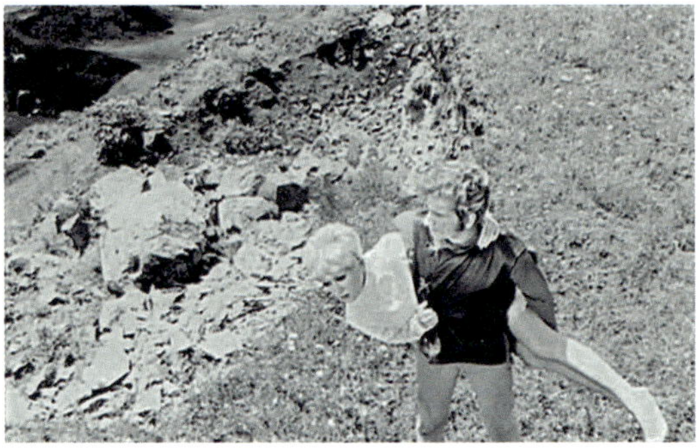

*Fando and Lis.*

The adult's hands directly approach the child's privates. Beyond the potential issue of censorship (though *Fando and Lis* goes very far in its representation), there is the fact that a film frame, no matter how spectacular, is only a piece in a sequence, whereas a painting has to express everything in a single image.

The second frame from *Fando and Lis* offers a stylized and metaphorical vision of the bodily communion of lovers, which reappears in several of pascALEjandro's paintings, notably in *All of Love.* The first difference one notices is the inversion of the partners. In the painting, it is the woman who carries her lover with his feet suspended in the air. Also, in the painting the lovers are naked and joined in full sexual intercourse (even though we don't see their genitals). In the film, the sexual relation is stylized through the peculiar and suggestive position of the lovers, which evokes at once a union of bodies (the girl's legs seem to come out of the man's hips) and a fellowship of souls (one lover carries the other).

The most striking thing one notices in these two comparisons is, of course, the contribution of the colors to the paintings in relation to the black-and-white film—and just how vivid these colors are. The tragedy of abuse in no way restricts the shimmering of these emphatically symbolic tones: the assailant stands in grey; the walls and the door to which he will drag the girl are blood red; black streaks of shadow soil the blue ground from which the child dressed in yellow and orange will soon be lifted. Orange, a warm color, runs its gamut in the painting *All of Love*, from the body of the woman to the shade of the sky. At the top of this monochrome, red graces only the woman's hair (plausibly an echo of the poet Stella Díaz, who was Alejandro's first lover and who indeed sported such hair in real life, as we see in *Poesía sin fin*). Here too, the ground is turquoise, but it occupies only a small portion of the frame: the lovers have already abandoned reality to lift off toward the ecstasy of the orange sky. This very evocative way of arranging colors in pascALEjandro's paintings comes from Pascale Montandon-Jodorowsky. Her work is not that of a colorist but rather of an artist in her own right, who offers a reading of the drawing through her use of color. This color is all the more striking in that the background has been purged of details, and the tones diffuse through the canvas in large swaths that command our eye.

### *The Holy Mountain*

*The Holy Mountain* is a color film whose tones explode in certain scenes. Nevertheless, at the time it was made (1973) the treatment of color on celluloid remained tightly linked to what one was filming (scenery, costumes) and, in comparison to pascALEjandro's canvases, the film's colors, though very evocative, seem almost tame.

Even though the painting *Poetic Re-evolution* appears, in its very title, even madder than the frame of *The Holy Mountain* with which I am comparing it here, there is an obvious likeness between the two images: an aspect of ritual in the procession of the crowd, closely linked with the idea of death. One thus finds a similar spirit in these two images of a crowd bearing aloft a body (which is innocence). The swarm of bearers is united in a single brown color of bare skin (in the film) or in the grey tint of uniforms (in the painting). The white of the uplifted body stands out as a symbol of innocence against a tortured background: a drawing of flames in the painting and the remains of a destroyed pyramid in the film.

Visually, the painting is the stronger of the two images, as it has to express in a single frame what the film also expresses by other means: by the sound of the scene and the movement of the crowd which will eventually crucify and stone this body.

The next example presents two situations which are directly opposite, but which one cannot help associating. In the film, a group of young people has been shot to death by the dictator's policemen, and little birds symbolically take flight from their mortal wounds—this is life and purity taking flight. The scene is all the more striking for being presented as a static shot, like a painting. In the painting *Angelivorous Birds*, we also presume the winged victim to be pure—angelic even. And these carnivorous birds have come to devour him. Their outspread wings contrast

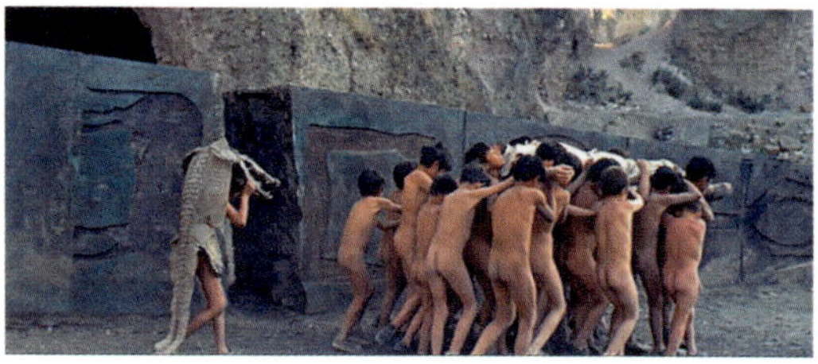

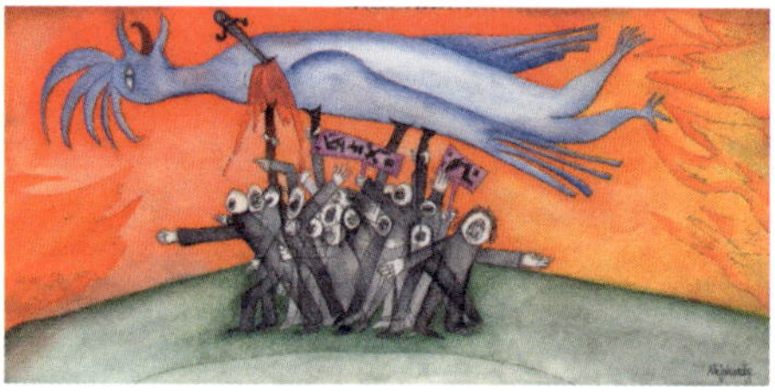

*The Holy Mountain.*
*Poetic Re-evolution* (2011).

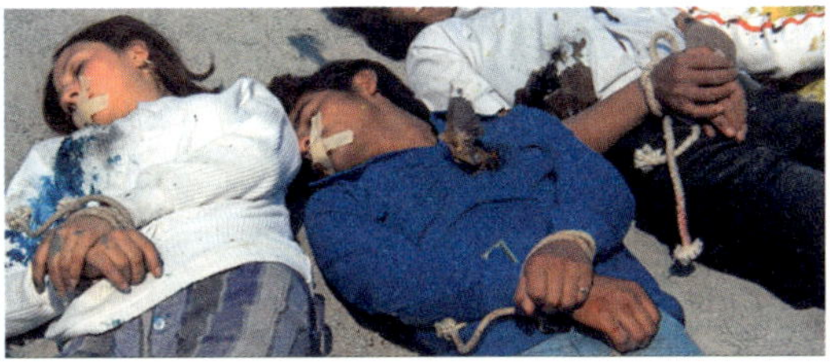 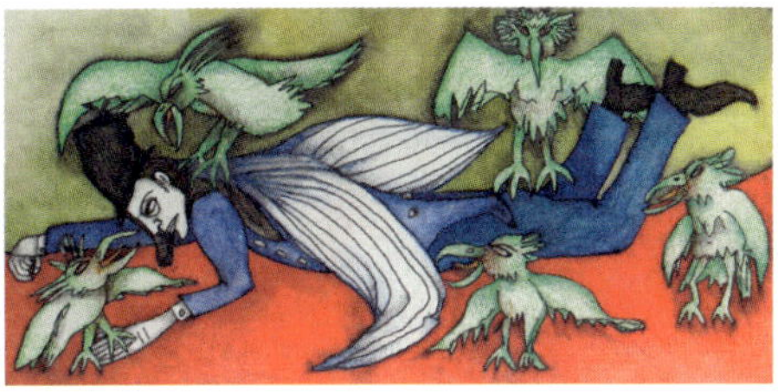

*The Holy Mountain.*
*Angelivorous Birds* (2010).

with those of the angel, crumpled. In such a context, it shouldn't surprise us that this time it's the ground that is red. The blue clothes of the man on the ground accentuate the connection with the film frame, which cultivates the same sensation of innocence being put to death.

There are many more examples that could be cited to demonstrate how Jodorowsky's visions as a filmmaker suffuse pascALEjandro's work, albeit in revitalized forms, screened though the language of painting and the colors of Pascale Montandon-Jodorowsky.

**Birth of *The Child Fireman***

We know it was Pascale who spurred Alejandro to take up drawing again. But at that moment they were still far from the birth of pascALEjandro, as we can see from the genesis of one of this artist's most famous paintings: *The Child Fireman*, which would later serve as the poster to *La Danza de la realidad*.

Pascale Montandon-Jodorowsky recalls:

"In the very beginning, long before Alejandro had written the film script, he wrote a collection of three tales originally meant to be published in Spain under the title *Tres cuentos mágicos (para niños mutantes)*. The first tale speaks of Alejandro's childhood as a "child fireman," an episode he later narrated in *La Danza*. The tale is much more a dream vision than a reconstruction of childhood memories, but Alejandro really wanted me to do the cover illustration for the book. Another difficulty for me was that

I had to paint this cover figuratively, whereas my work over the years had evolved more toward abstraction.
I started making drawings and preparatory sketches and, as I went along, Alejandro would make suggestions and specify his vision of what he wanted. In the end I managed to convince him to do the drawing himself, and I promised to do the colors.
That's what gave birth to the drawing that later served for the film poster and, in a certain way, initiated our collaboration".[2]

Beyond the interest of the anecdote, it is illuminating to retrace the origins of this painting. Pascale, following Alejandro's indications, indeed began to draw the father and son in firemen's uniforms being carried off in a kind of whirlwind which, in a first colored version, entirely obliterates the father. At this stage, the work almost looks like a battle between figurative art (the child) and abstraction (the whirlwind). In redoing the drawing himself, Alejandro abandoned the idea of the whirlwind in favor of these flames which, in a superb stroke, he depicted with human bodies seeming to be consumed within. Above the figures of the father and the child whom he holds affectionately by the shoulder, a circle of butterfly-angels sketches a strange halo. The portrait seems at once tender and terrifying while it radiates a surprising sweetness. The flames, whose color extends the orange swath of the ground, appear under control. The very calm stance of the two characters dispels any notion of danger, even though the child's outspread arms betray an emotion not shared by the father—as in the earthquake sequence of *Poesía sin fin*. The warm colors conceived by Pasacle, far from the dark whirlwind of her second sketch, would become one of pascALEjandro's trademarks.
This painting predates the film *La Danza de la realidad*, for it was made in 2009, at a time when Alejandro had yet even to write

2. Unpublished interview with the author.

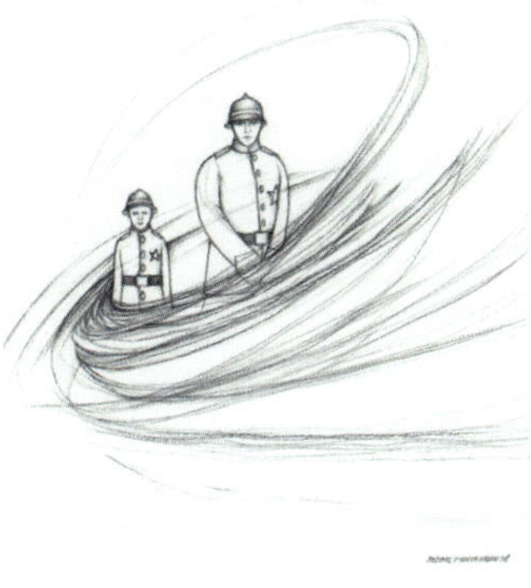

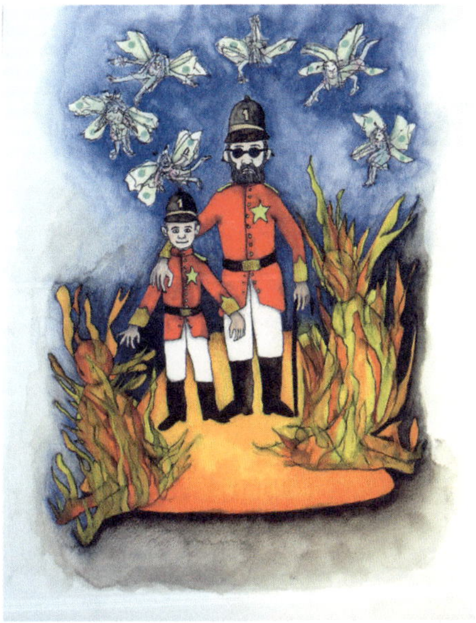

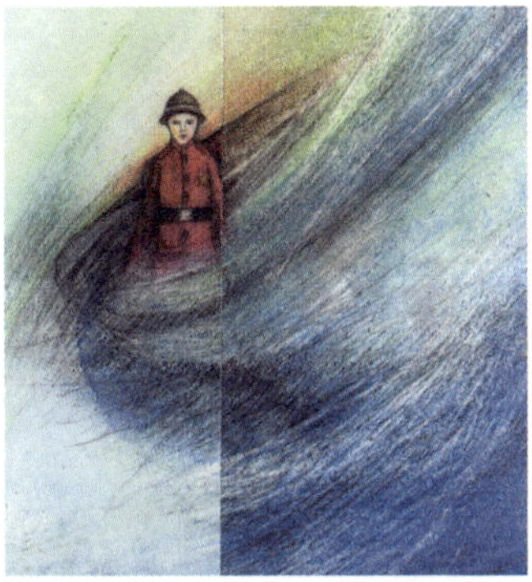

*The Child Fireman* (2008).
*The Child Fireman* (2009) *featured on the 2013 poster.*

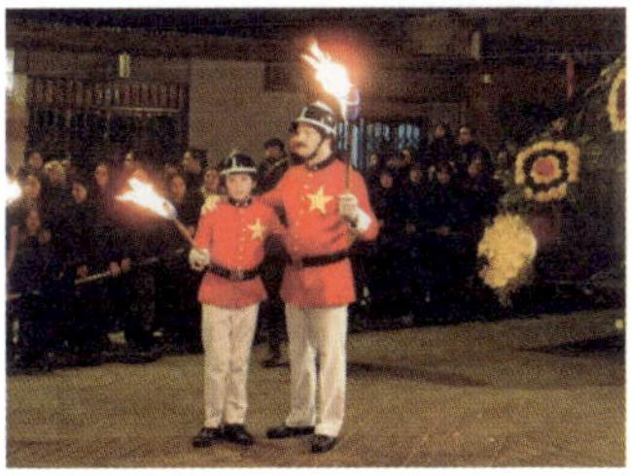

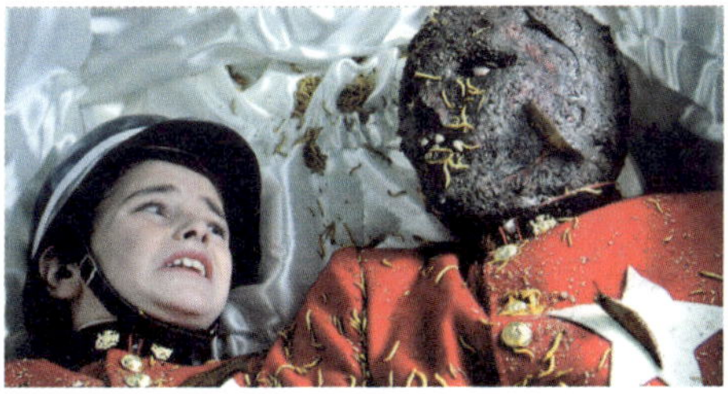

*La Danza de la realidad.*

his screenplay. It was only after the film was finished that the idea arose of using *The Child Fireman* for its poster. But, in the meantime, one might infer that this painting of pascALEjandro's exerted a certain influence on the making of the film.
One finds in this painting the same predilection for bright colors and the same decision to depict the characters looking directly at

the spectator, which is more common in painting (the figures face us) than in cinema where a look-to-camera reminds the spectator of his position and disrupts the willing suspension of disbelief. In the film, the flames feature in this sequence only as a fully mastered element, confined to the tips of torches, but the shadow of death remains strongly present: it broods in the nightmarish vision of the little boy, who believes he has woken up next to a worm-eaten corpse that menacingly turns towards him.

Strangely, the little boy in the painting does not have the features of a child. His face evokes a combination of the child he used to be and the man he will become, in a way that anticipates one of the film's key narrative devices: in the film, a single image often juxtaposes Alejandro as the wise old man he is today and Alejandro as the child he once was, whom he comes to counsel and console. pascALEjandro's manner of drawing the protagonist will reappear in the preparatory painting for the first poster of *Poesía sin fin*.

**pascALEjandro and the autobiographical diptych**

In the first painting linked to *Poesía sin fin*, the protagonist appears in a bust-length portrait, carrying on his shaved head the famous "burning butterfly" of creation, which is mentioned several times in the film but never appears on screen. pascALEjandro's later painting, made after the film was finished for the film's official poster, likewise takes up this motif of the butterfly. In a three-quarter back-view, a figure whose silhouette recalls that of the actor Adan Jodorowsky walks along a beach releasing a stream of butterflies from his bag, mirroring the many poems delivered orally throughout the film but never written down on paper.

This example of the butterfly aptly demonstrates—in relation to Jodorowsky's two autobiographical films—that pascALEjandro is in no wise an illustrator or a storyboard author. No painting of pascALEjandro's actually represents a scene from the film. pascALEjandro's works remain independent. This is not to say that the paintings and the films do not interact with each other,

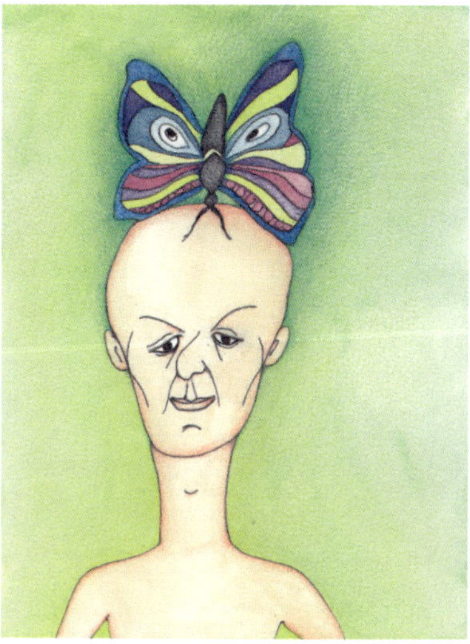

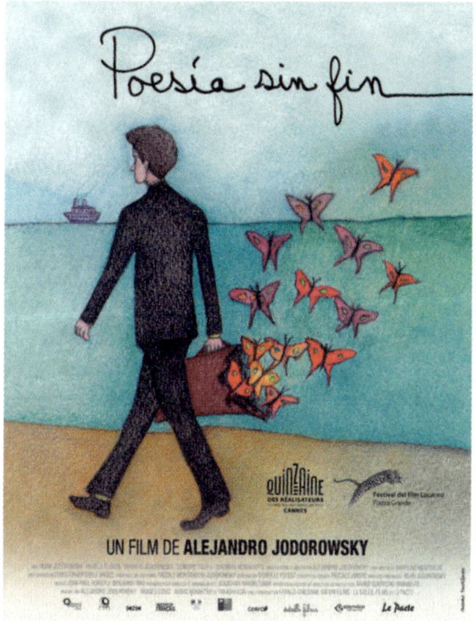


*Poesía sin fin* (poster draft, 2014).
*Poesía sin fin* (official poster, 2016).

but rather that they meet in more of a discrete, diffuse way than might be expected.

The paintings and the films indeed share a certain number of emblematic figures, such as the Pierrots or the yogis who meditate half naked. But these figures, who reappear often in pascALEjandro's canvases, are too archetypal to be taken as references to *La Danza de la realidad* or *Poesía sin fin*. The major themes of the films—poetic creation and the difficulty of a child's relationship with his parents—are never directly addressed in the paintings. Certainly, the childhood world at the heart of *La Danza* is also one of pascALEjandro's major themes as a painter. But this is simply because Alejandro frequently represents his and Pascale's childhoods in his drawings for pascALEjandro, just as he often finds inspiration in his love for Pascale.

The influence of pascALEjandro's paintings on Jodorowsky's cinematic diptych is rather to be found elsewhere, notably in the latter's stylized approach to color. In *La Danza*, this influence is

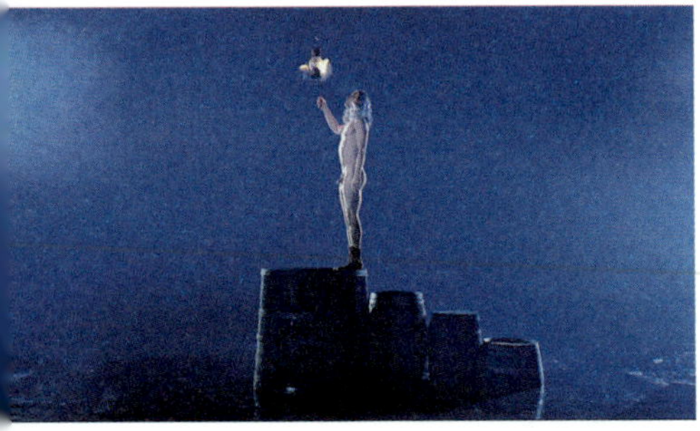

*La Danza de la realidad.*

still timid, with the exception of a handful of emblematic scenes, such as the death of Alejandro's maternal grandfather while perched atop alcohol barrels to light a lamp, depicted in a blue monochrome. In *Poesía*, this stylization of color becomes the norm: the embrace with the dwarf in a red atmosphere which recalls the young woman's menses; the violet boat at the end, which fades into the offing on a milky ocean; the white of the Pierrot costume against the red of the carnival dancers. This last example is all the more notable in that its play of colors also relies on costumes designed by pascALEjandro. For the rest, the principal part of the work on the colors indeed took place during post-production. Pascal and Alejandro spent weeks on the color grading (much longer than usually required) going over each image and each detail of each image. "By changing the color, you can completely change the meaning of a scene,"[3] says Alejandro, who, naturally, listed pascALEjandro in the credits of *Poesía sin fin* for its work on the colors: a way of expressing gratitude for its contribution and opening new doors for an artist who is still young, still up-and-coming.

pascALEjandro's influence on Jodorowsky's films nevertheless seems to go beyond this particular stylization of color. pascALEjandro has developed an entire method of reinventing reality which suffuses Jodorowsky's cinema. This might be one of the reasons why his autobiographical diptych appears calmer than his previous films. This is not to say that pascALEjandro's paintings offer a vision purged of violence. On the contrary,

3. Interview conducted by Philippe Rouyer and Michel Ciment for *Positif* magazine, n° 668, October 2016.

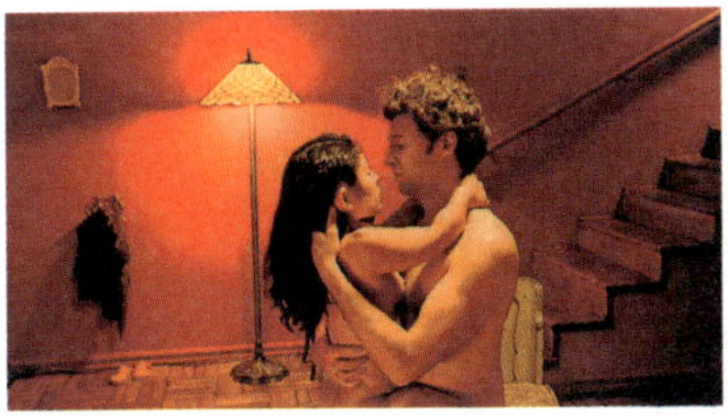 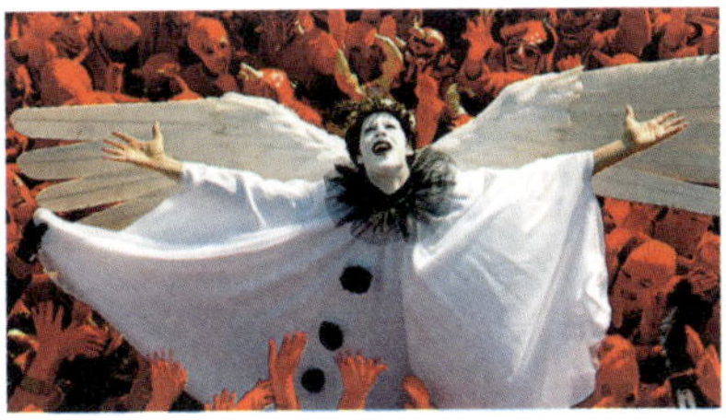

*Poesía sin fin.*

violence is everywhere in a majority of the paintings. But in each instance it is held at bay, filtered by the gaze of the artist who, like Alejandro in his two most recent films, looks inward to find "something sublime to show the spectator. You have to escape from social problems to arrive at a pure form of artistic expression. With all the emotion that this entails."[4]

To verify pascALEjandro's influence, we might return to the example of *The Child Fireman*. In the final painting as it was used for the poster of *La Danza*, the halo of grey figurines above the two characters adds a certain softness to the scene. It is as if the characters were under the protection of these celestial presences. Nothing of the sort appears in the film during the firefighter sequence. But in the film's closing scene, as Alejandro leaves his native town by boat with his parents, the reverse shot shows him on the pier in his fireman uniform surrounded by life-size photographs of all the persons we have met during the film. The gray and white silhouettes stand in contrast to his red fireman's jacket, as on the film poster. Whether favorable or unfavorable to Alejandro, all appear beside him, tutelary ghosts of the child whom it is important to "keep in your heart," as the devastating voiceover of today's Alejandro recommends during the film's last images.

Notice that "keep the child in your heart" is a saying that precisely describes the pictorial work of pascALEjandro.

4. Ibid.

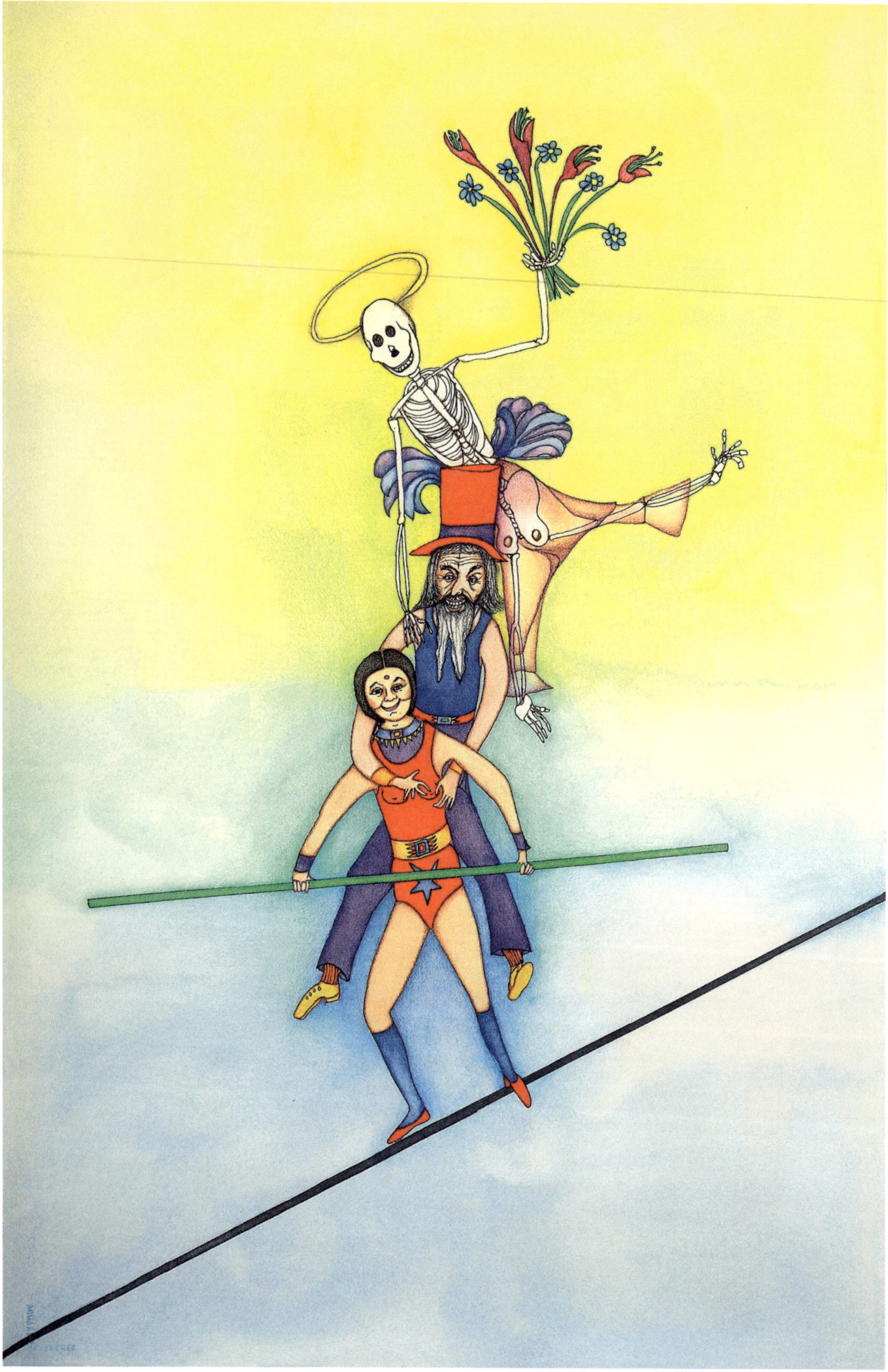

*Alegría! Alegría! Alegría!* 2017
102 × 65 cm

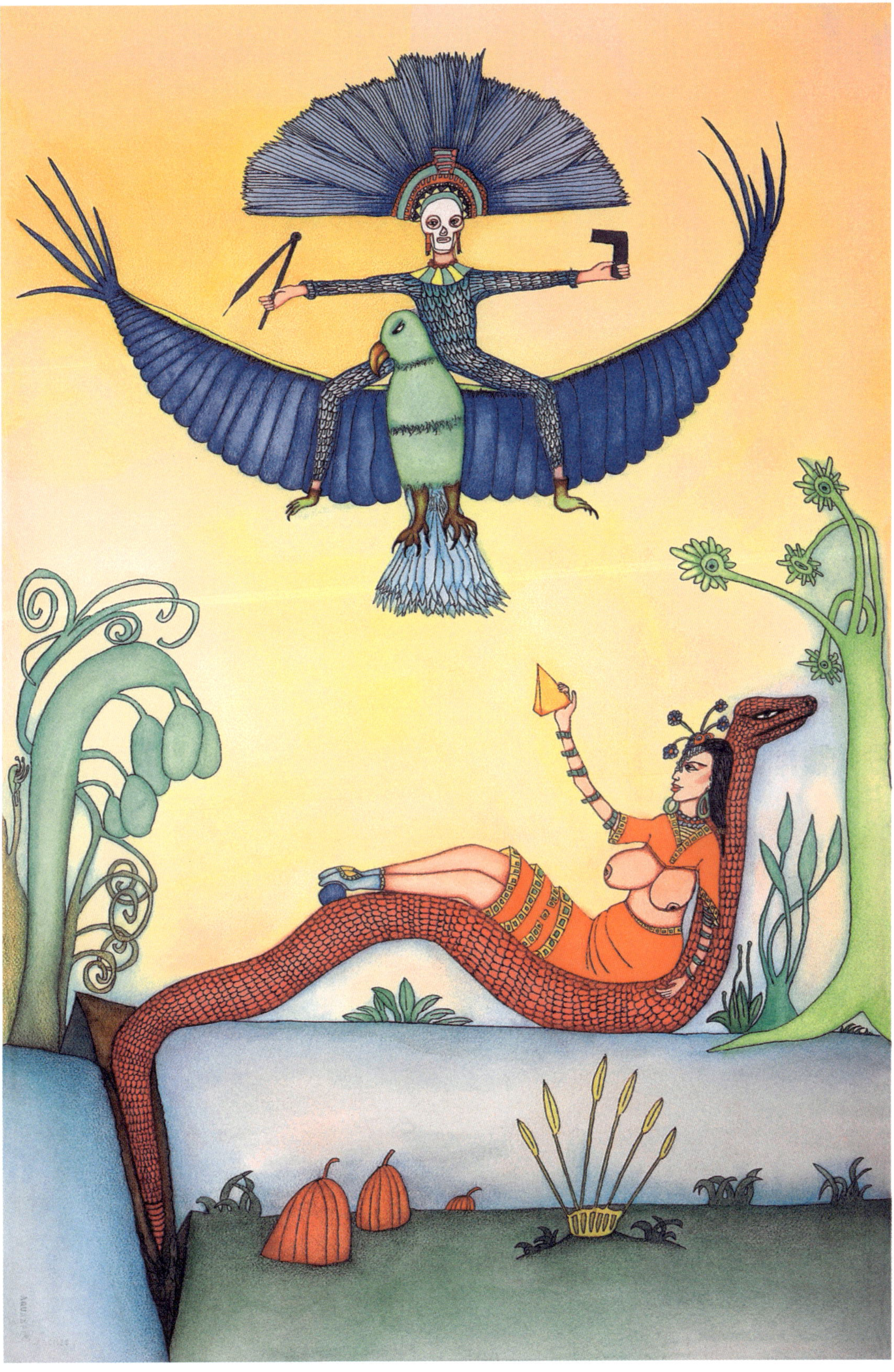

*Mythic Couple*, 2017
102 × 65 cm

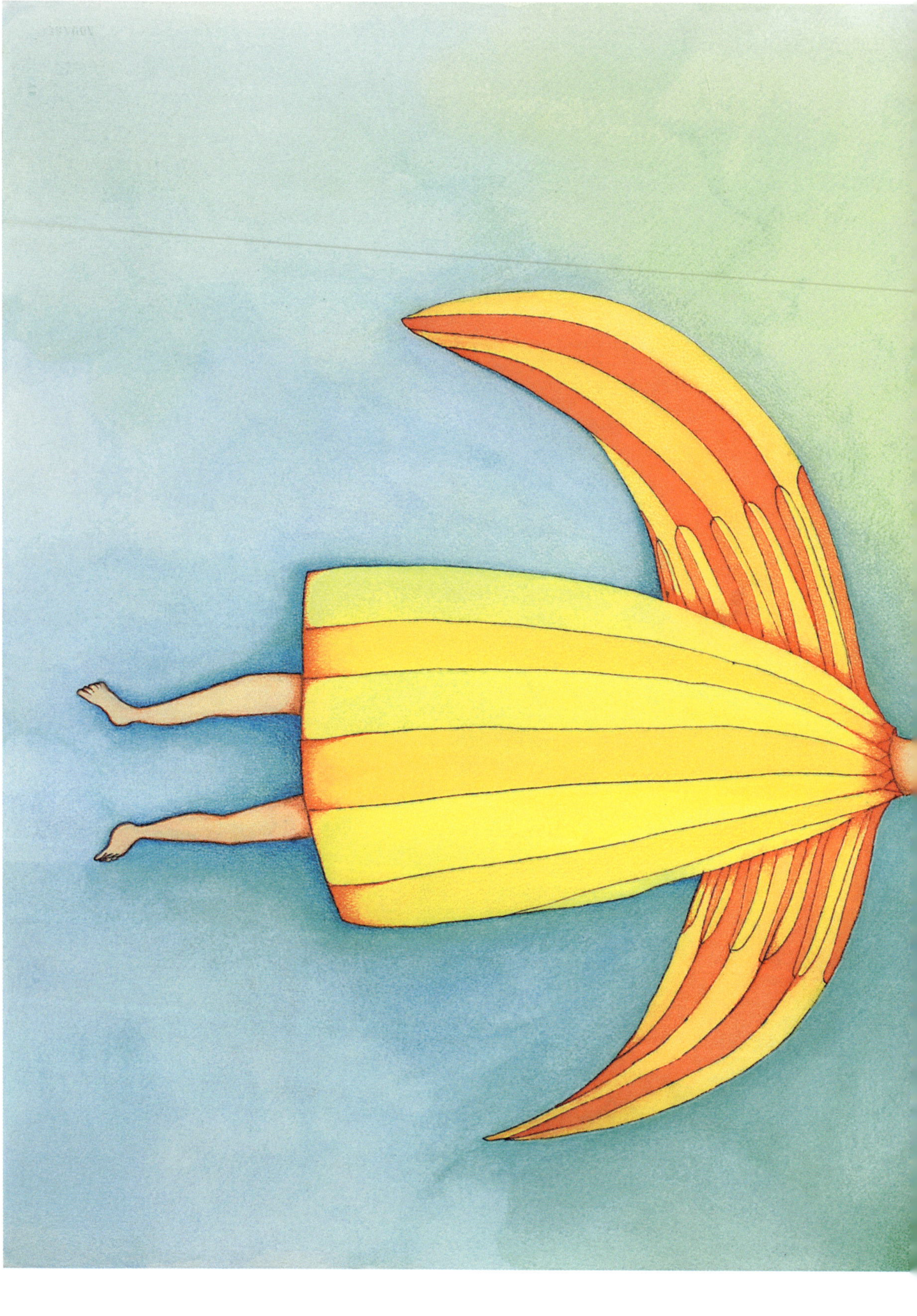

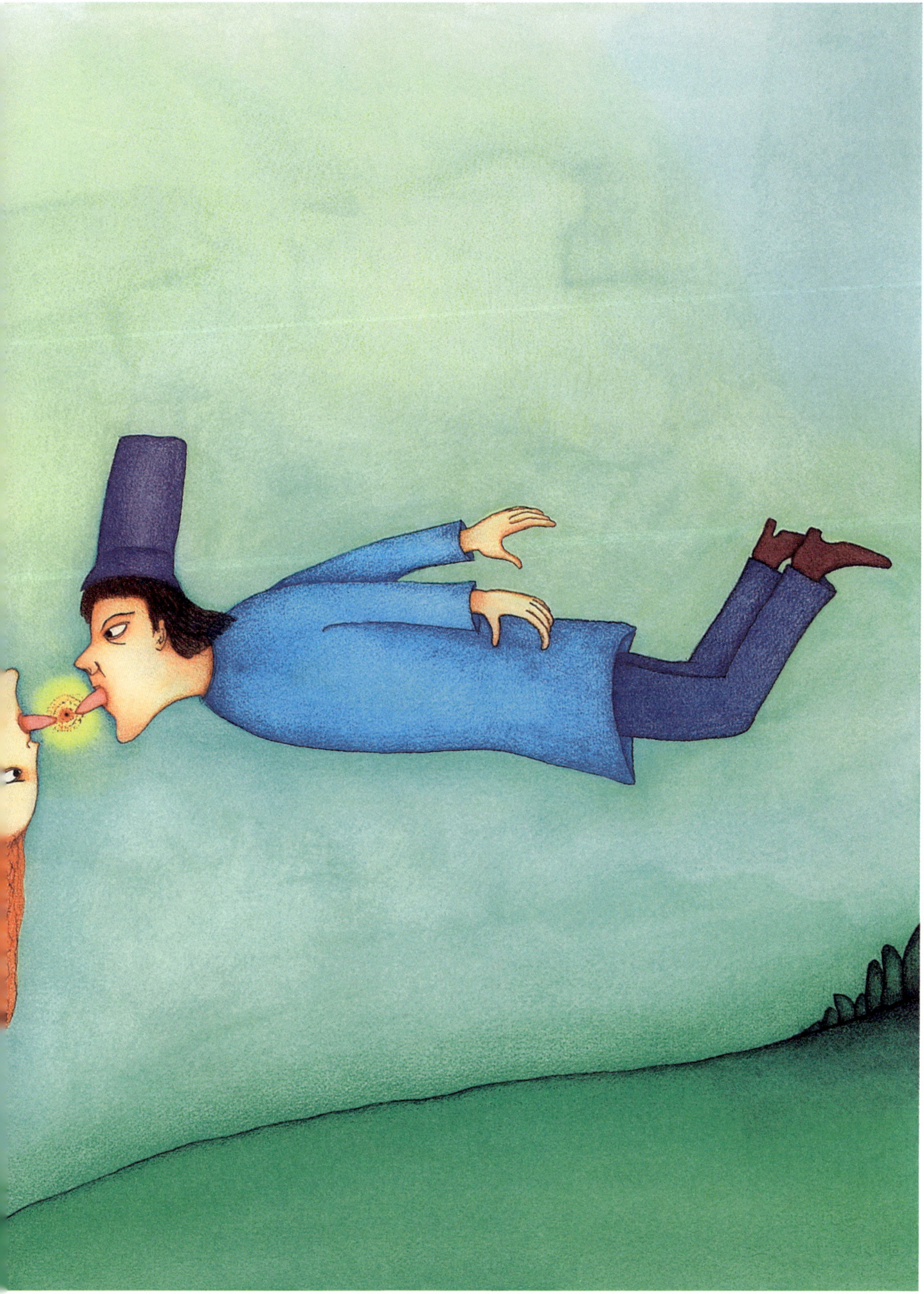

*The Essential Point*, 2016
65 × 102 cm

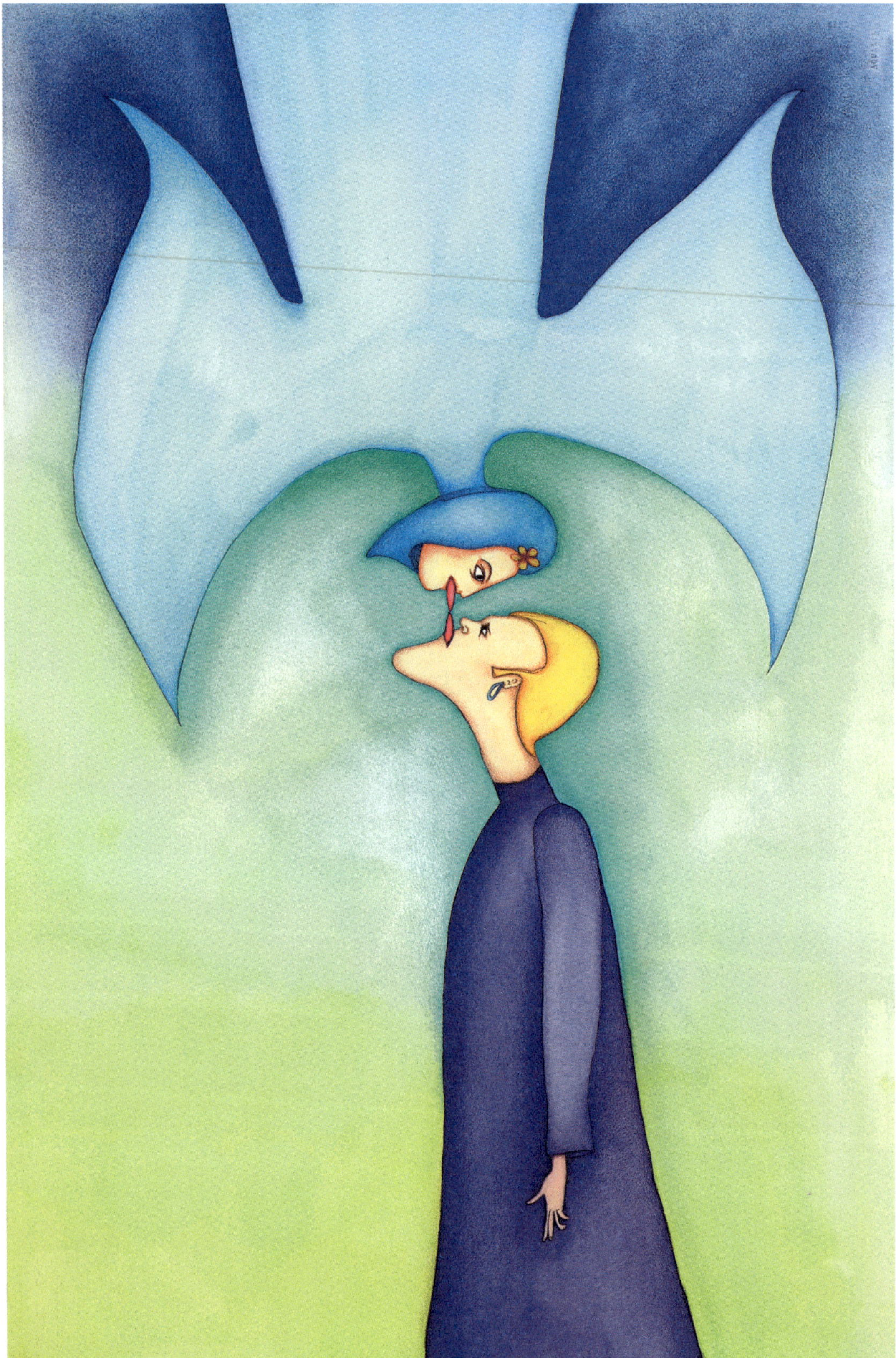

*Beyond*, 2016
102 × 65 cm

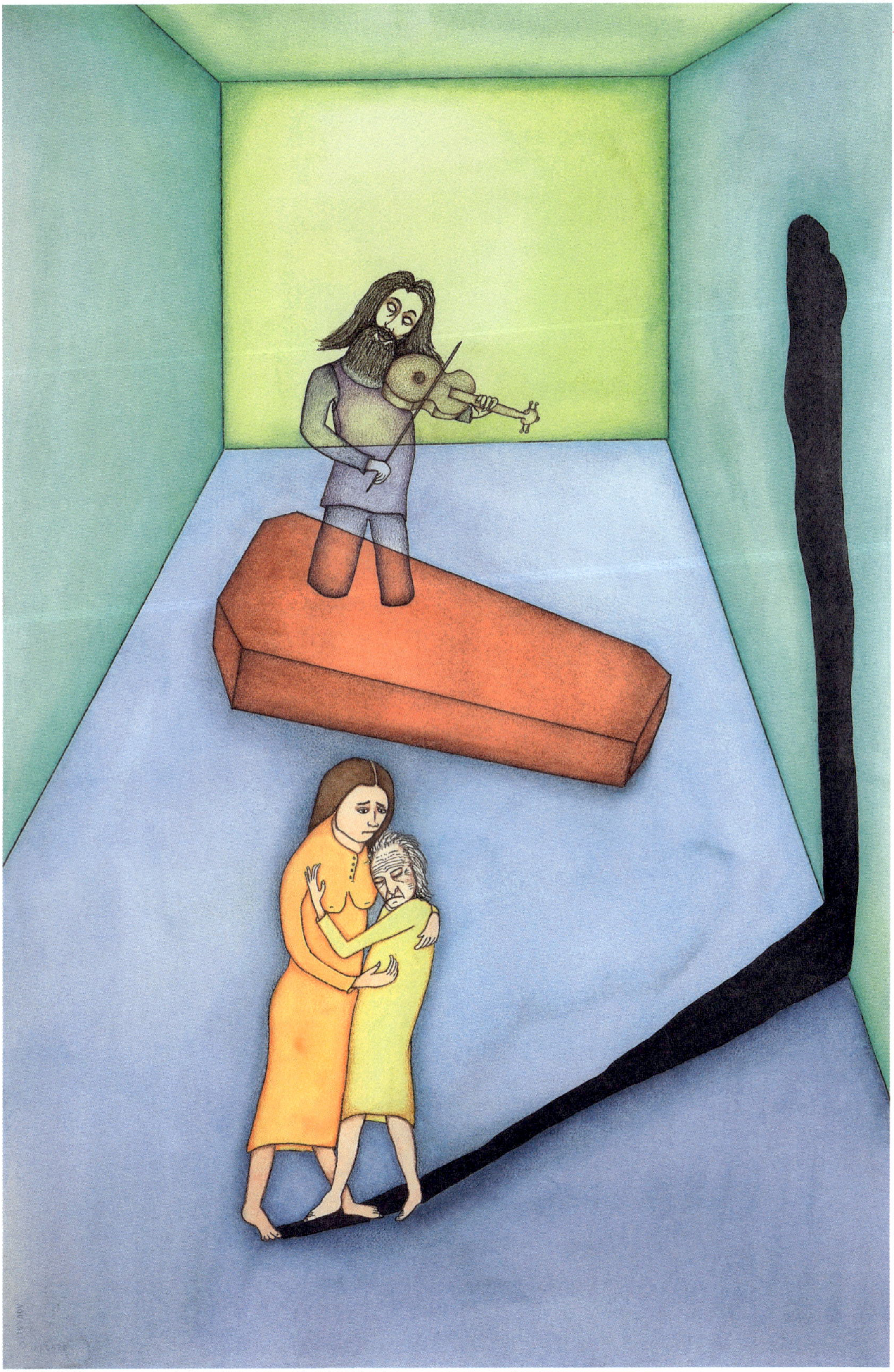

*Farewell*, 2017
102 × 65 cm

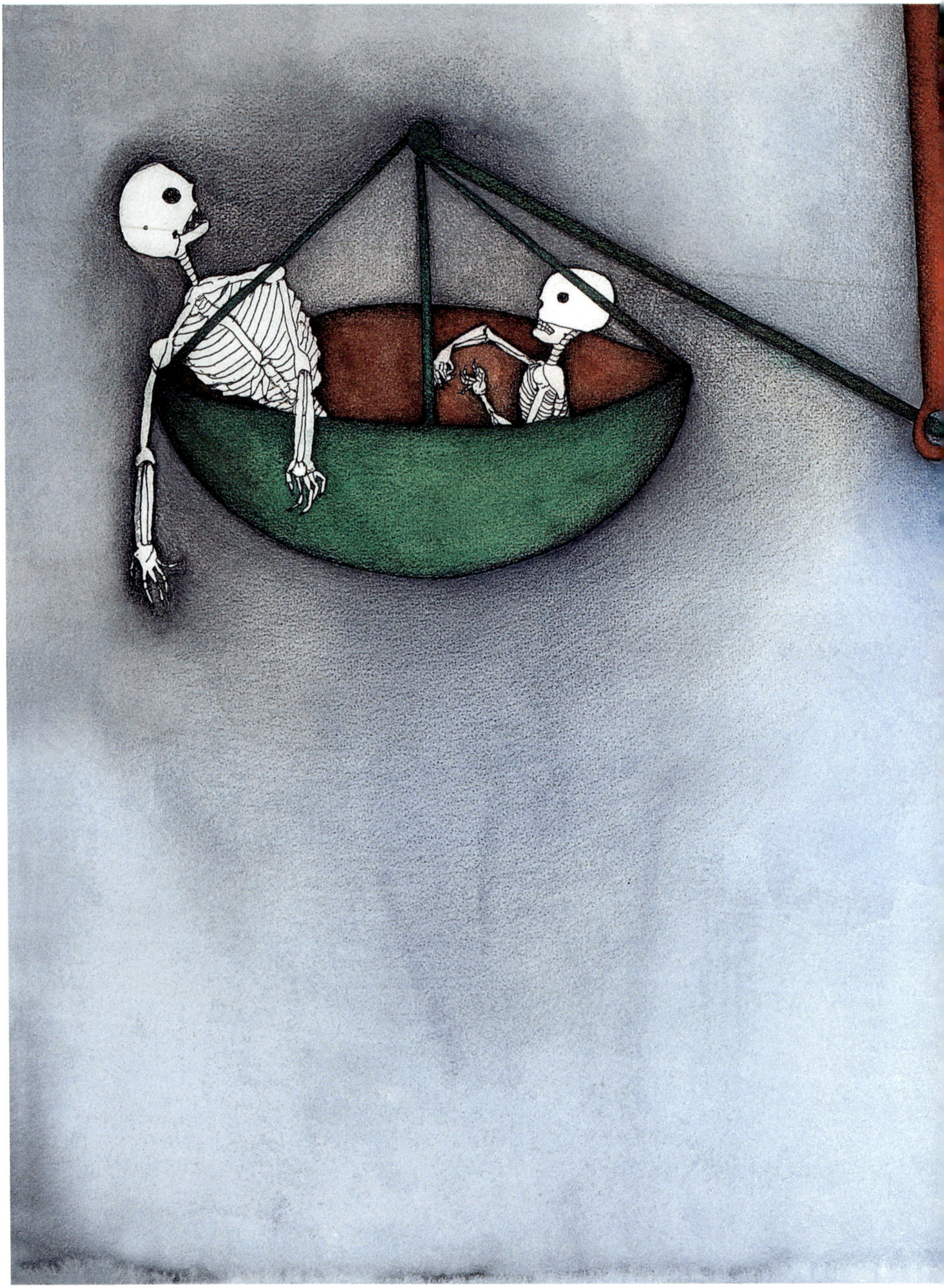

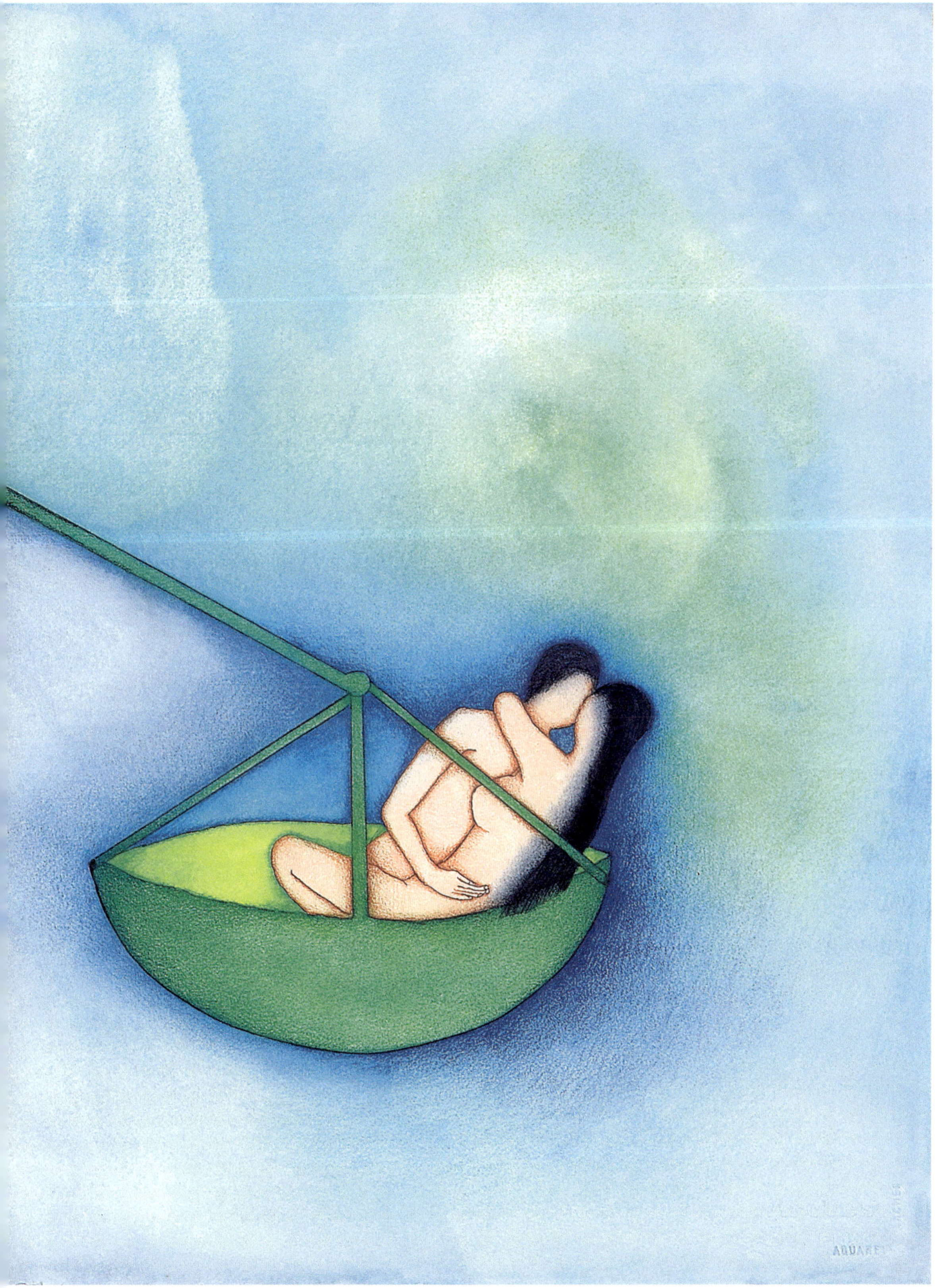

*The Weight of Love*, 2016
65 × 102 cm

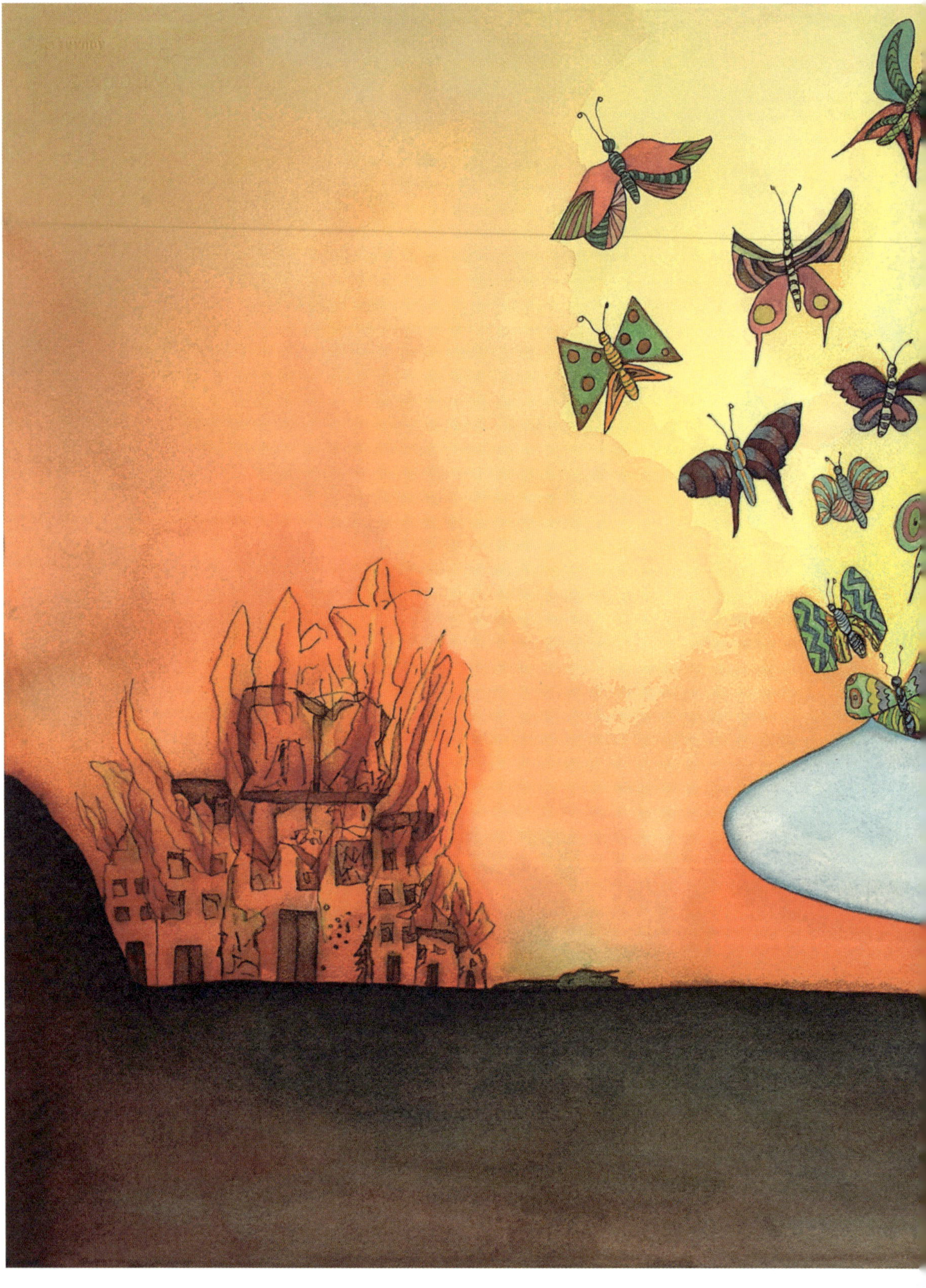

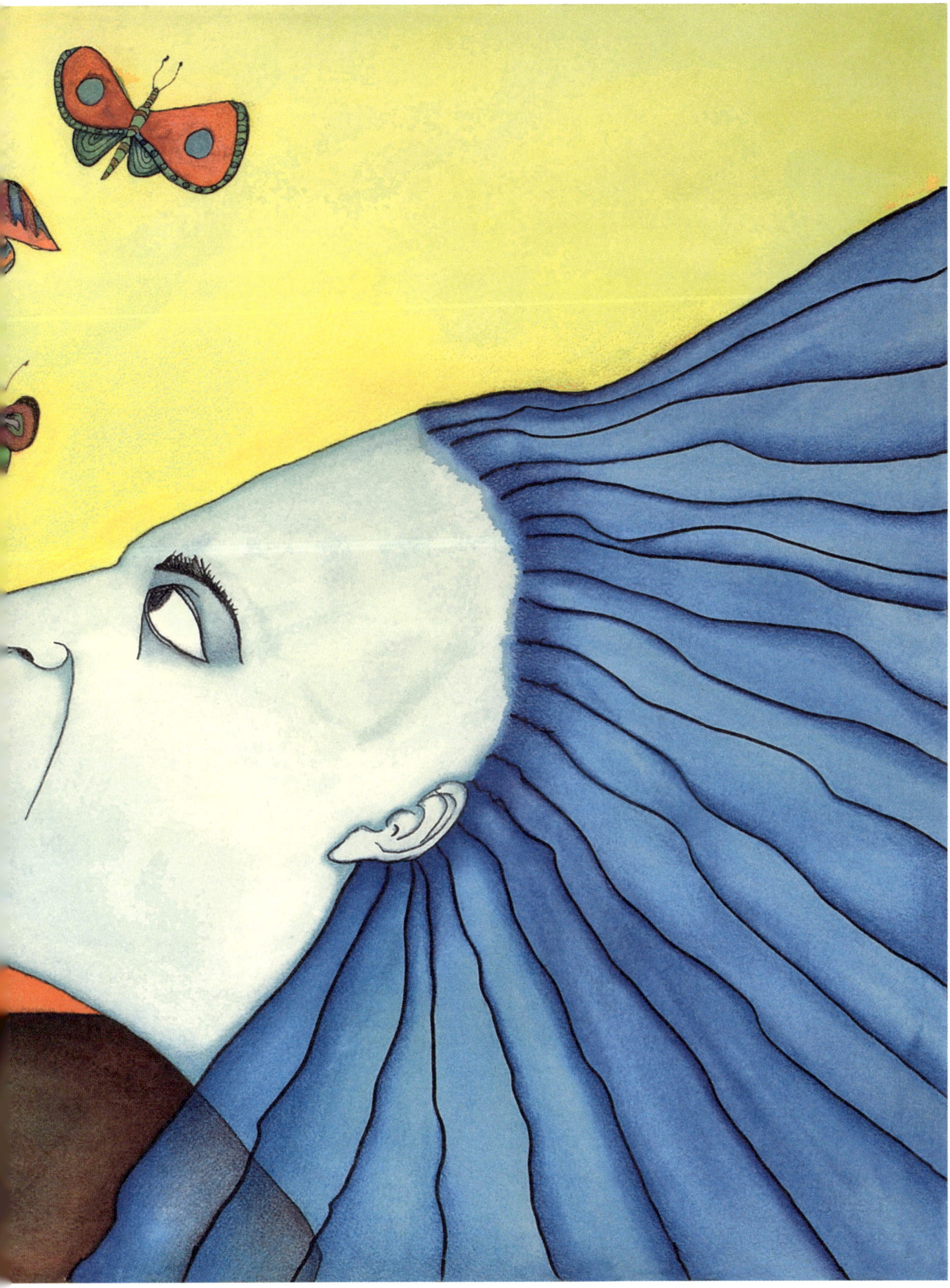

*The Cry of the Soul*, 2016
65 × 102 cm

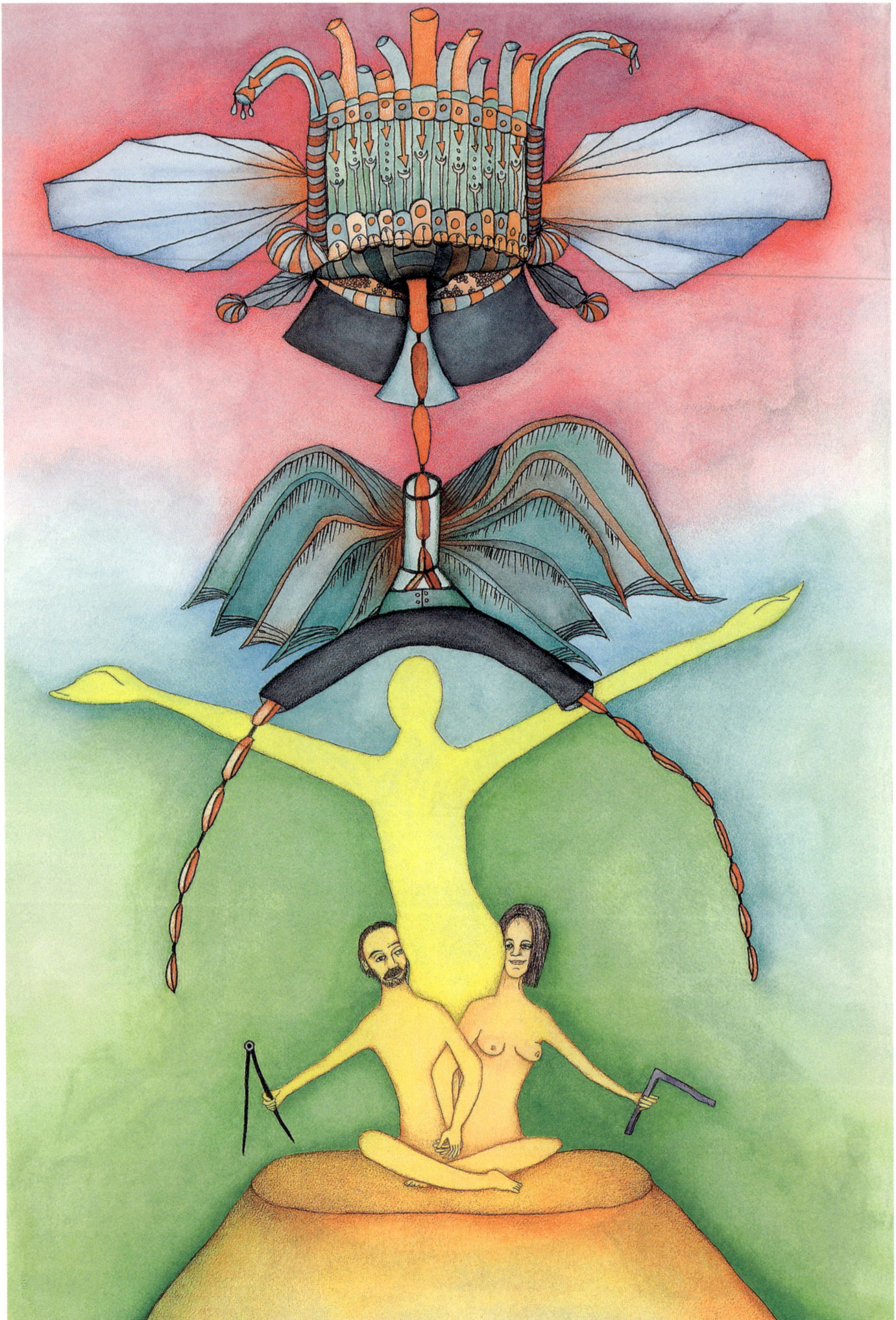

*Union Under Division*, 2016
102 × 65 cm

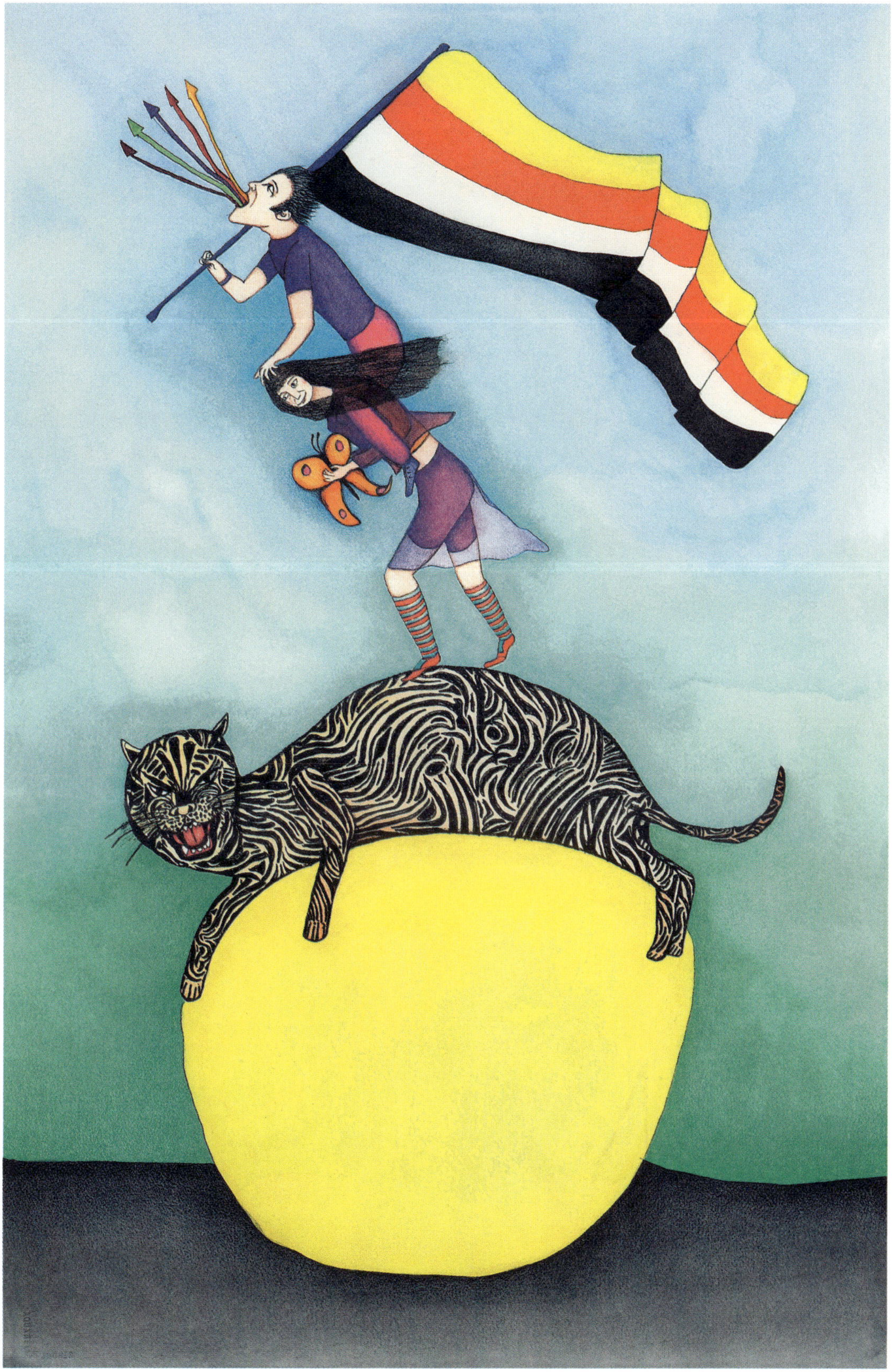

*Alchemic Re-evolution*, 2016
102 × 65 cm

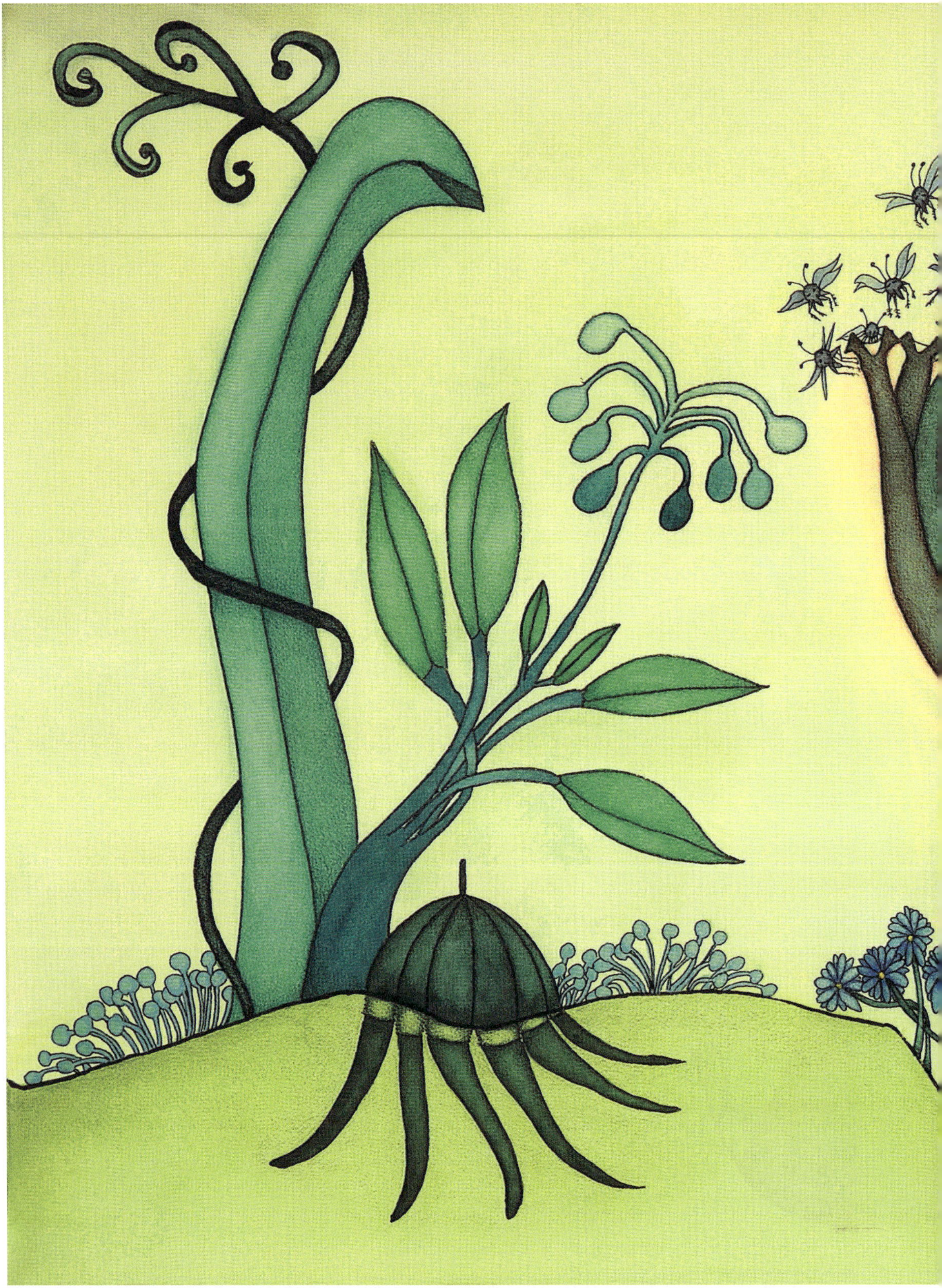

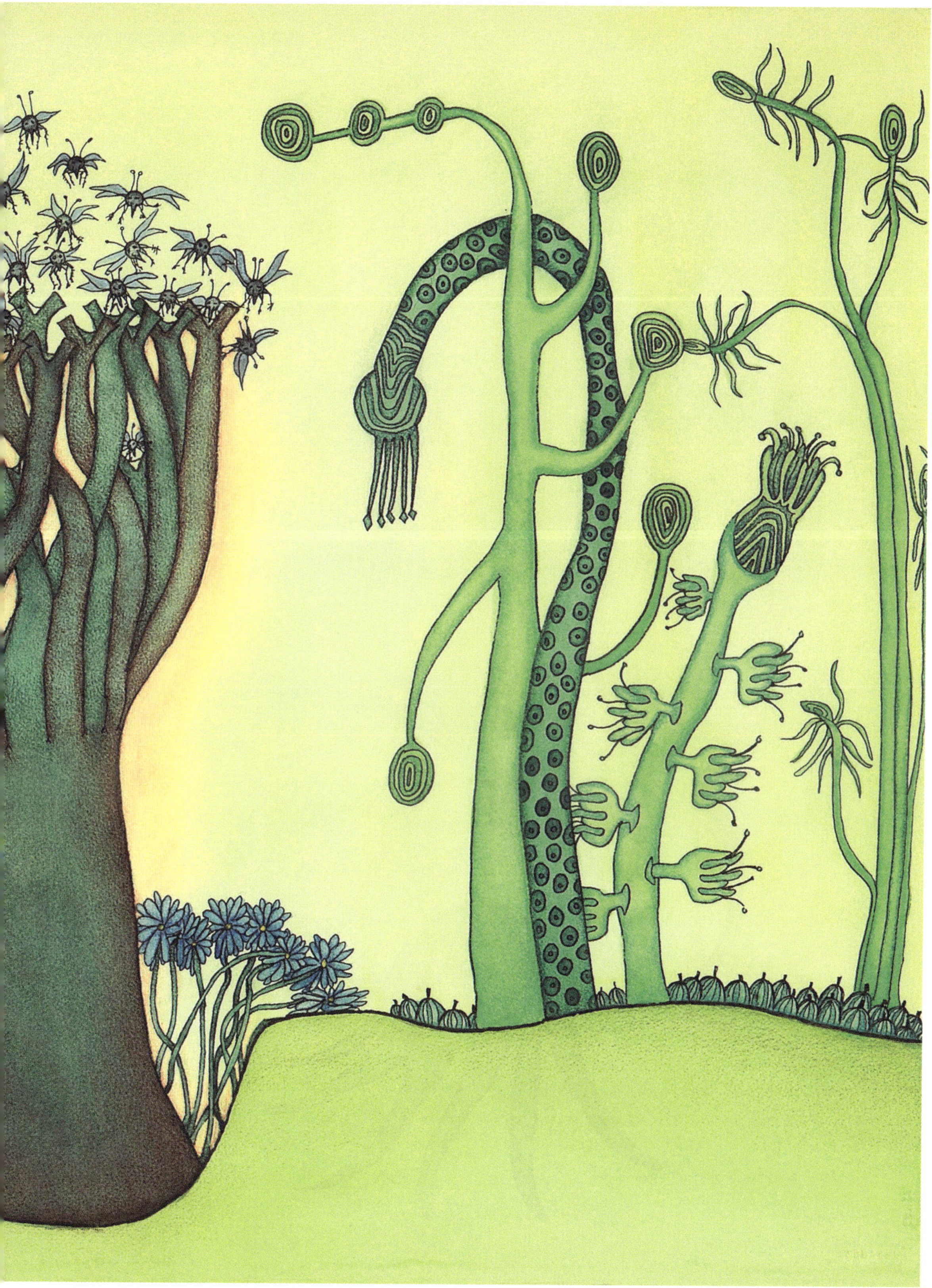

*Unstill Life*, 2017
65 × 102 cm

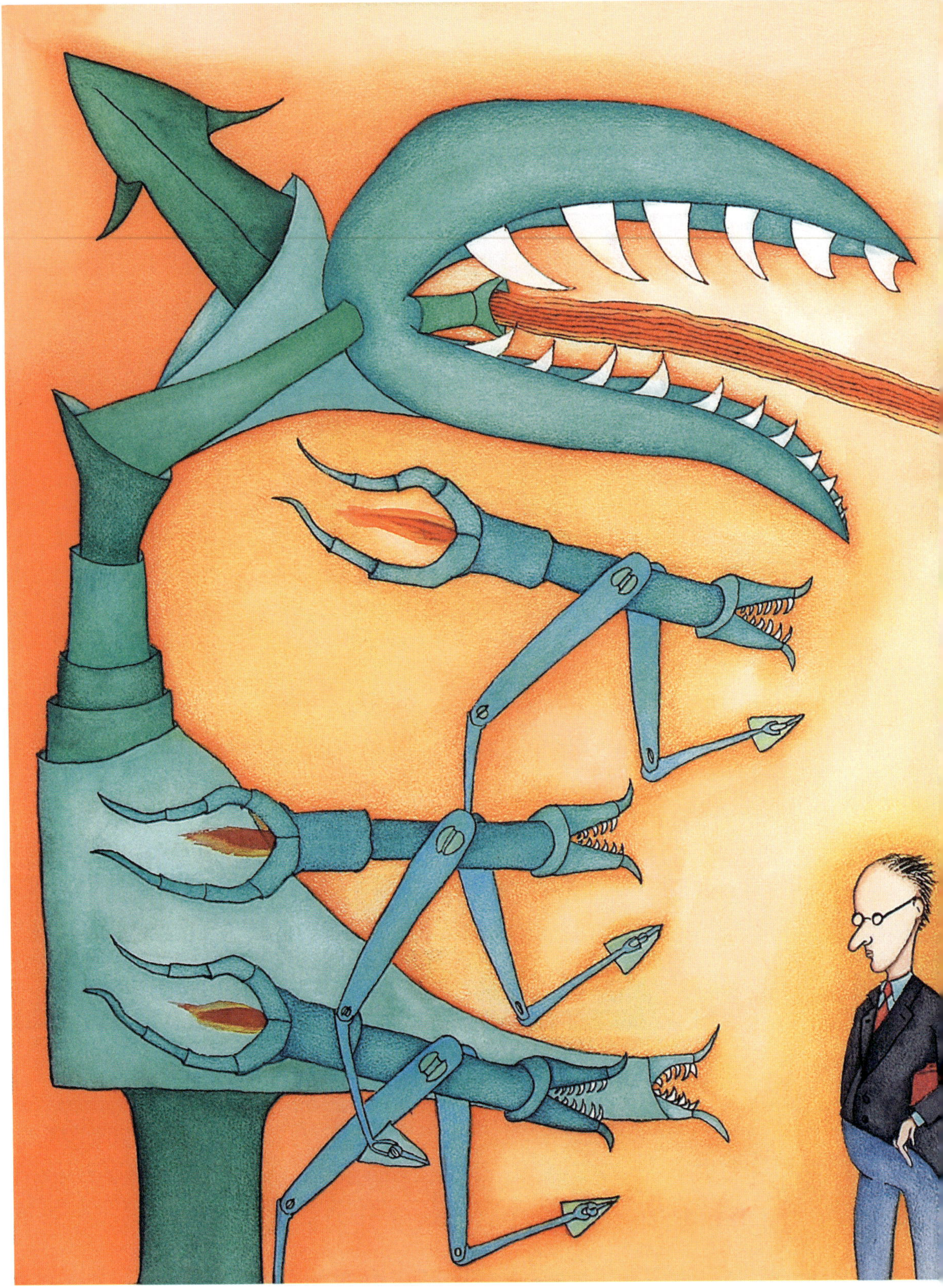

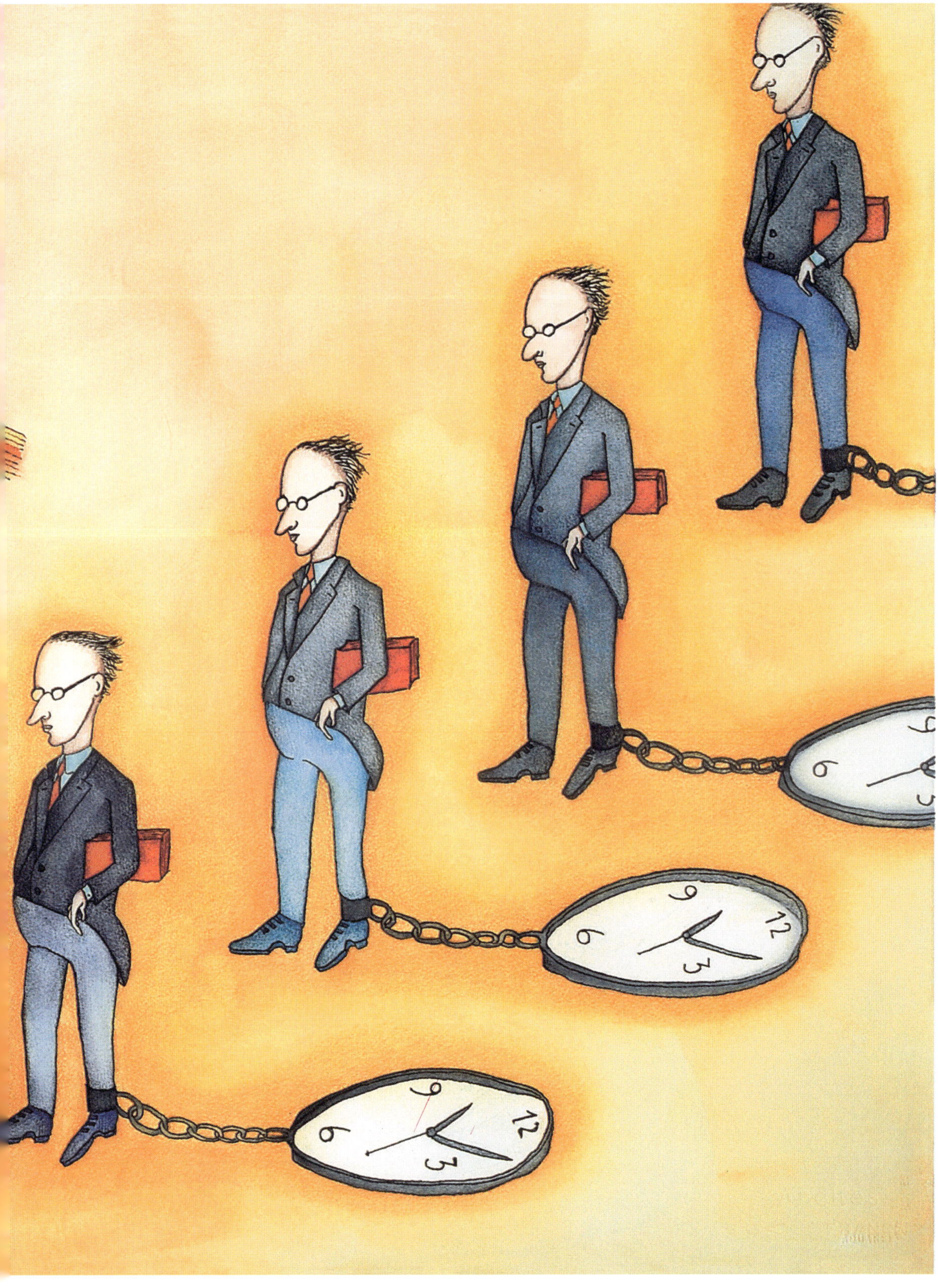

*The Way the World Goes*, 2017
65 × 102 cm

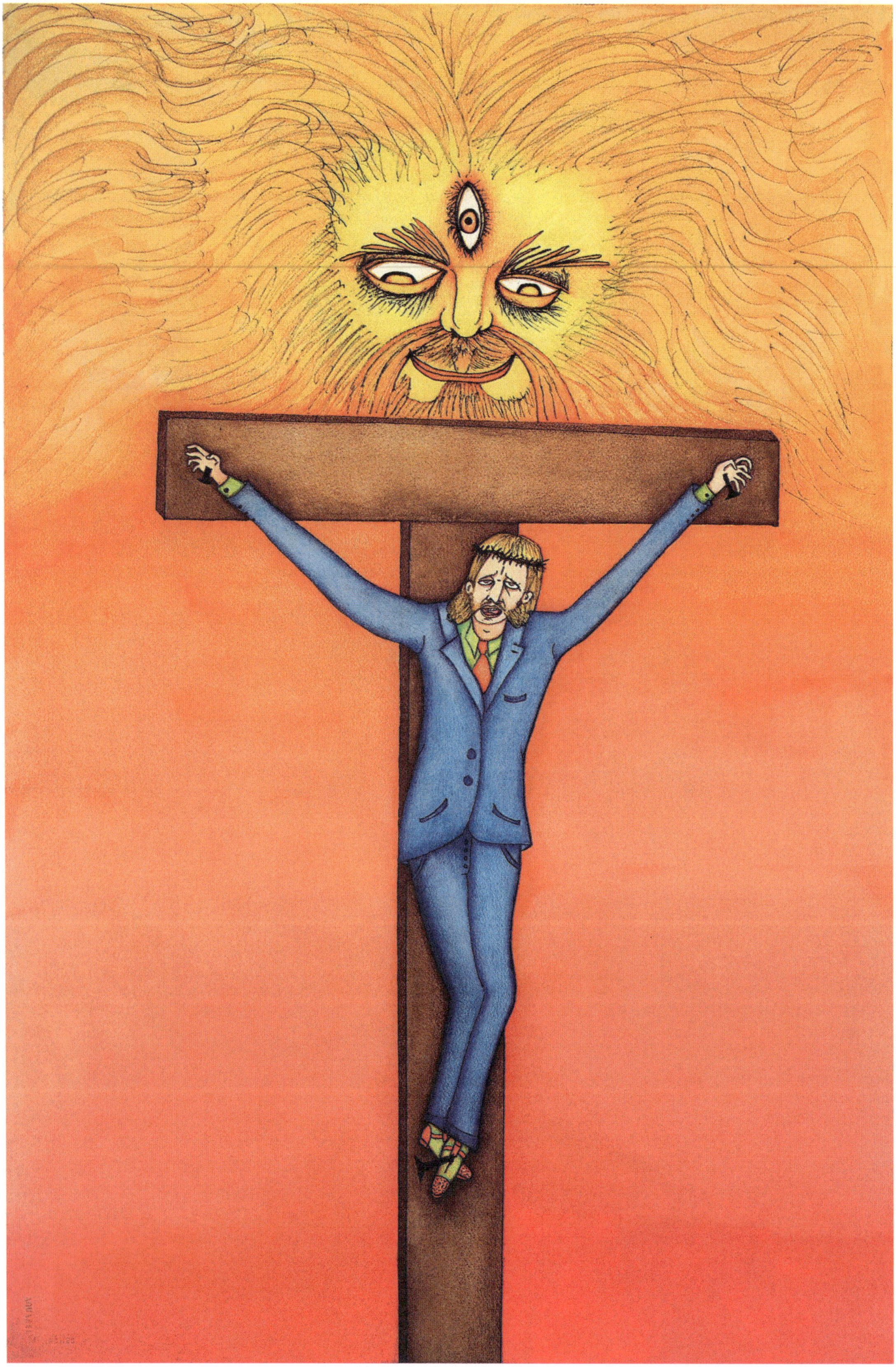

*Father, Why Hast Thou Forsaken Me?* 2017
102 × 65 cm

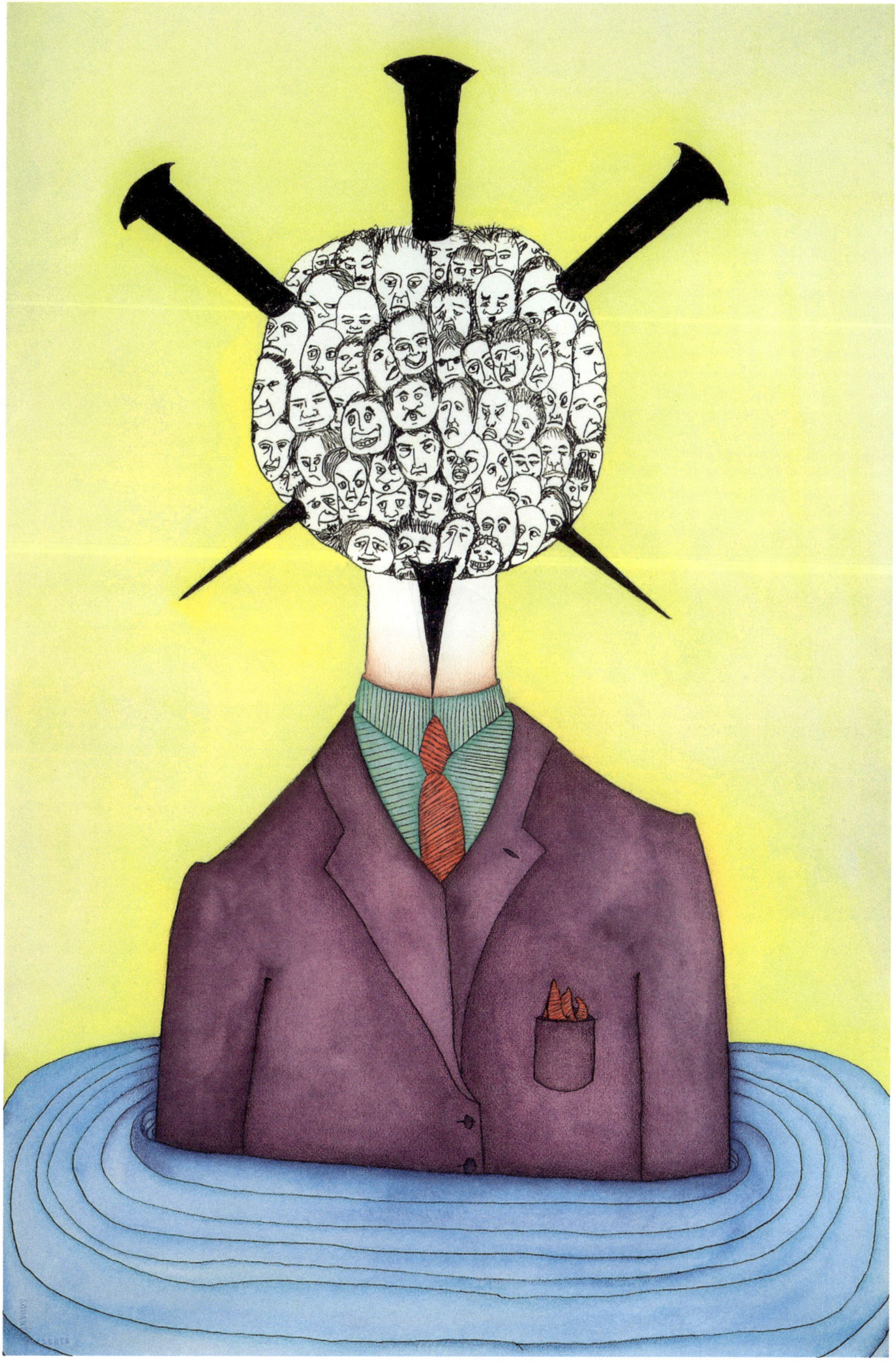

*The Man with a Thousand Egos*, 2016
102 × 65 cm

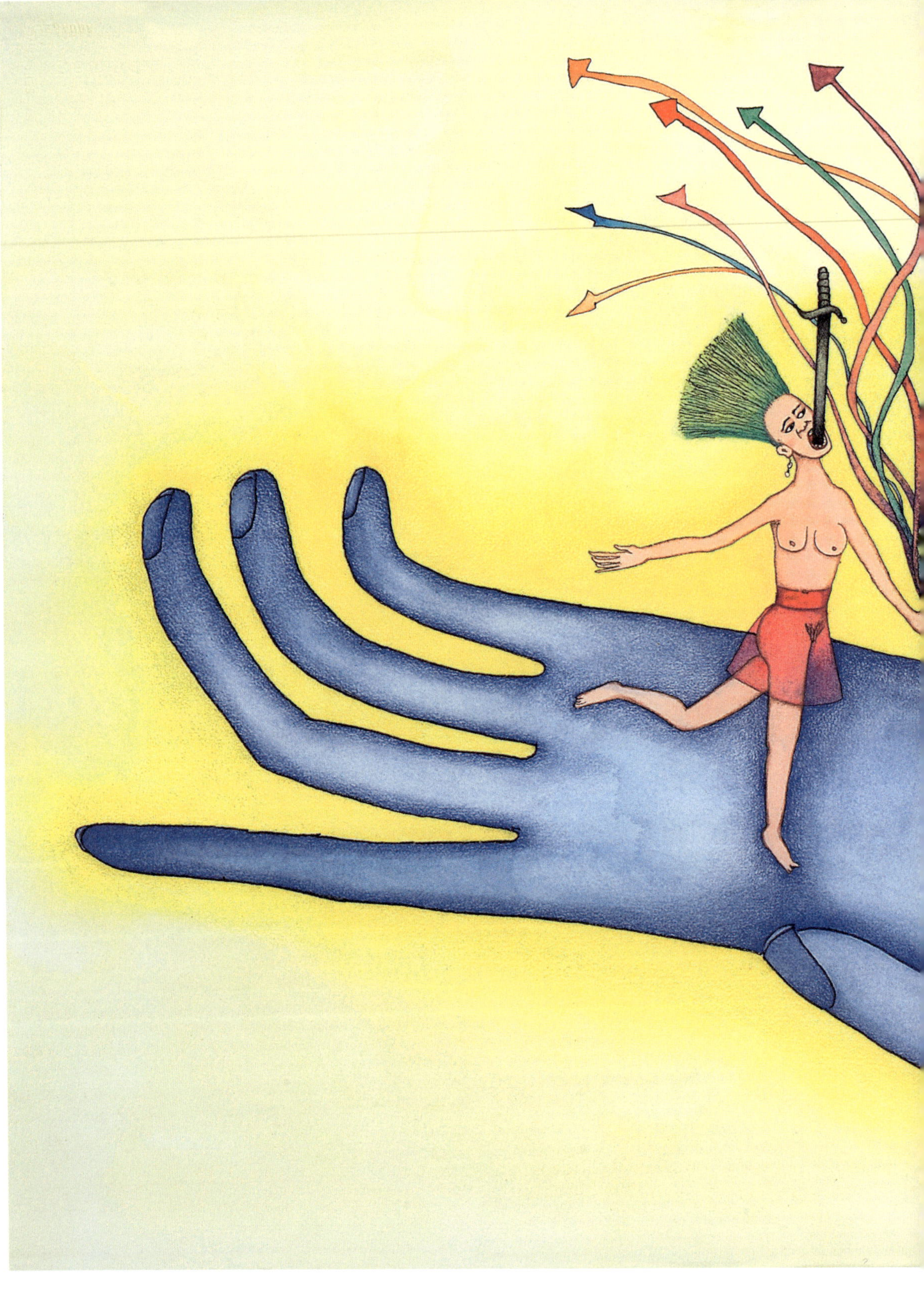

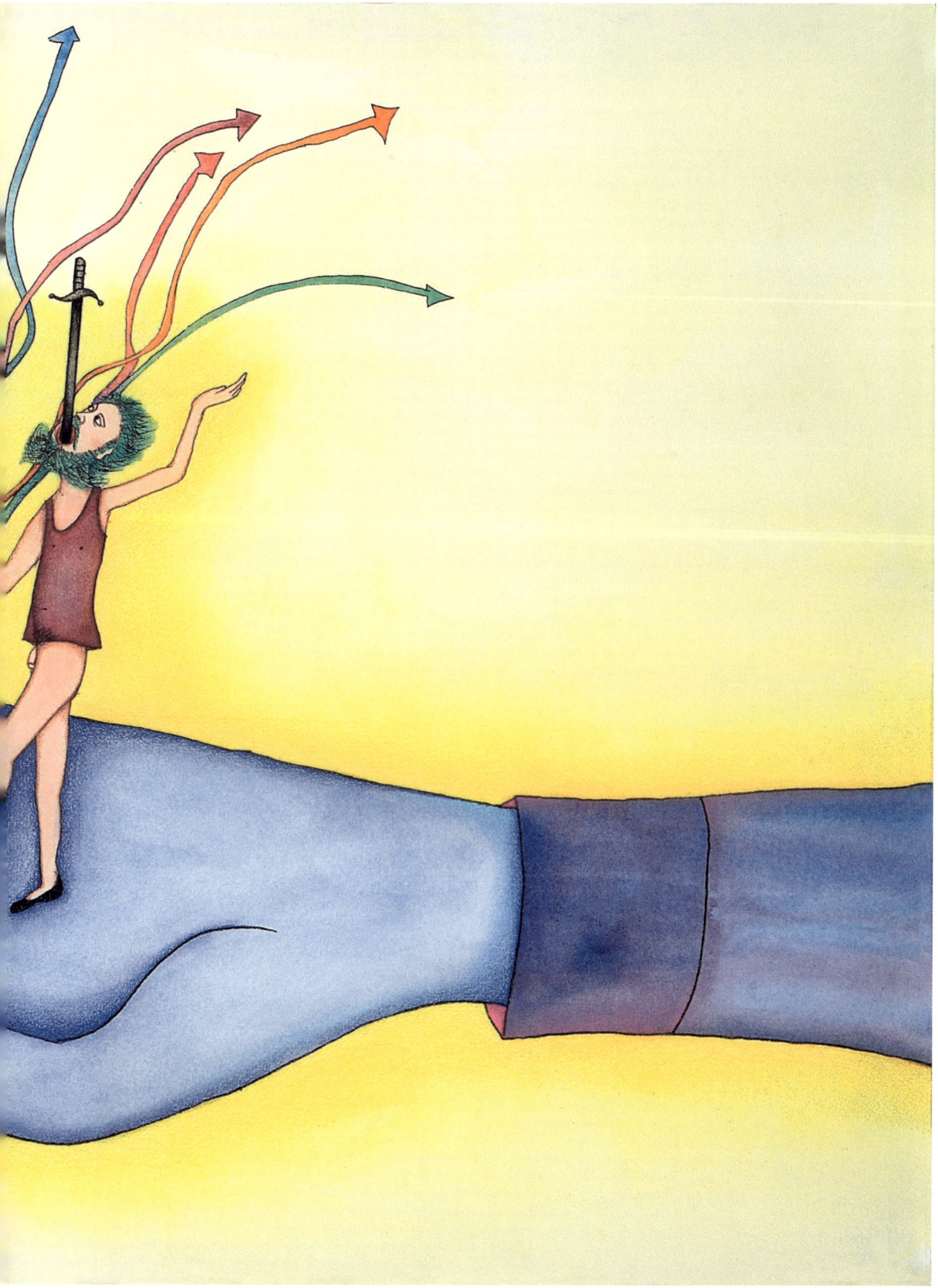

*Sword Swallowers in the Hand of God*, 2016
65 × 102 cm

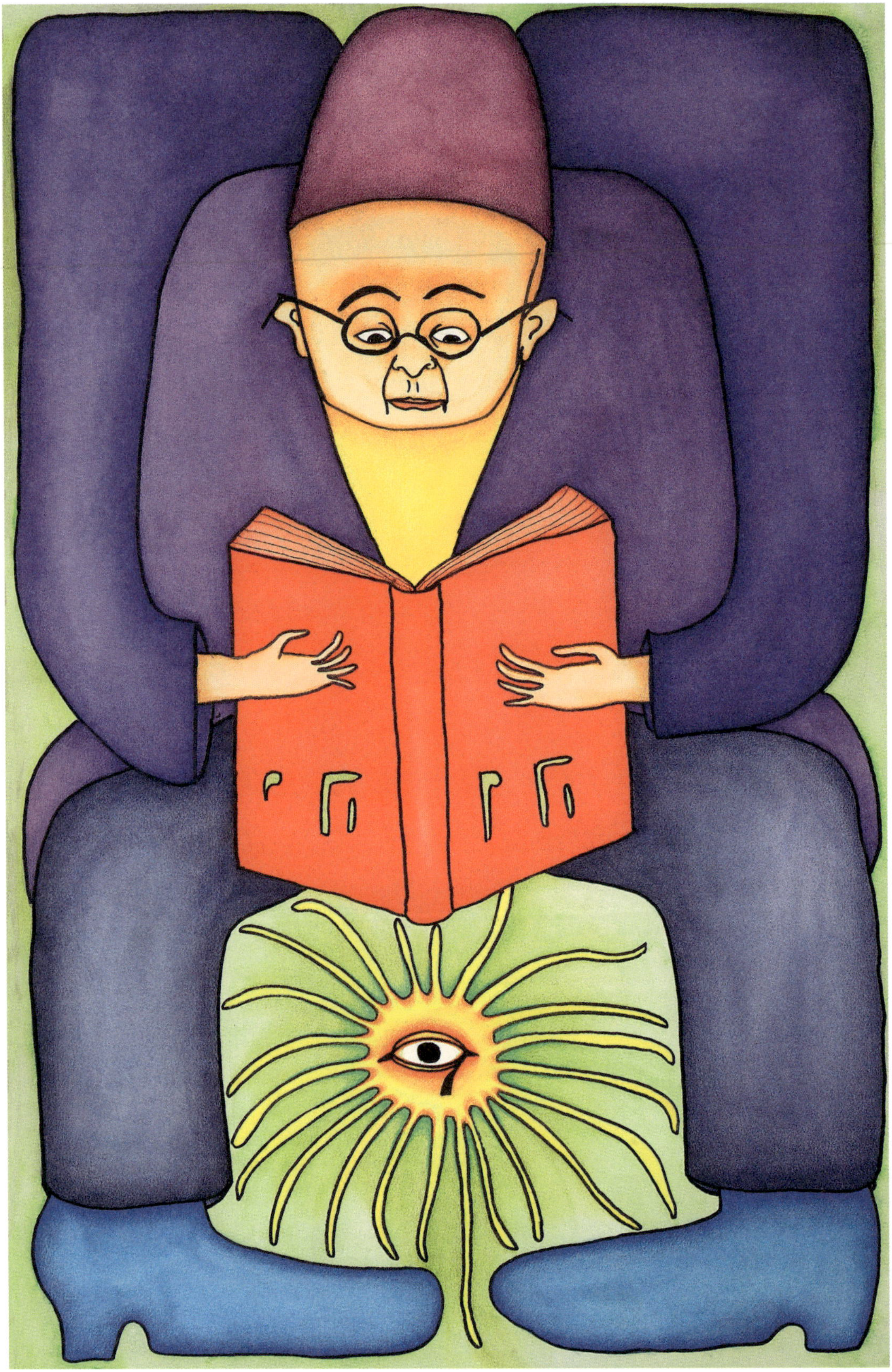

*Searching for What You Have*, 2016
102 × 65 cm

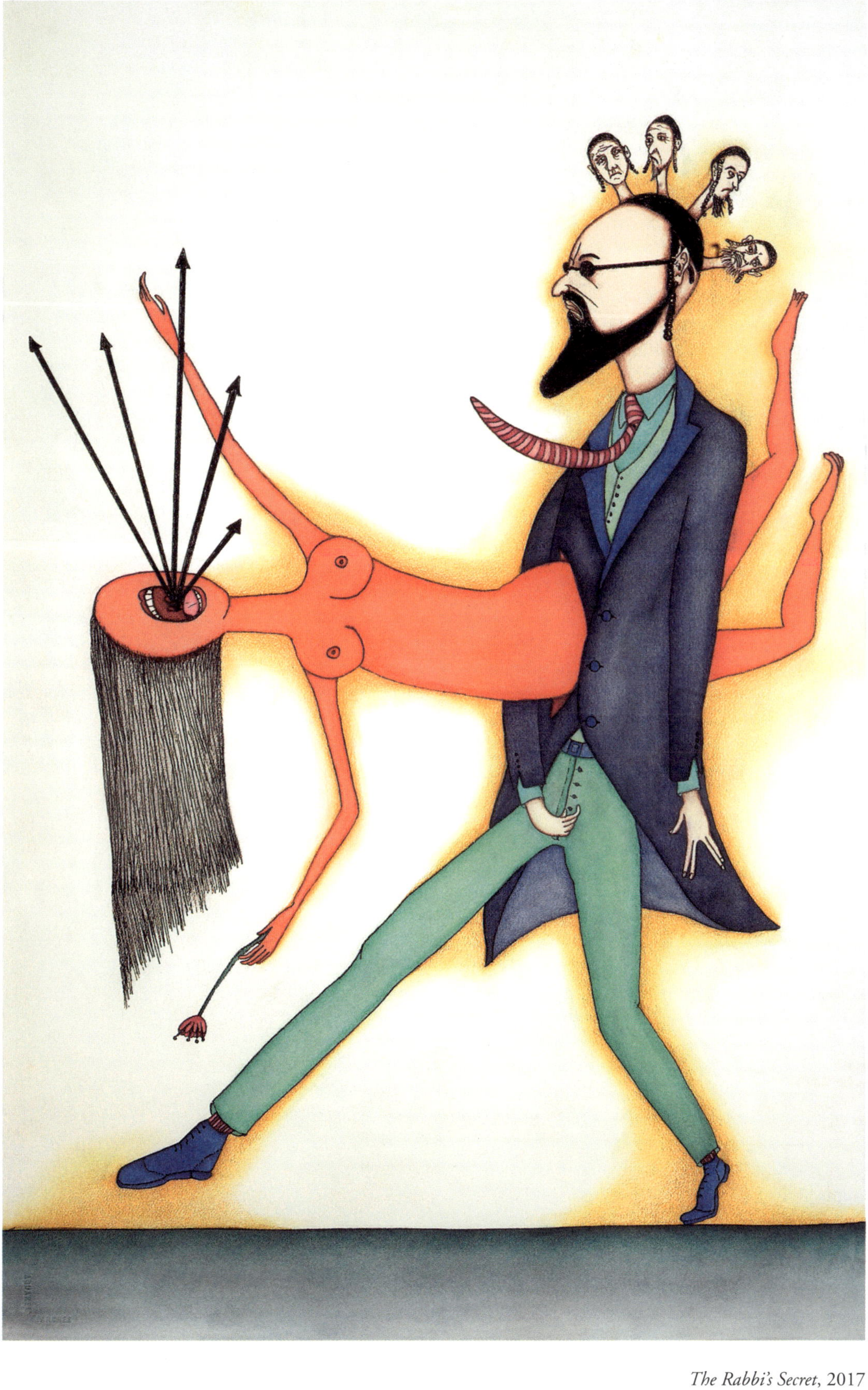

*The Rabbi's Secret*, 2017
102 × 65 cm

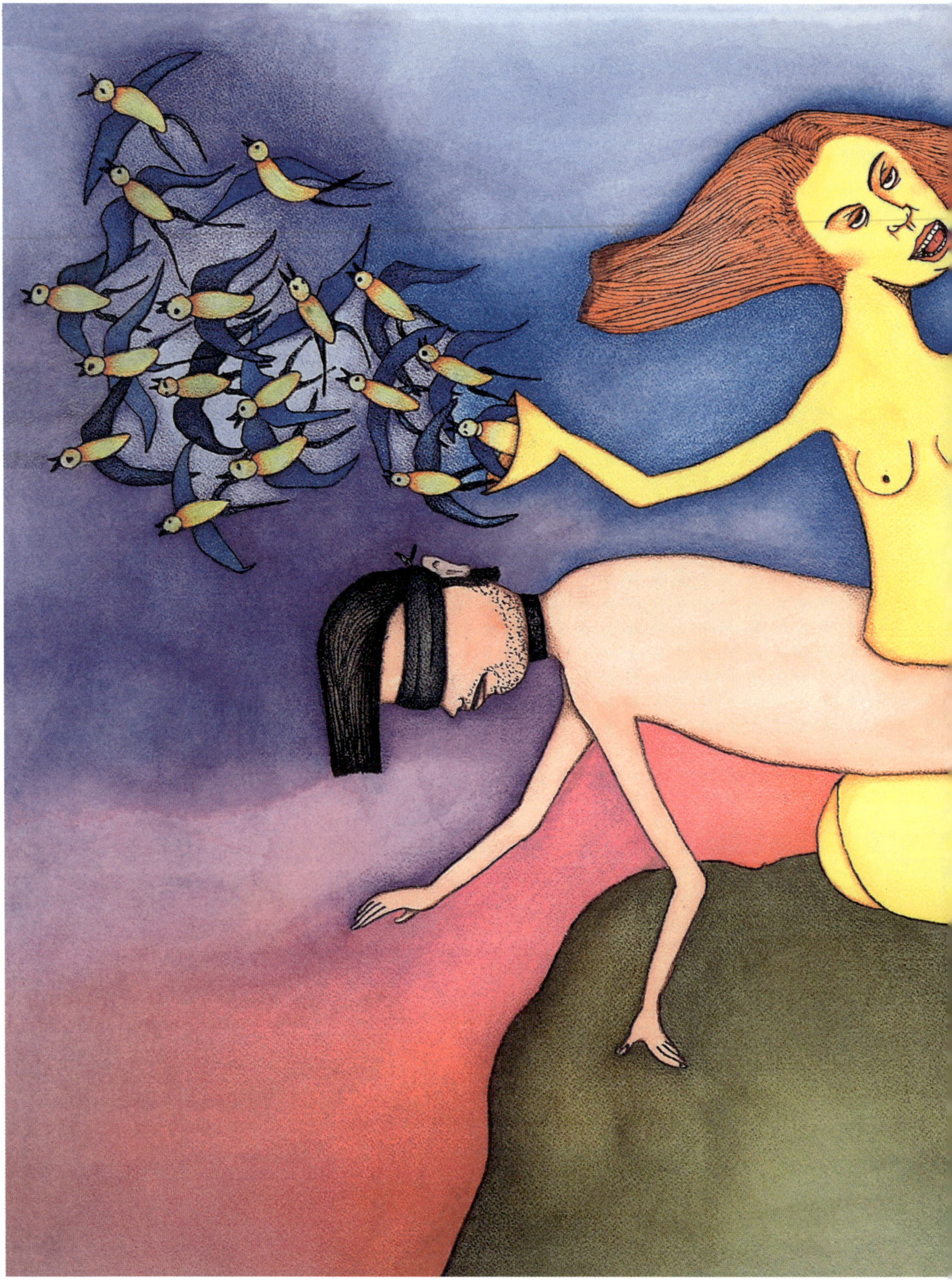

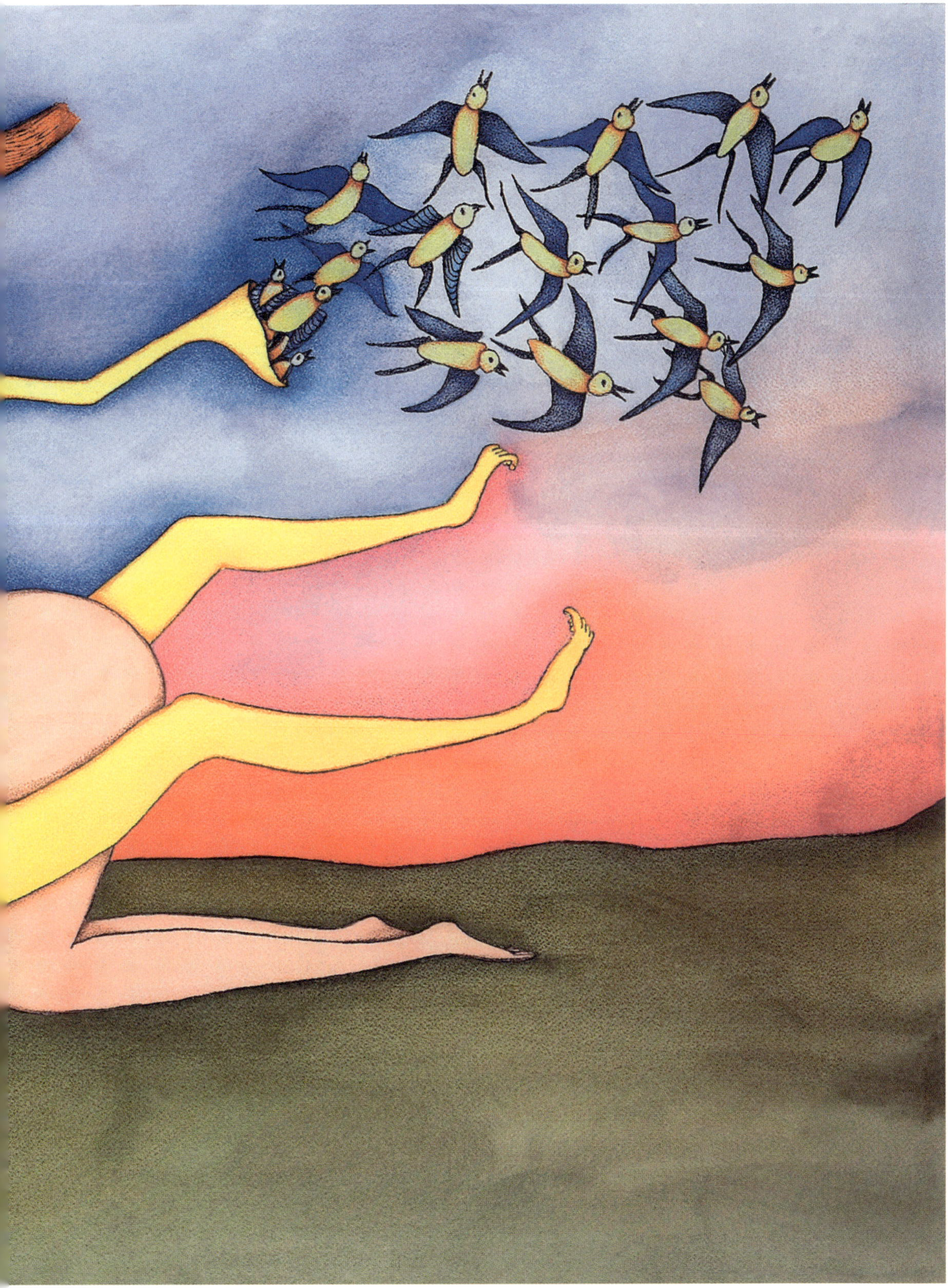

*Swallows for the Blind Man*, 2016
65 × 102 cm

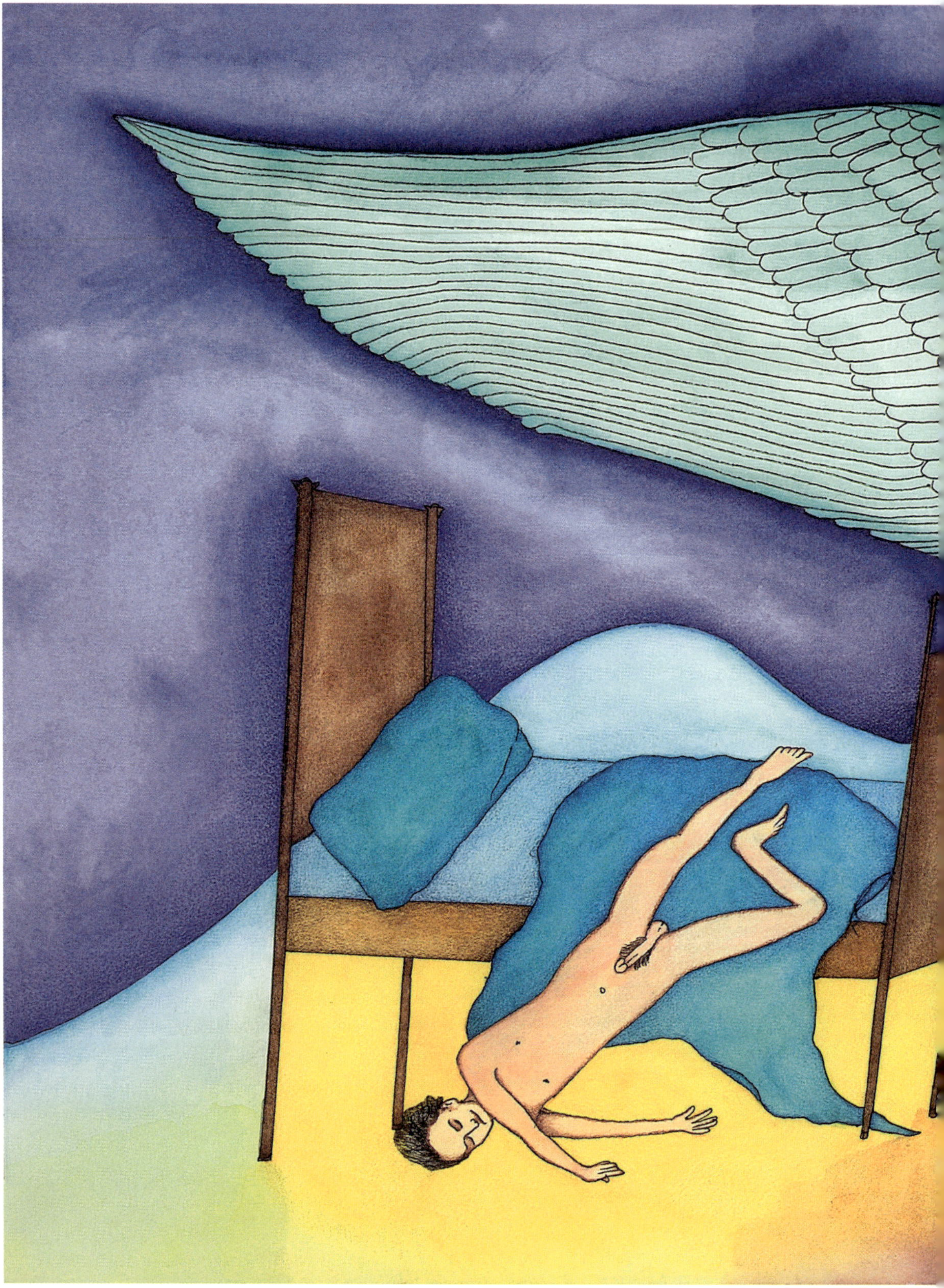

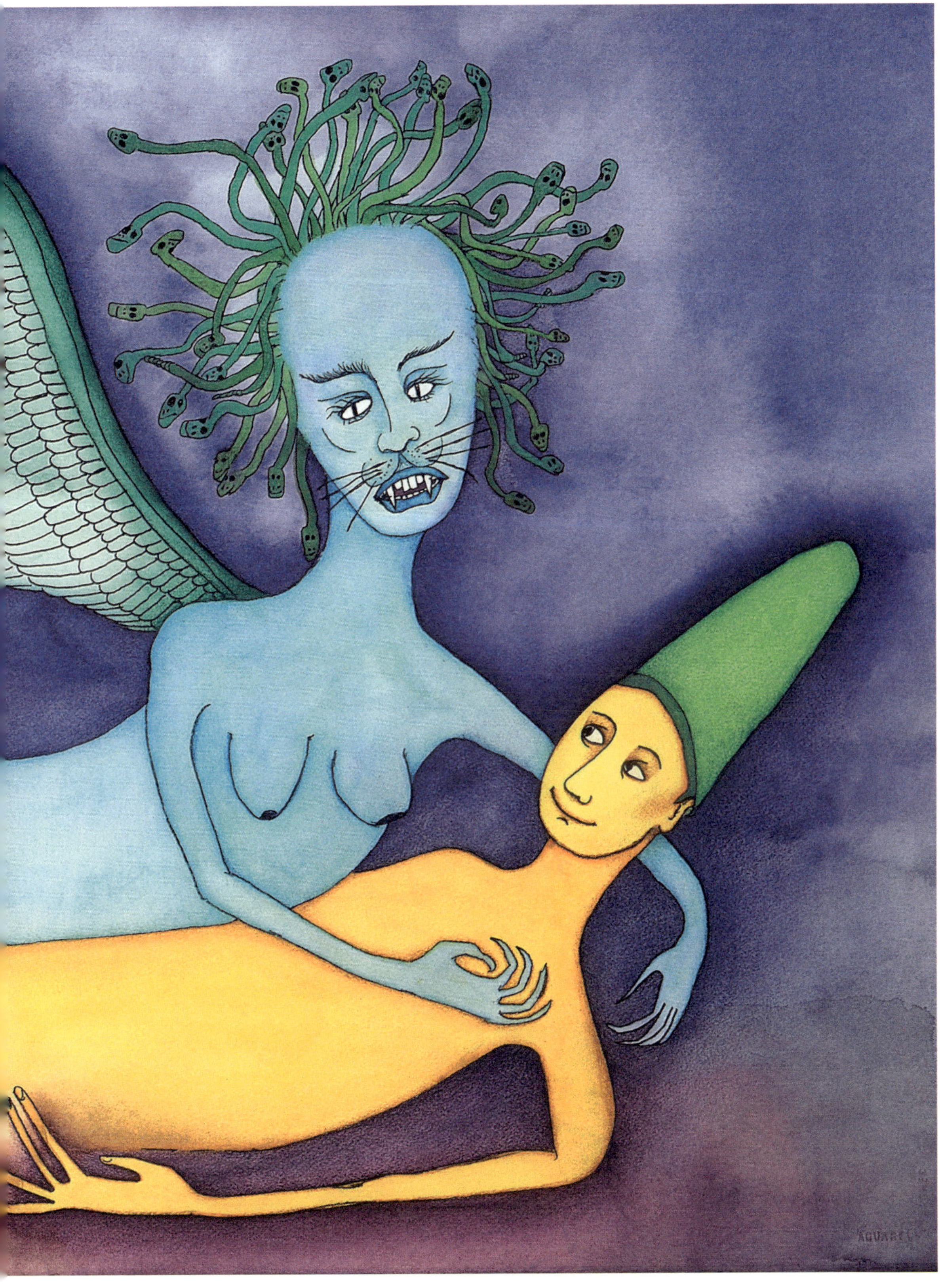

*Freud's Dream*, 2016
65 × 102 cm

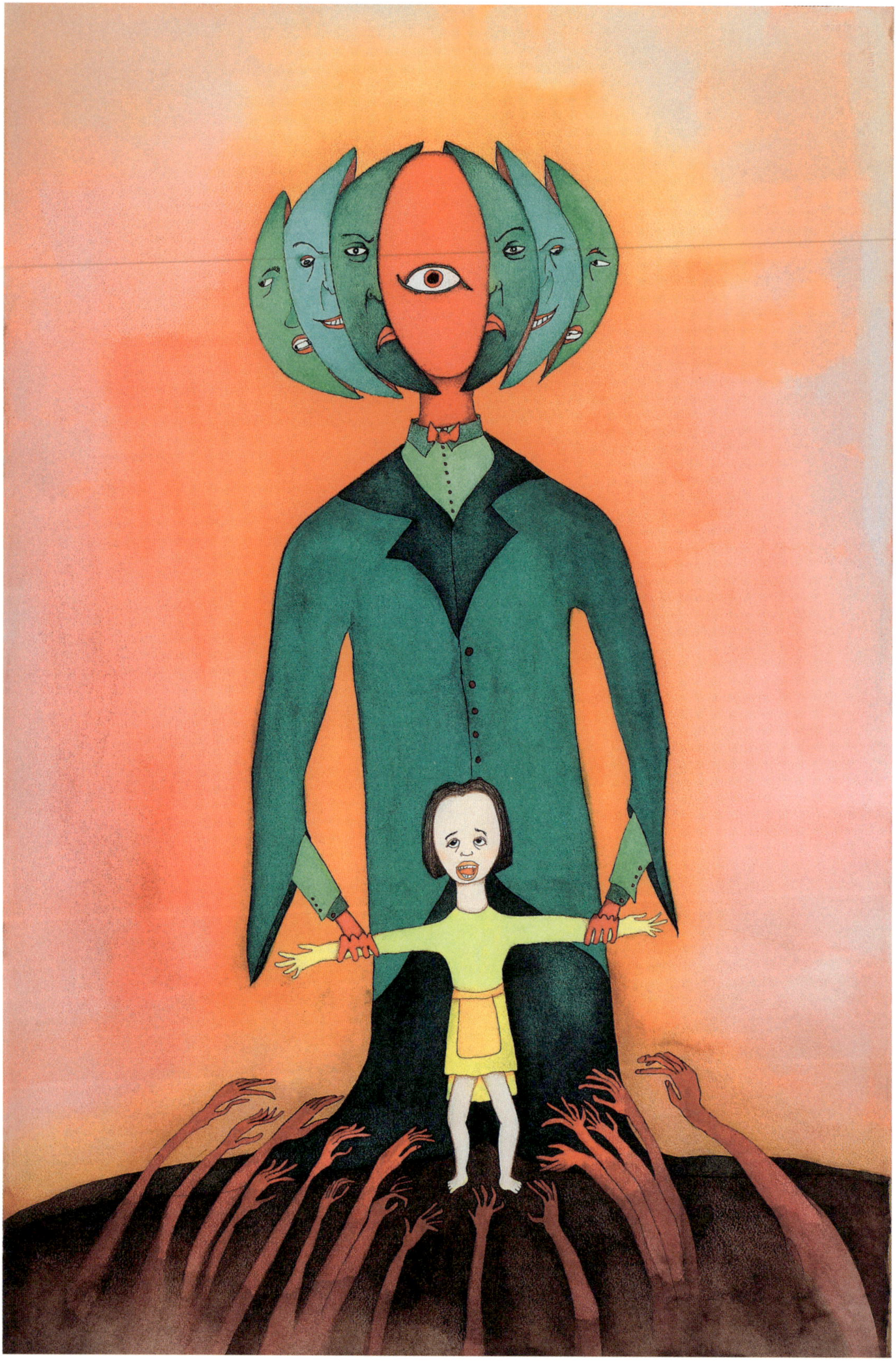

*Society Debut*, 2016
102 × 65 cm

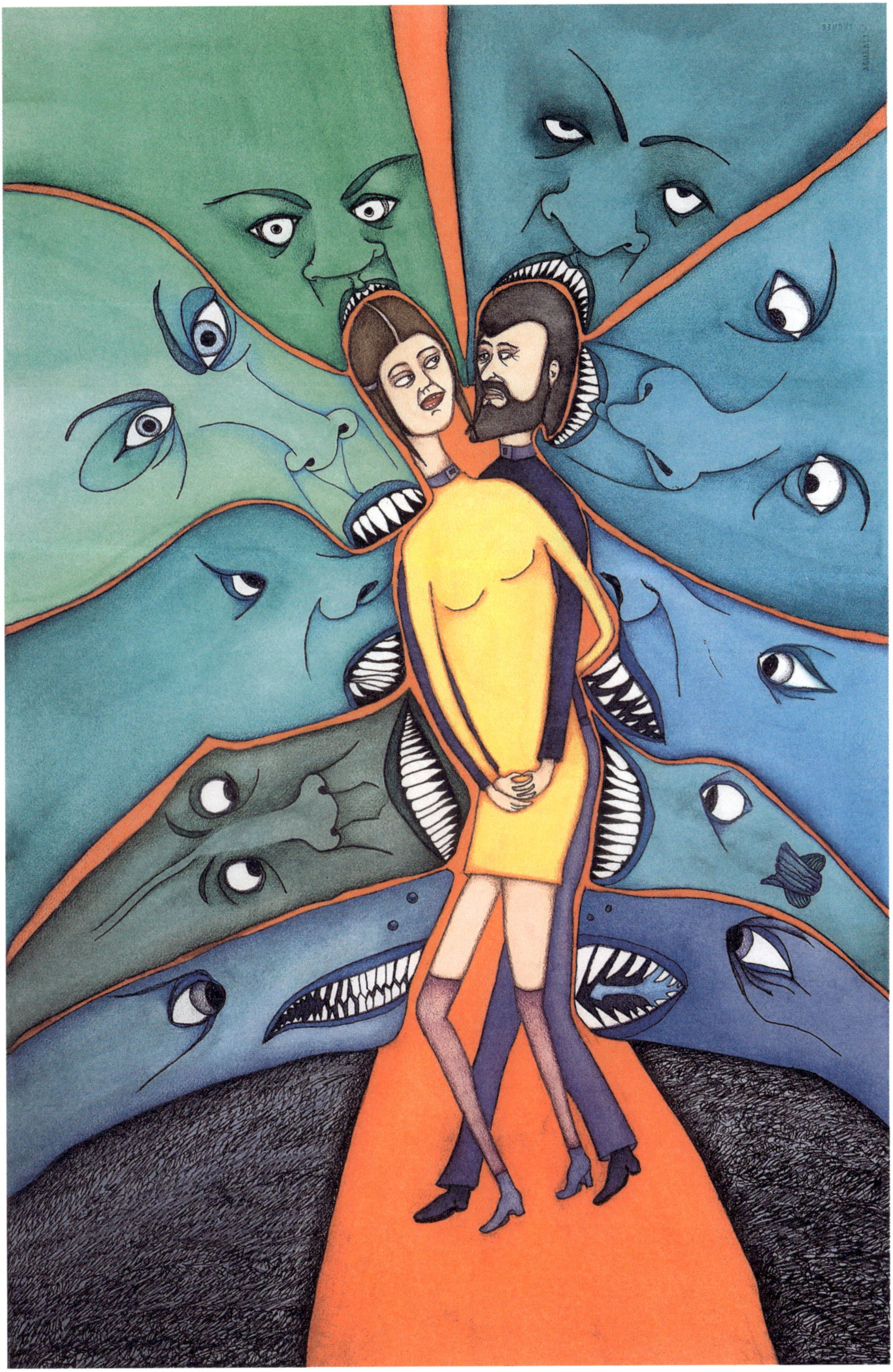

*The Anonymous Attack*, 2017
102 × 65 cm

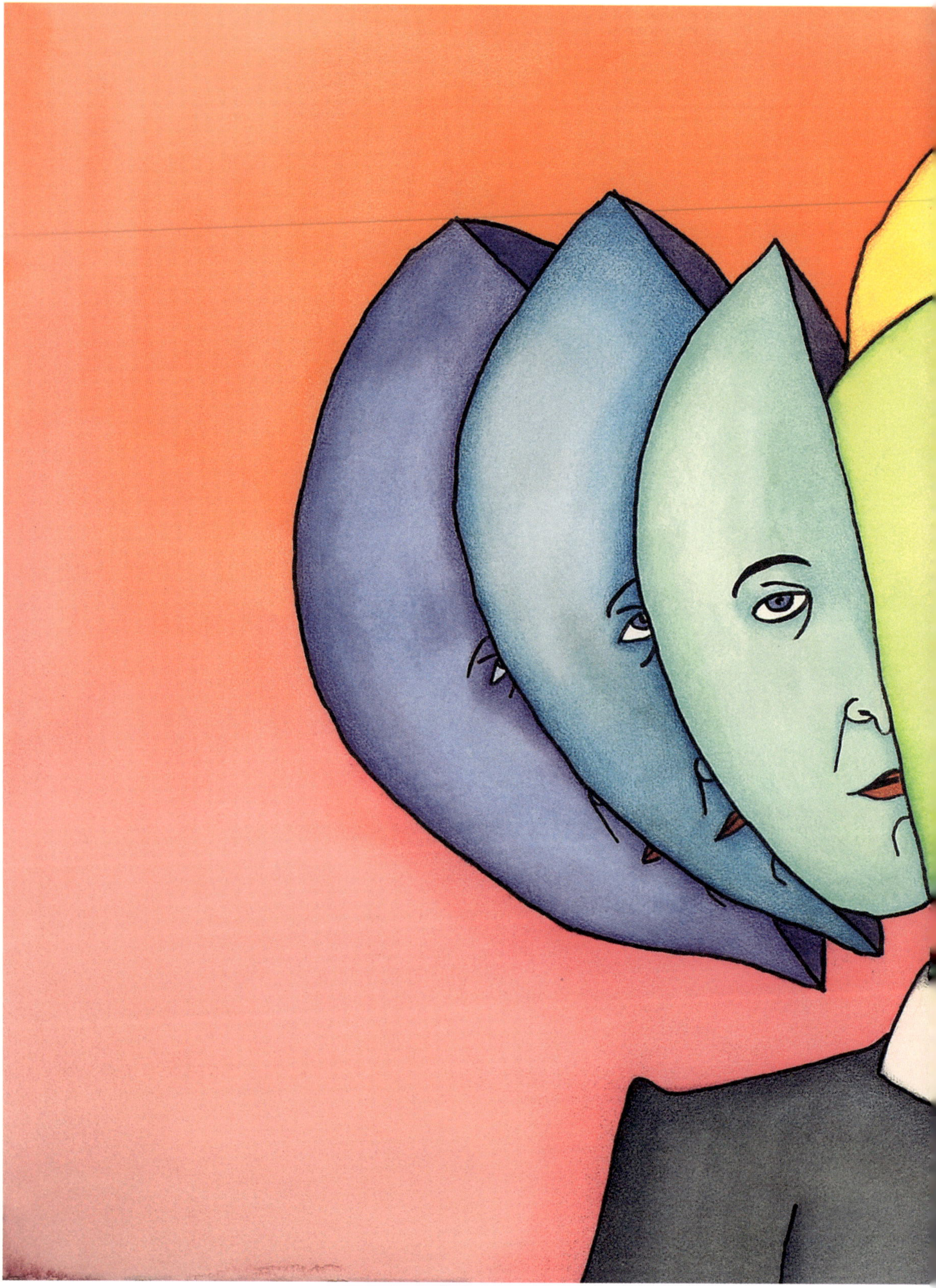

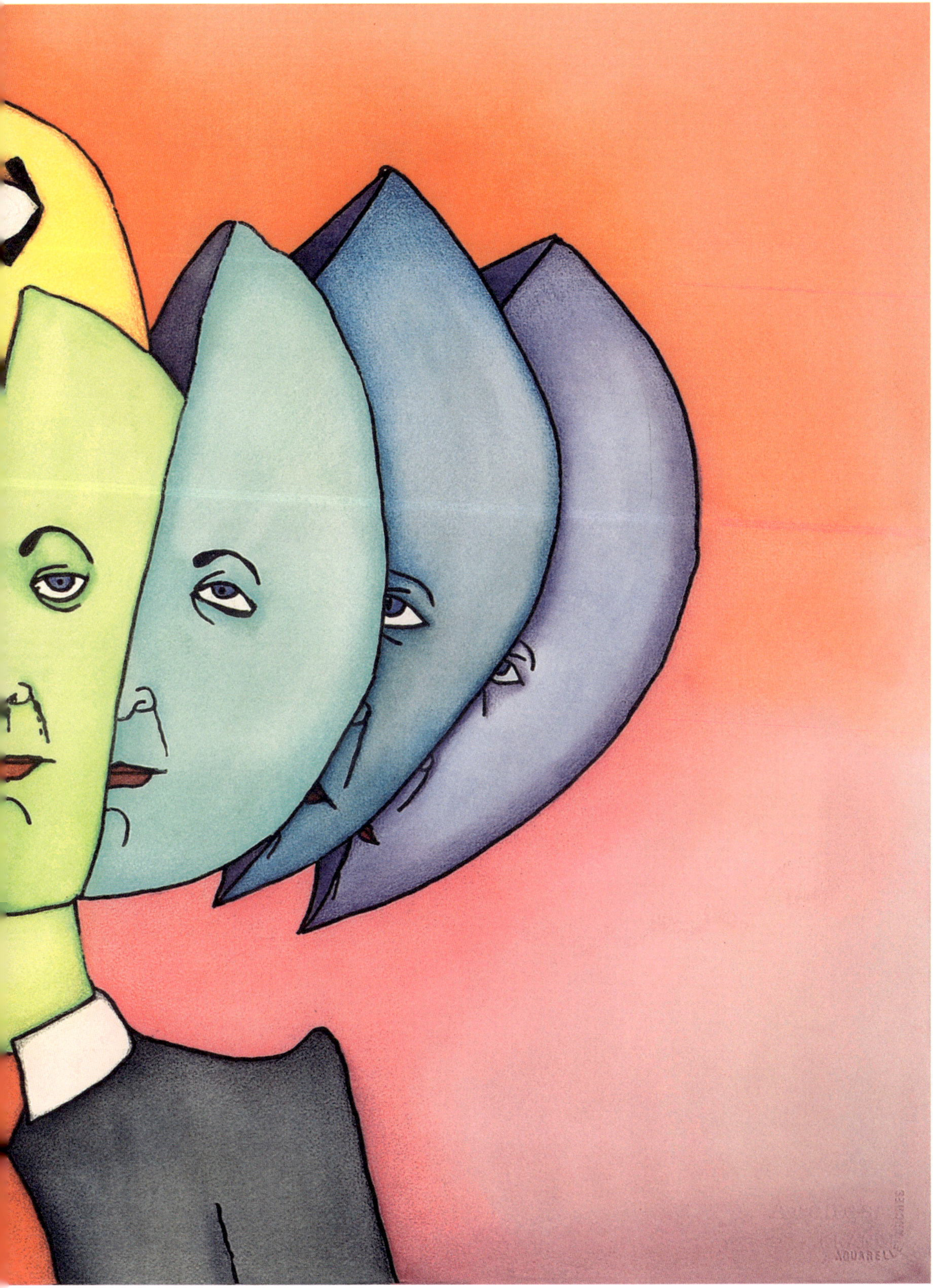

*Essential Being*, 2017
65 × 102 cm

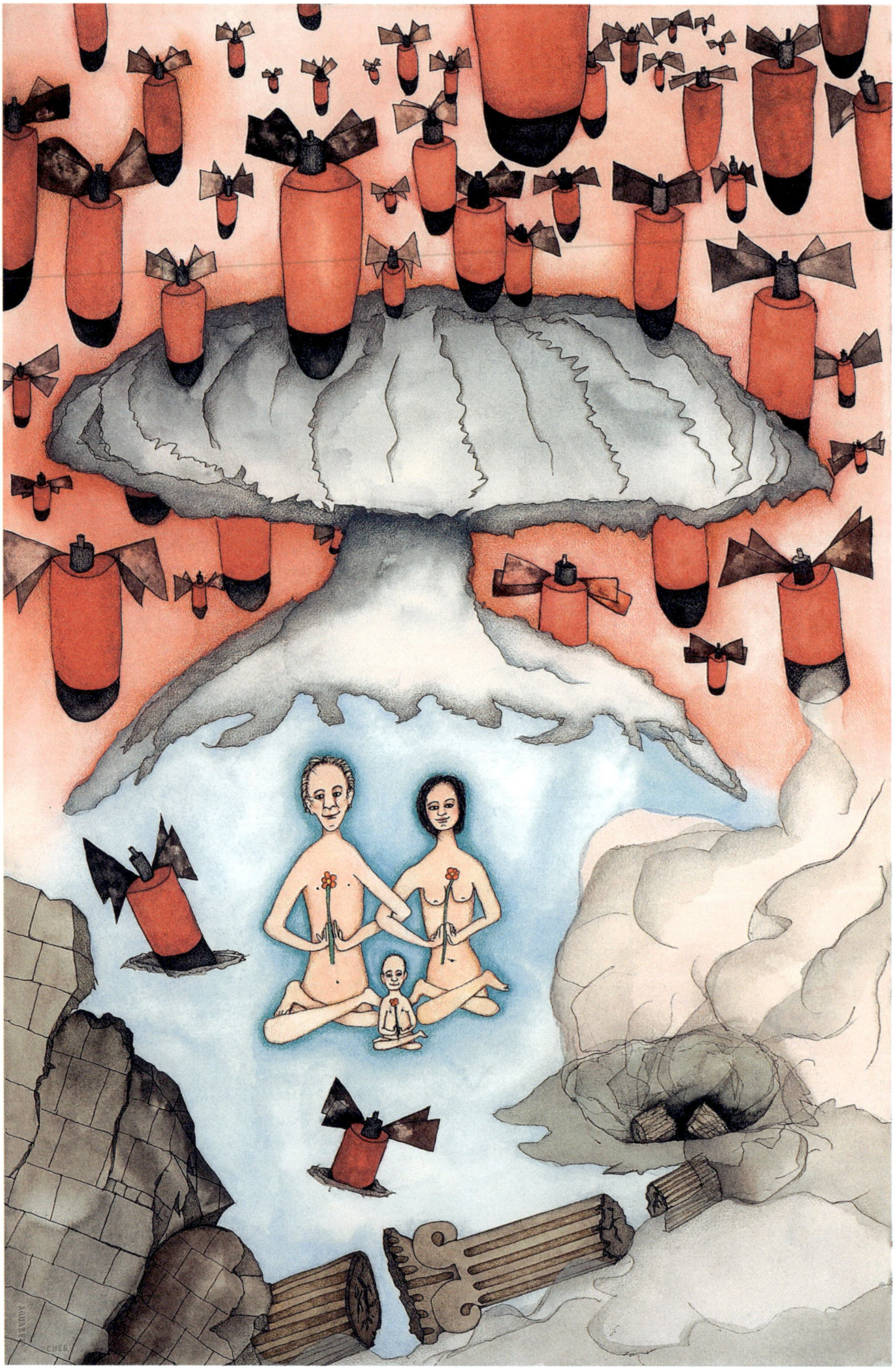

*Holy Family*, 2016
102 × 65 cm

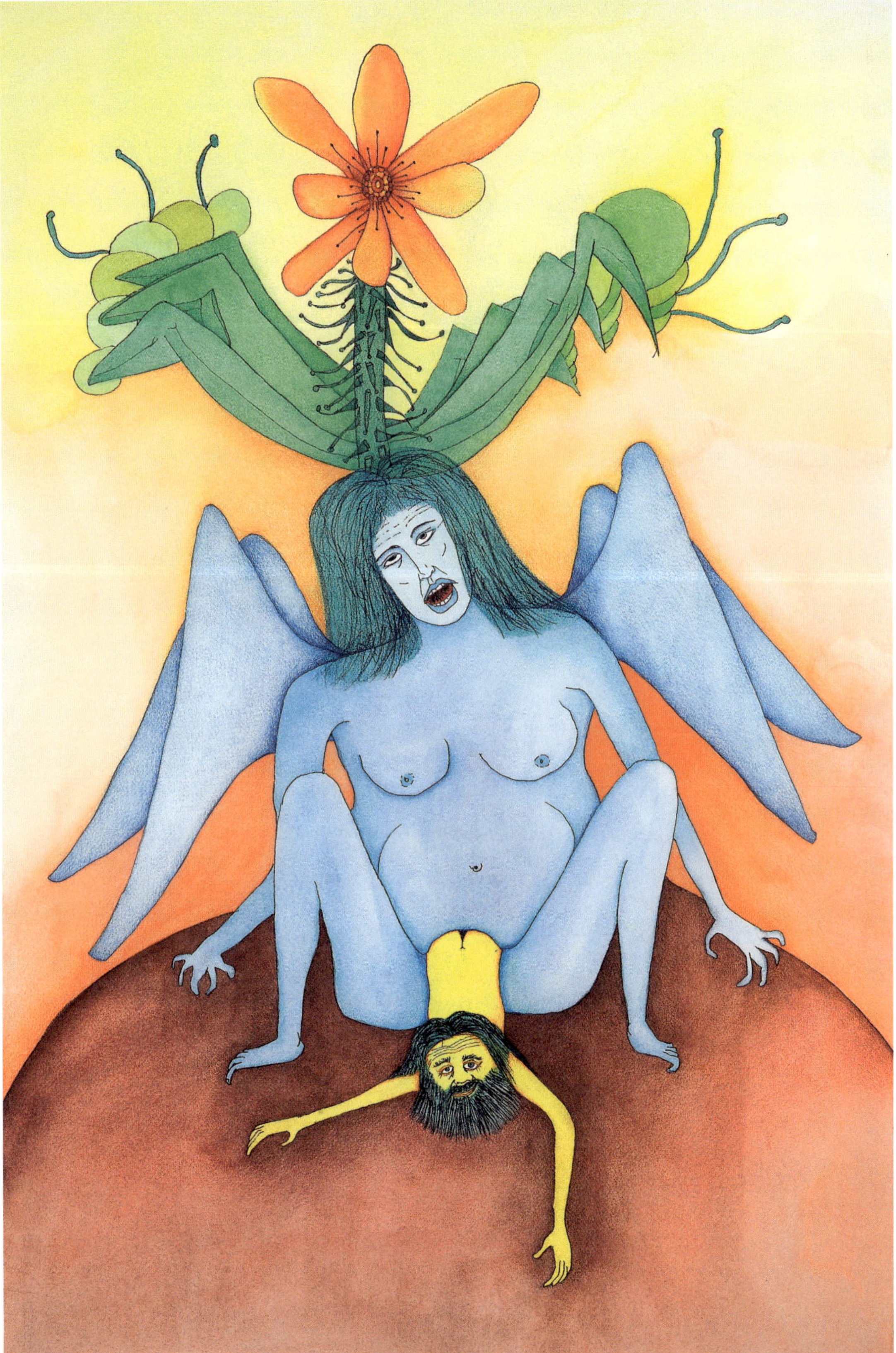

*Immaculate Conception*, 2016
102 × 65 cm

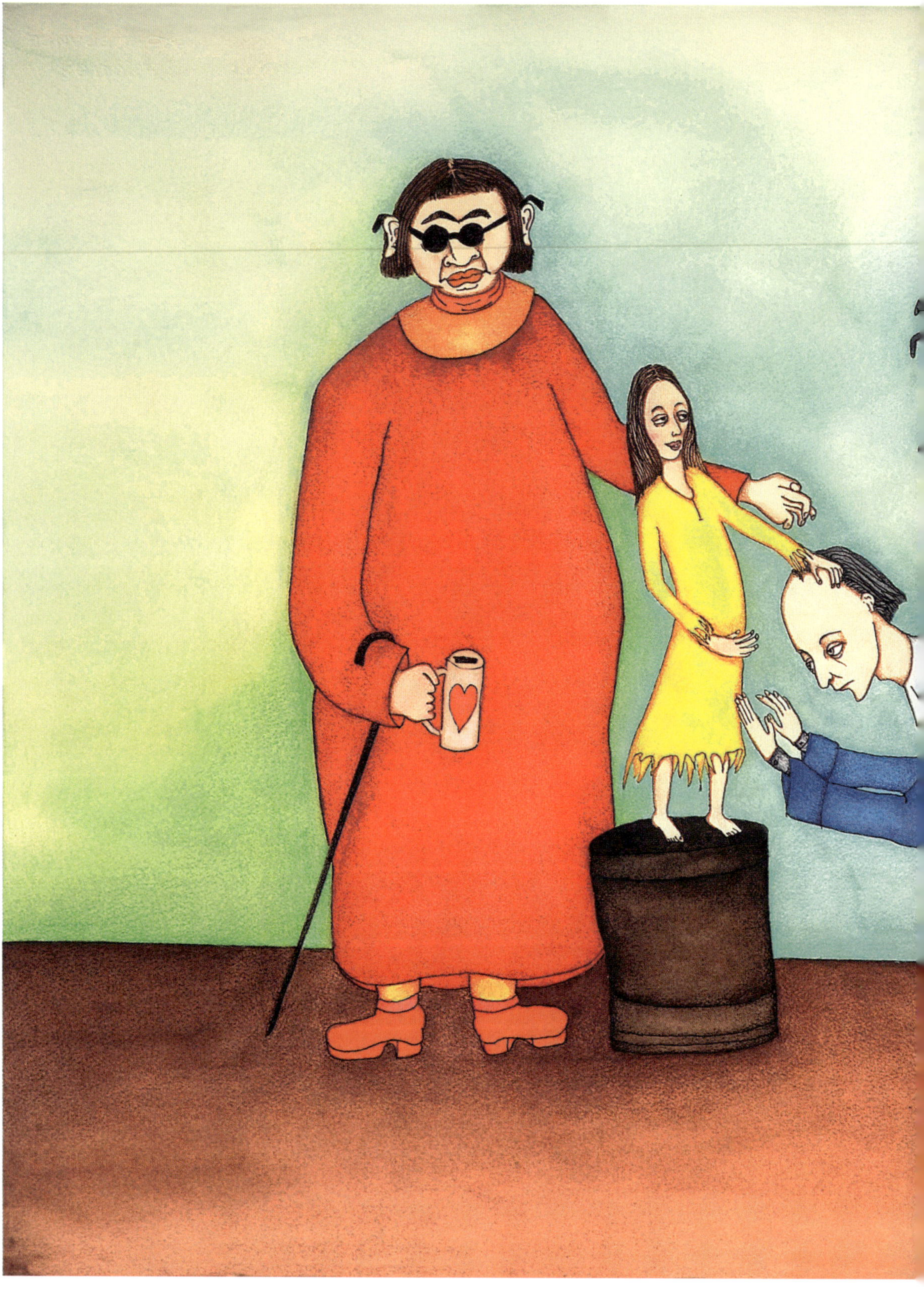

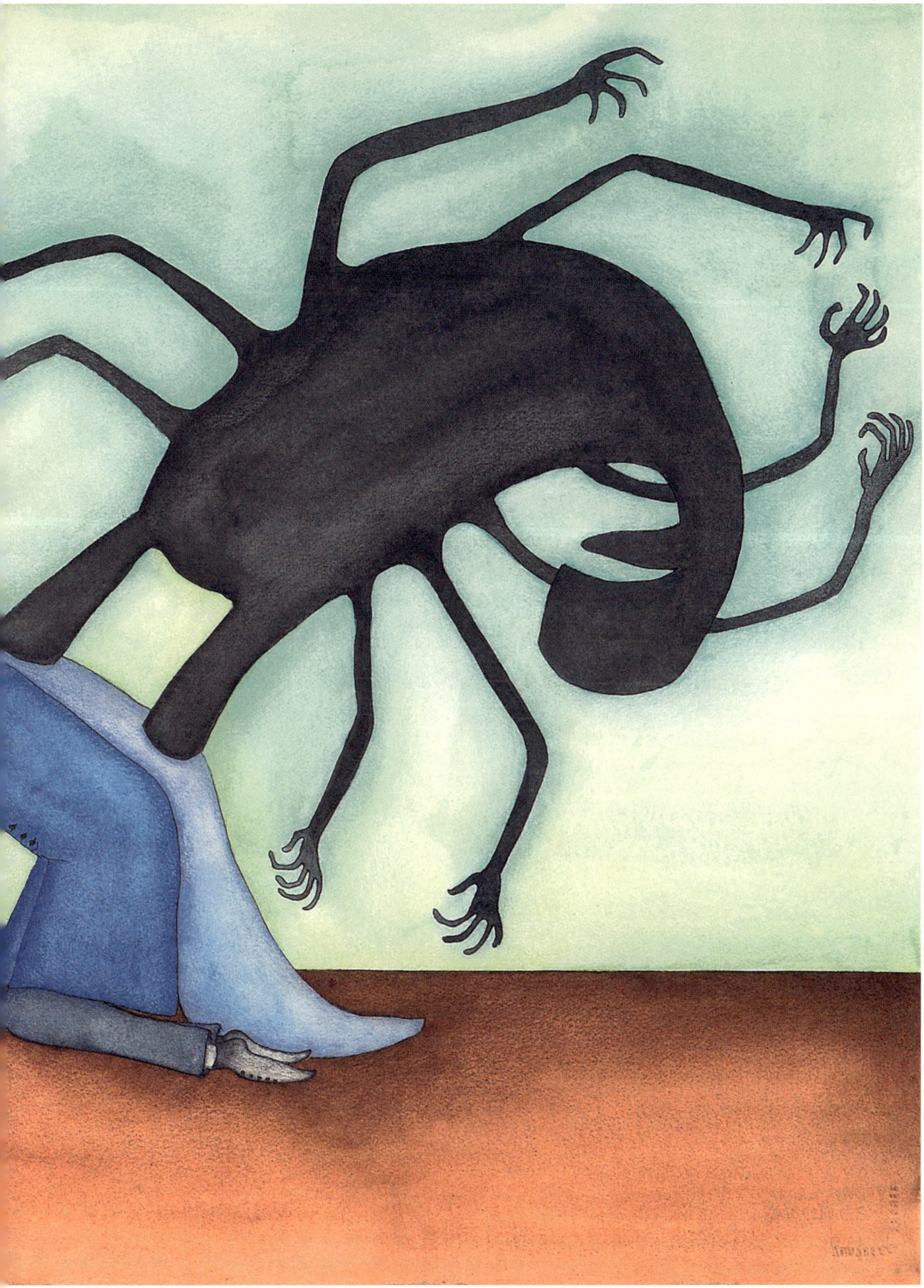

*The Tiny Exorcist*, 2017.
65 × 102 cm

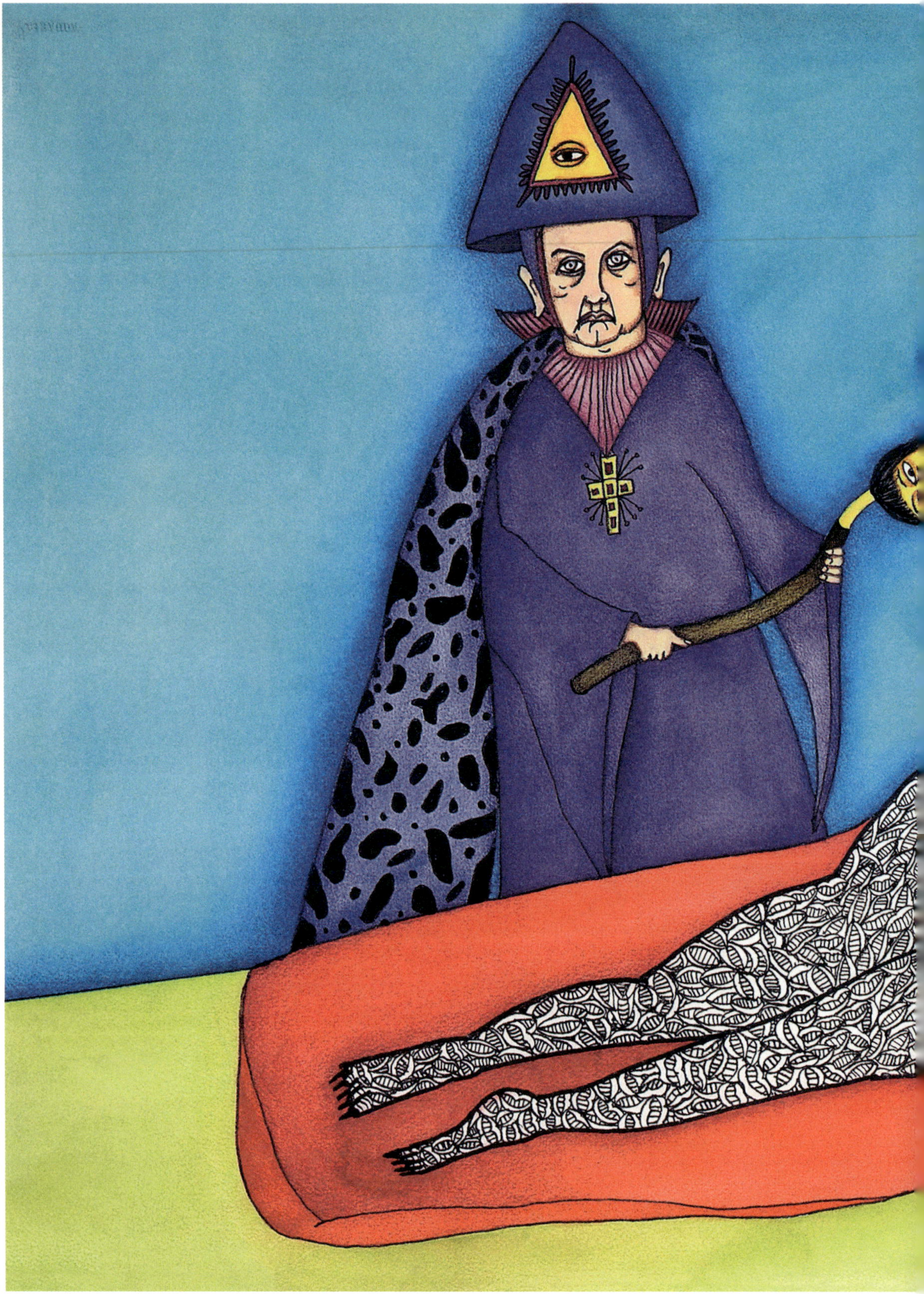

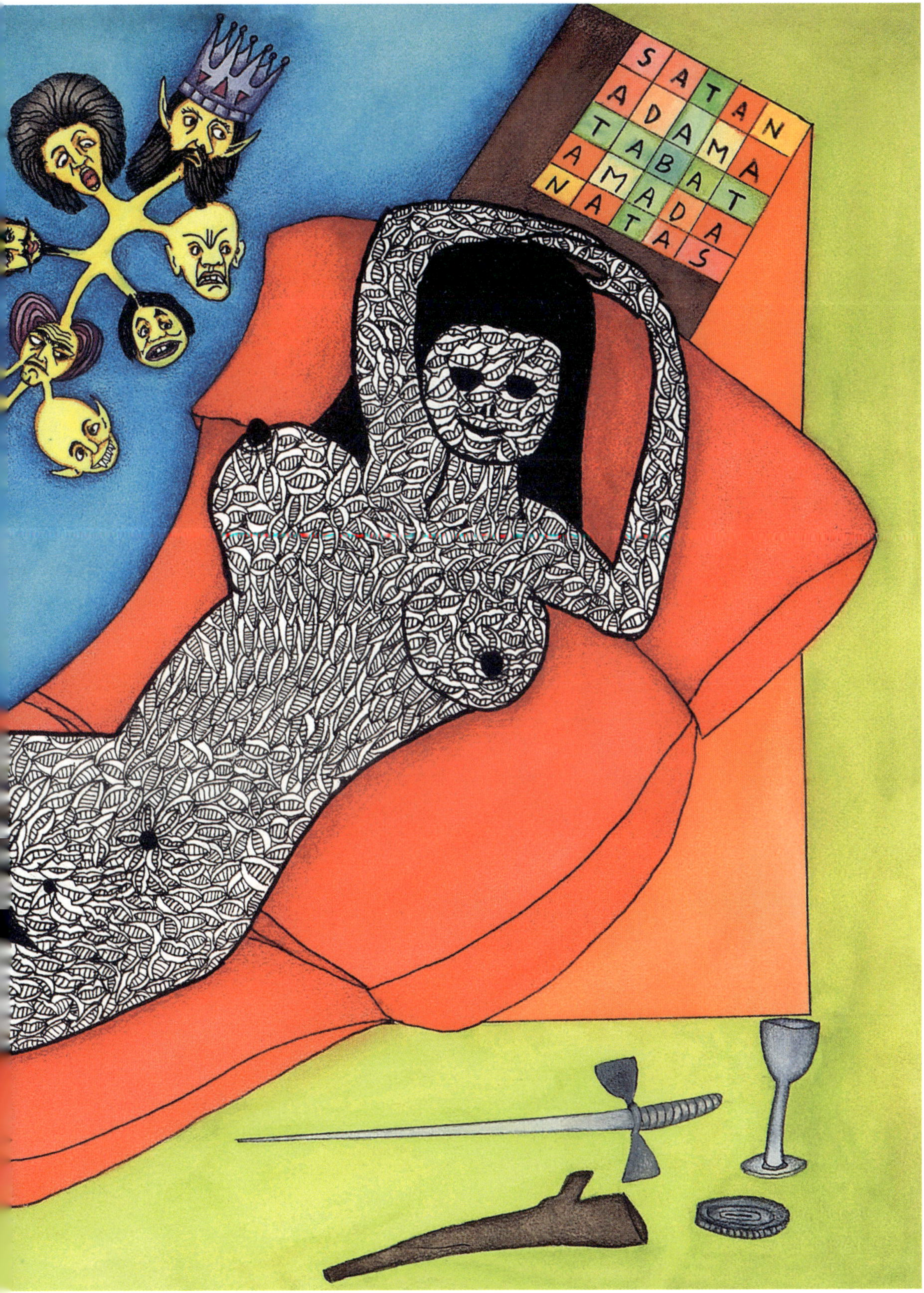


*Waking the Golem*, 2017.
65 × 102 cm

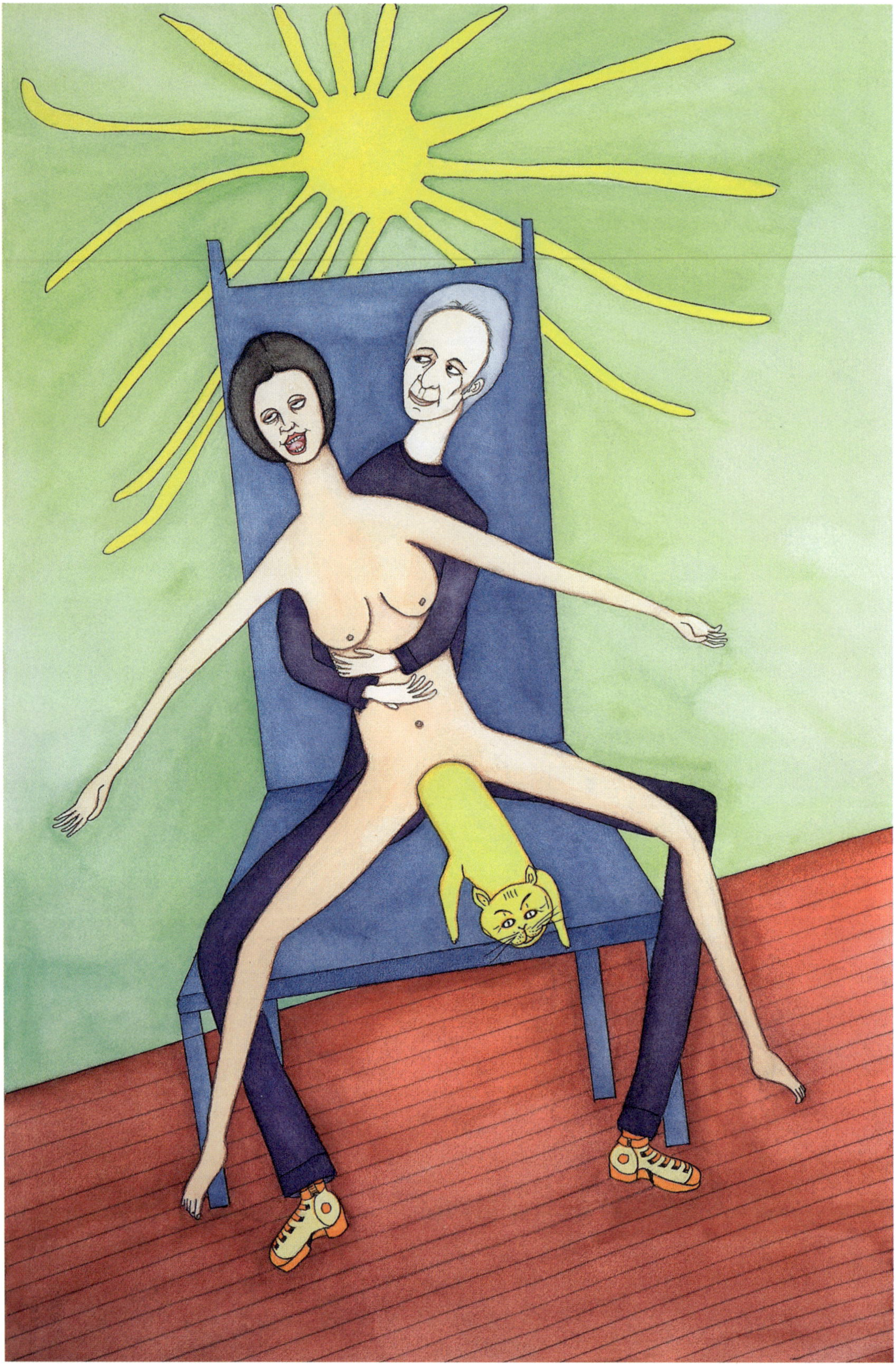

*The Messiah*, 2017.
102 × 65 cm

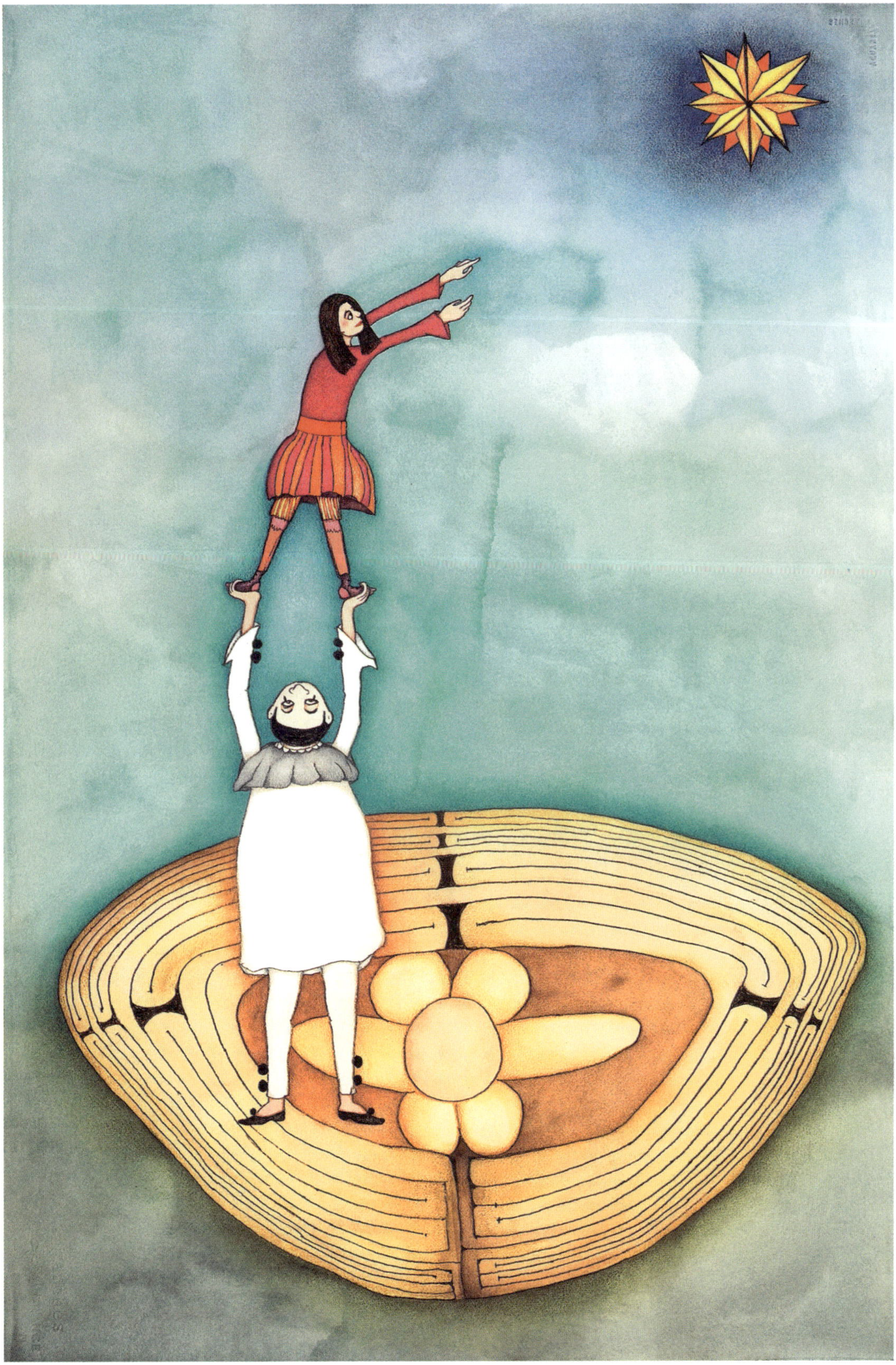

*The Promised Star*, 2016.
102 × 65 cm

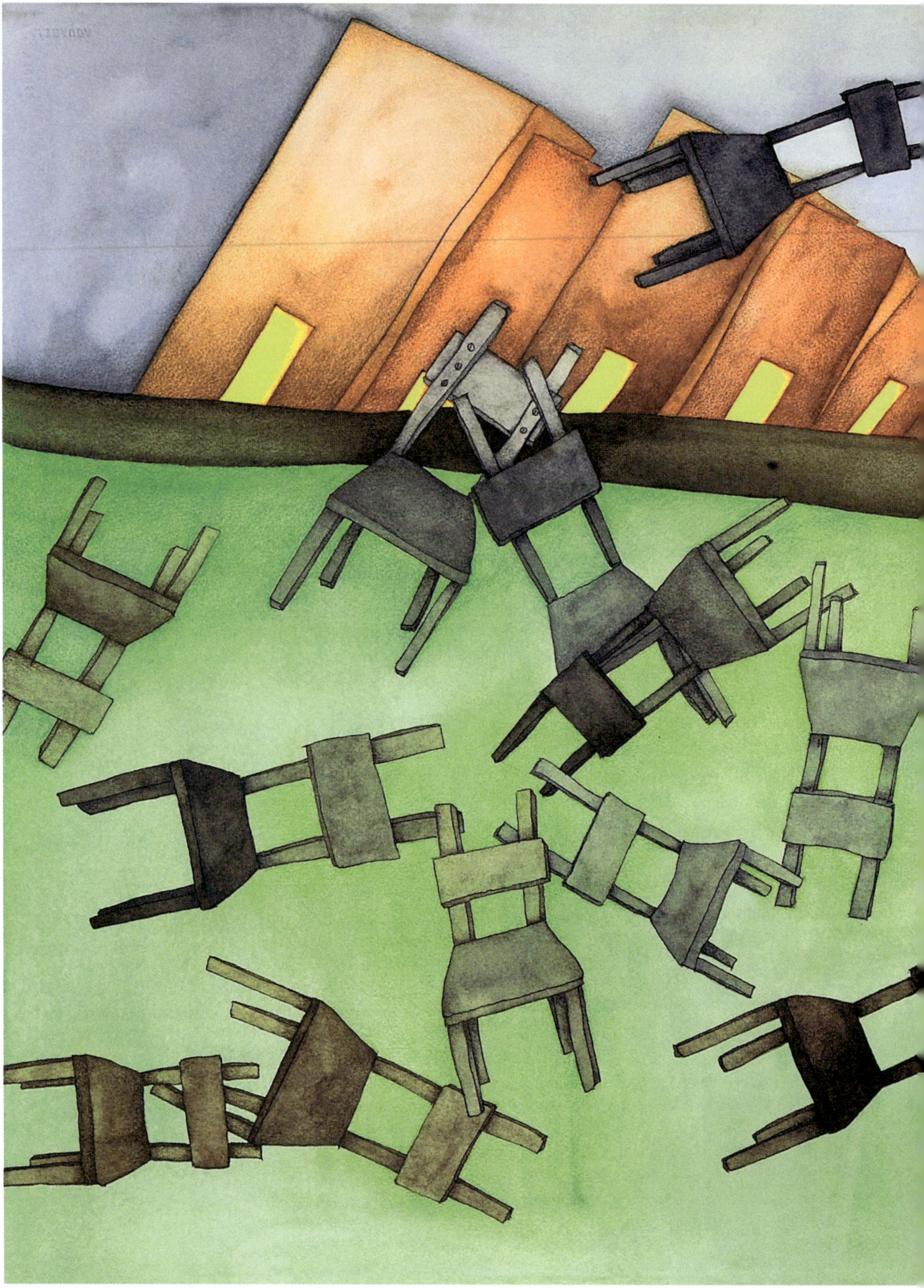

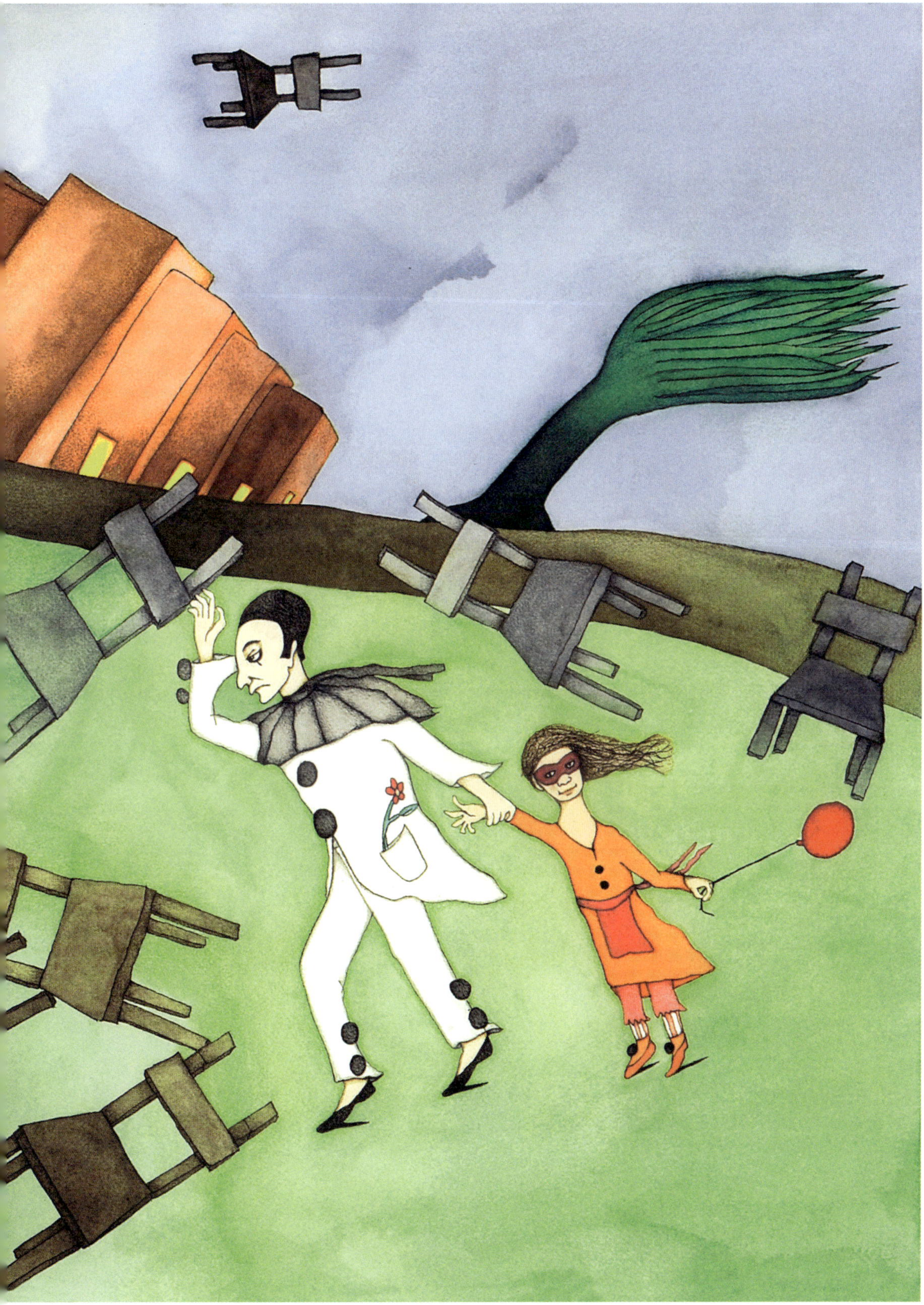

*March against Absence*, 2016.
65 × 102 cm

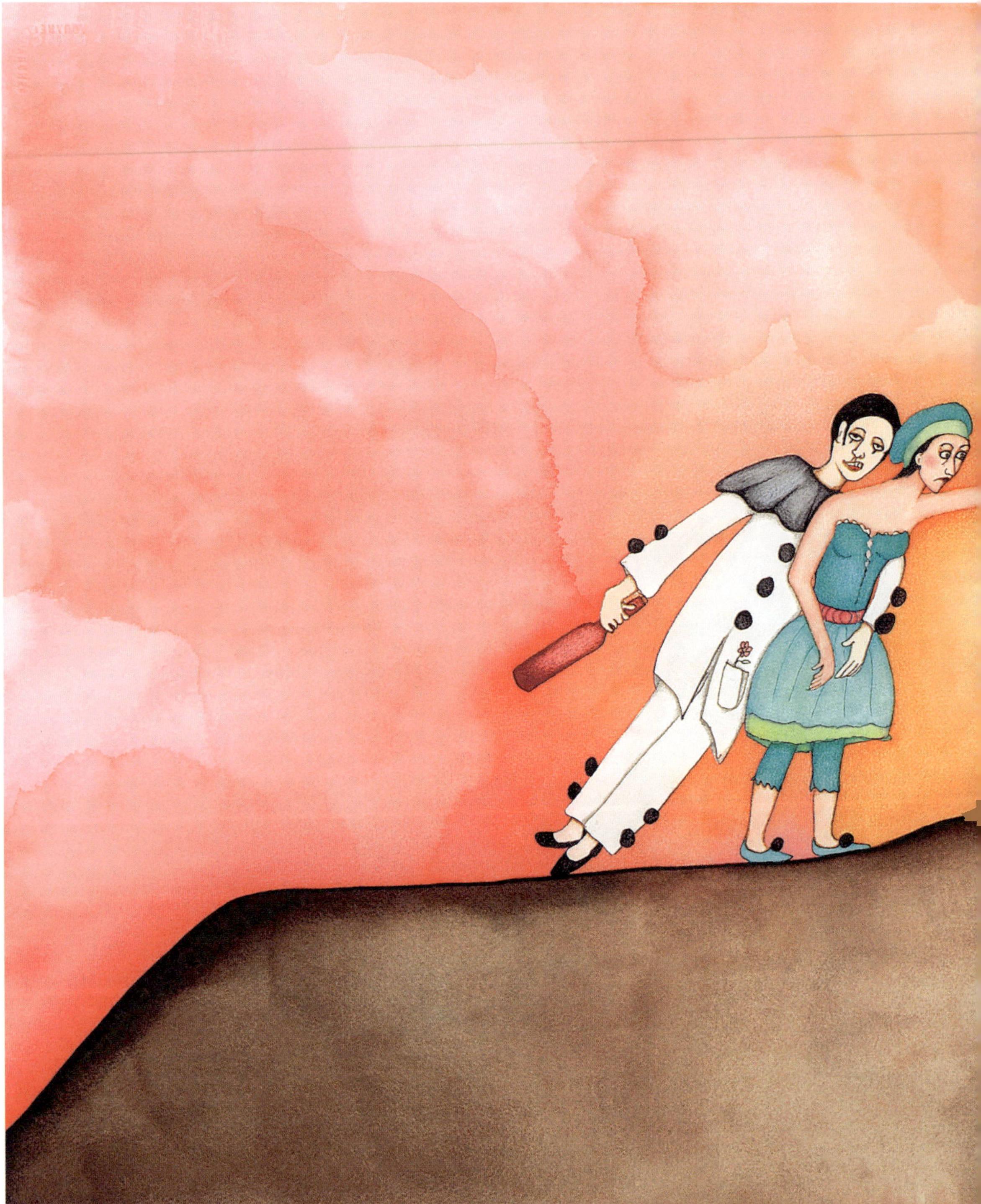

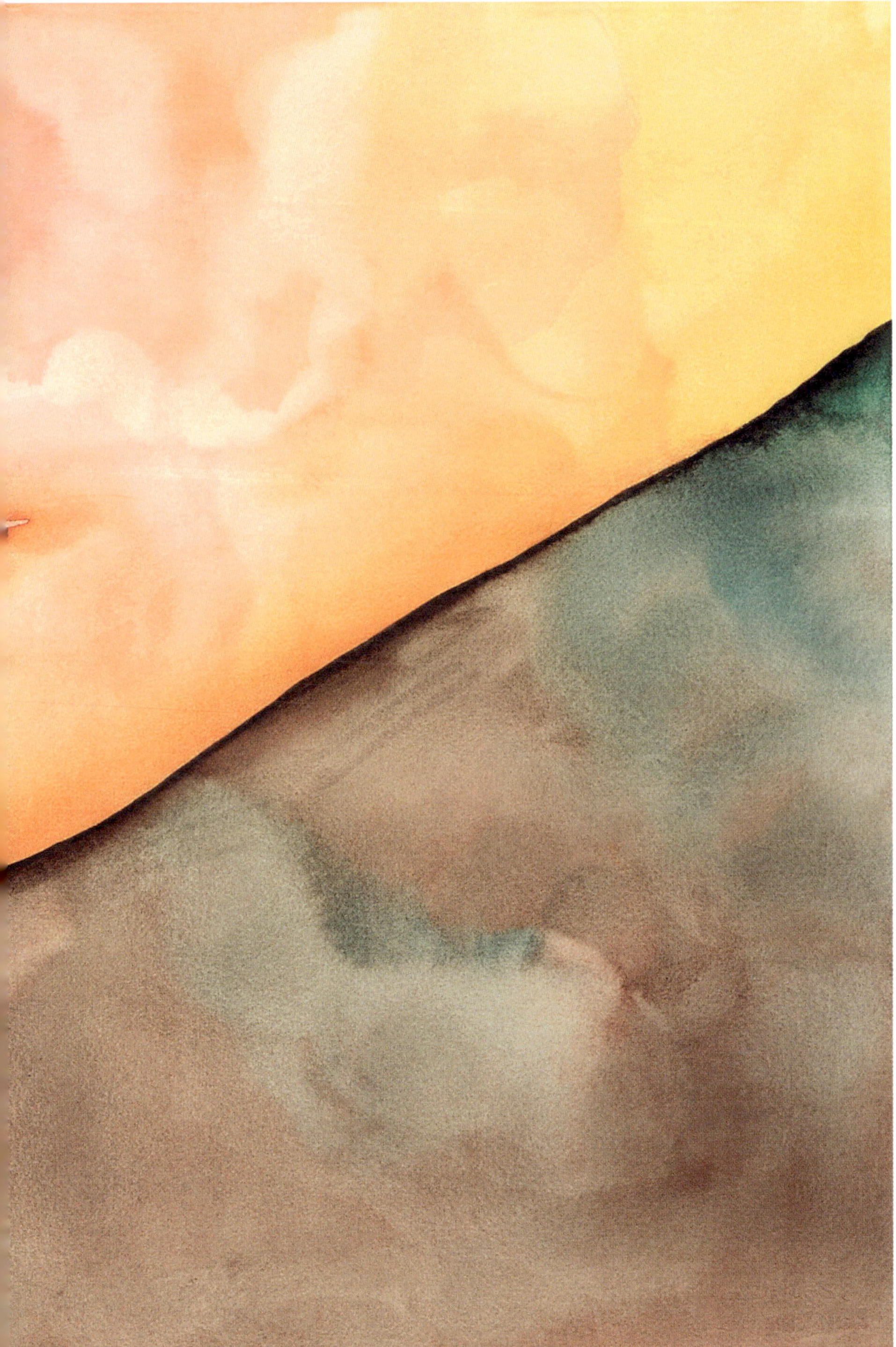

*Lost on the Horizon*, 2016.
65 × 102 cm

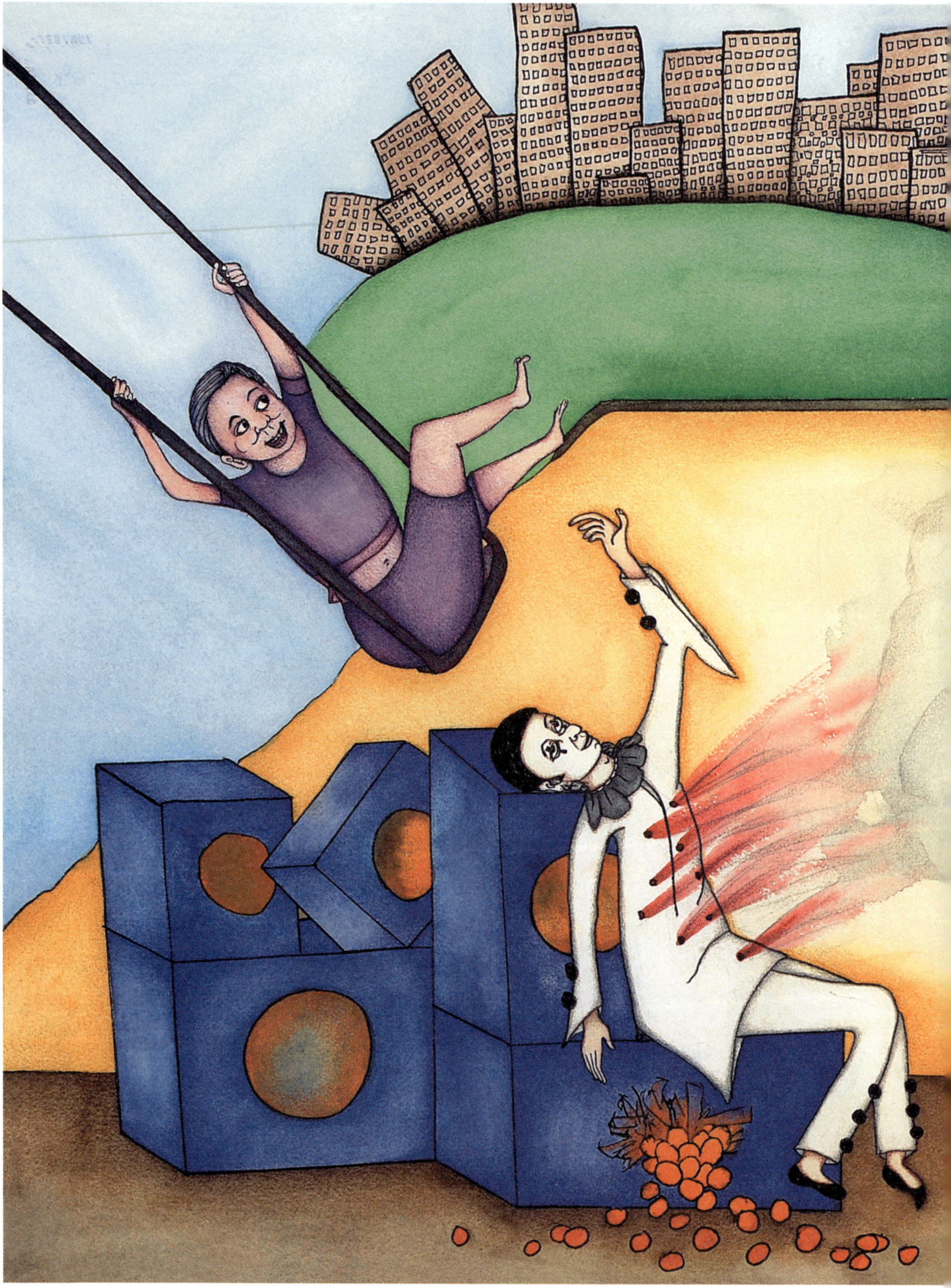

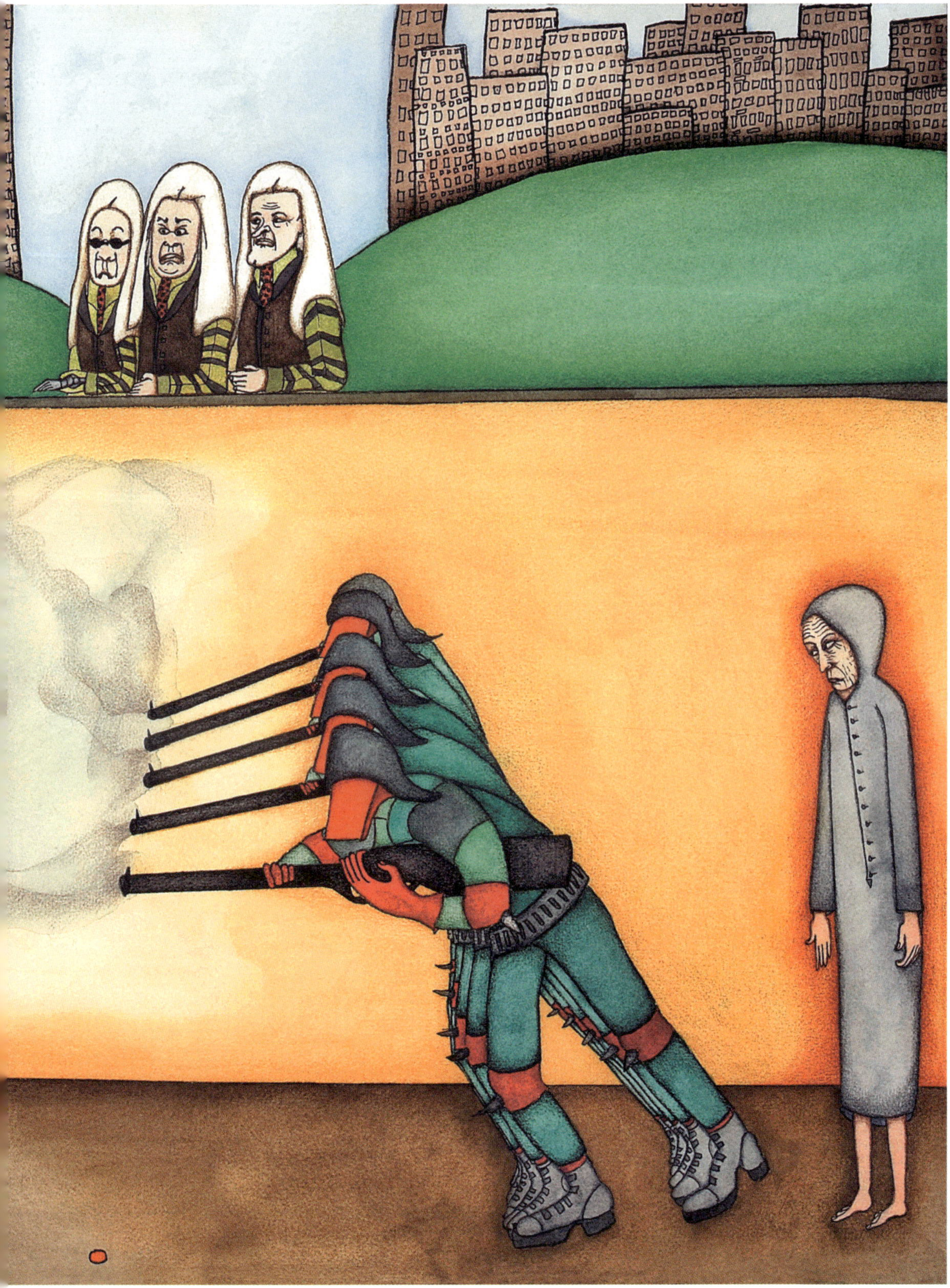

*The Last Poet*, 2016.
65 × 102 cm

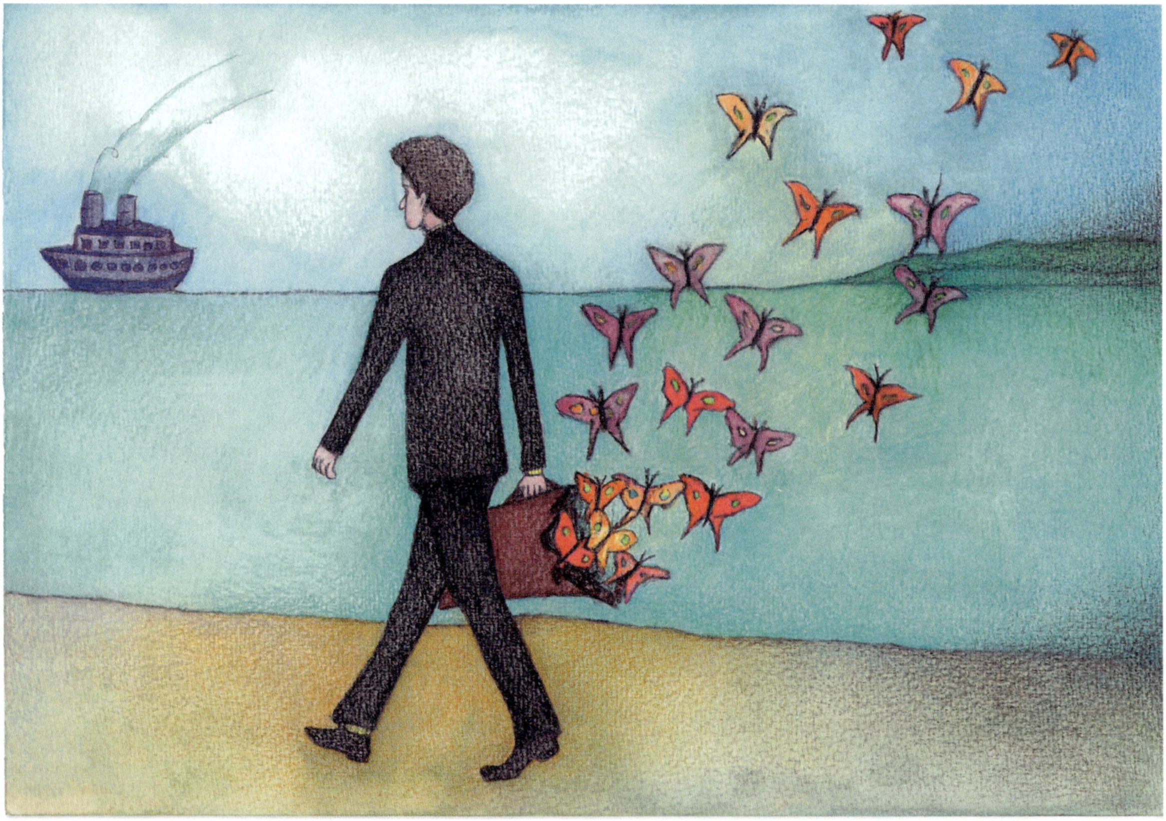

*Poesía Sin Fin*, (drawing for the official film poster), 2016
21 × 30 cm

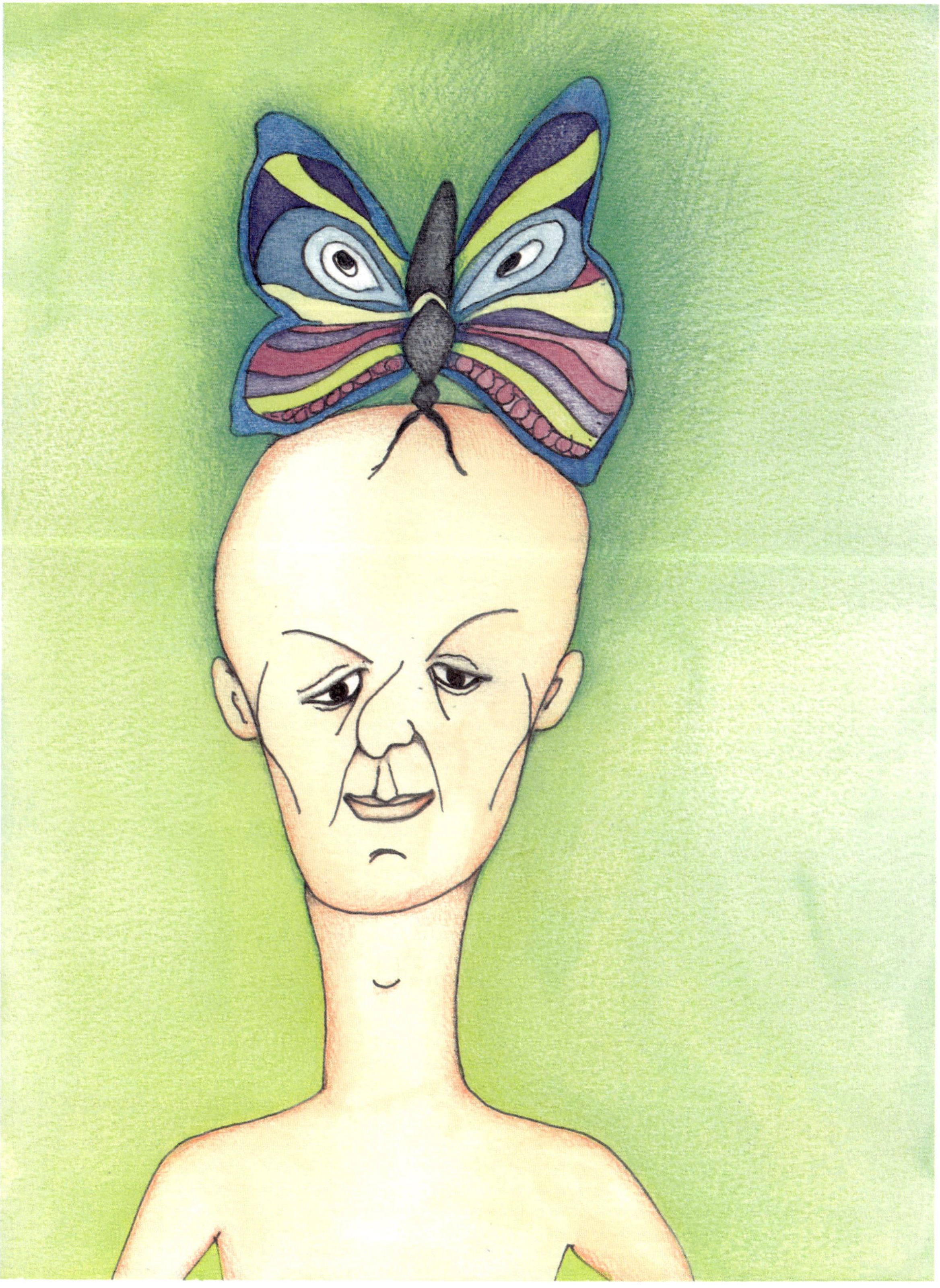

*The Beginning of Poetry*, 2015
30 × 21 cm

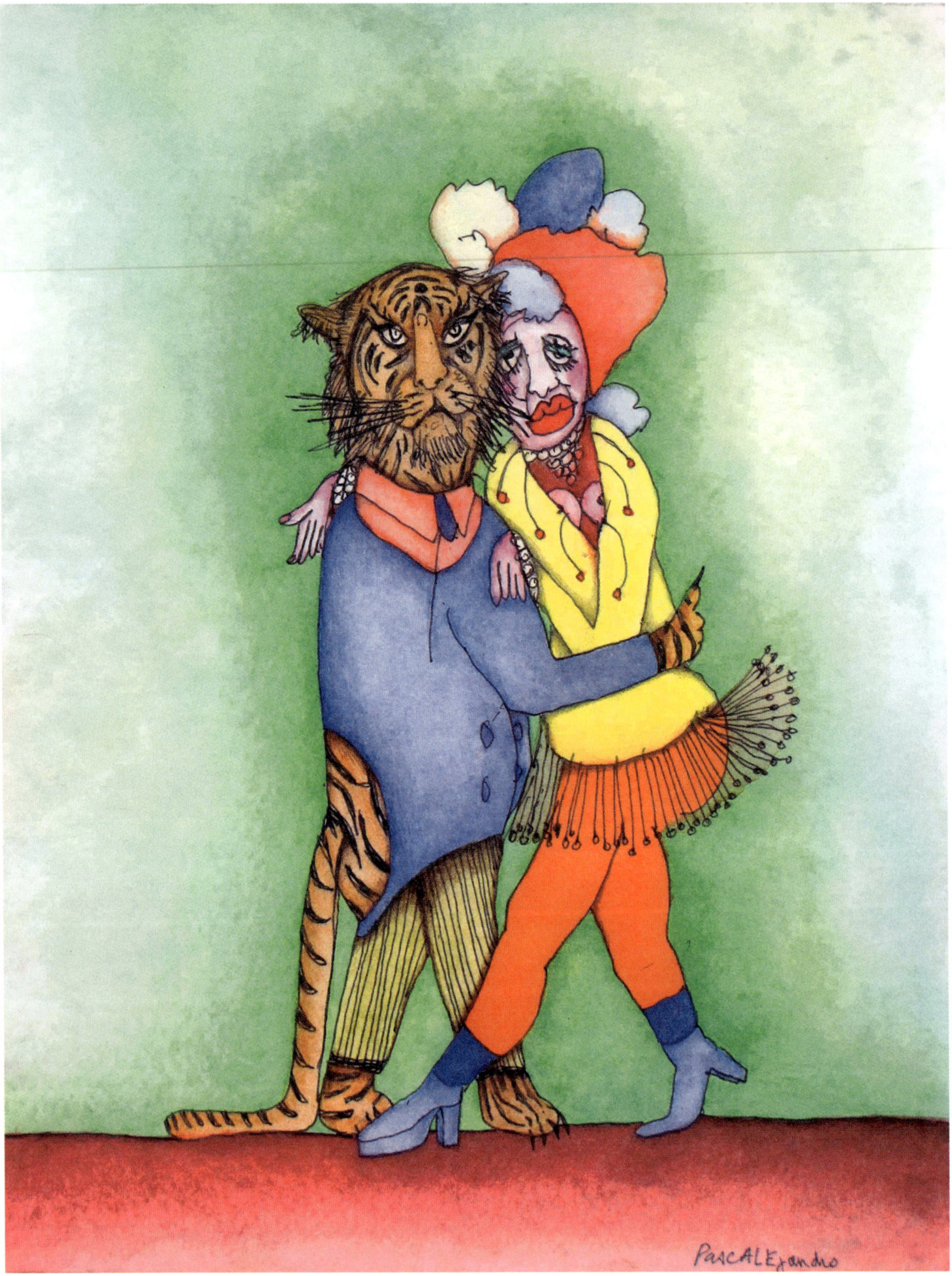


*The Tiger and His Whore*, 2014
41 × 31 cm

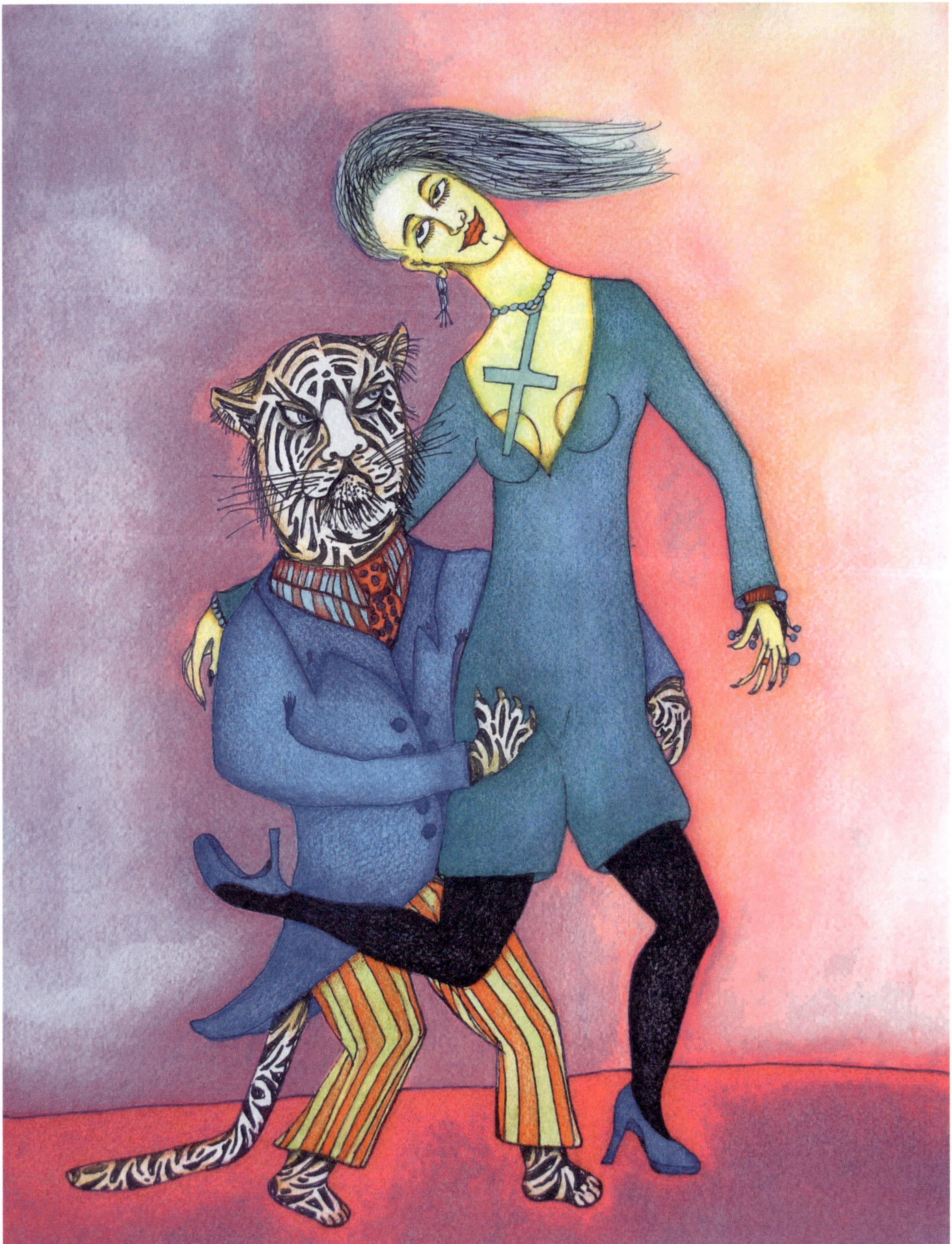

*Tiger Tango*, 2014
32 × 24 cm

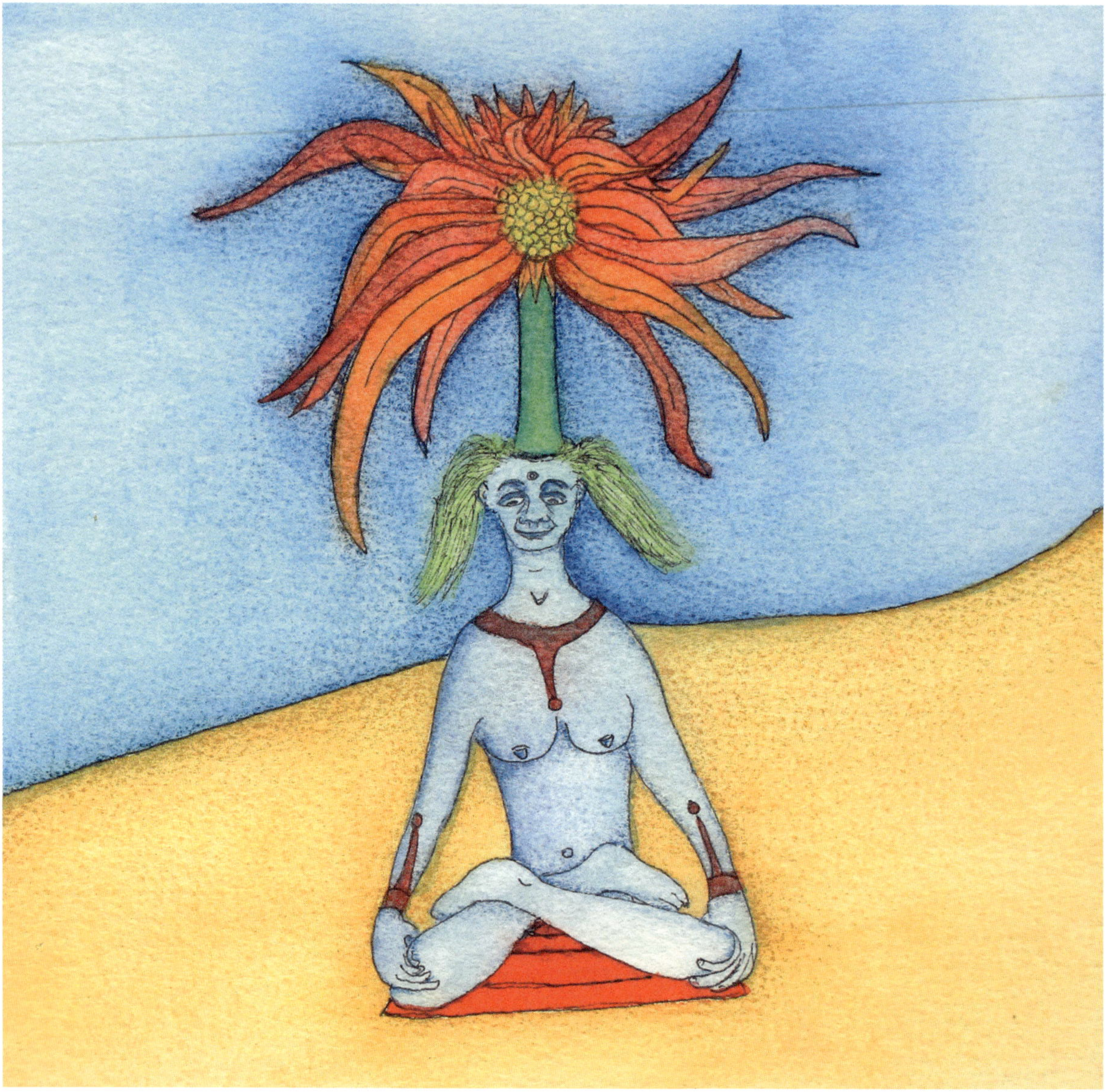

*Floral Yoga*, 2014
20 × 20 cm

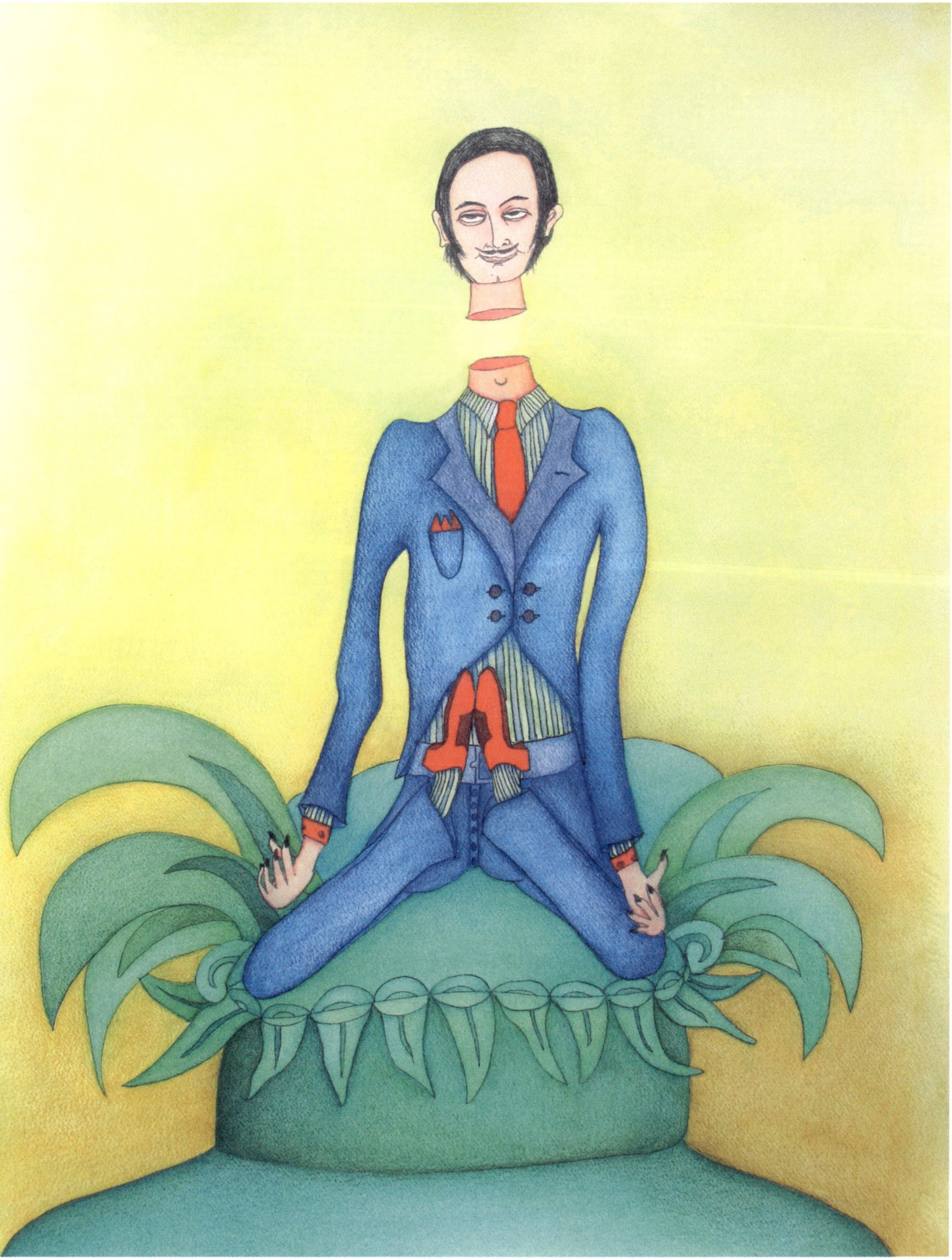

*Aristo-Yoga*, 2014
65 × 50 cm

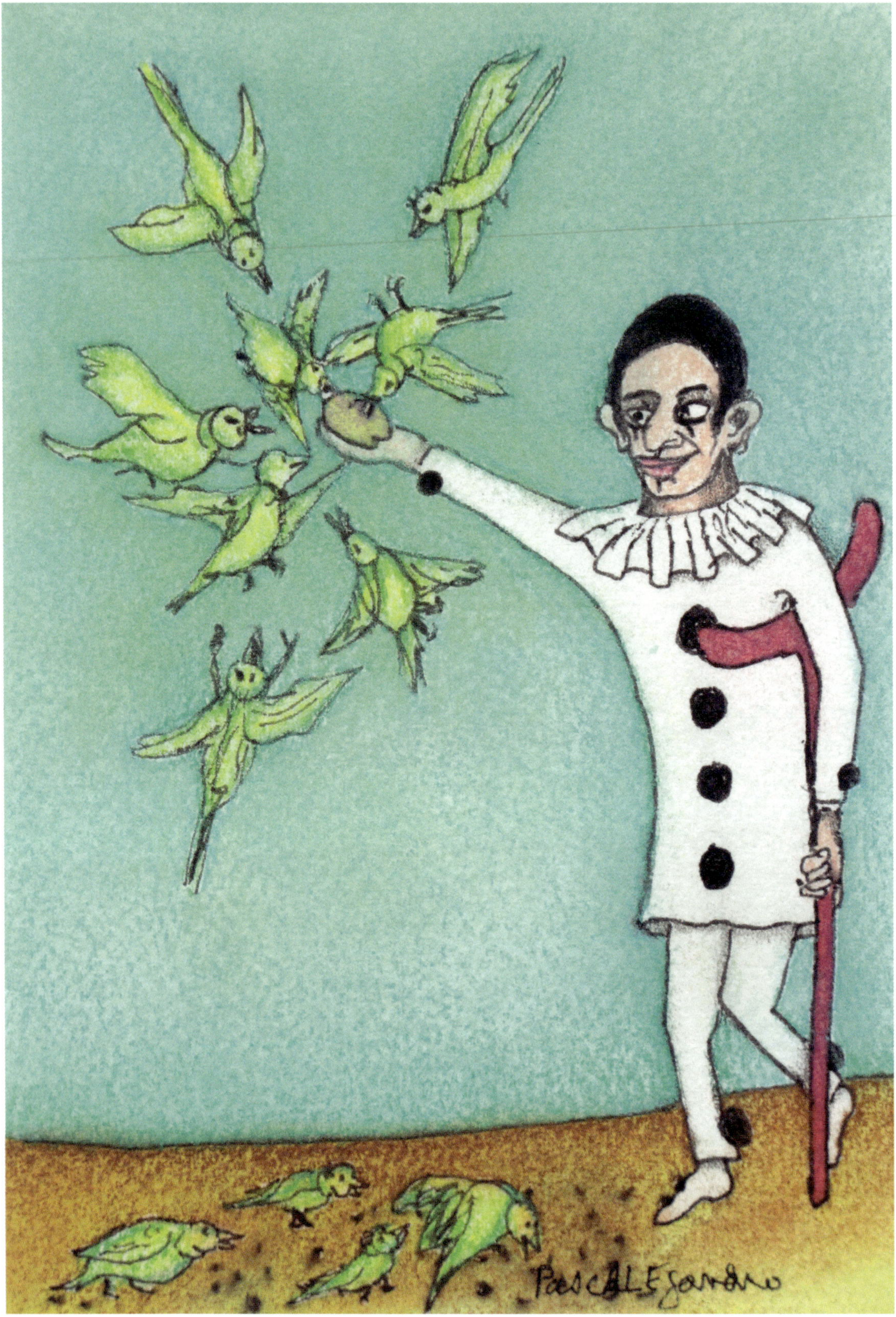

*Broken Leg, Happy Birds*, 2014
15,5 × 10,5 cm

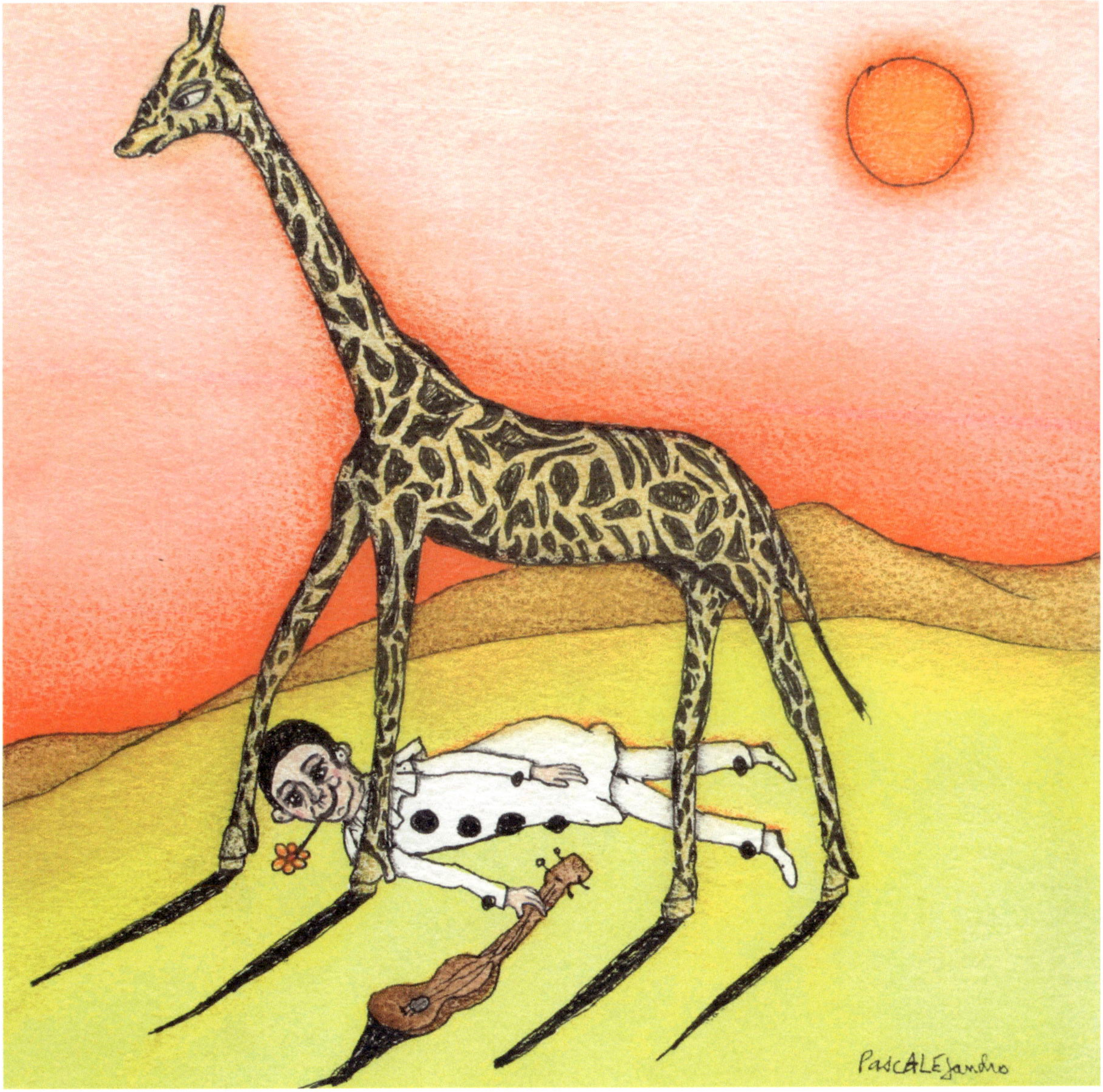


*In the Giraffe's Shadow*, 2014
20 × 20 cm

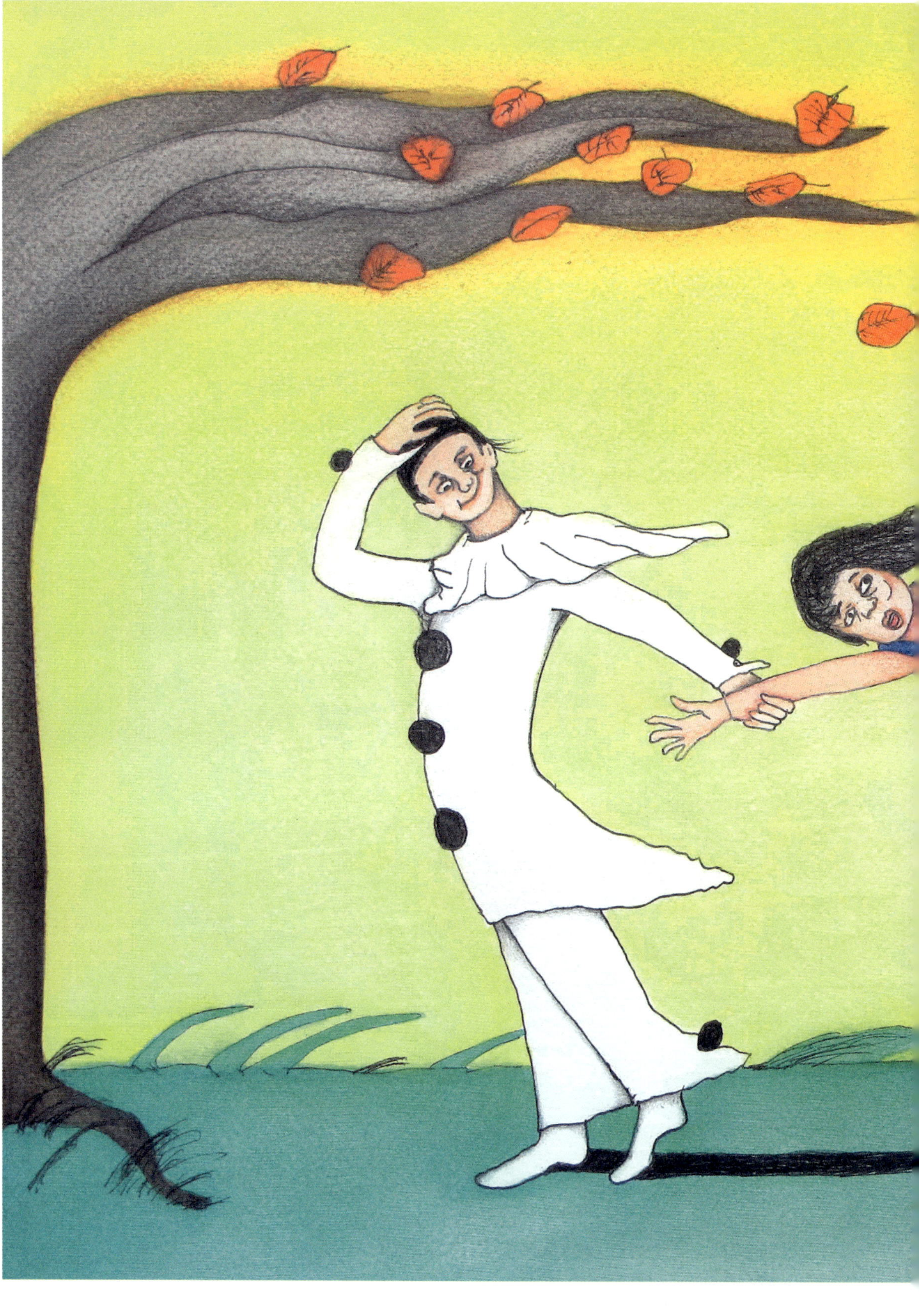

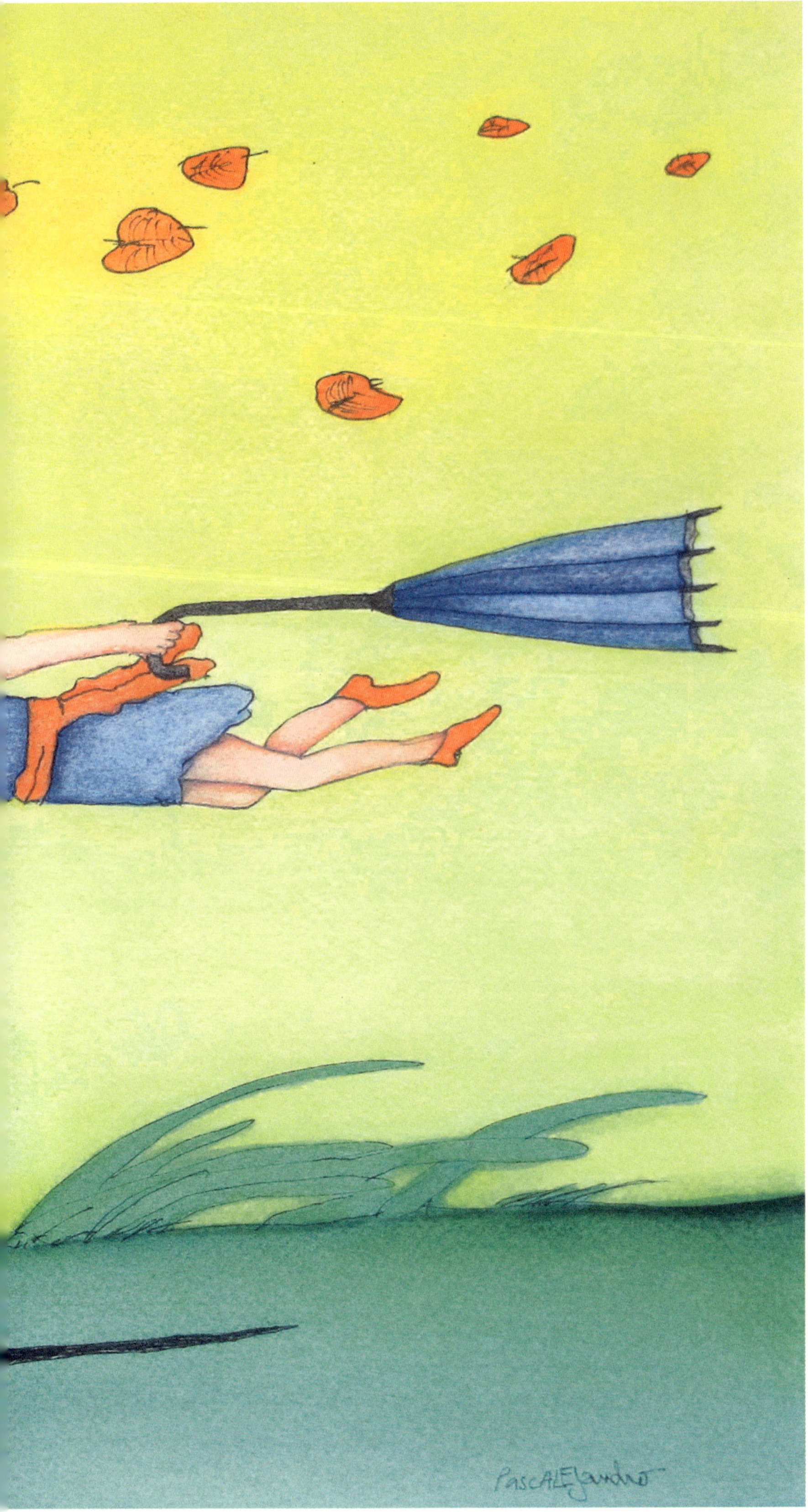


*The Wind of Love*, 2014
31 × 41 cm

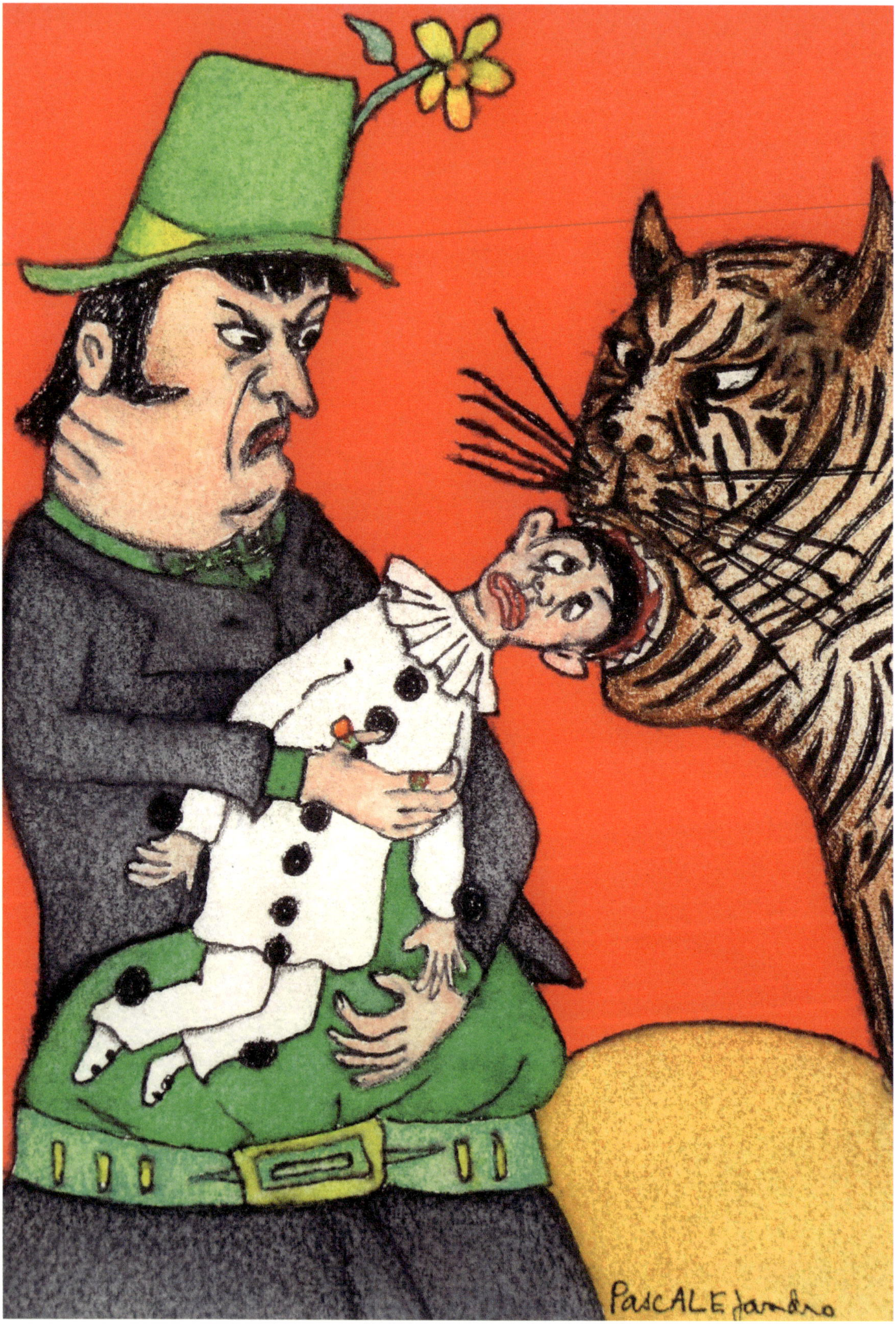


*Raising Little Pierrot*, 2014
15,5 × 10,5 cm

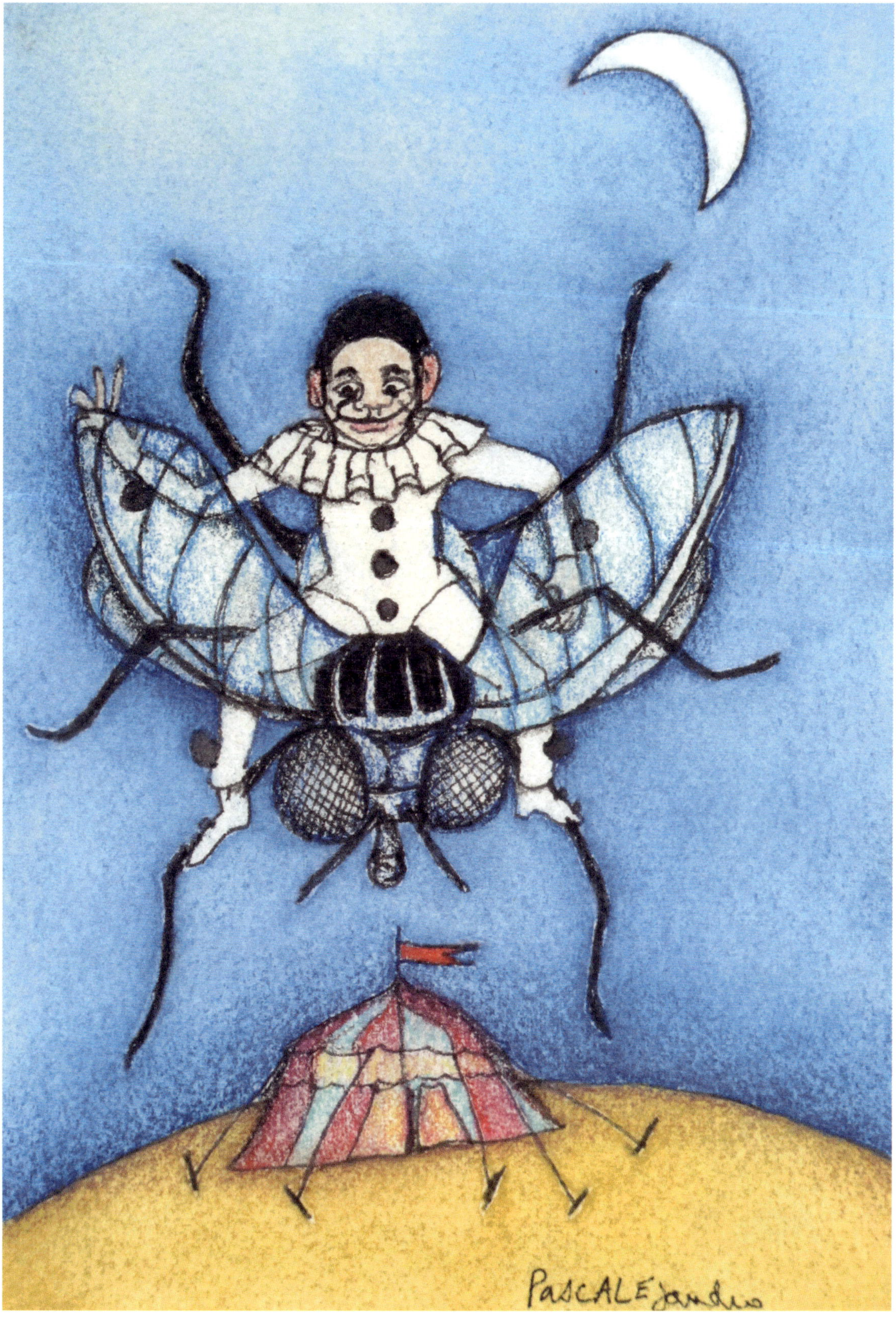


*Pierrot on a Fly*, 2014
15,5 × 10,5 cm

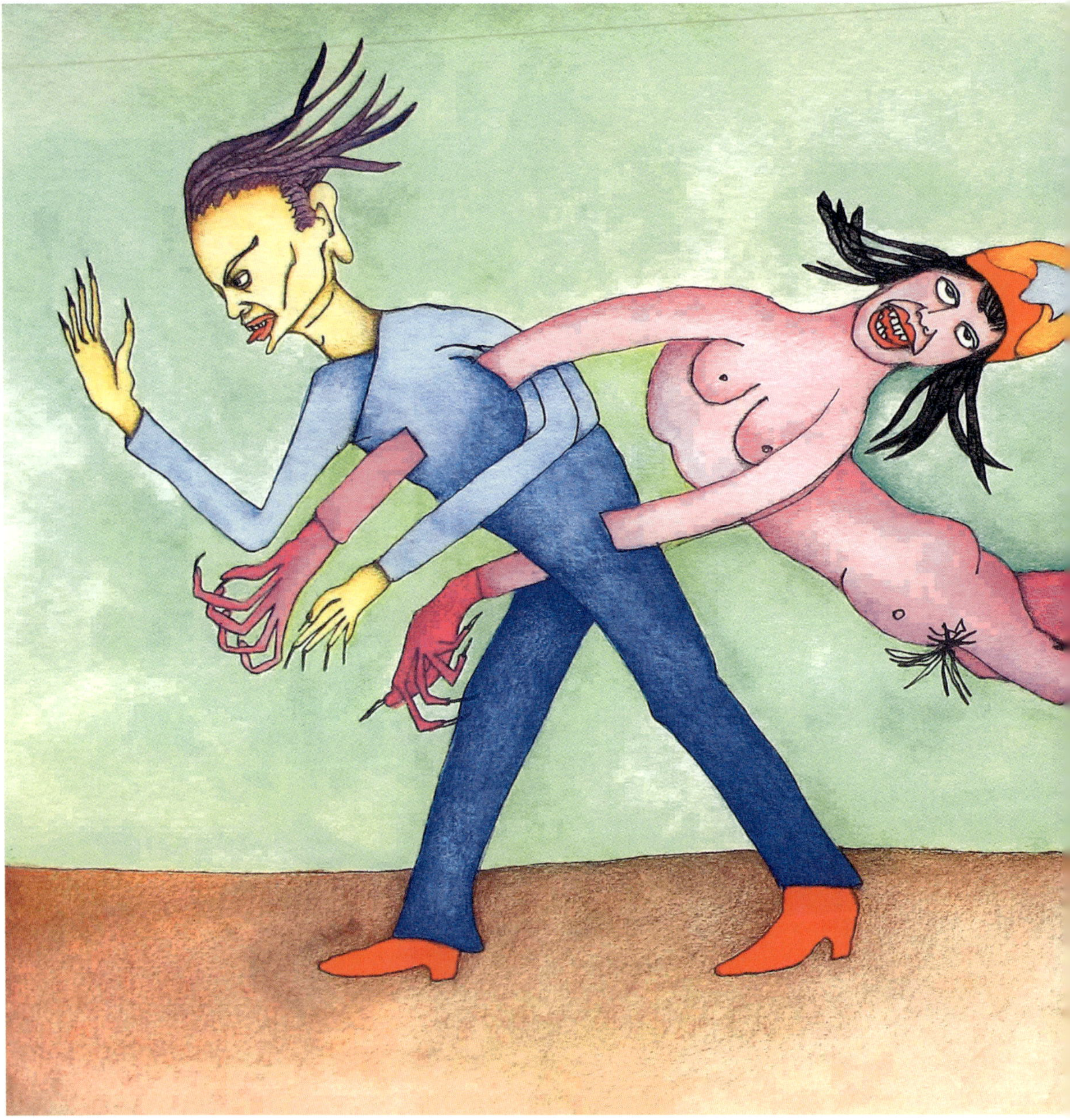

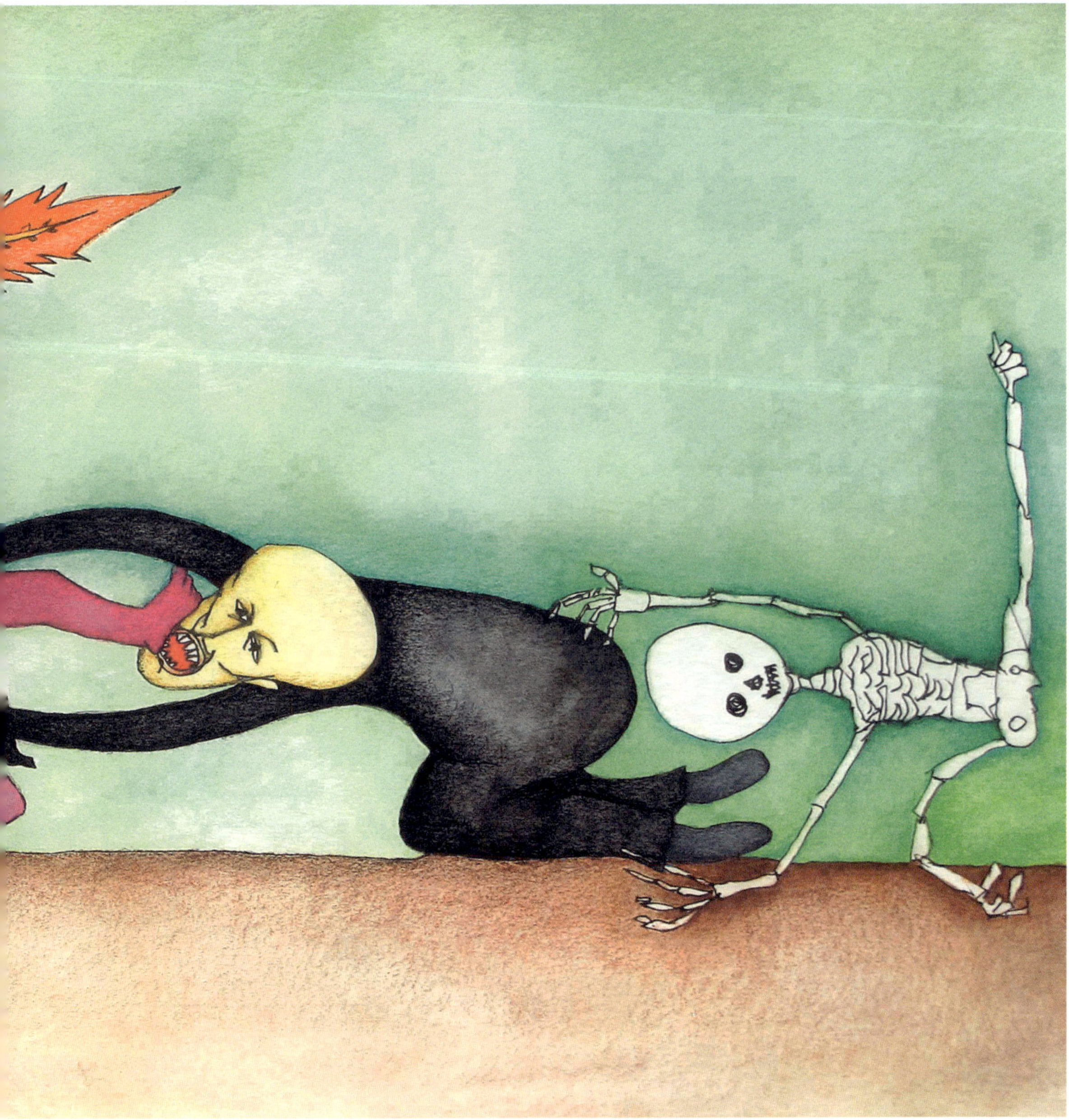

*The Weight of the Past*, 2014
30 × 60 cm

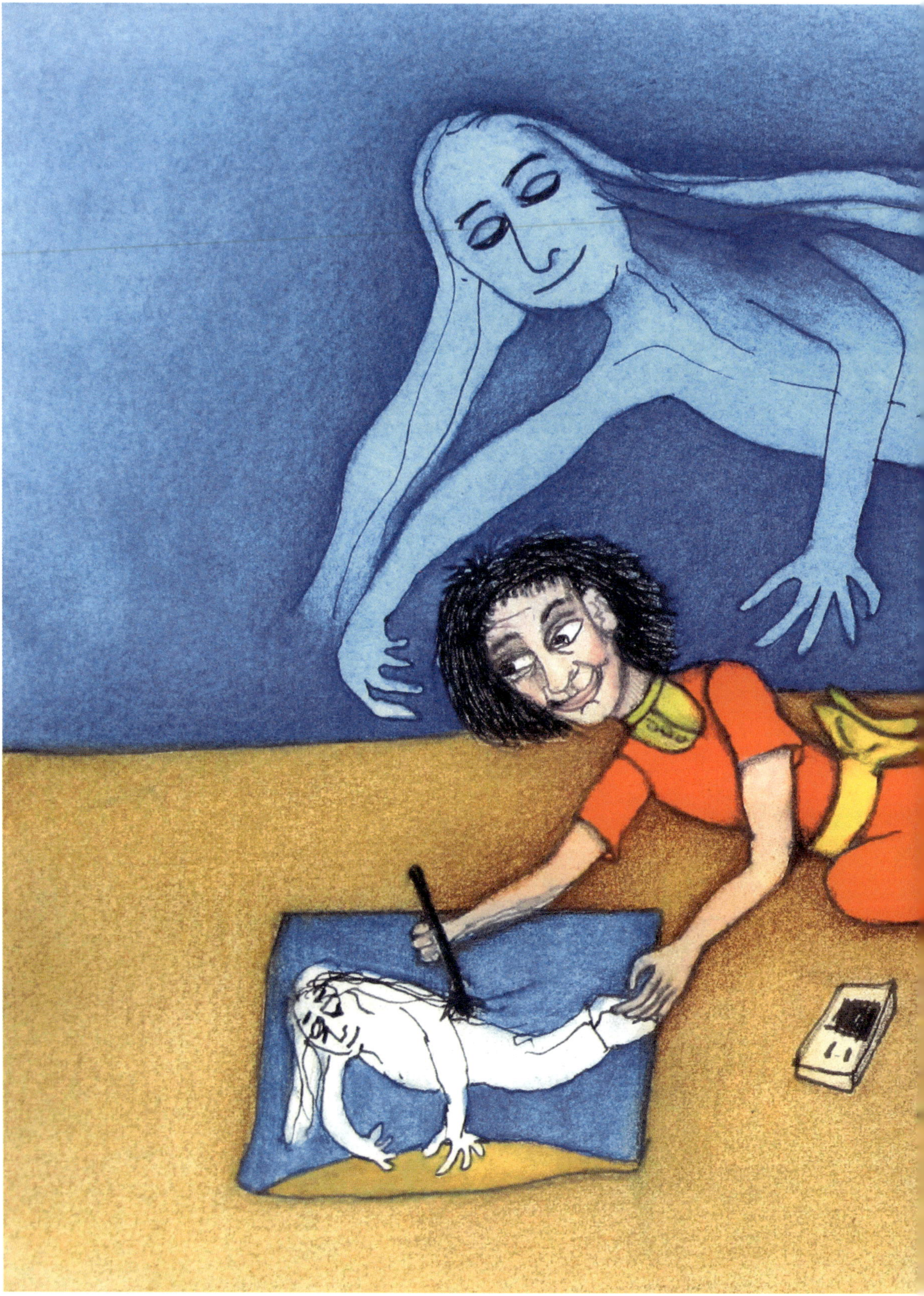

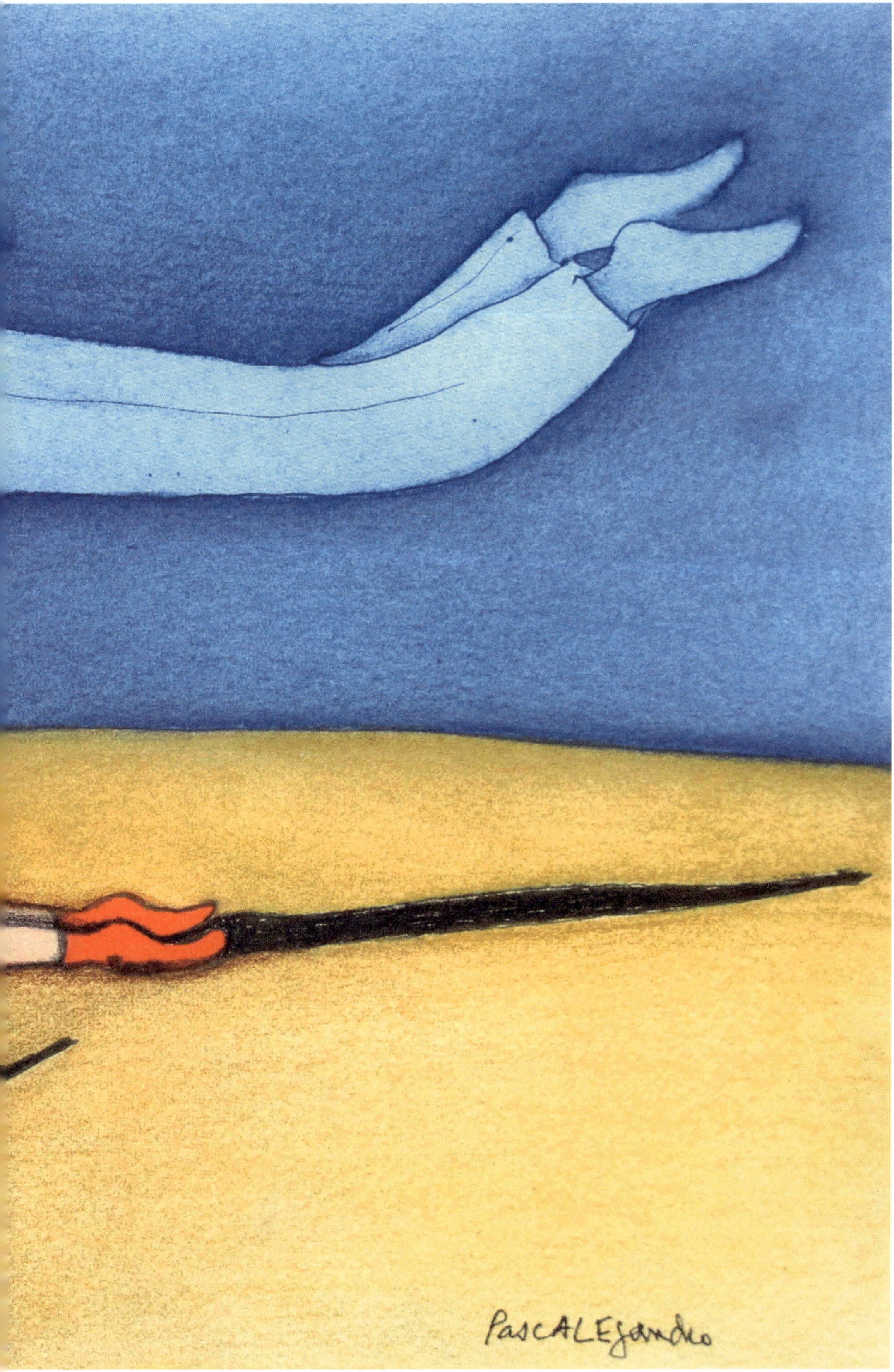


*Drawing and Presence*, 2014
18 × 26 cm

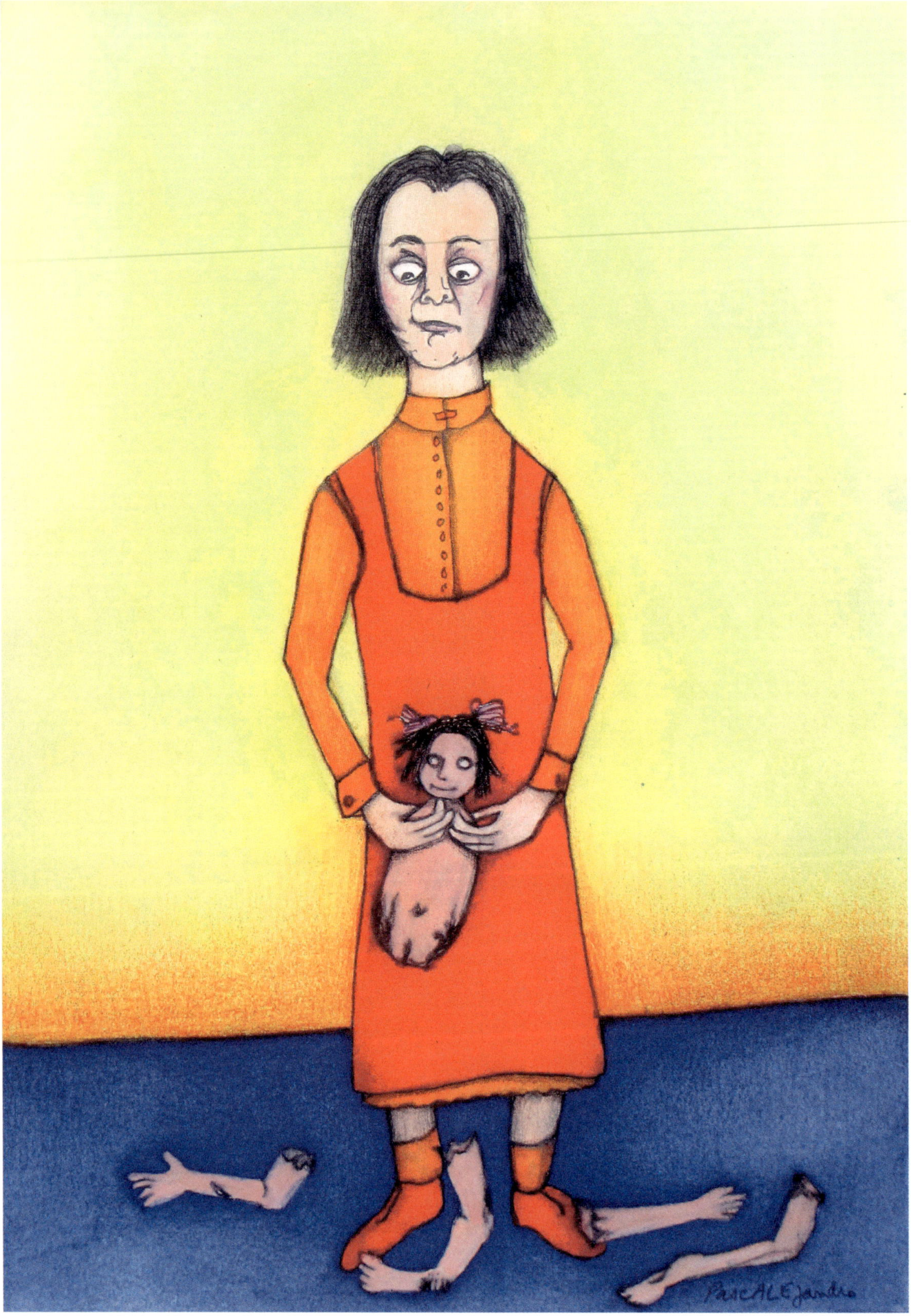


*My Dear Doll*, 2014
26 × 18 cm

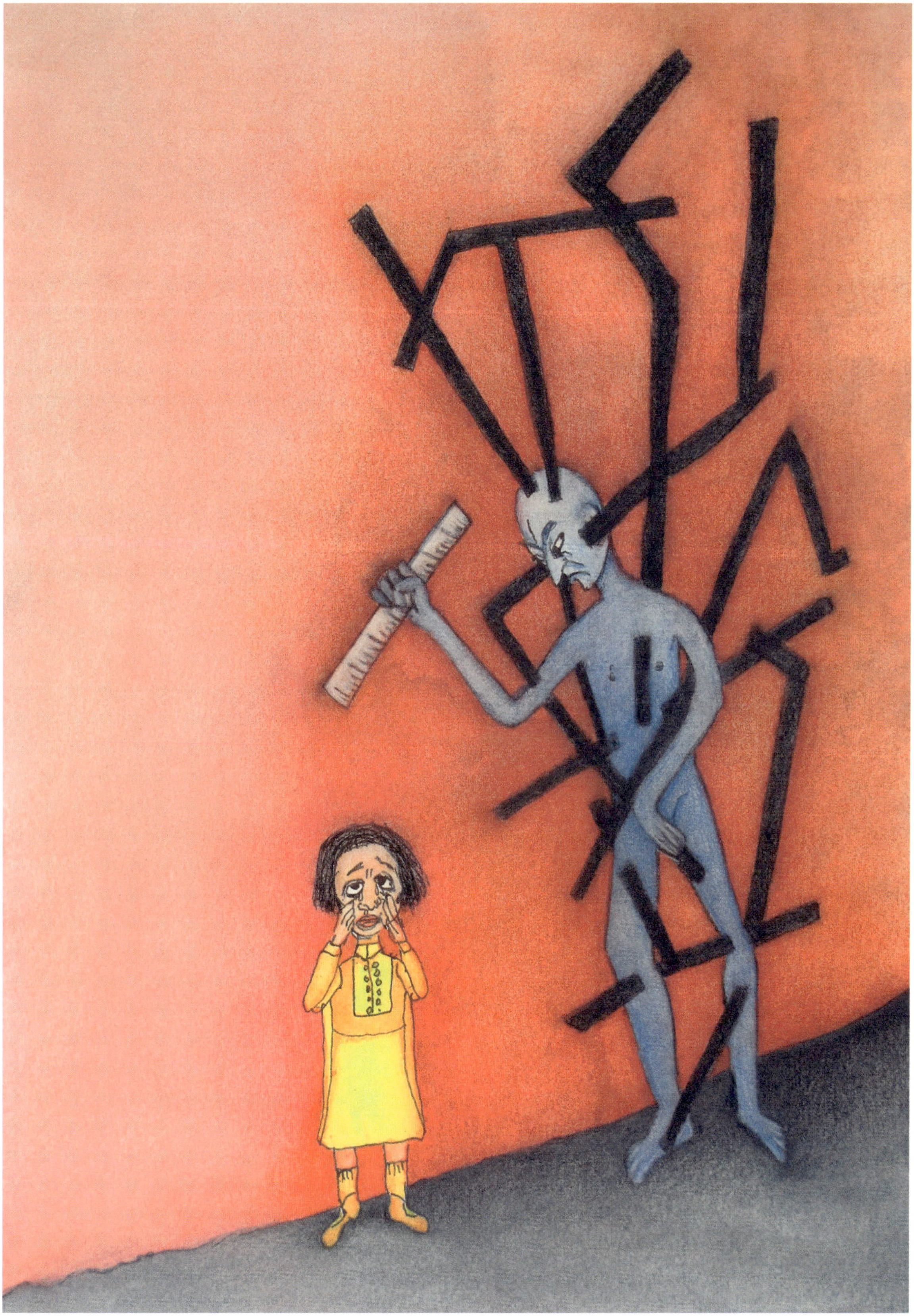

*The Mathematics Lesson*, 2014
26 × 18 cm

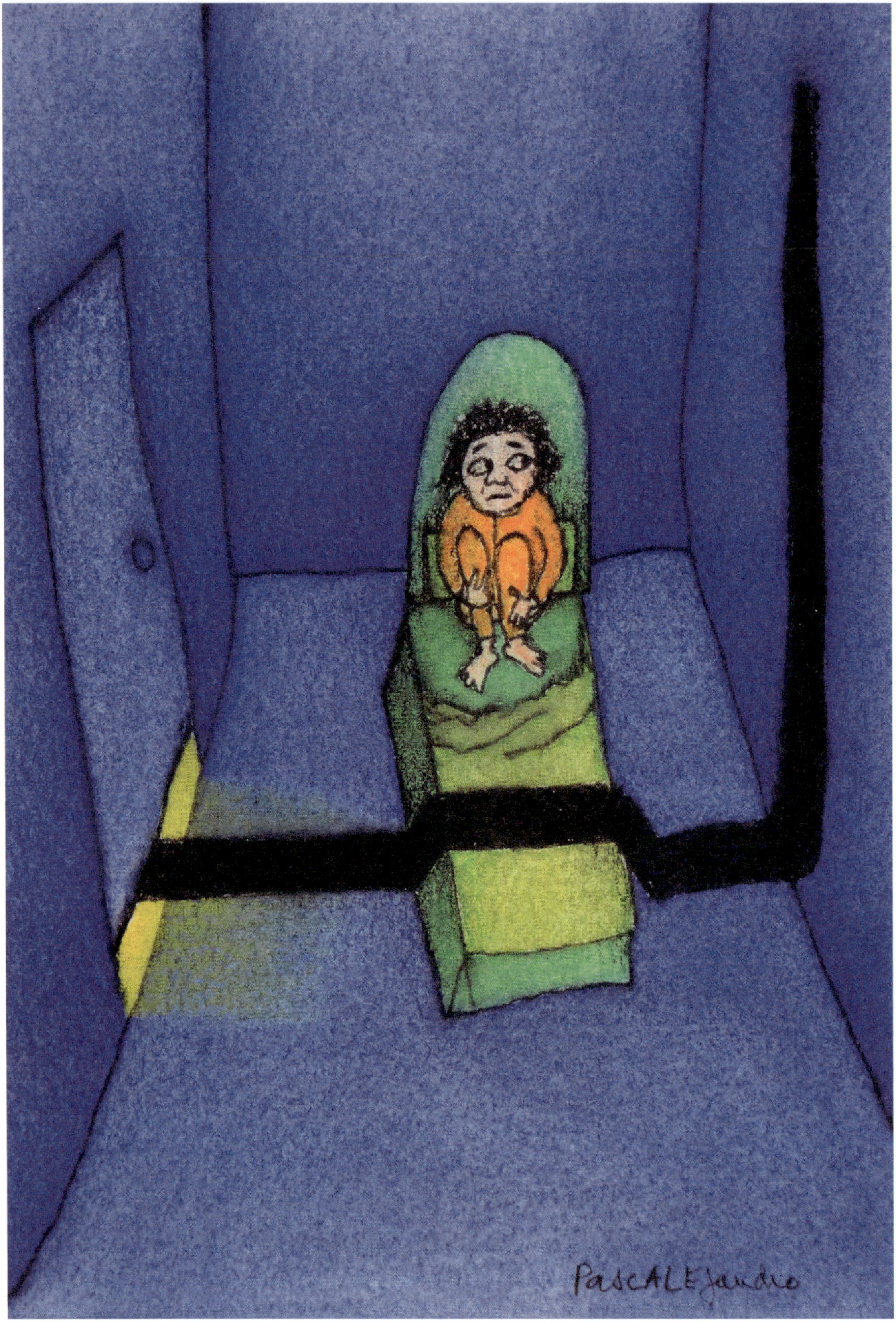


*Visiting Shadow*, 2014
15,5 × 10,5 cm

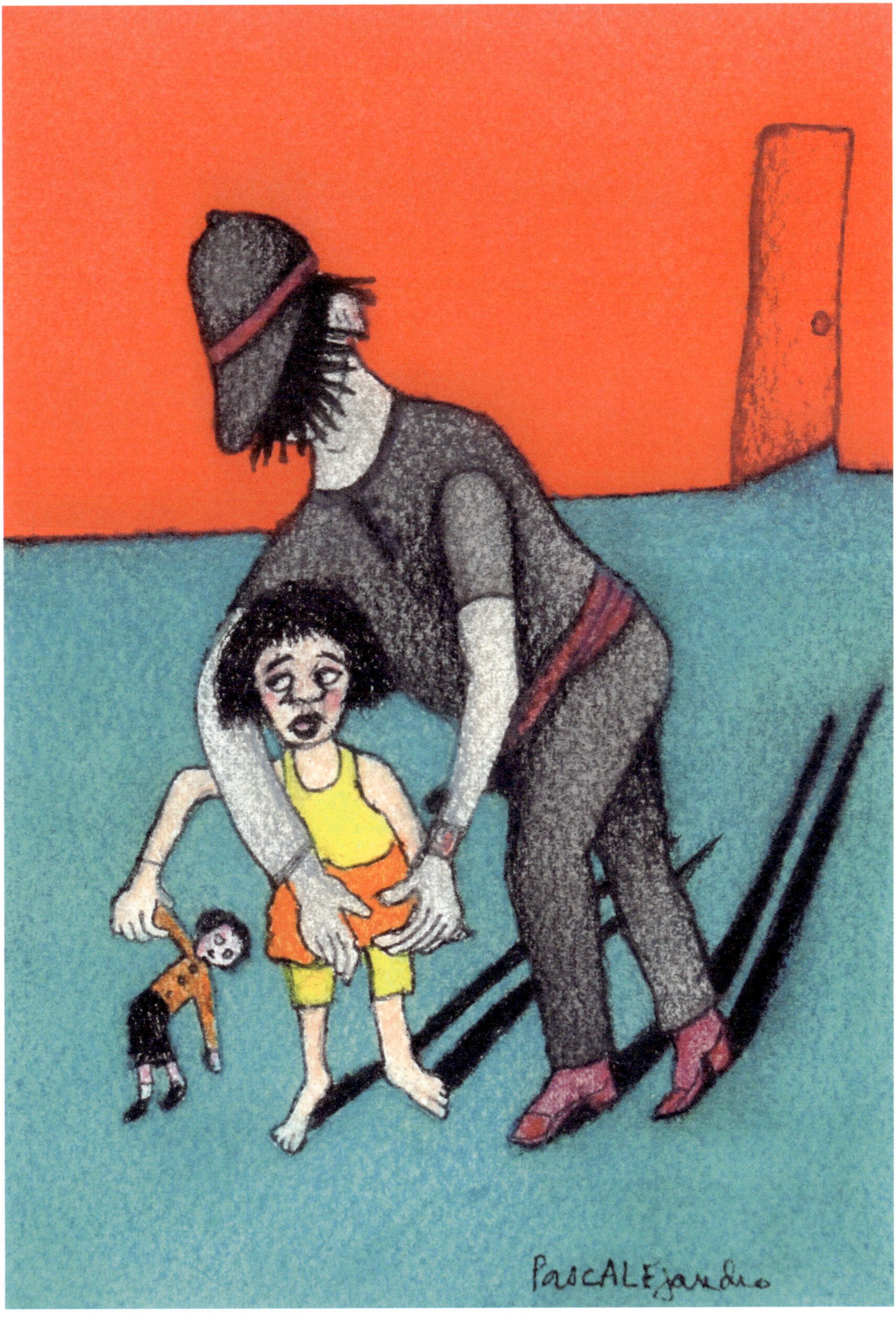


*Abuse*, 2014
15,5 × 10,5 cm

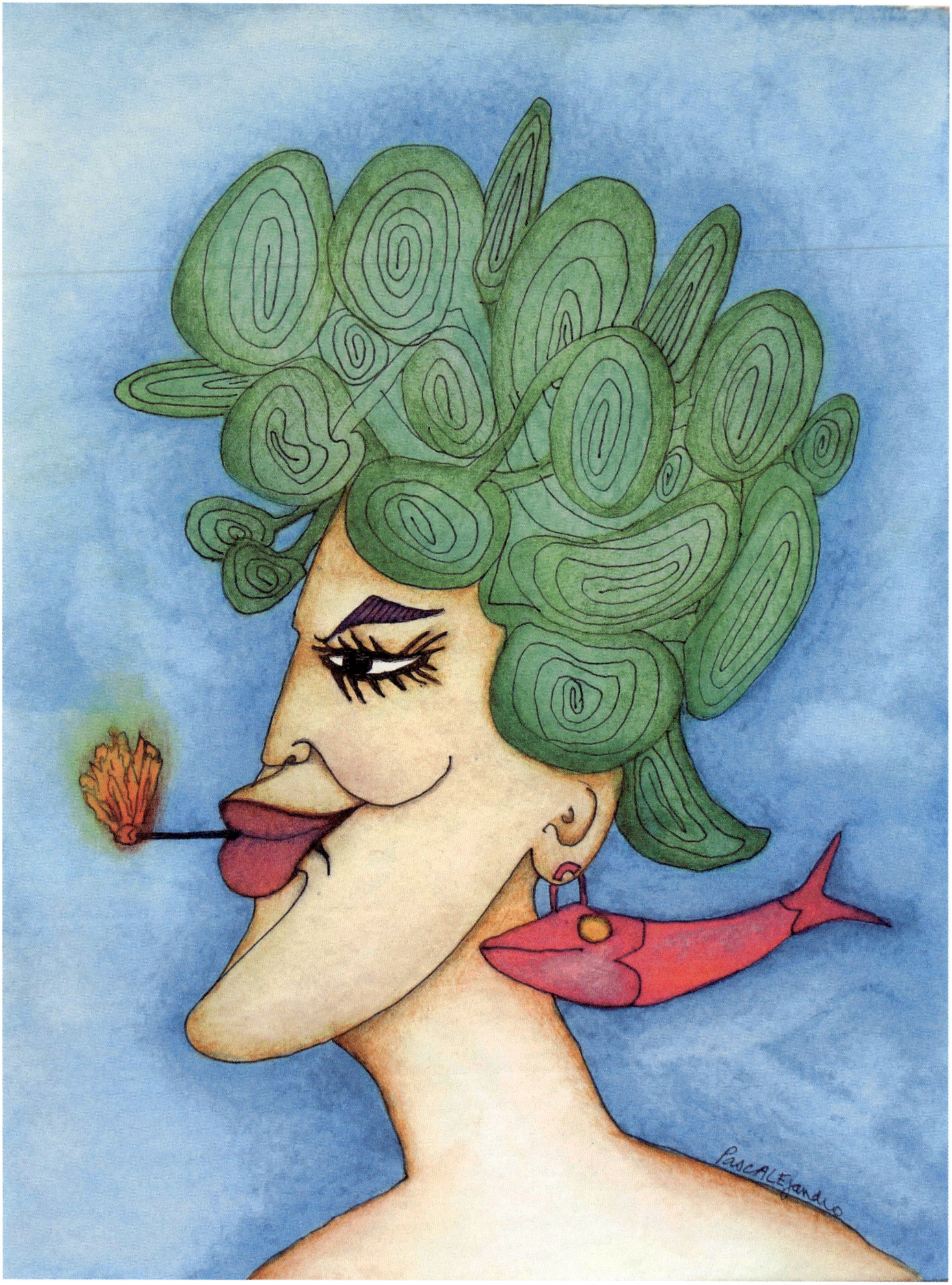


*A Diva*, 2014
32 × 24 cm

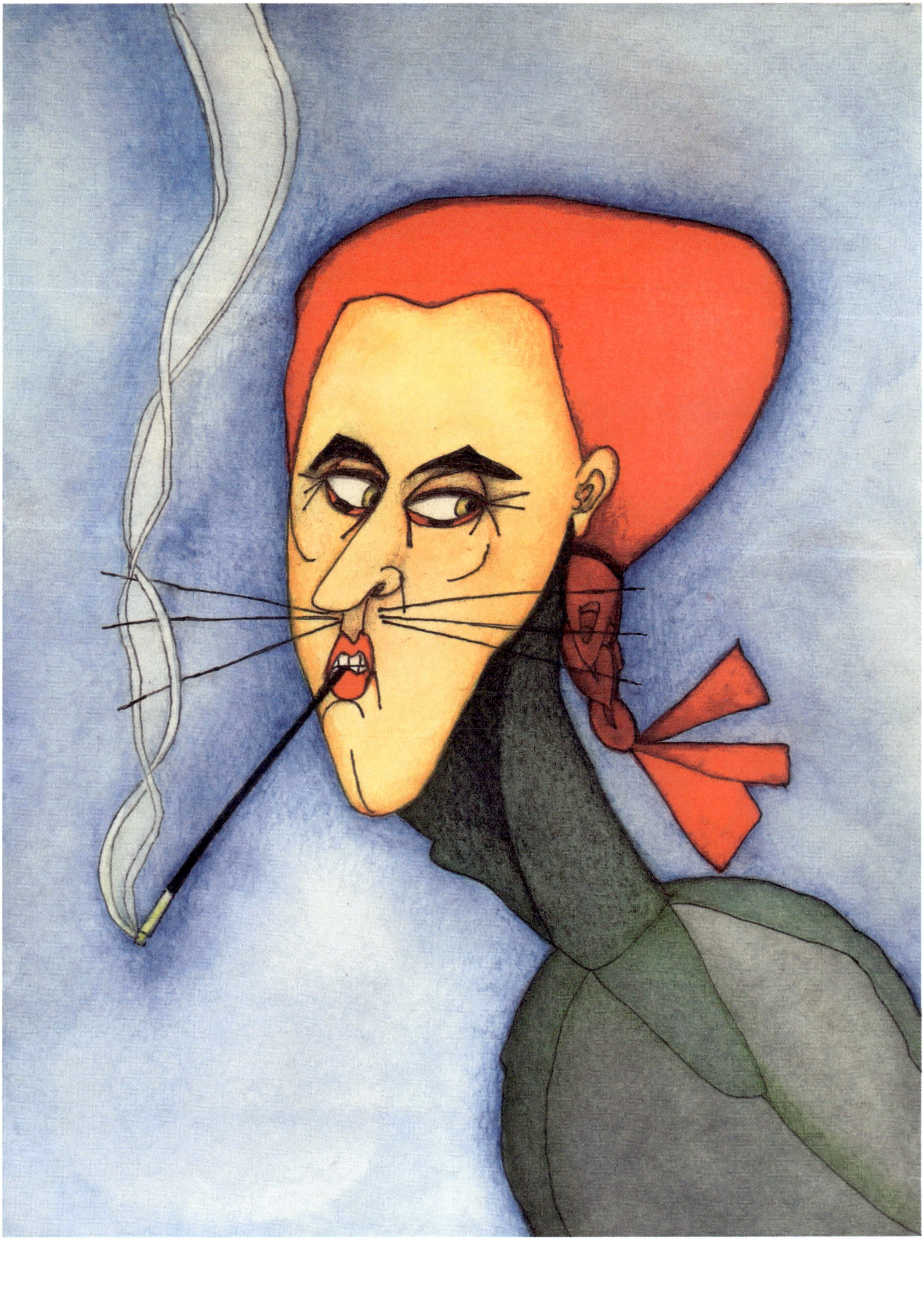

*The Duke of Marmalade*, 2014
32 × 24 cm

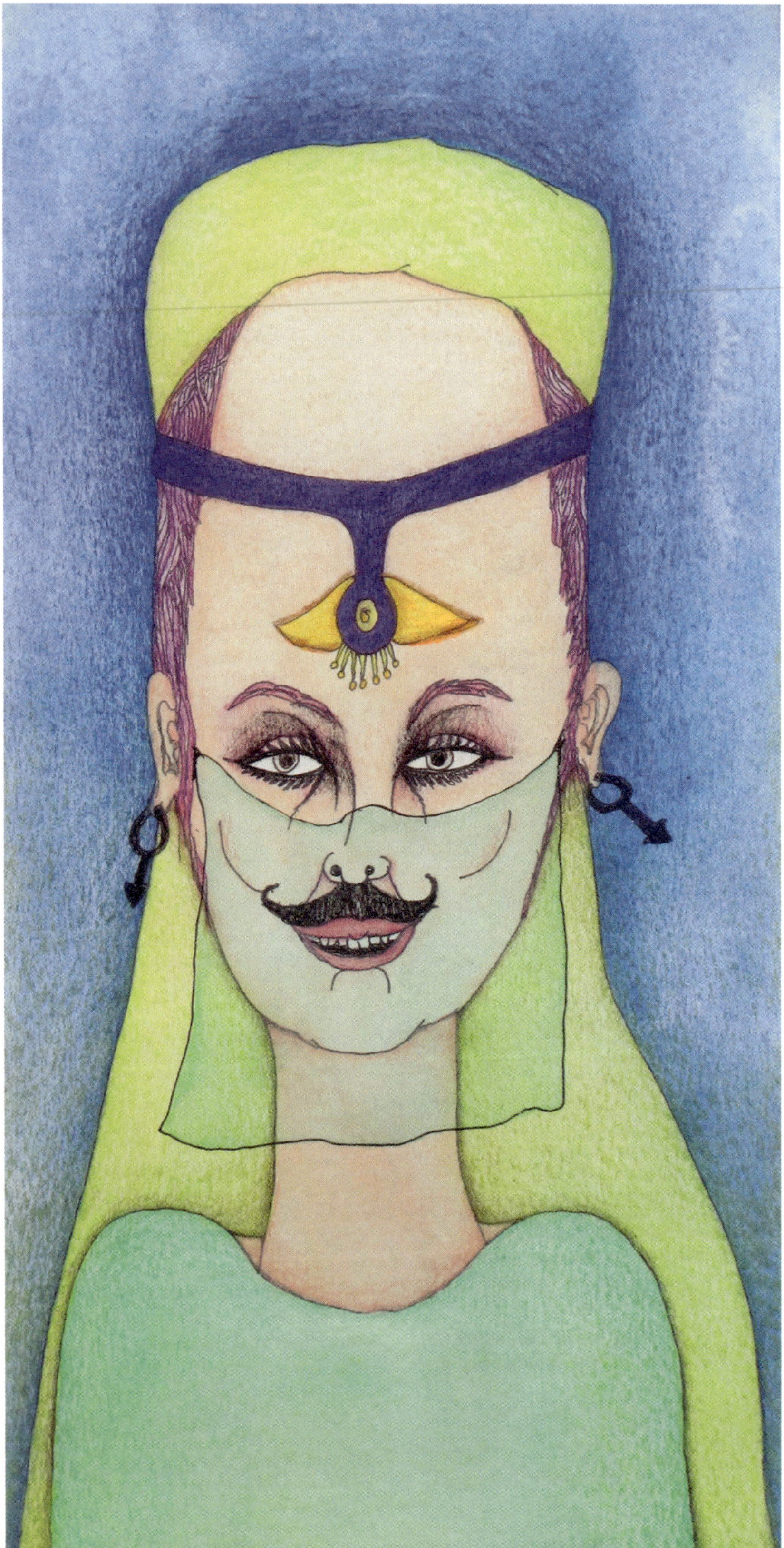


*Mustachioed Fiancée*, 2014
40 × 20 cm

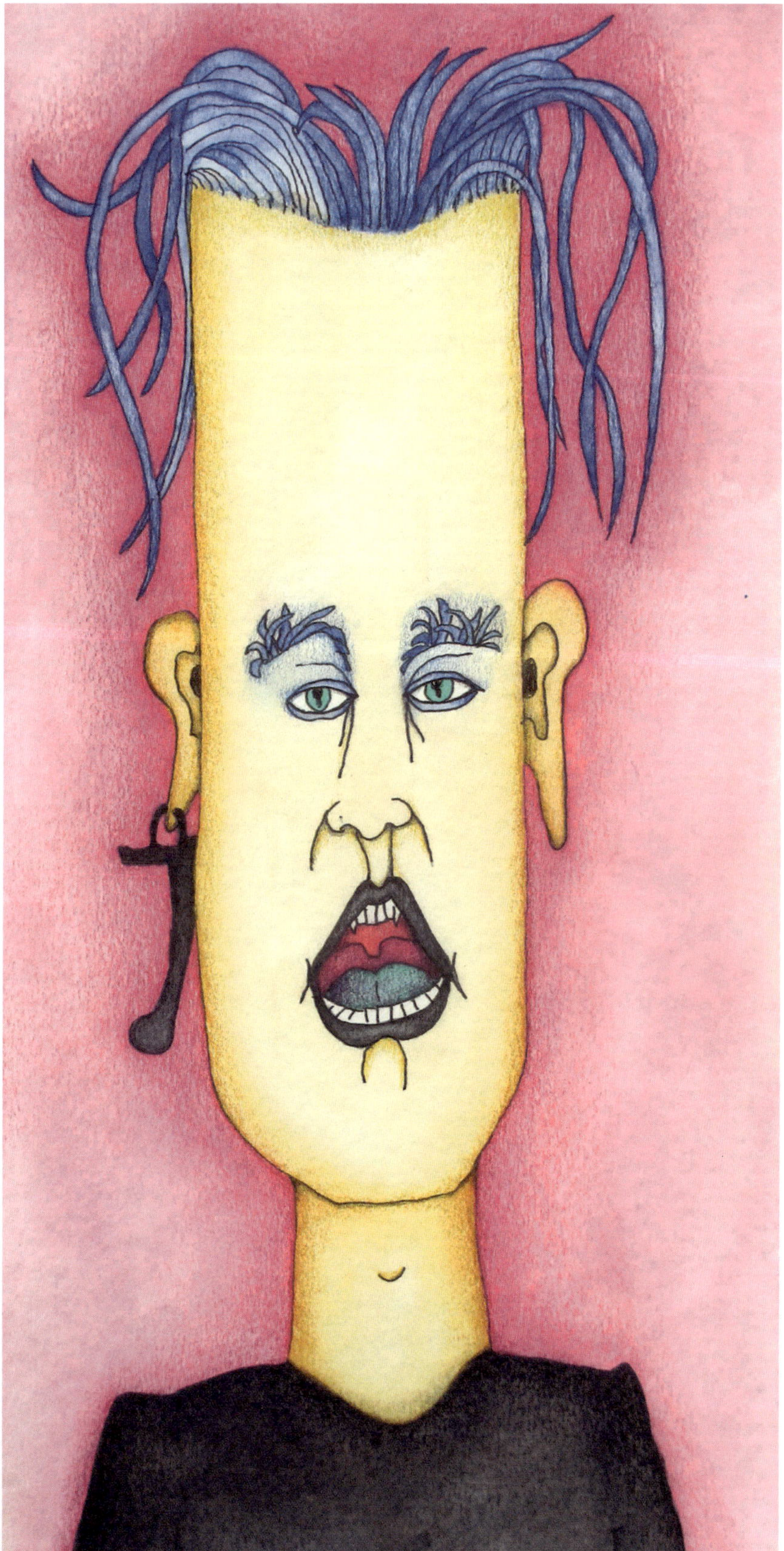

*Banana Boy*, 2014
40 × 20 cm

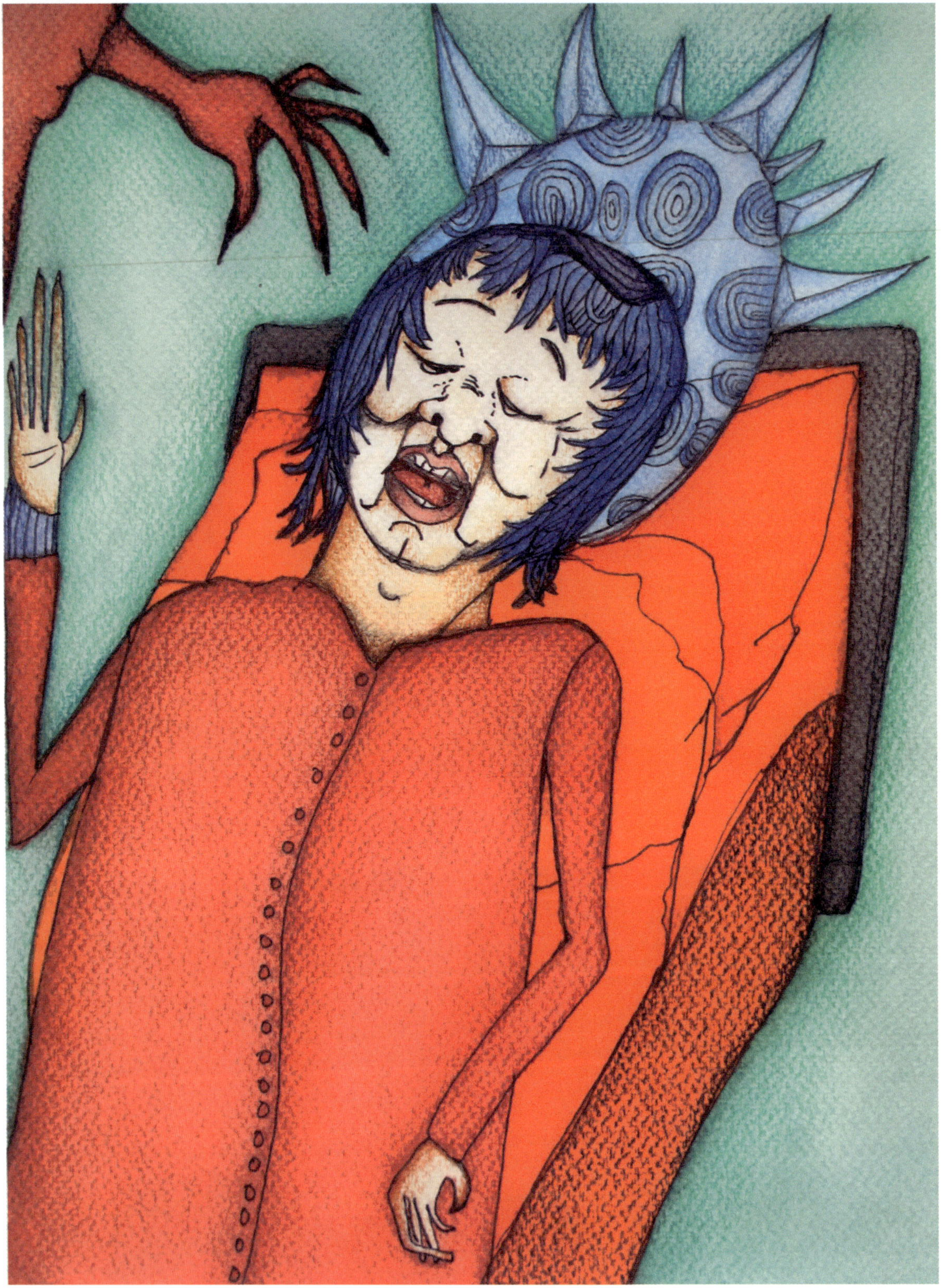

*Agony*, 2014
29 × 21 cm

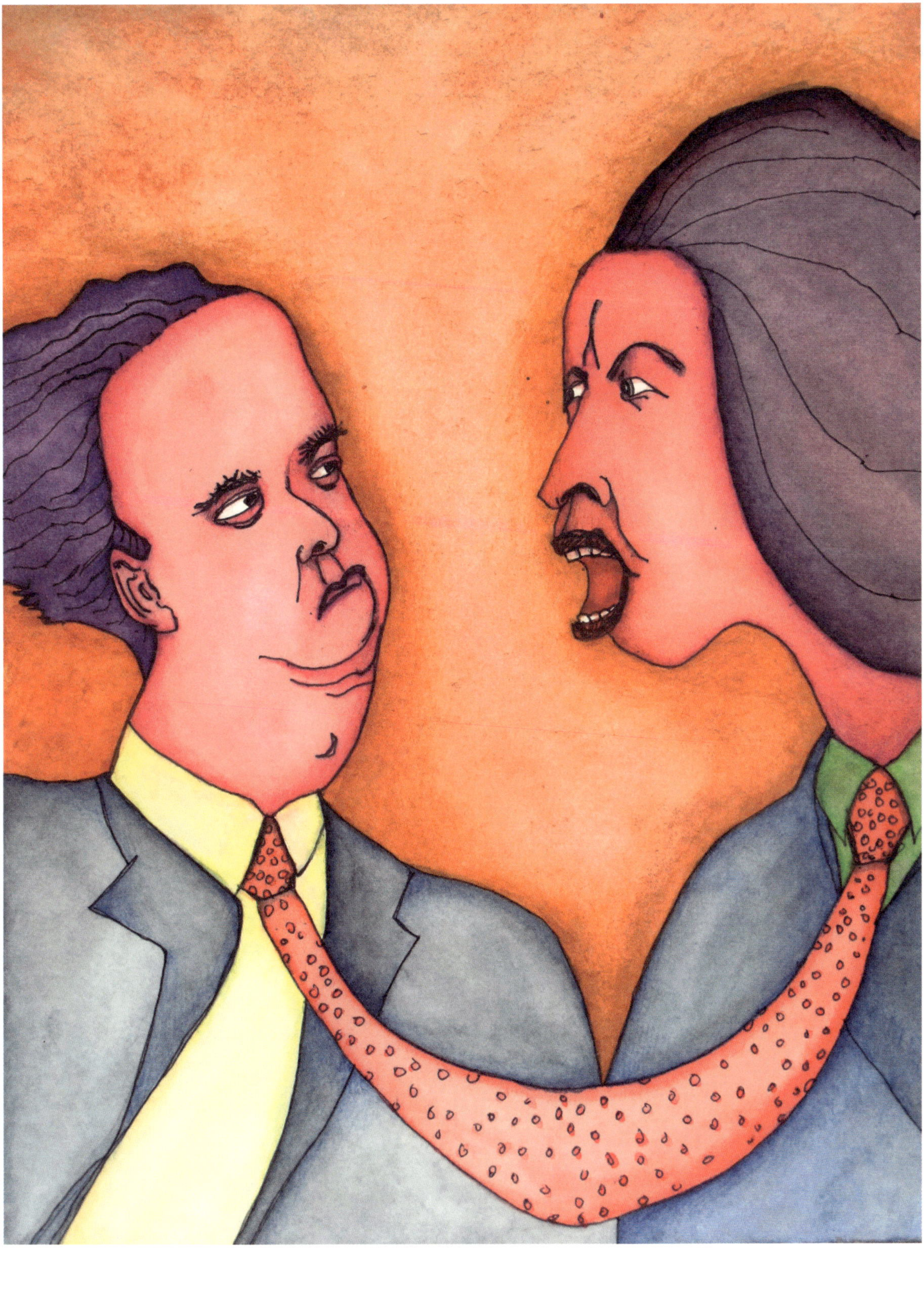

*Joined at the Tie*, 2014
32 × 24 cm

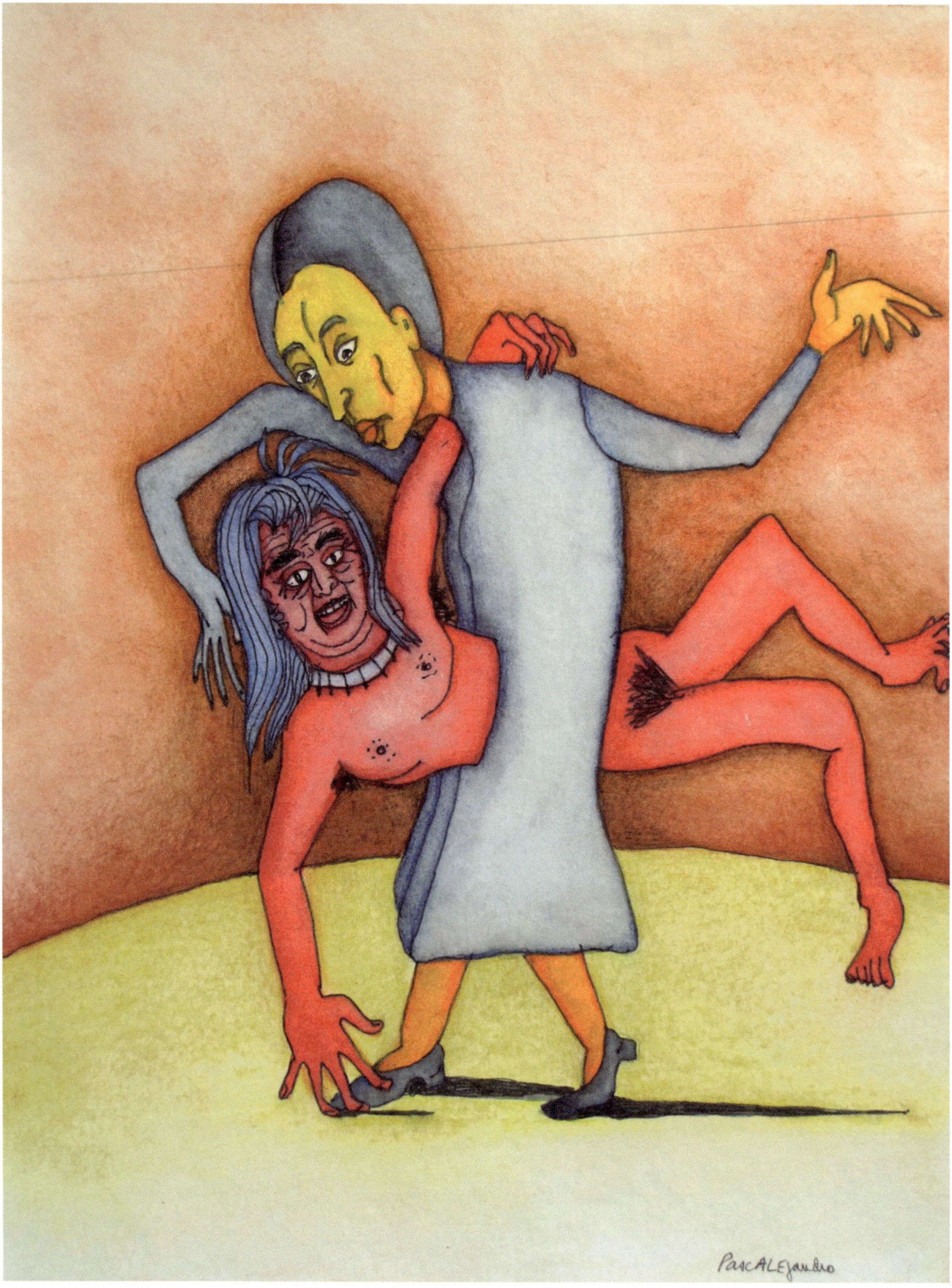


*My Poor Youth*, 2014
32 × 24 cm

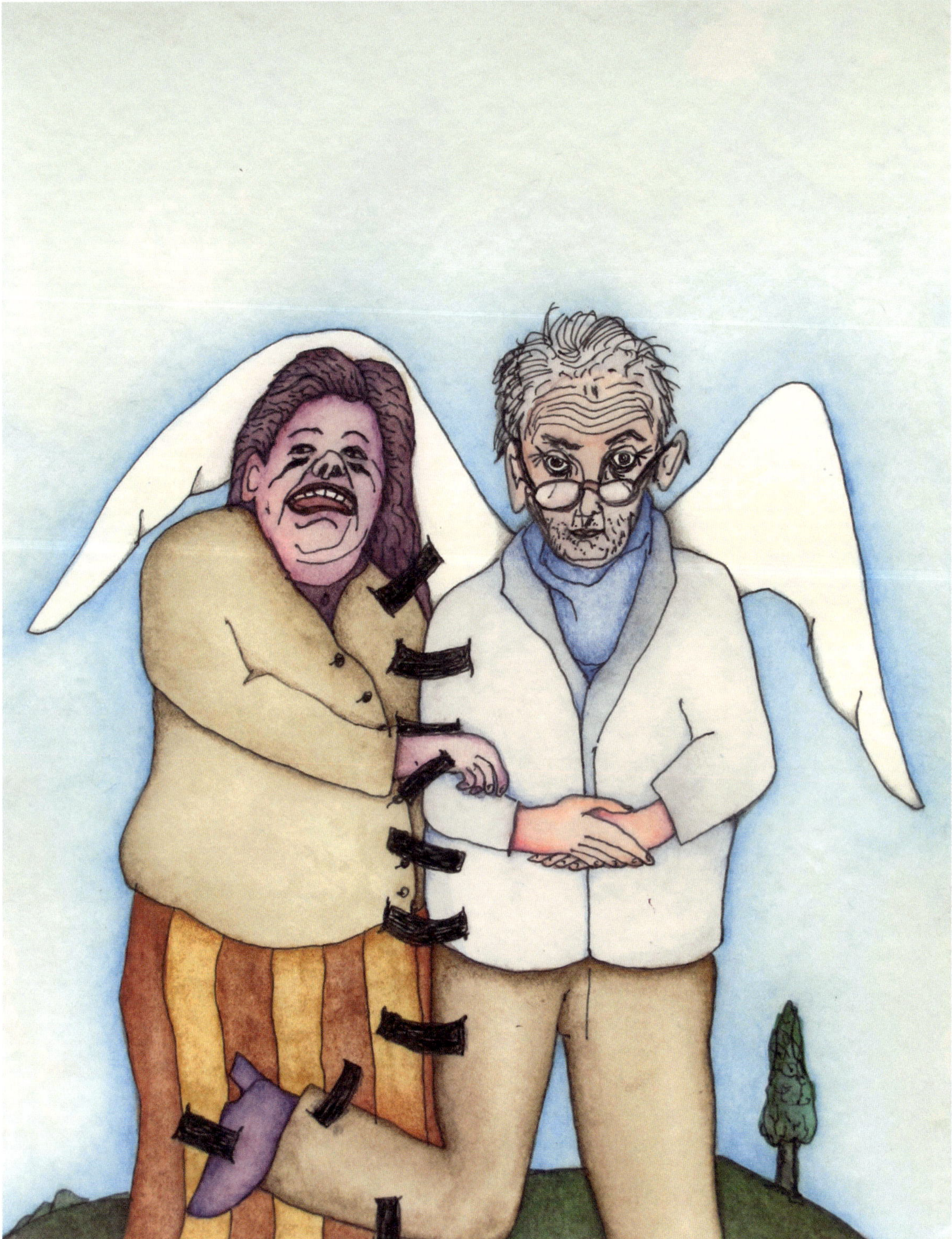

*The Widow*, 2014
32 × 24 cm

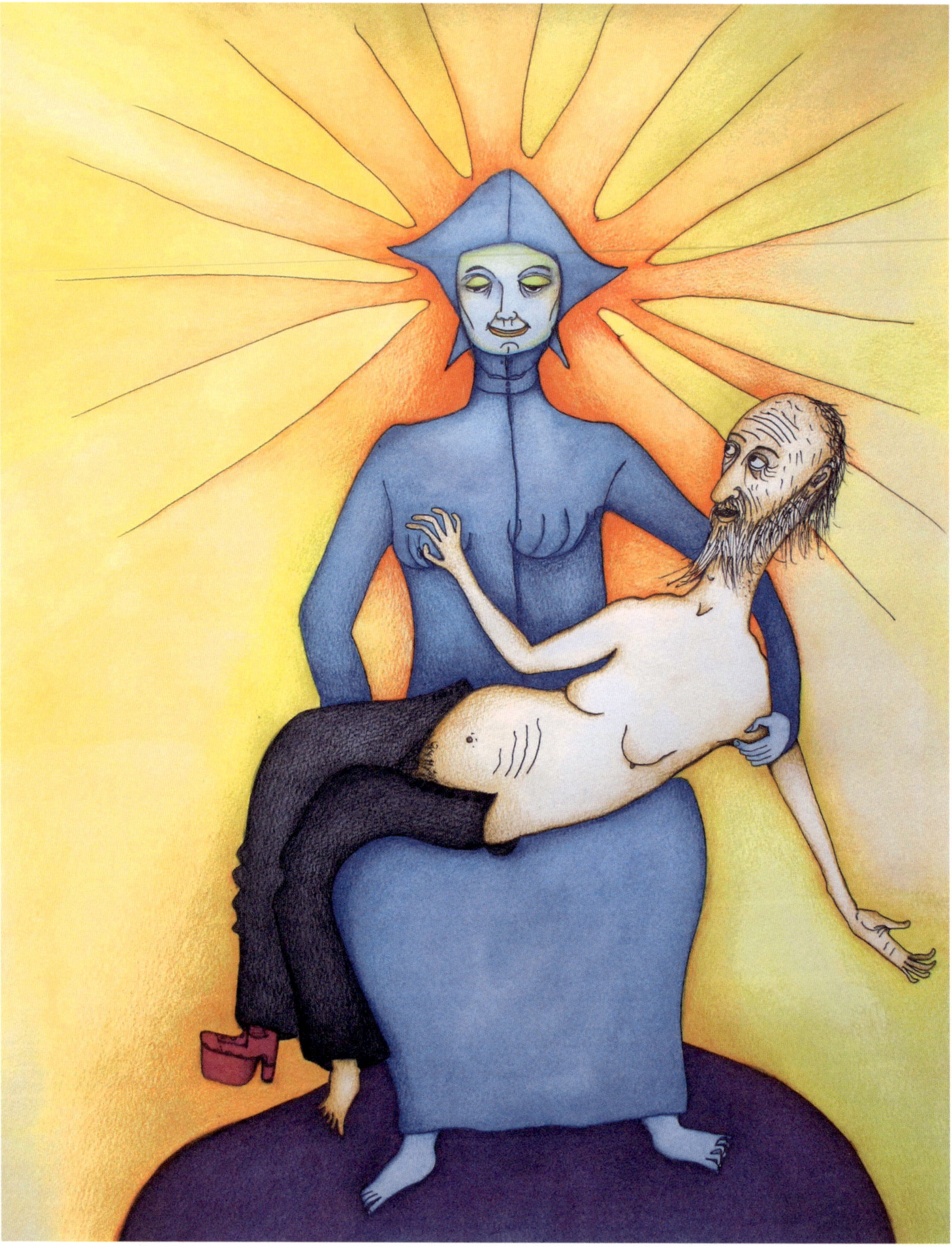

*The Grandfather's Virgin*, 2014
65 × 50 cm

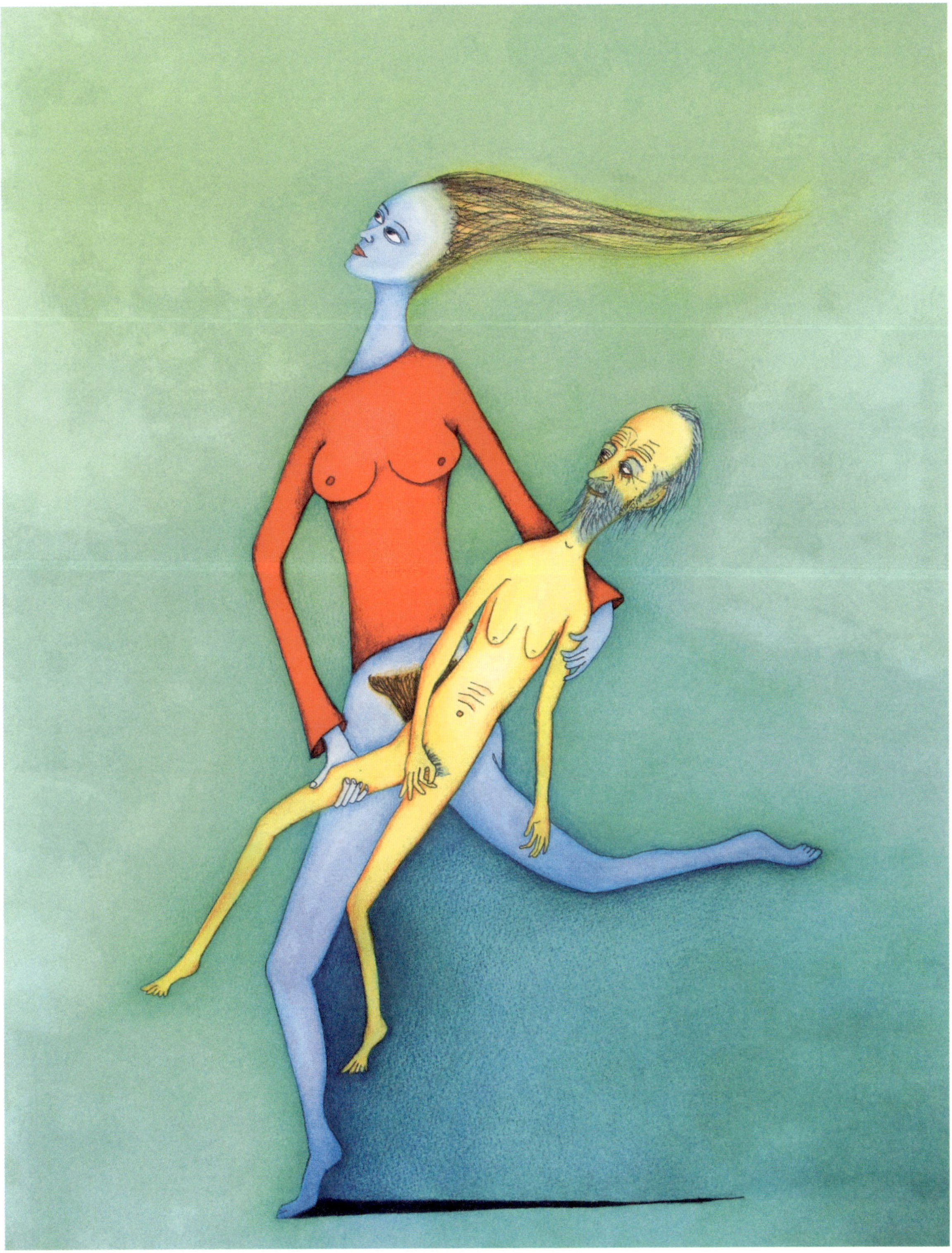

*Happy End*, 2014
65 × 50 cm

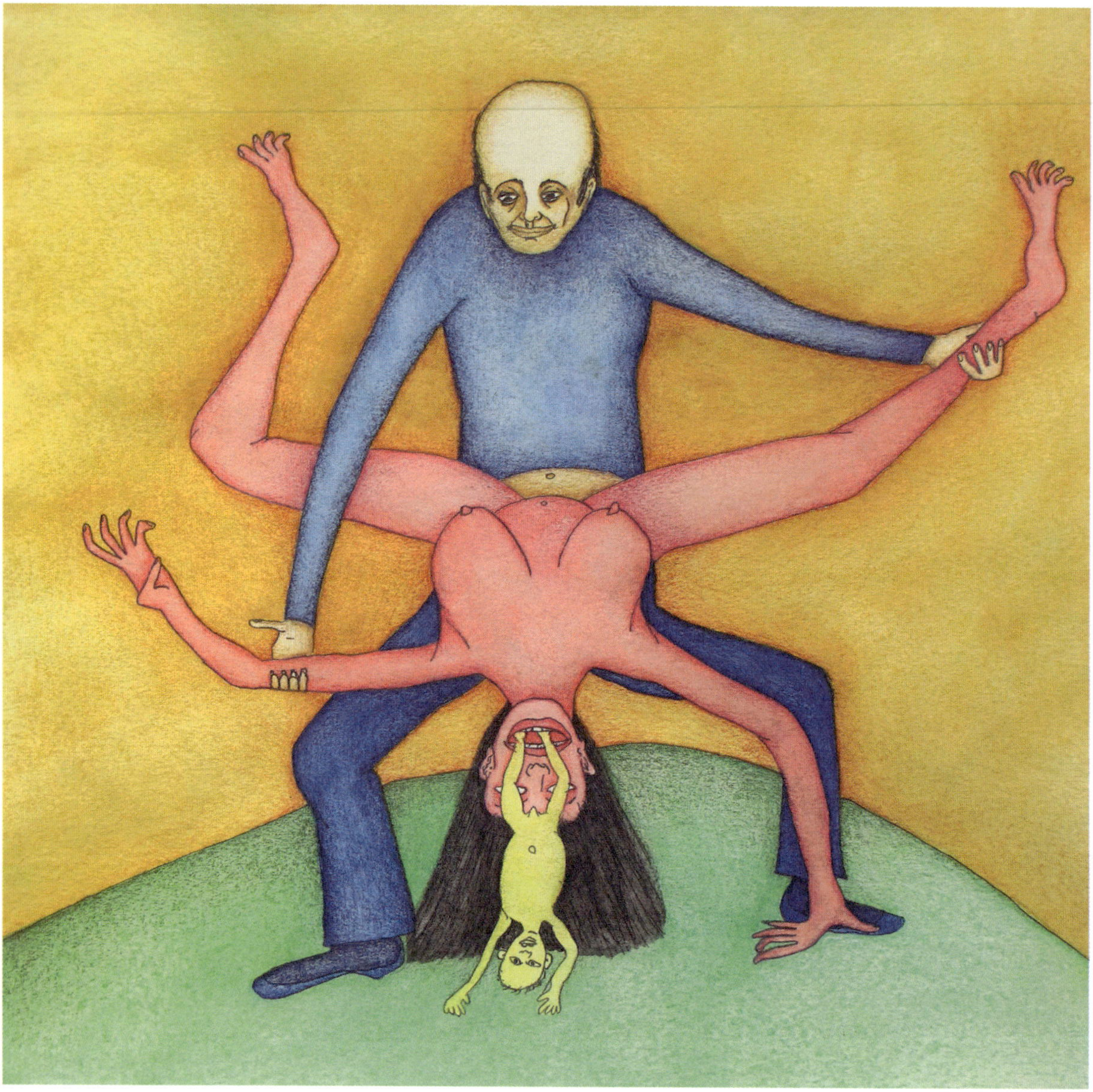

*The Birth of the Word*, 2014
32 × 24 cm

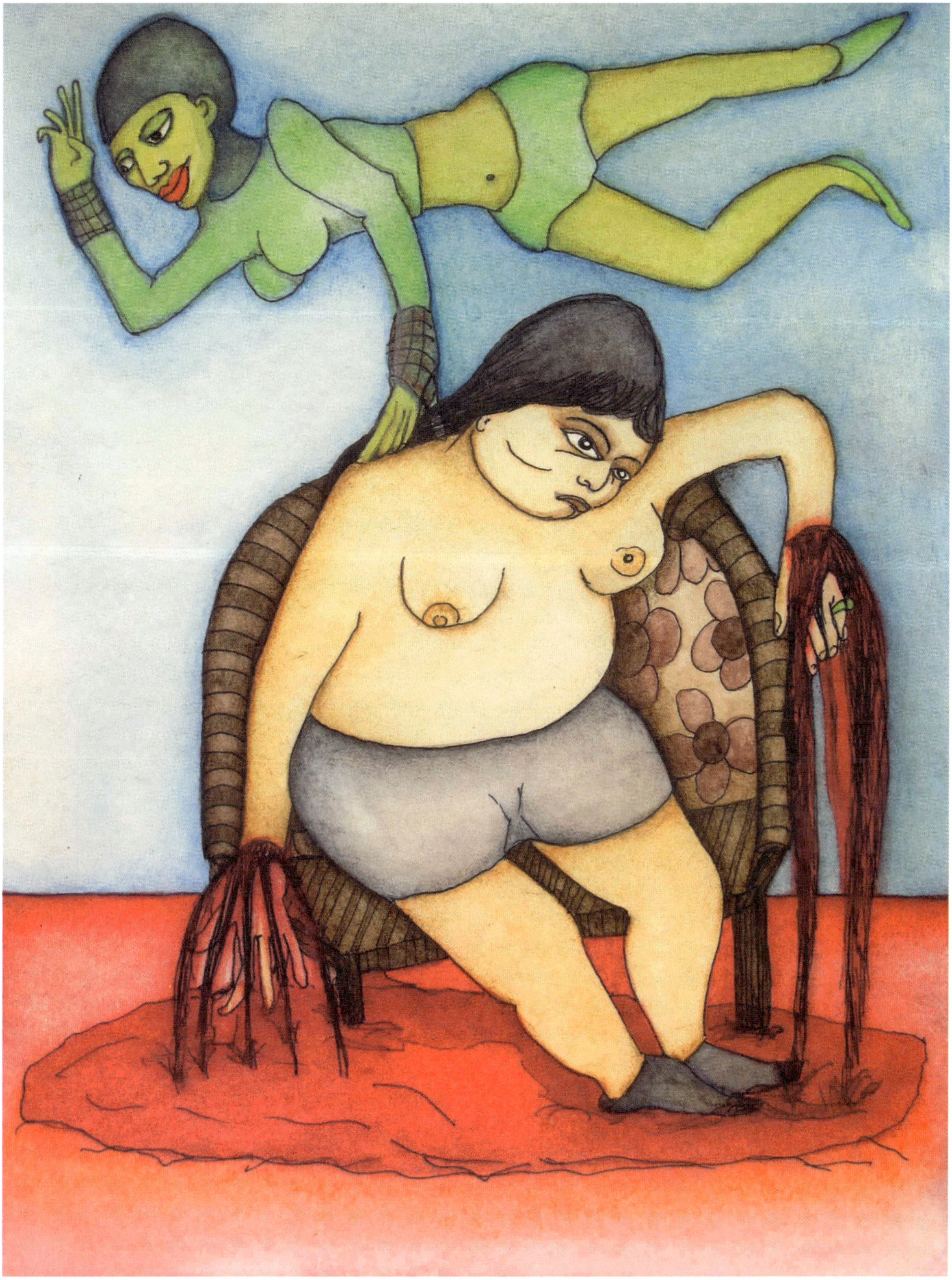

*Circus Suicide*, 2014
40 × 40 cm

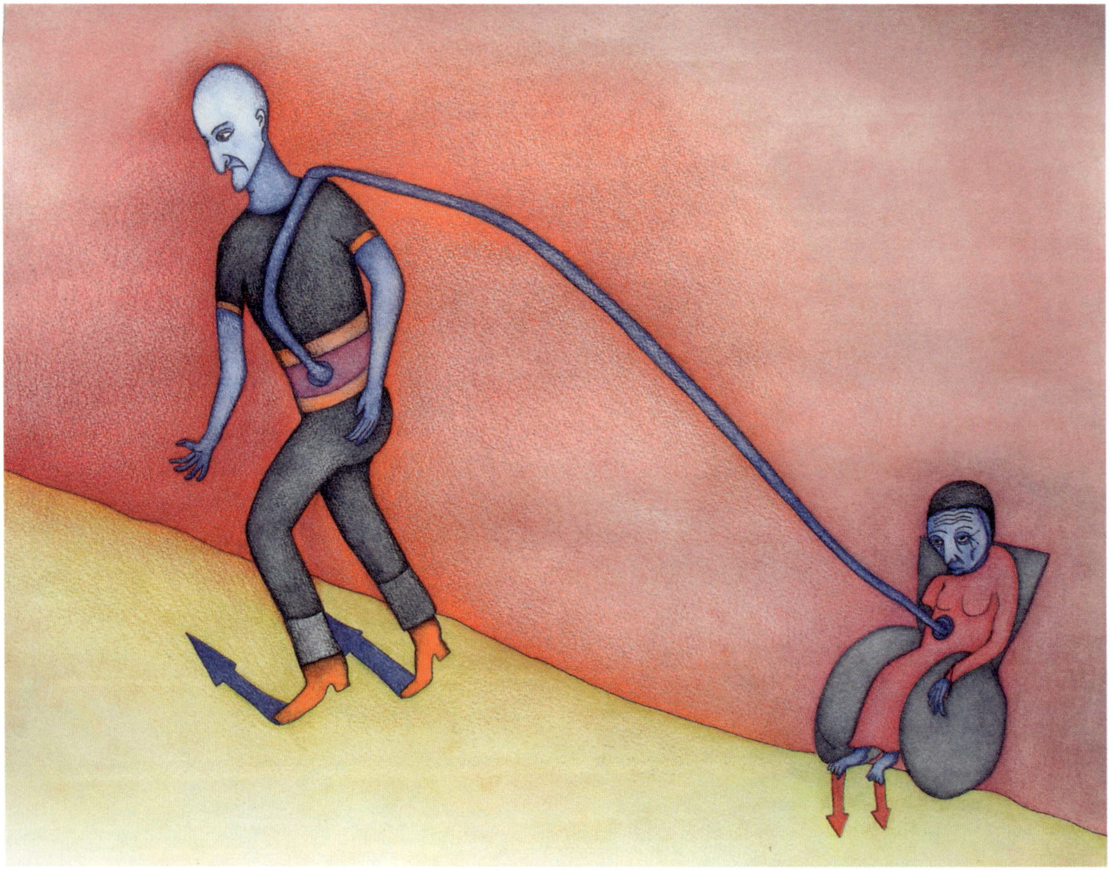

*Umbilical Leash*, 2014
50 × 65 cm

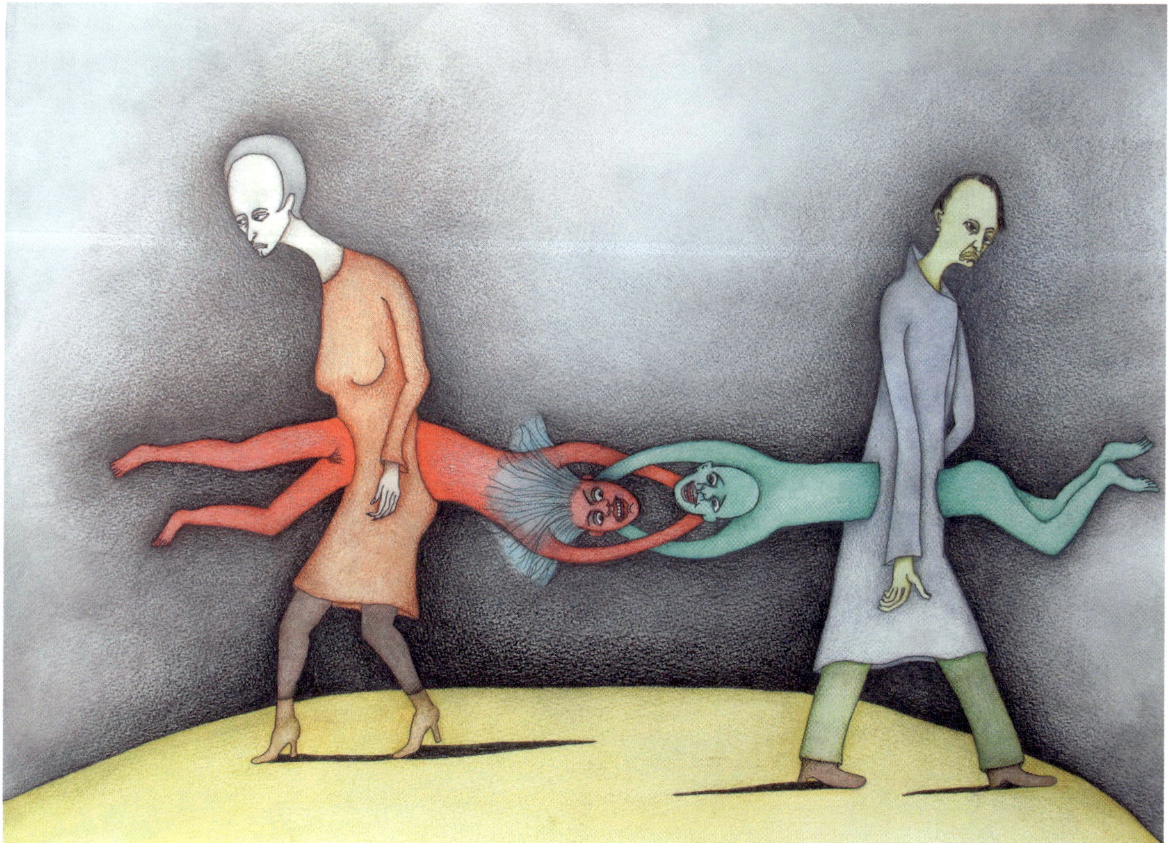

*Separation*, 2014
50 × 65 cm

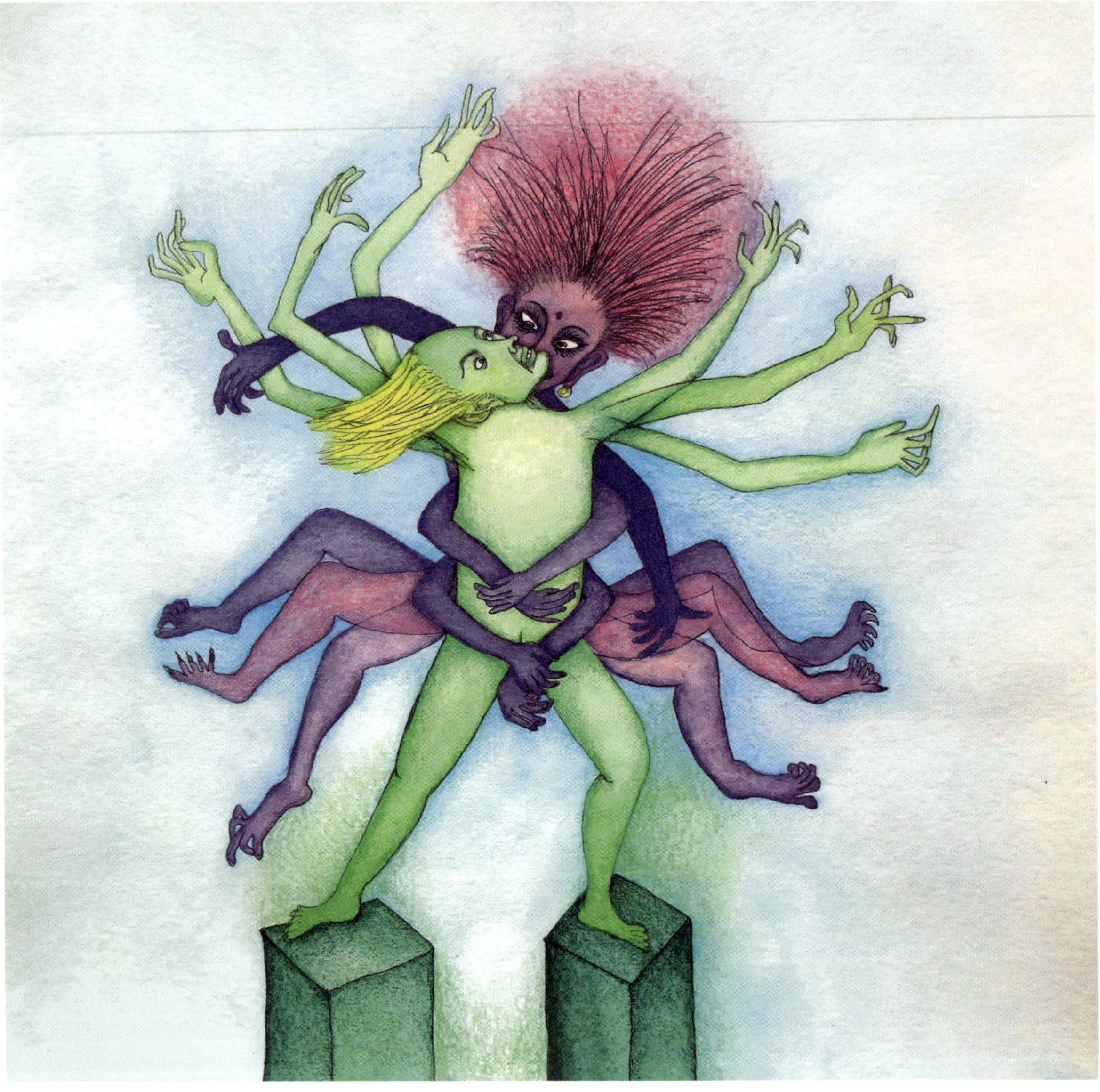

*Coito Divino*, 2014
40 × 40 cm

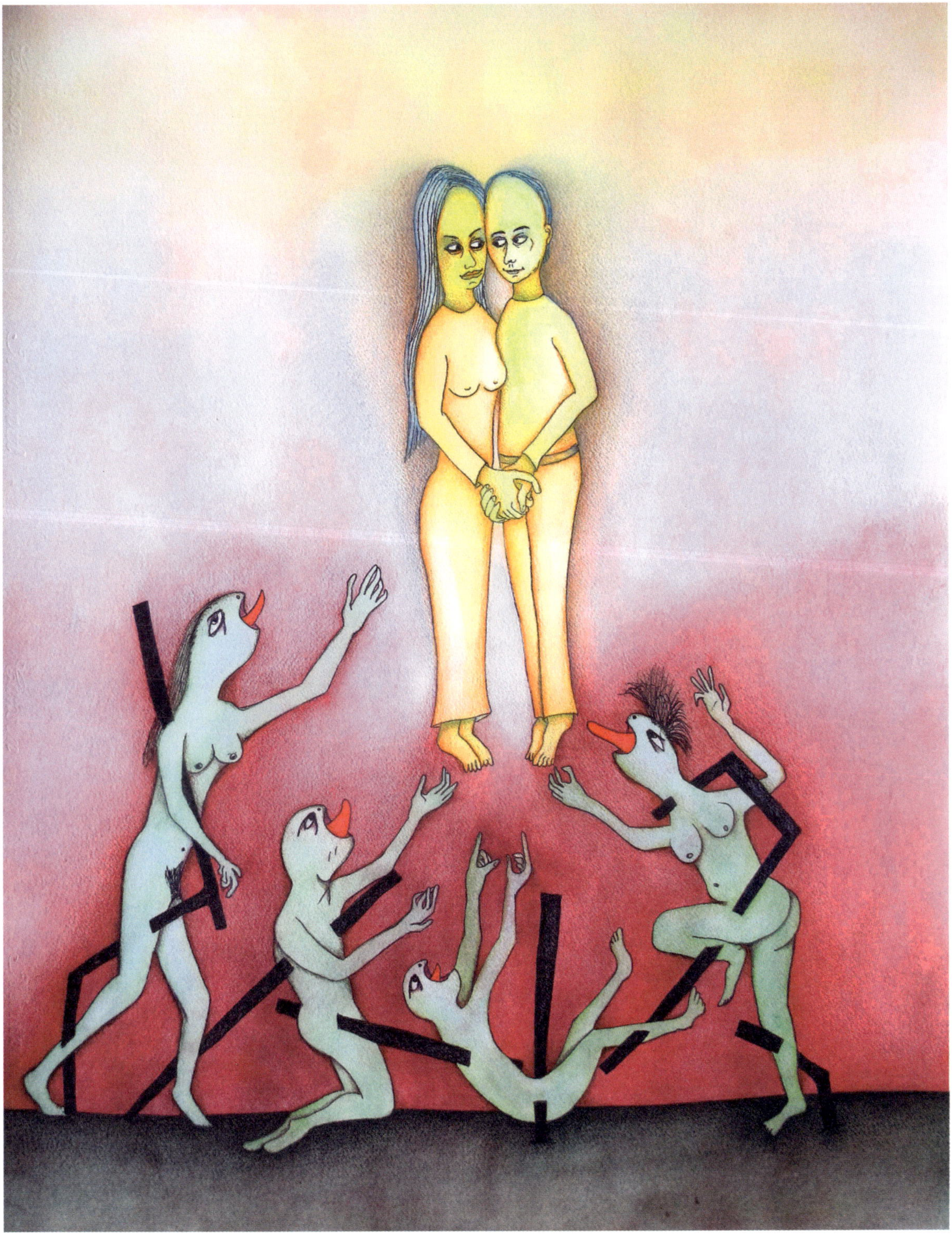

*Our Love*, 2014
65 × 50 cm

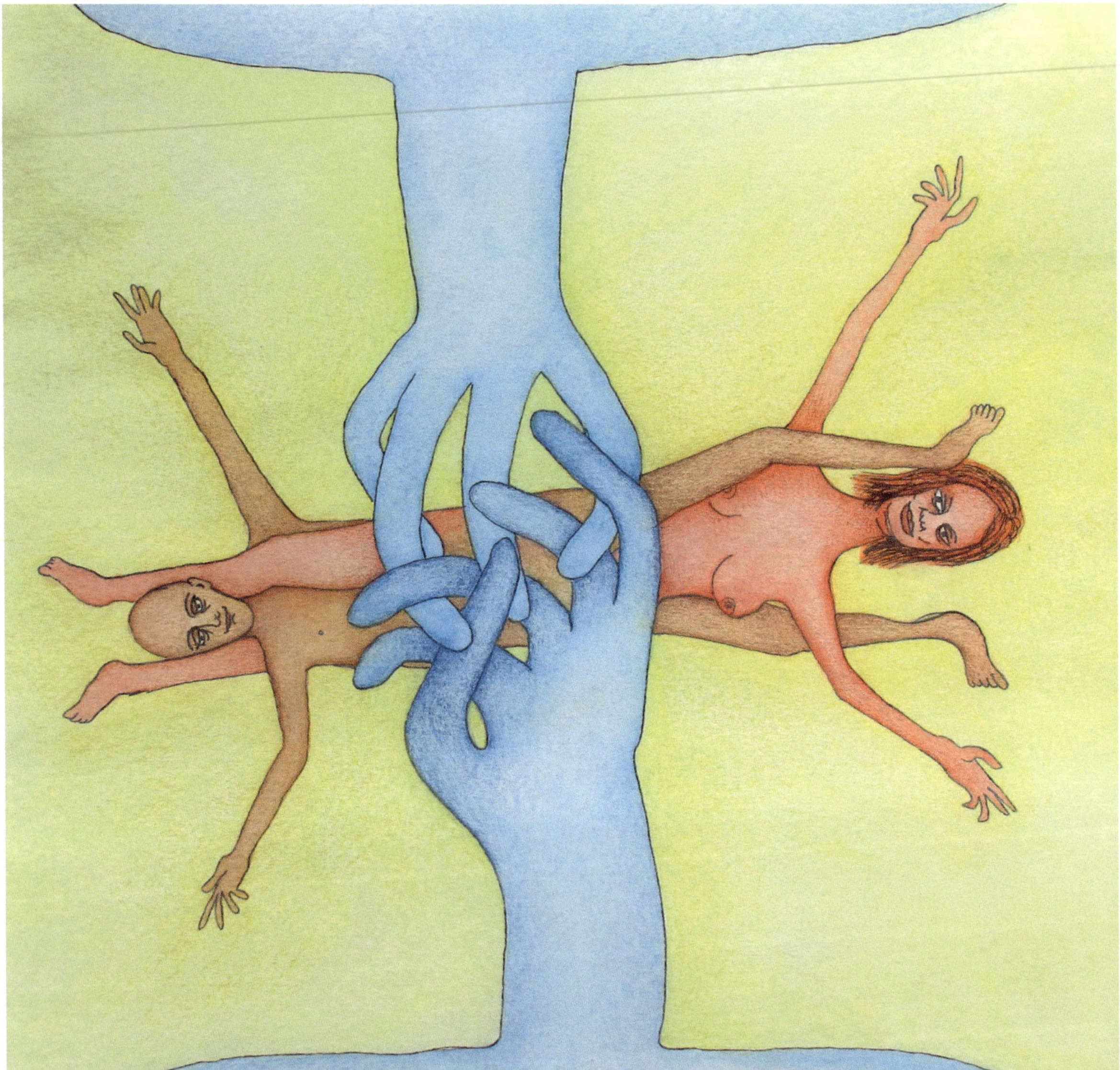

*Adam and Eve*, 2014
40 × 40 cm

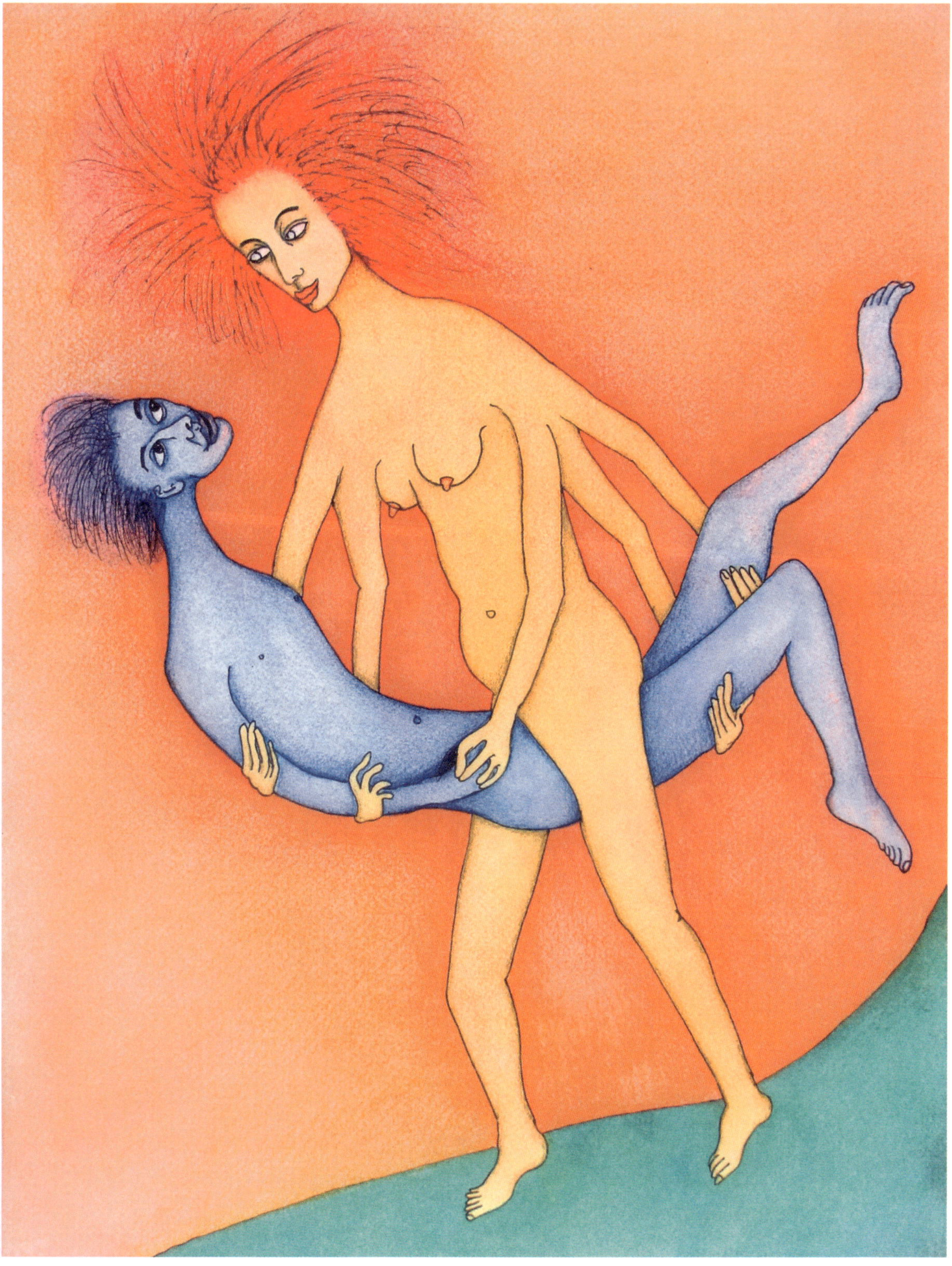

*All of Love*, 2014
41 × 31 cm

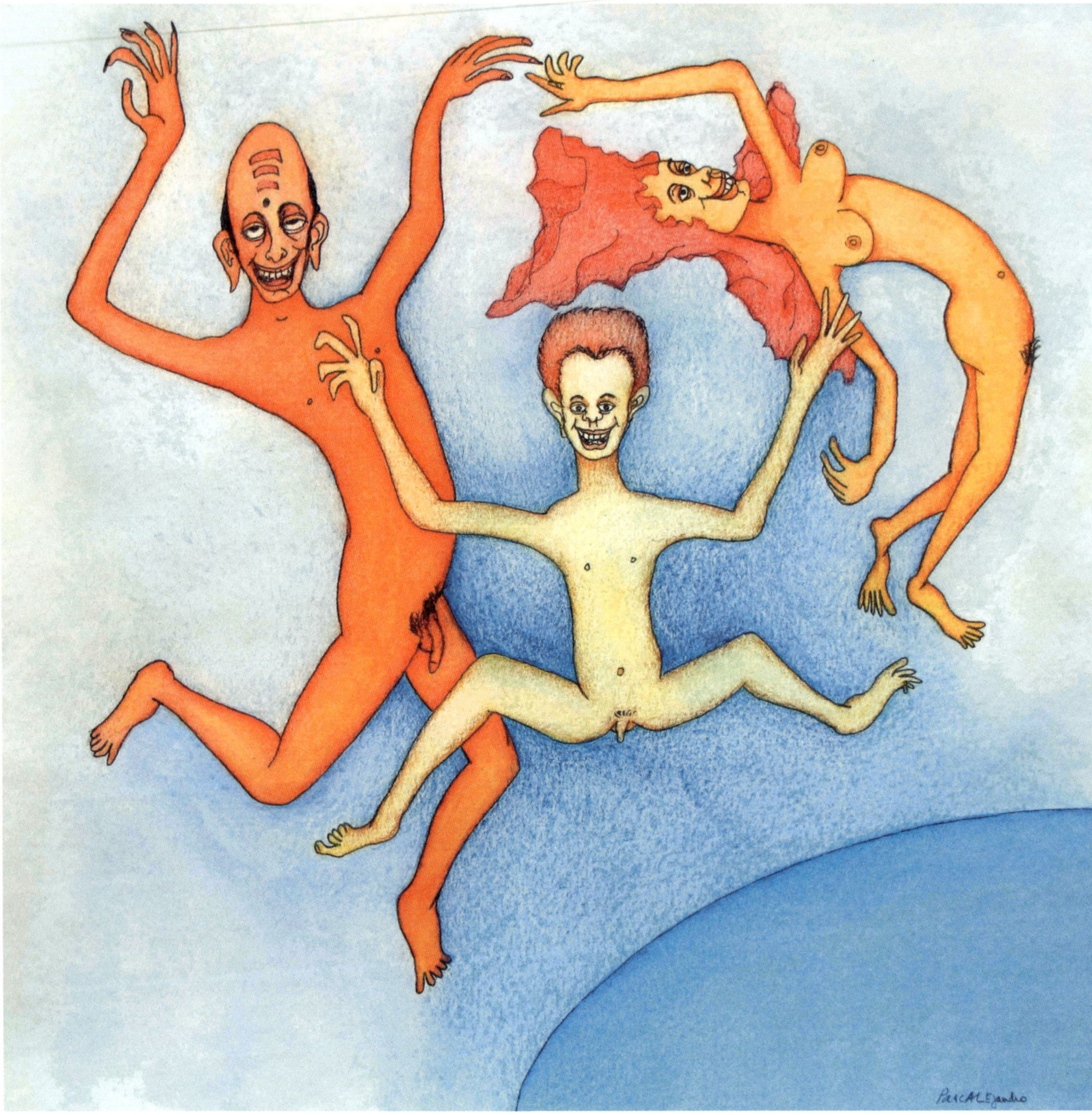

*Alegría! Alegría! Alegría!* 2014
40 × 40 cm

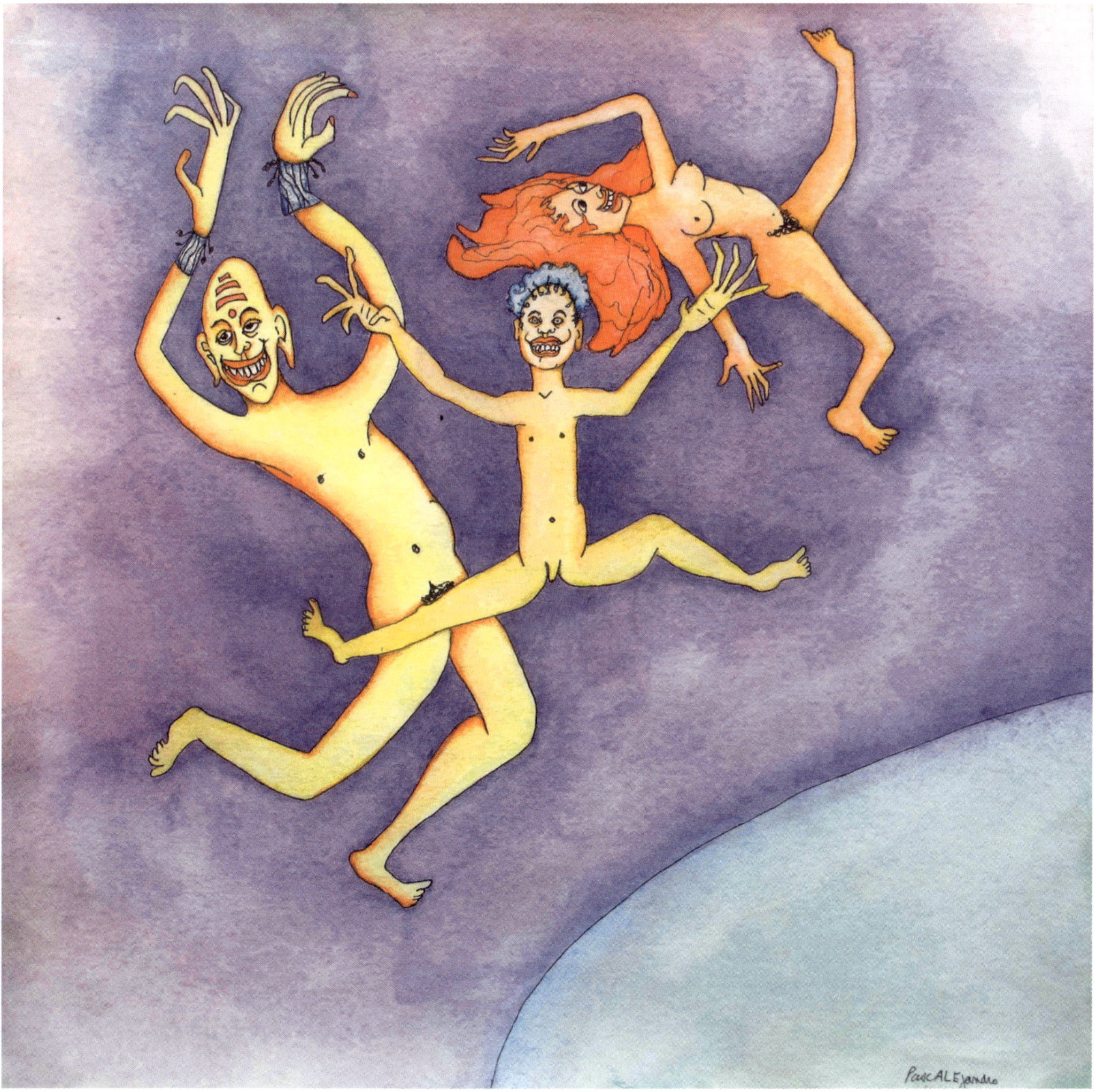


*Joy, Joy!* 2014
40 × 40 cm

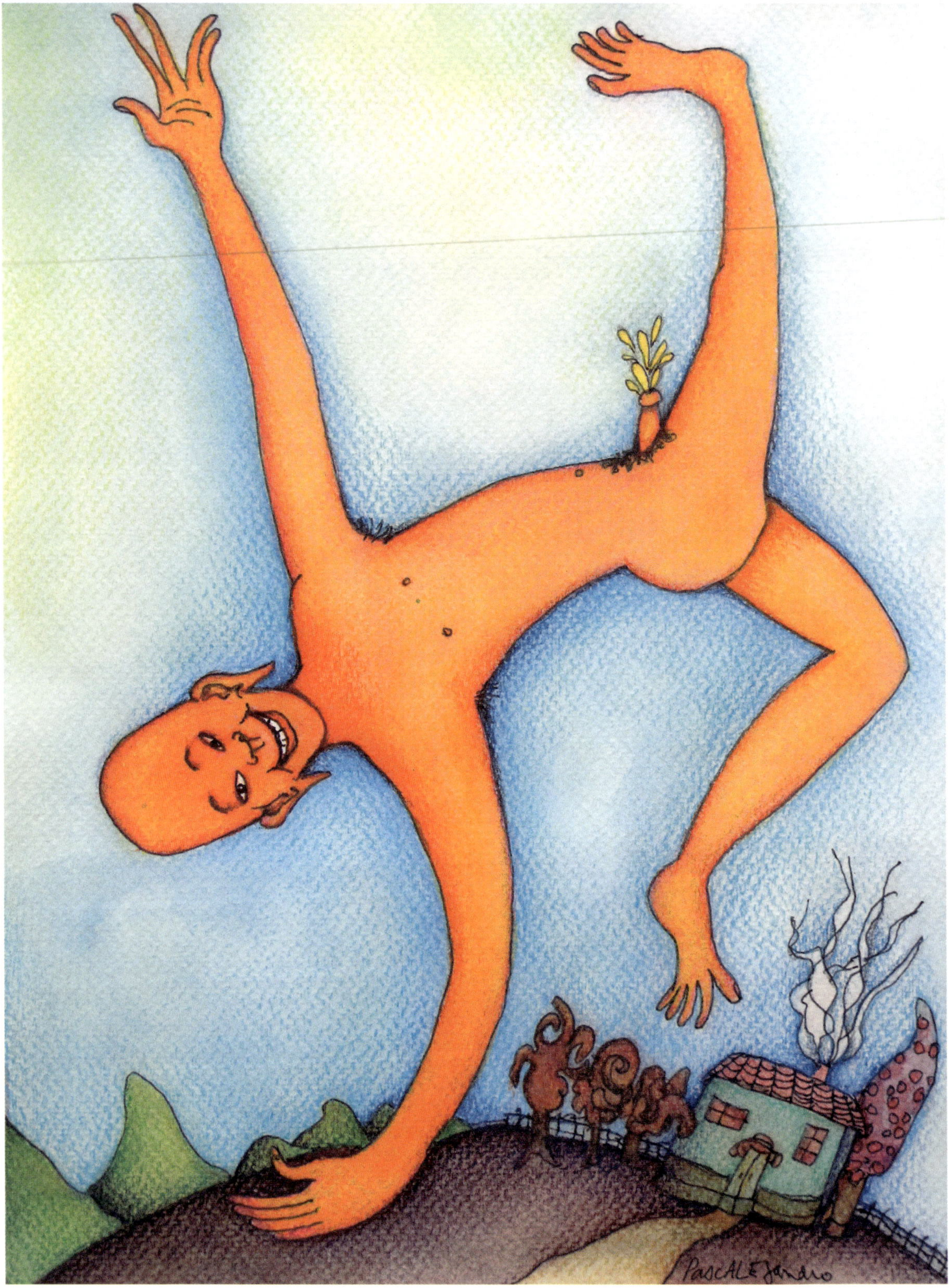

*Happiness*, 2014
29 × 21 cm

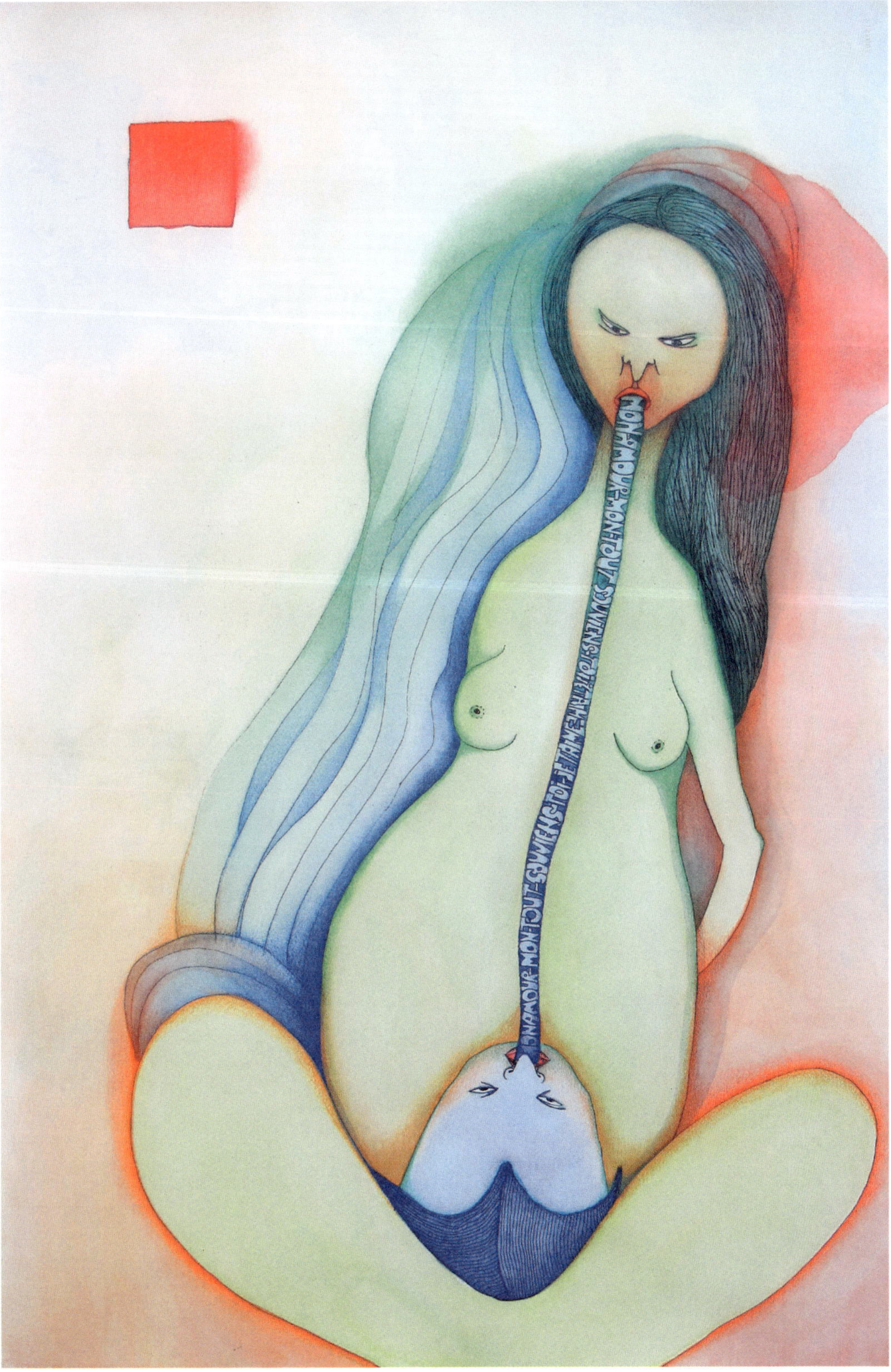

*Communicating Vessels*, 2012
102 × 65 cm

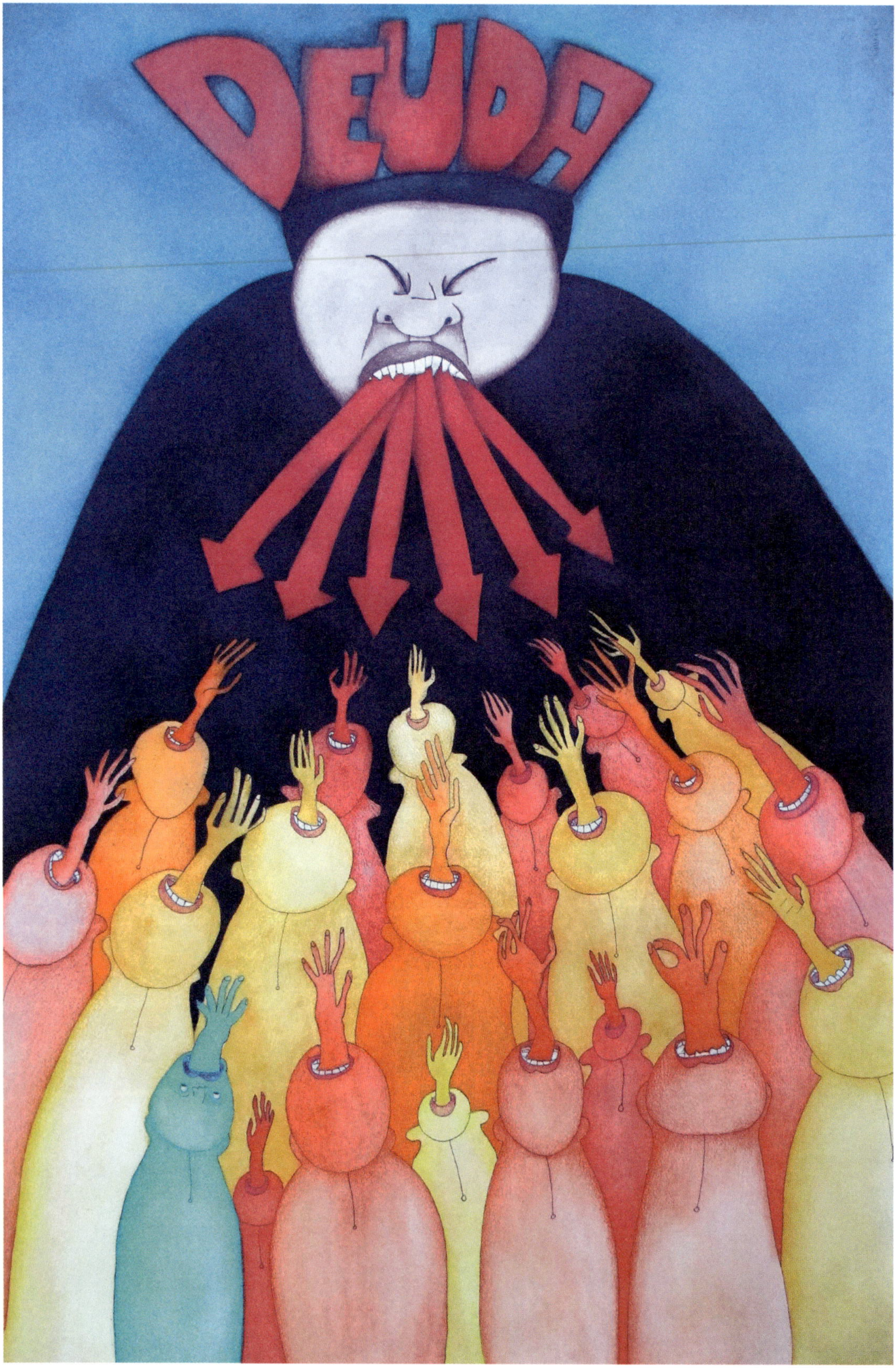


*Debt*, 2012
102 × 65 cm

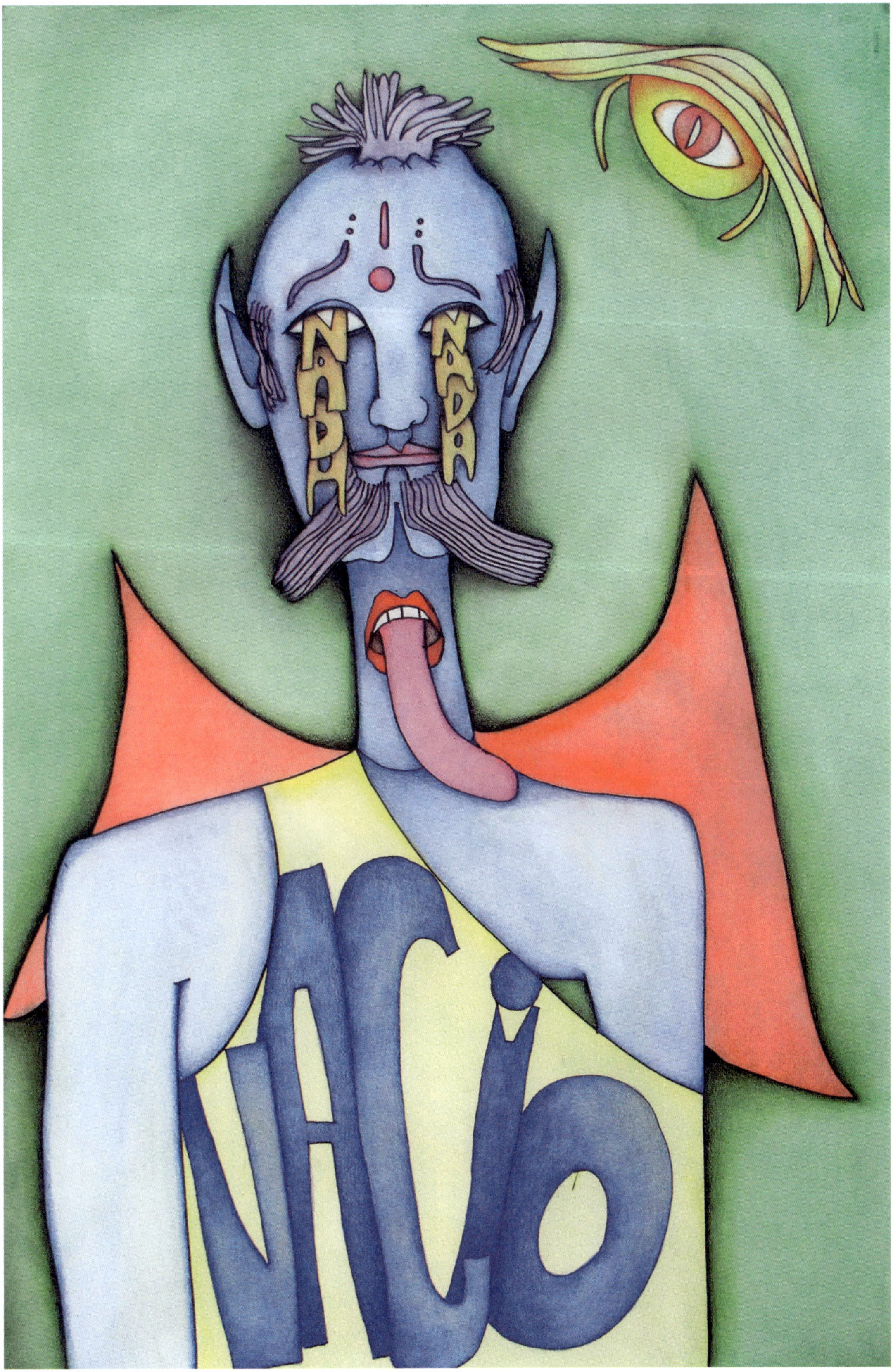


*VACIO*, 2012
102 × 65 cm

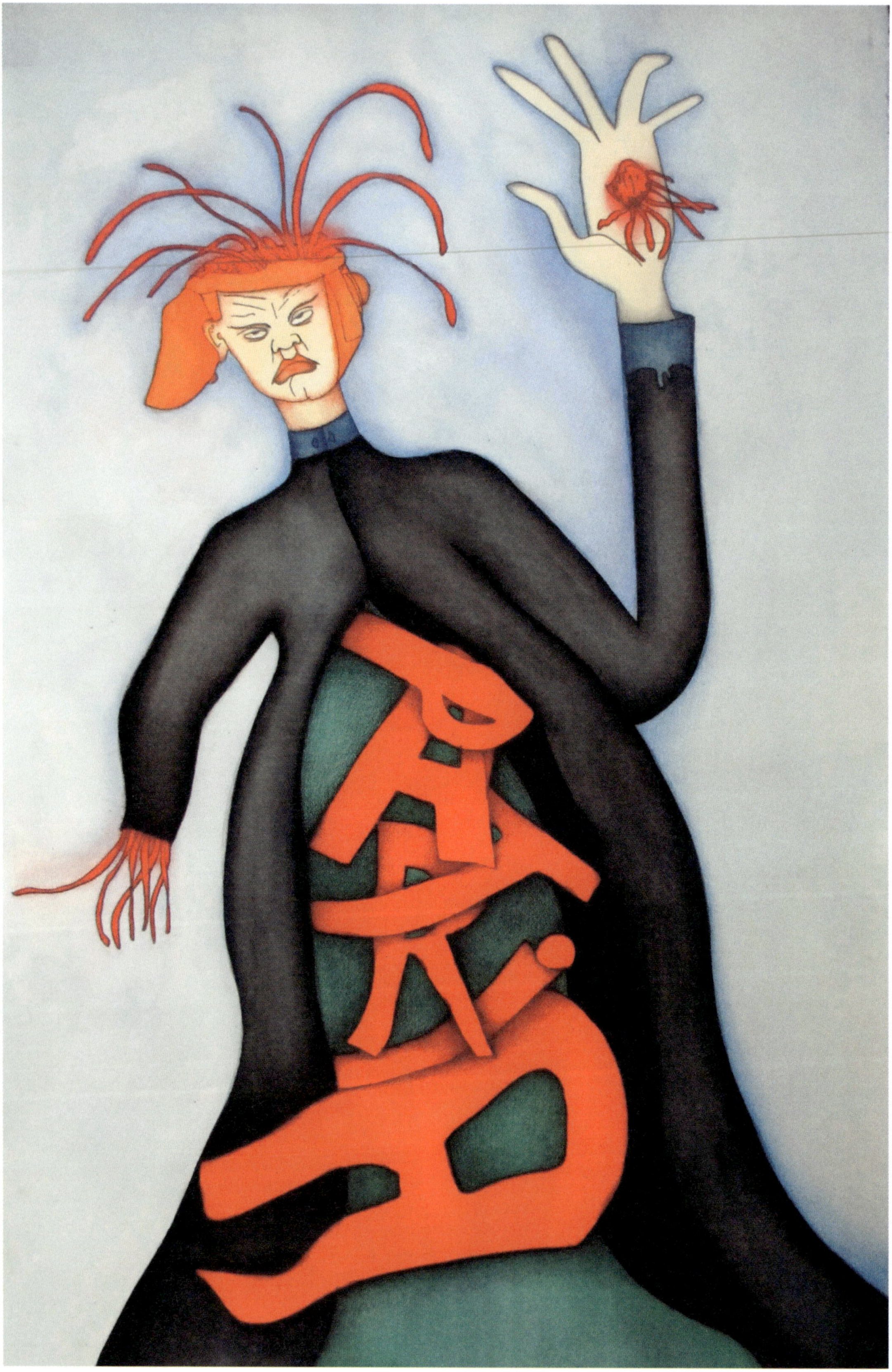


*PATRIA*, 2012
102 × 65 cm

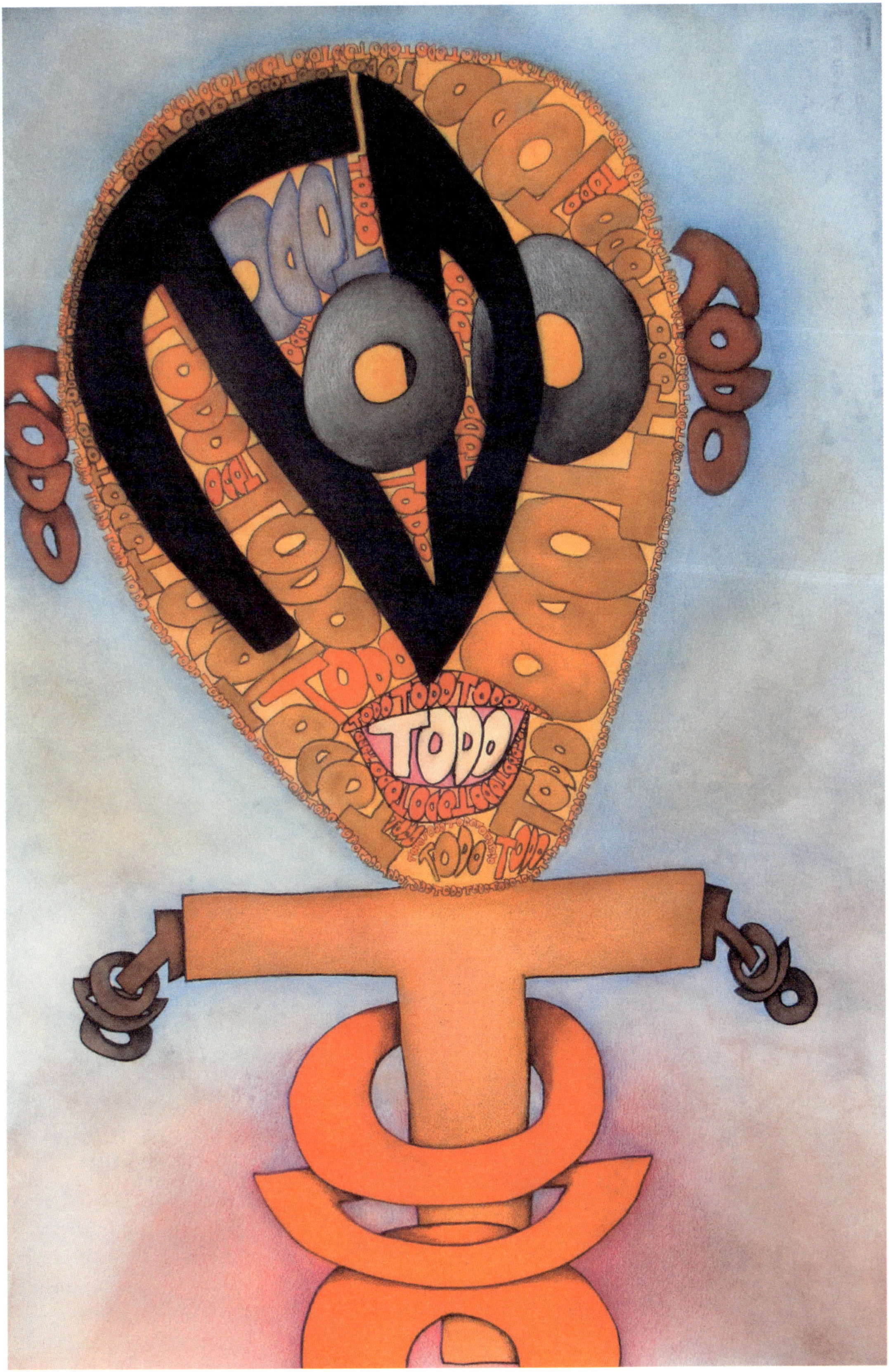


*TODO*, 2012
102 × 65 cm

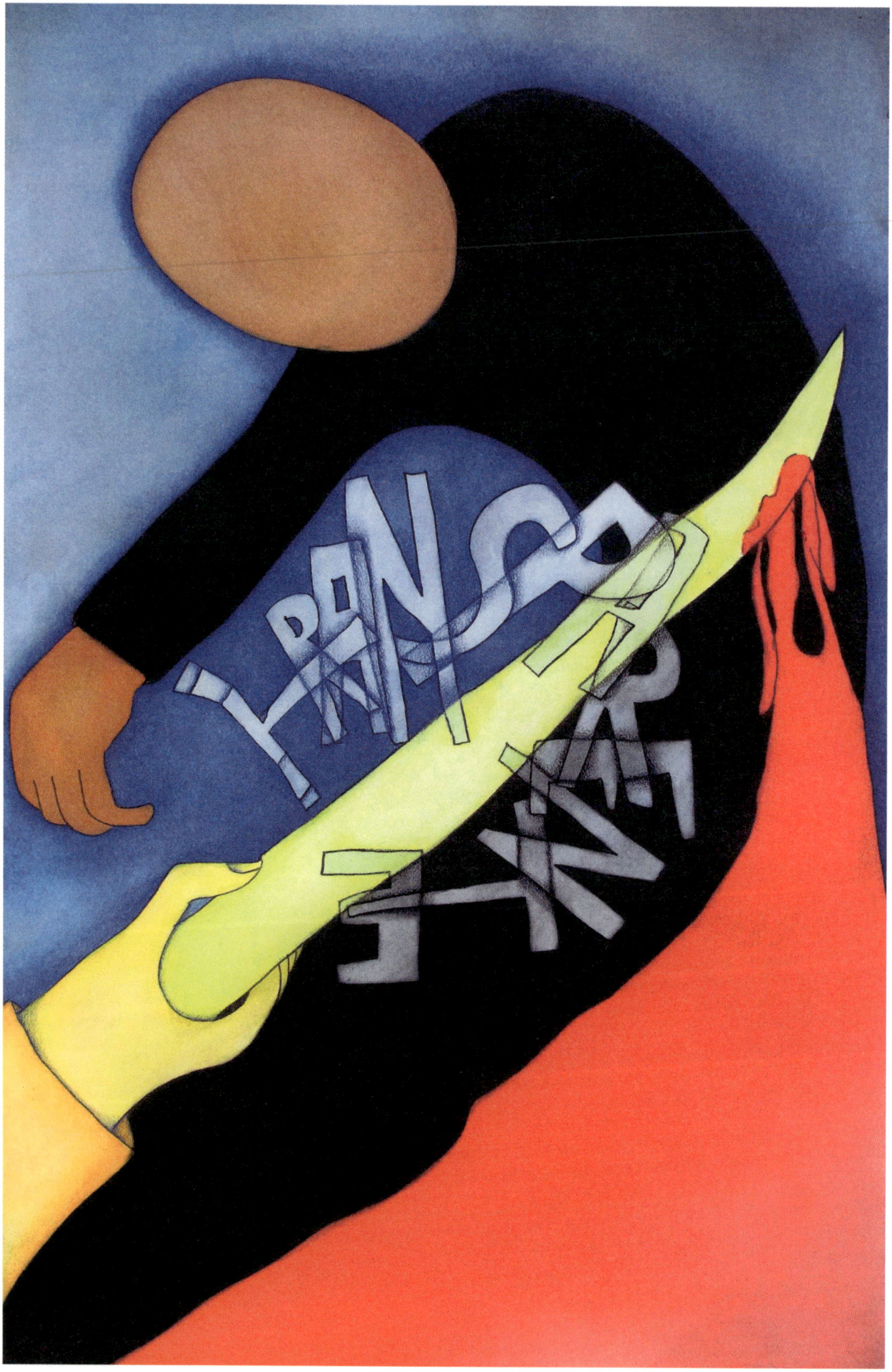

*TRANSPARENTE*, 2012
102 × 65 cm

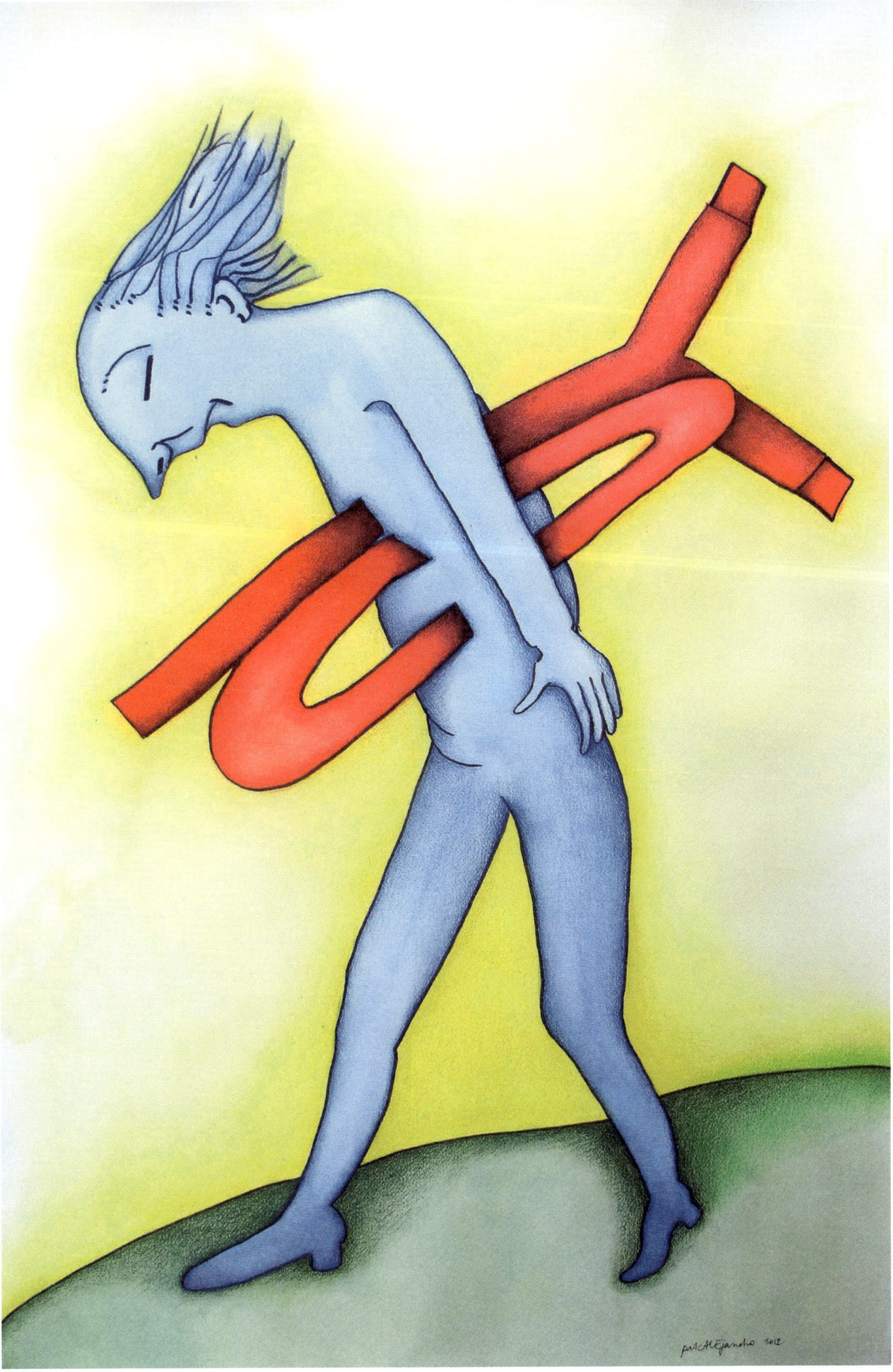

*YO*, 2012
102 × 65 cm

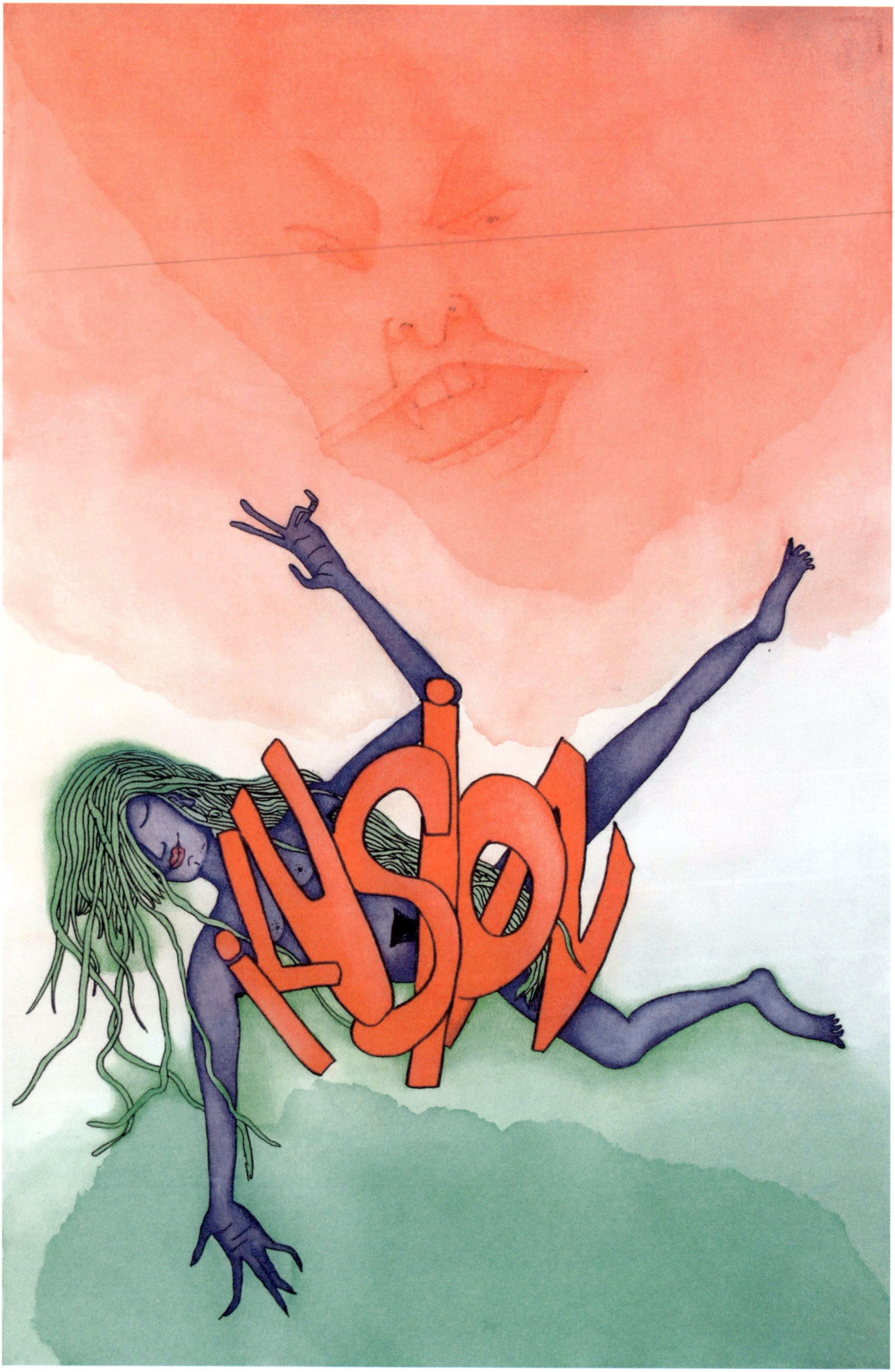


*ILUSION*, 2012
102 × 65 cm

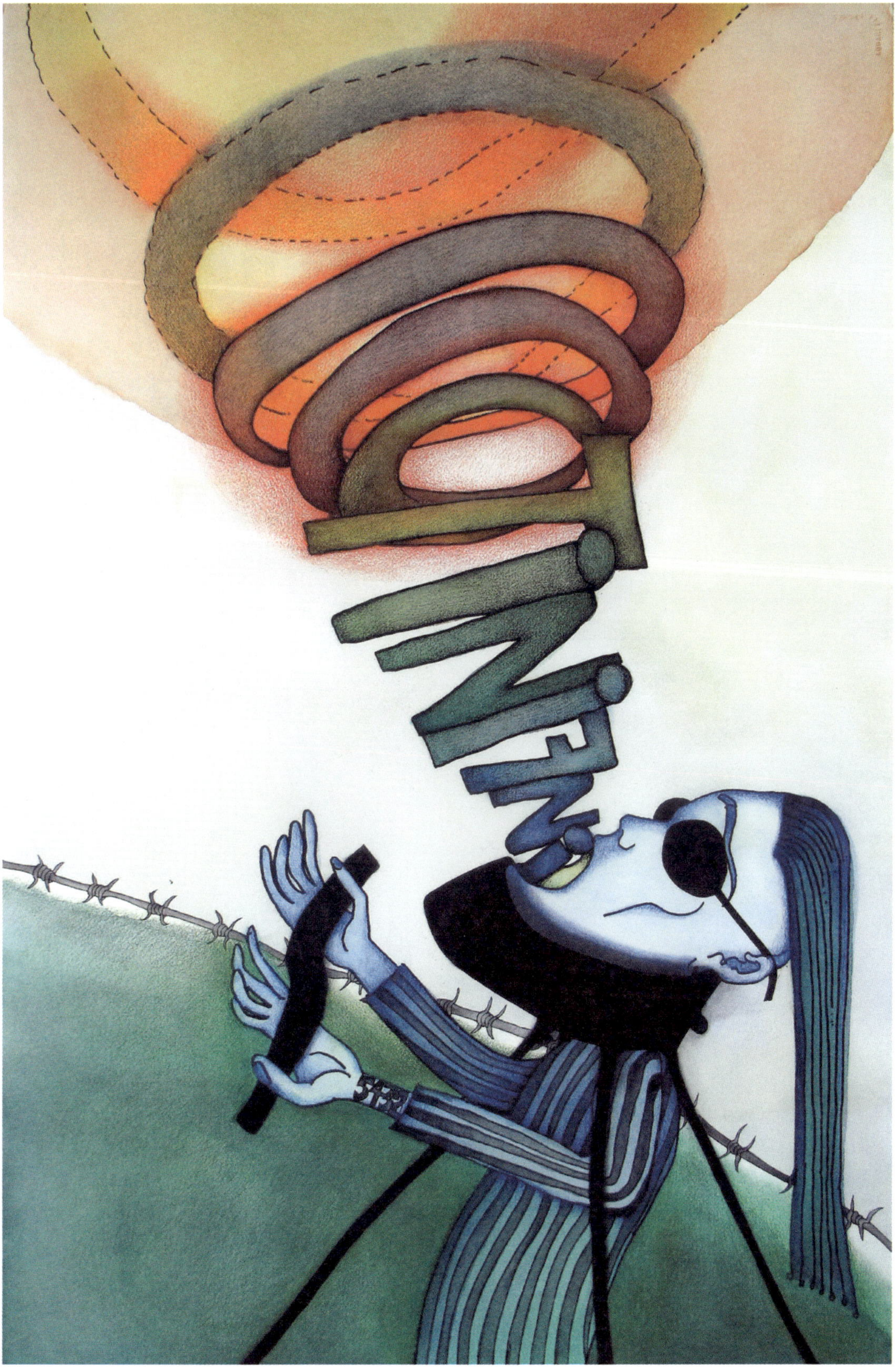

*INFINITO*, 2012
102 × 65 cm

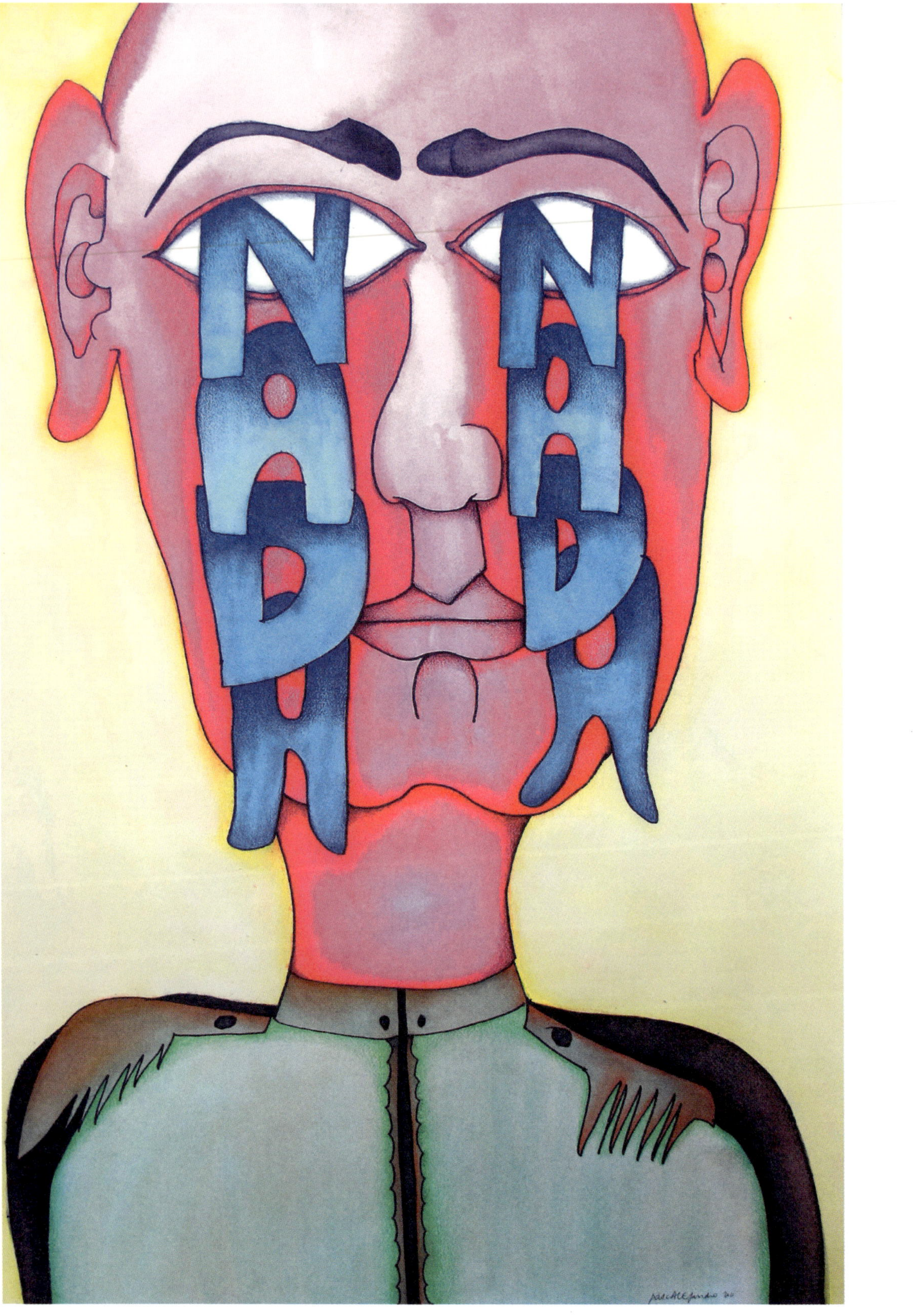

*NADA*, 2012
102 × 65 cm

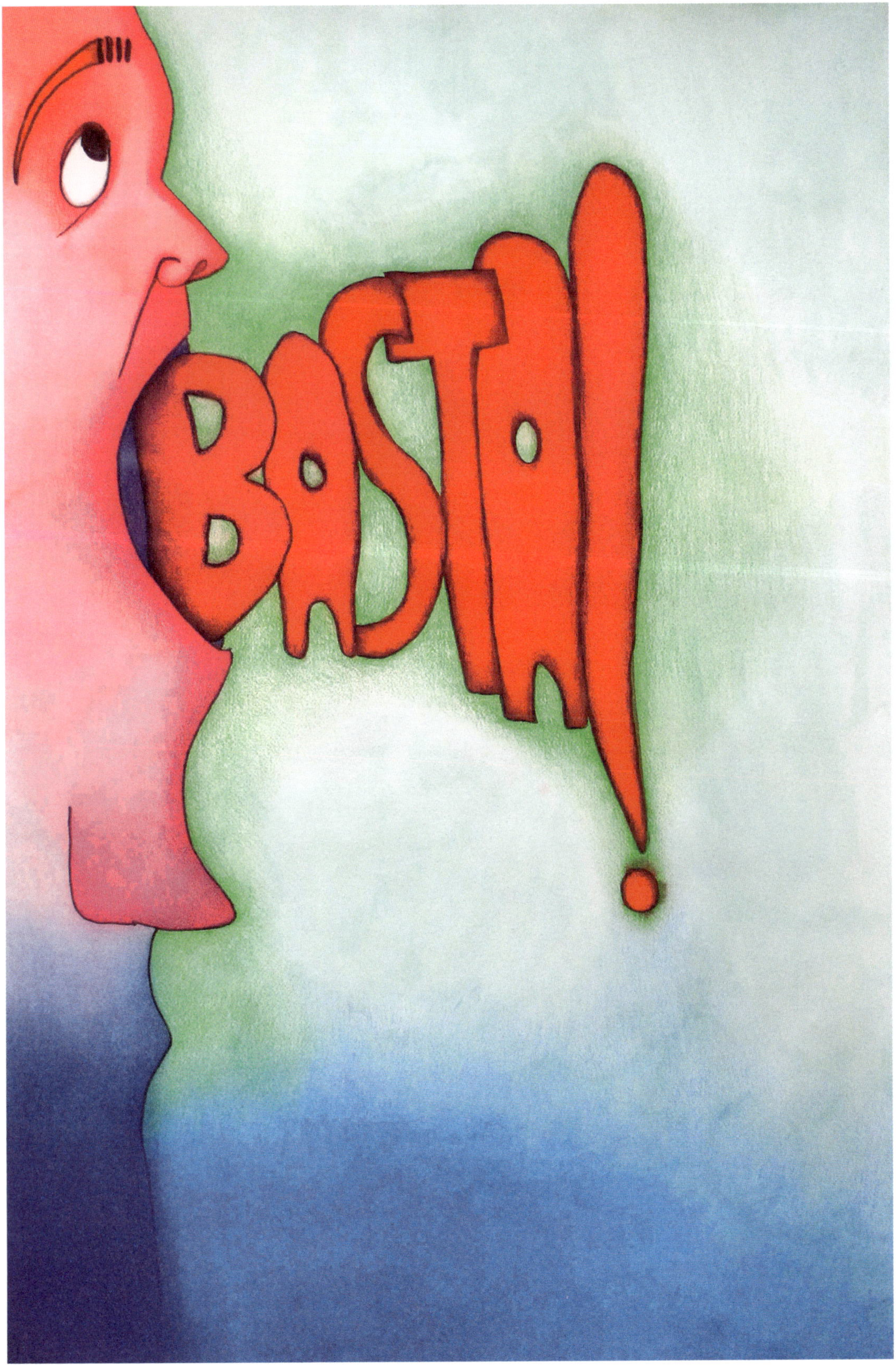


*BASTA!*, 2011
102 × 65 cm

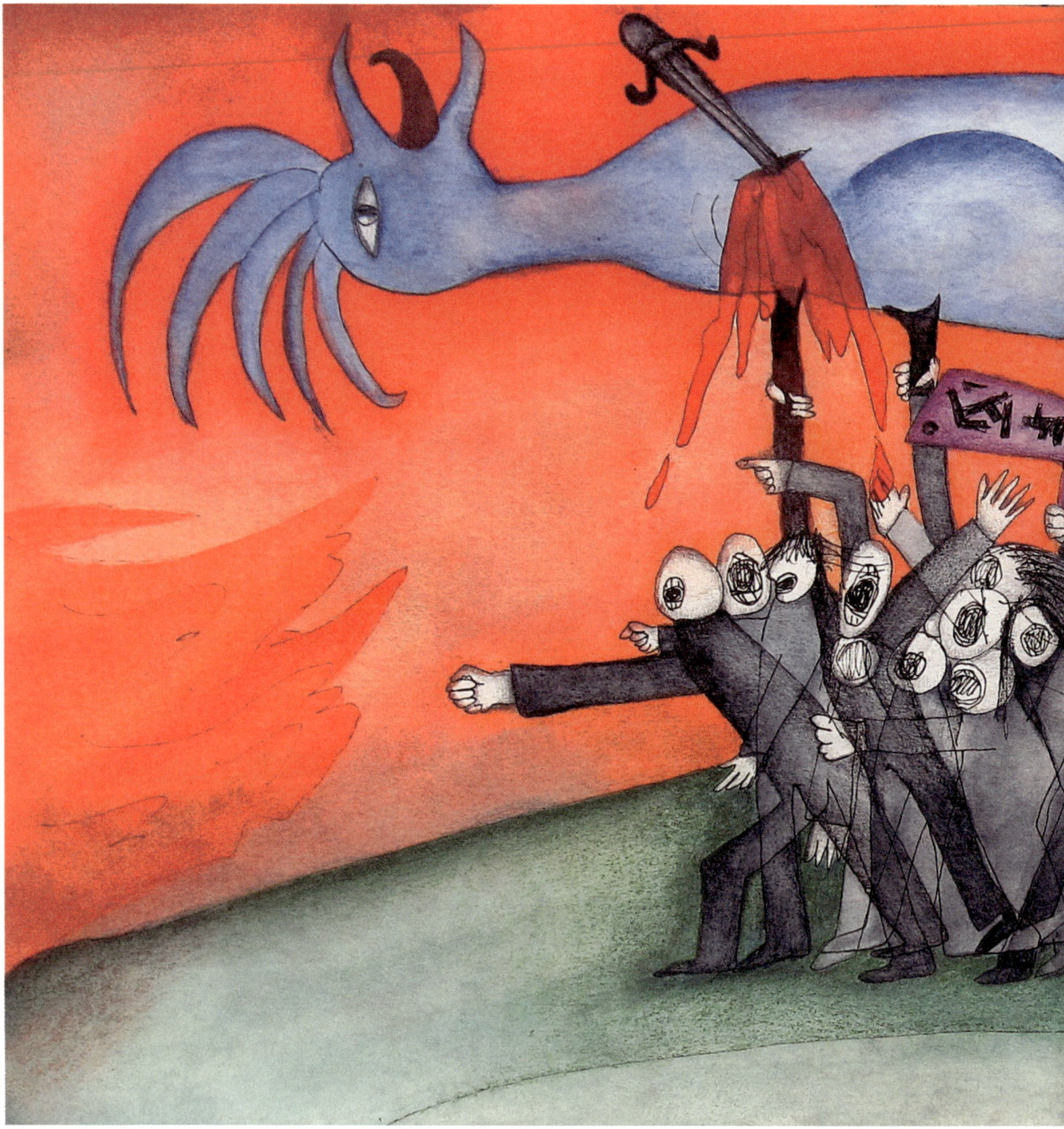

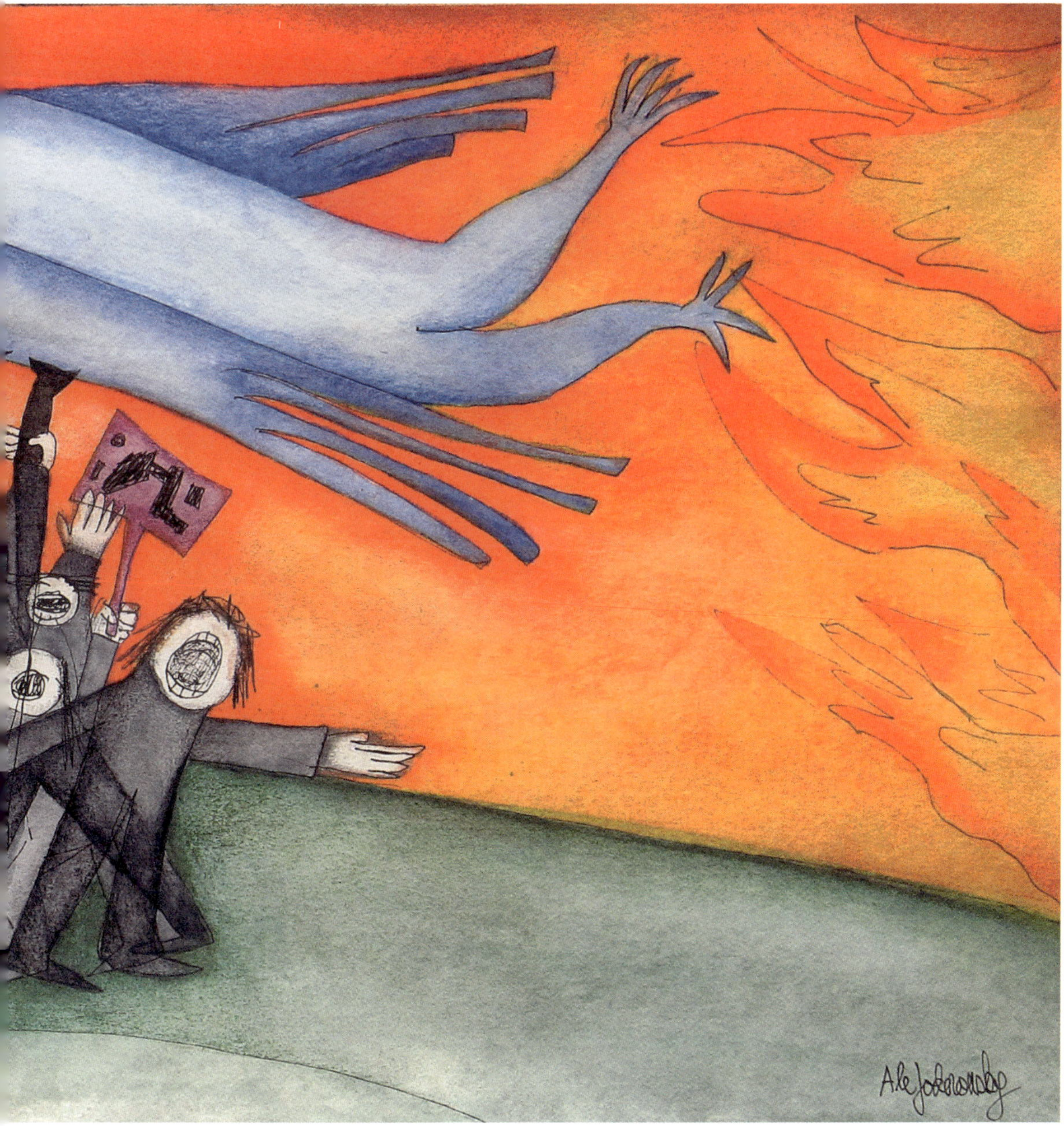

*Poetic Re-evolution*, 2011
30 × 60 cm

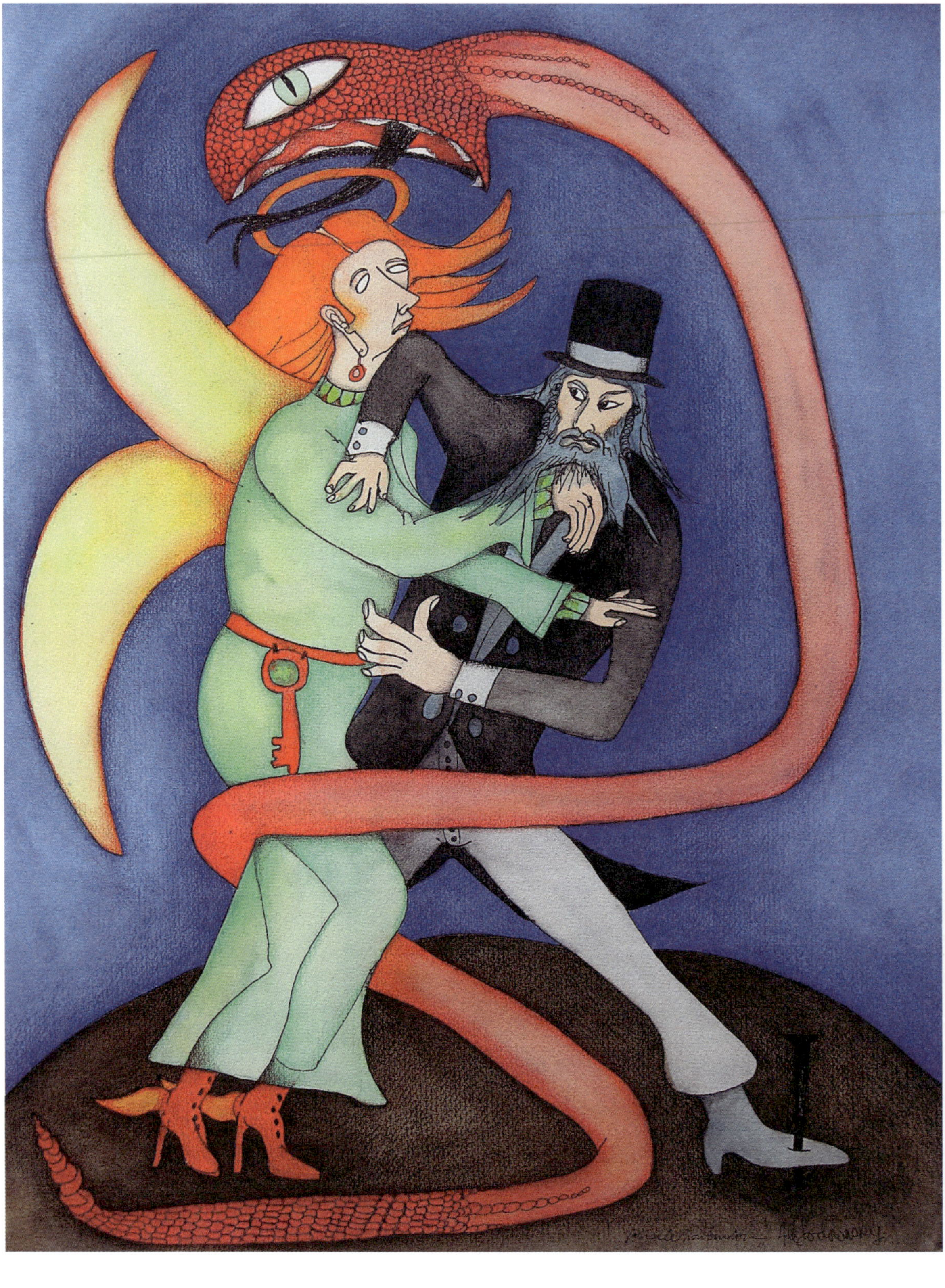

*Wrestling with the Angel*, 2011
56 × 42 cm

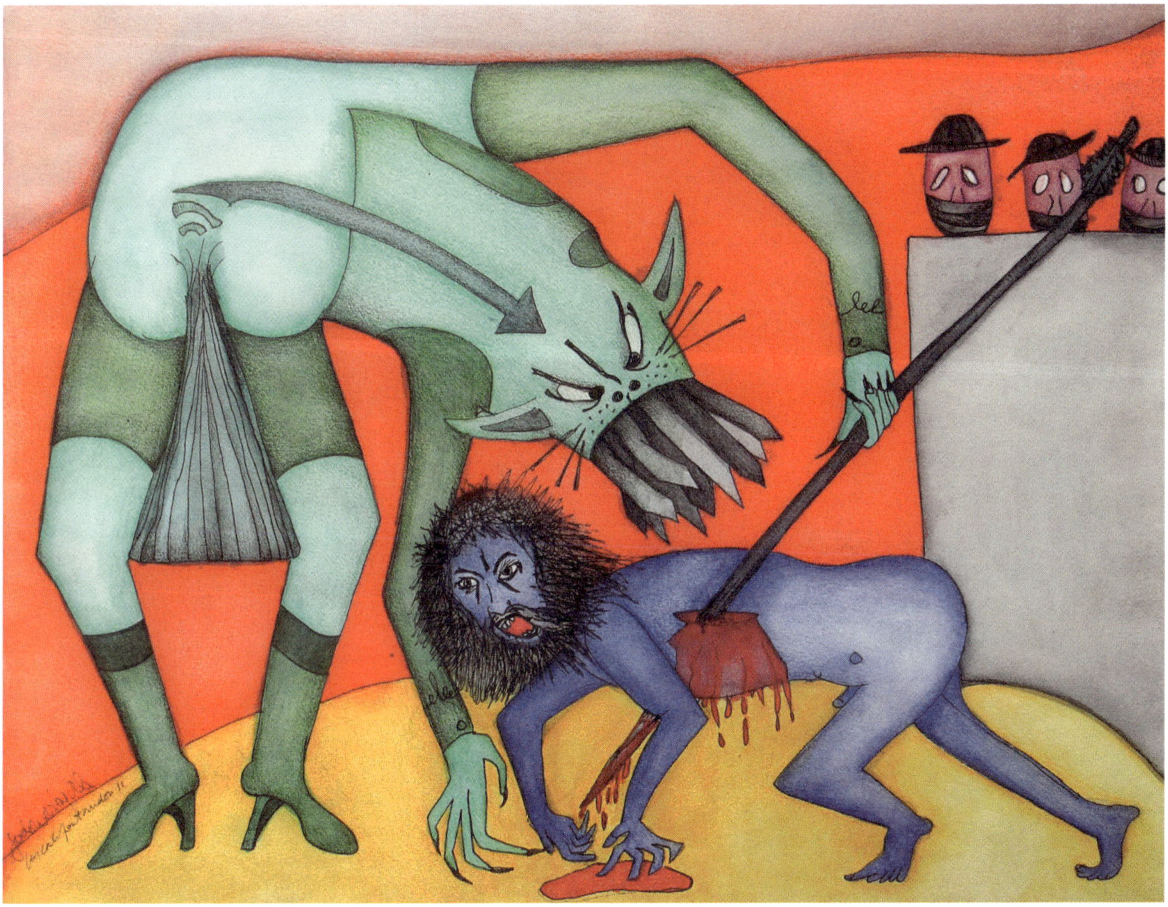

*The Beast's Revenge*, 2011
32 × 41 cm

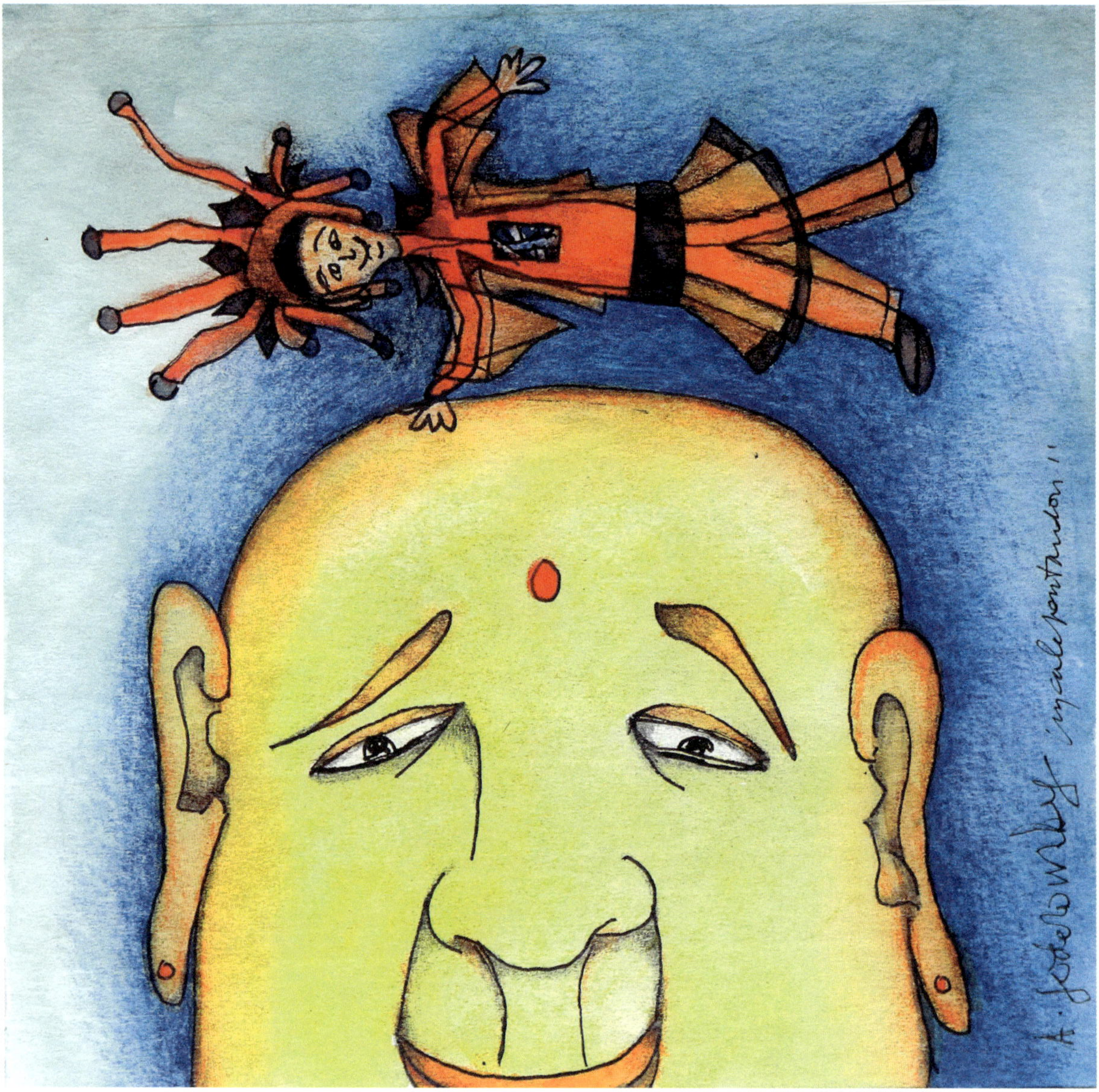

*The Buddha and His Mastered Ego*, 2011
15 × 15 cm

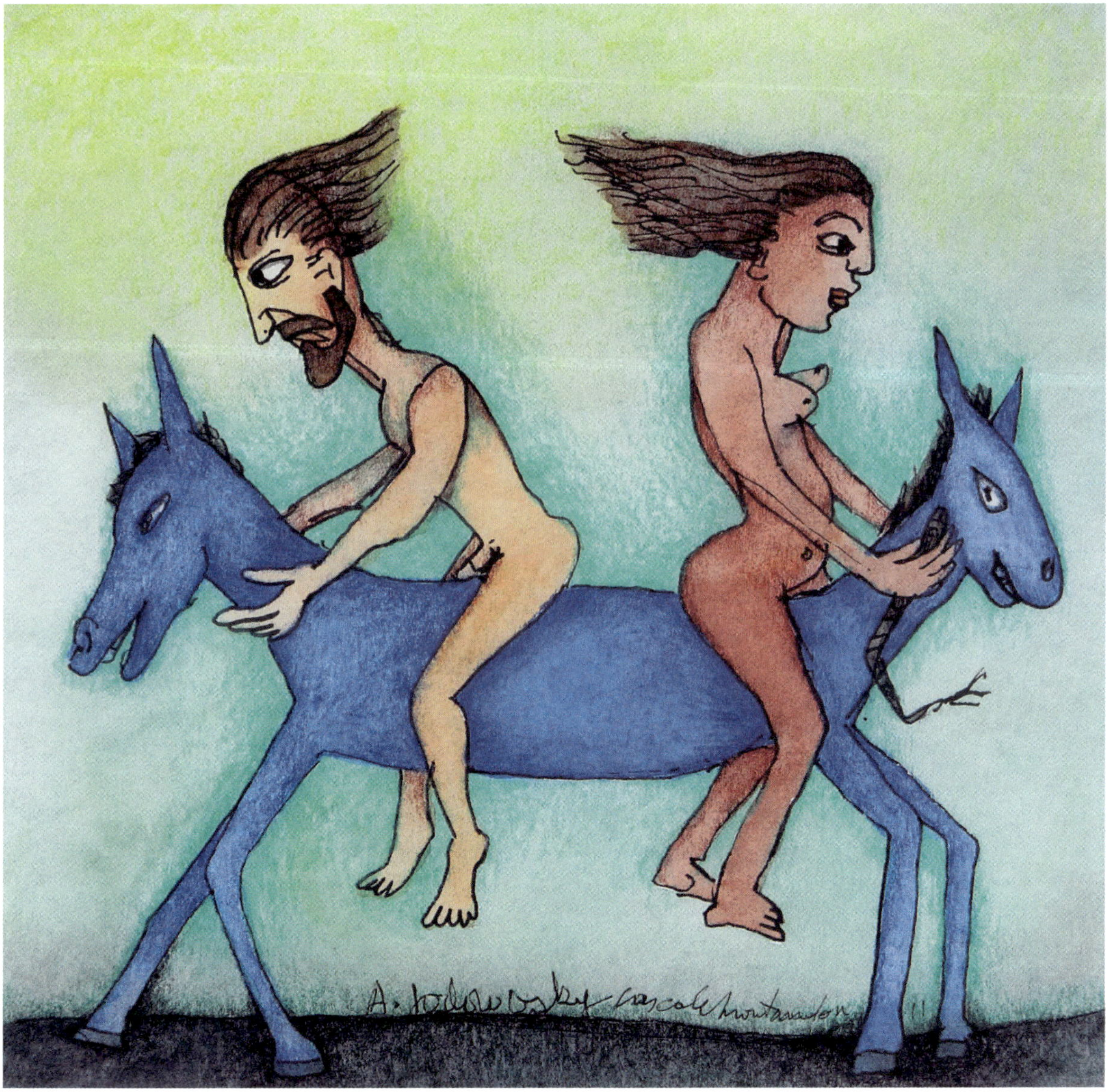

*Couple in Crisis*, 2011
15 ×15 cm

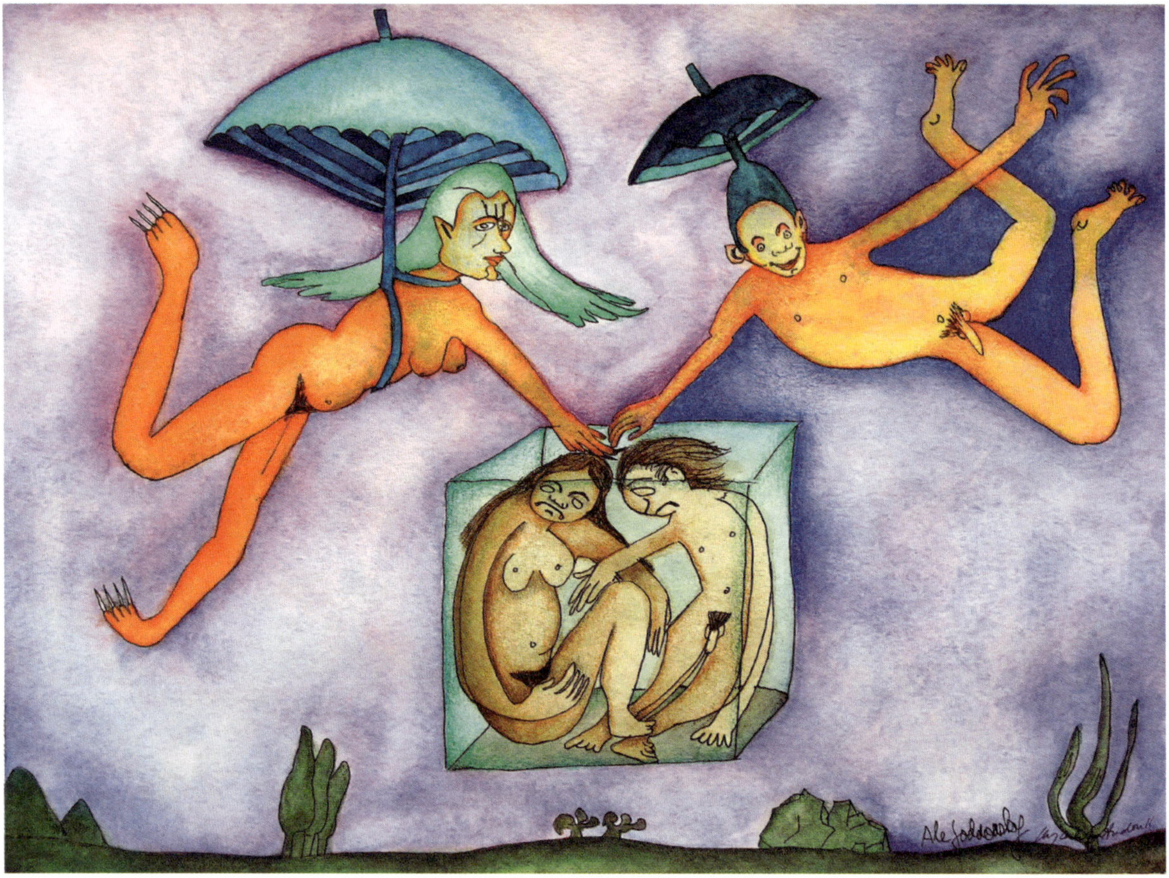

*Joyful Balancing on Sadness*, 2011
32 × 41 cm

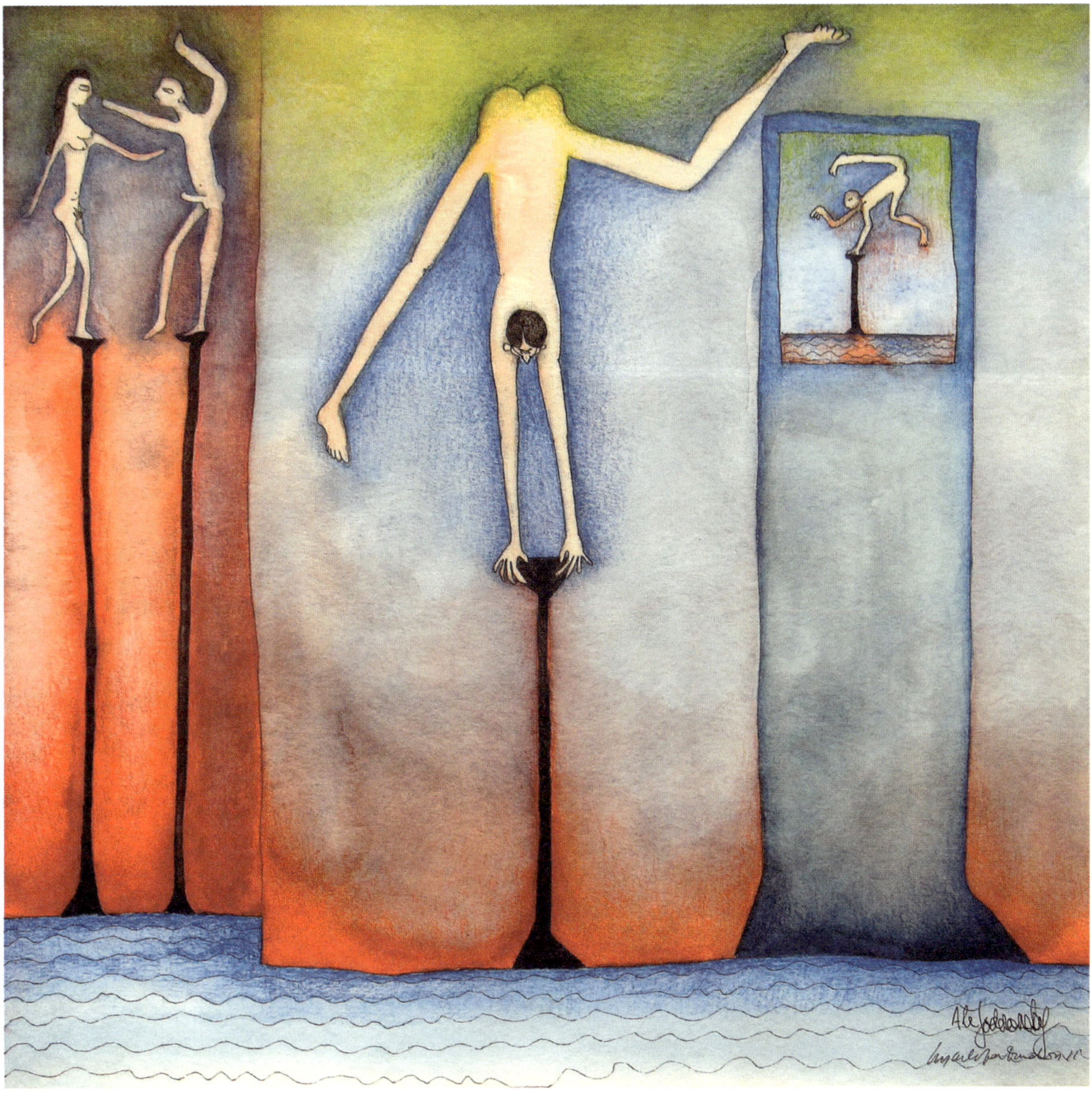

*Balancing near Water*, 2011
40 × 40 cm

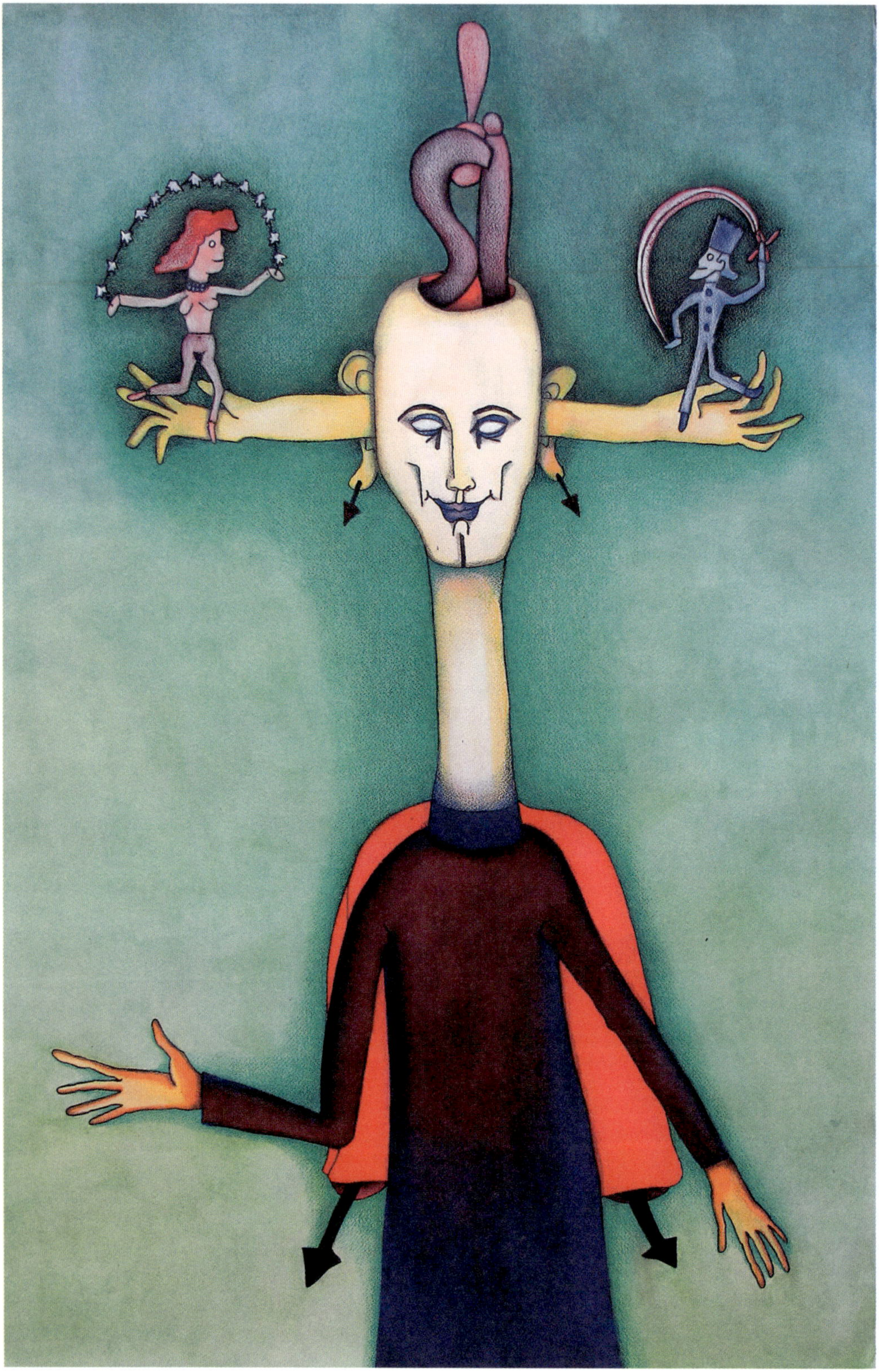

*The Magician*, 2011
102 × 65 cm

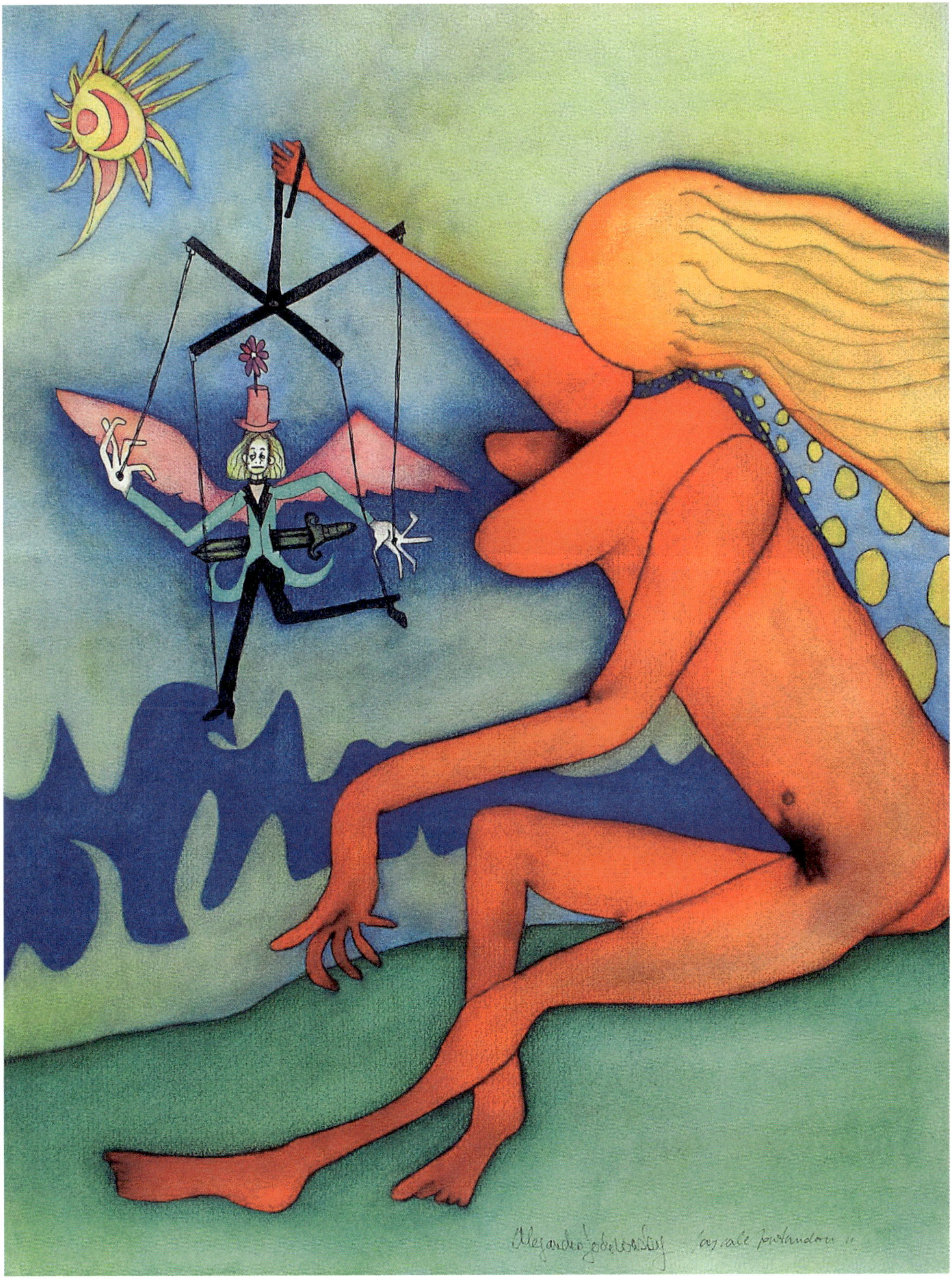

*Wounded Puppet*, 2011
56 × 42 cm

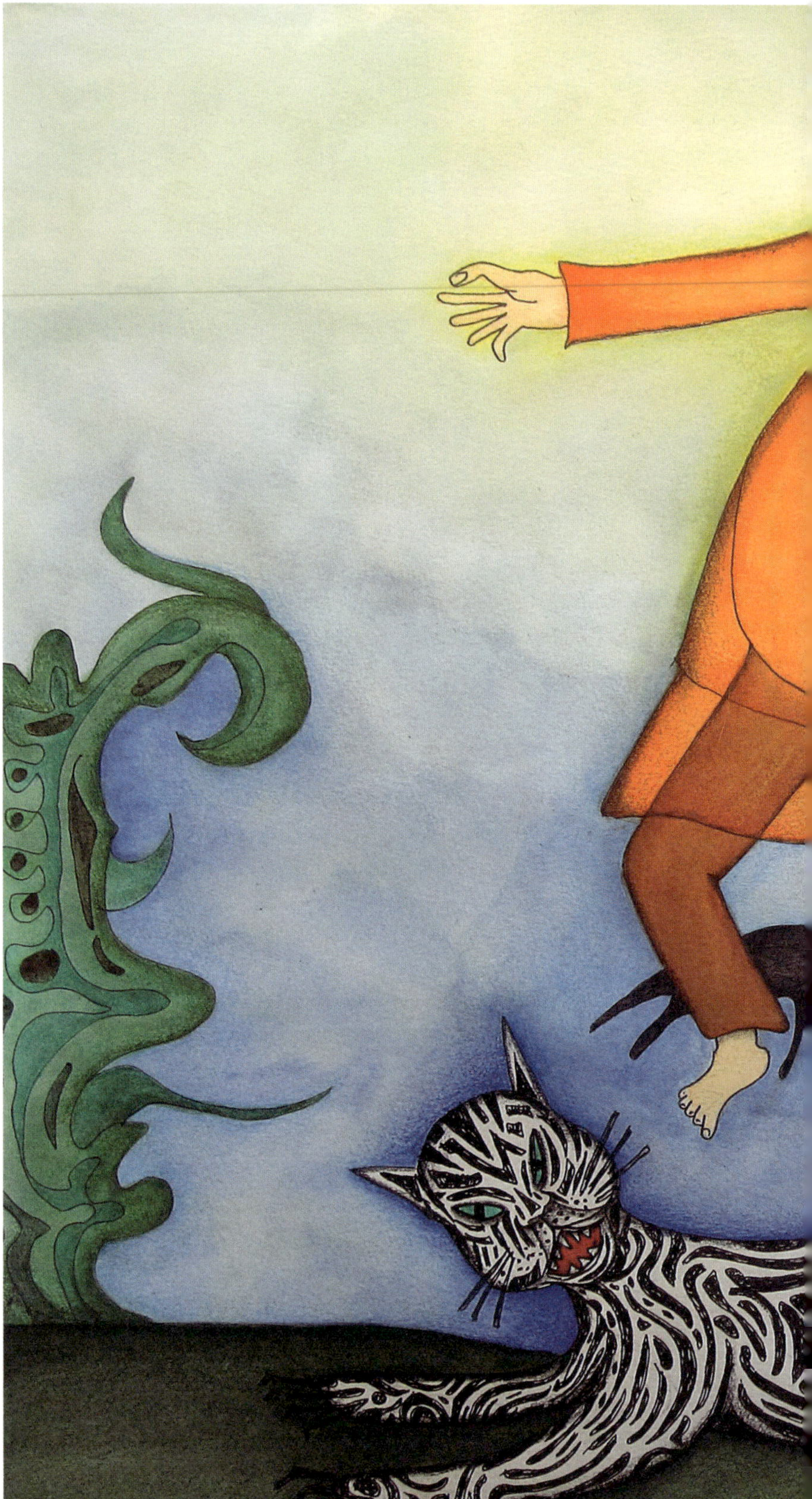

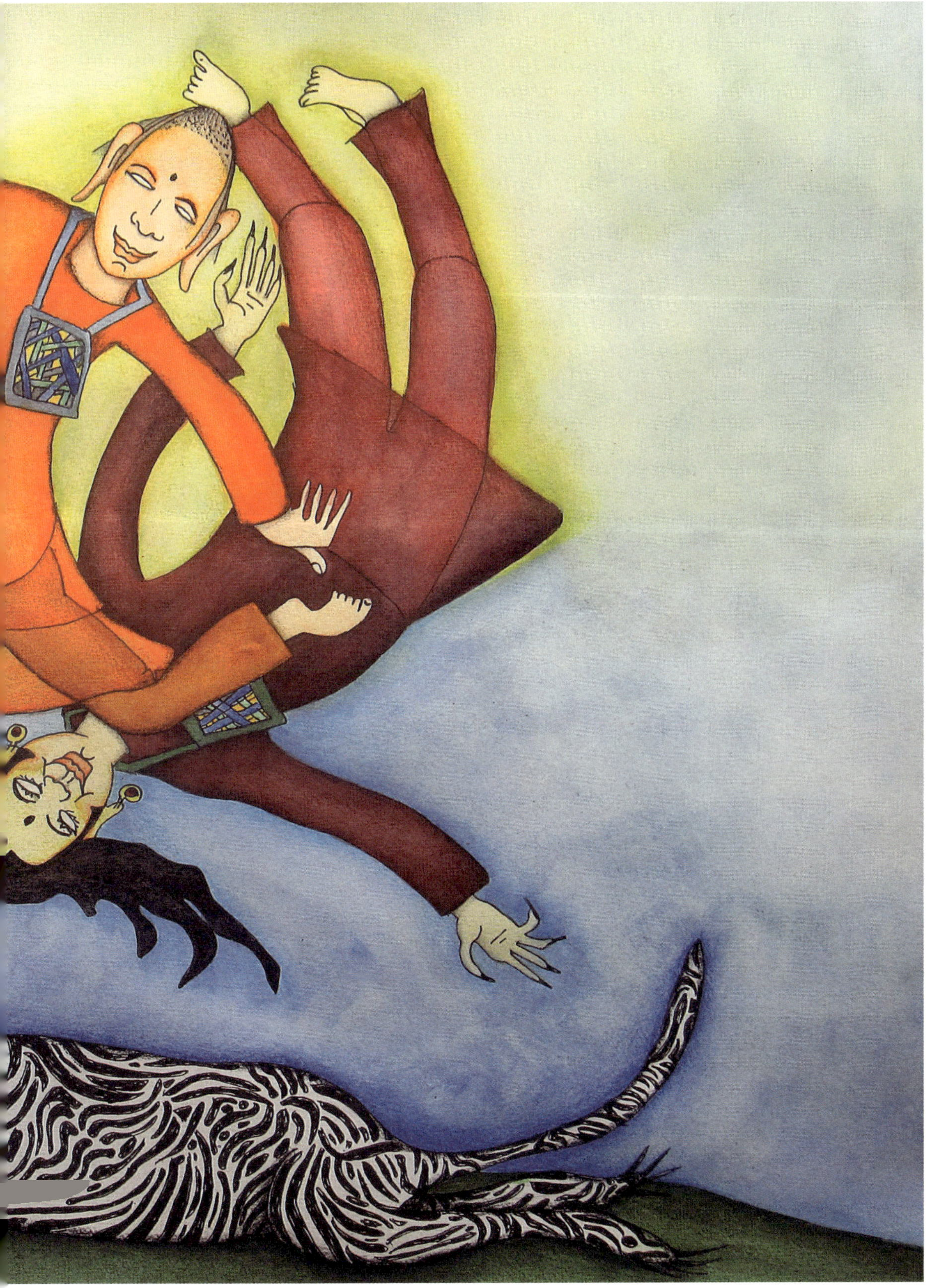

*Dancing on the Tiger*, 2011
50 × 65 cm

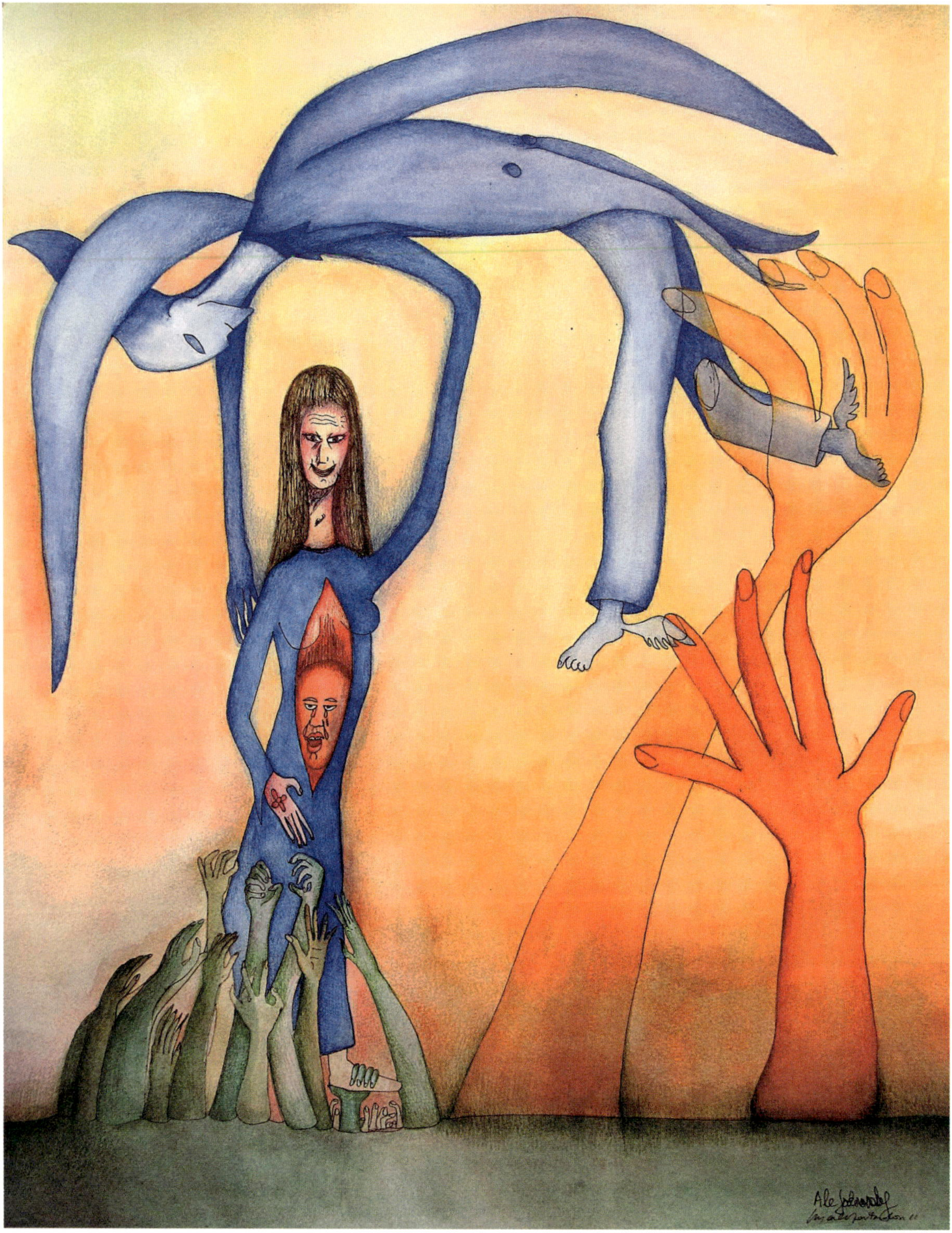

*Body, Soul and Mind*, 2011
65 × 50 cm

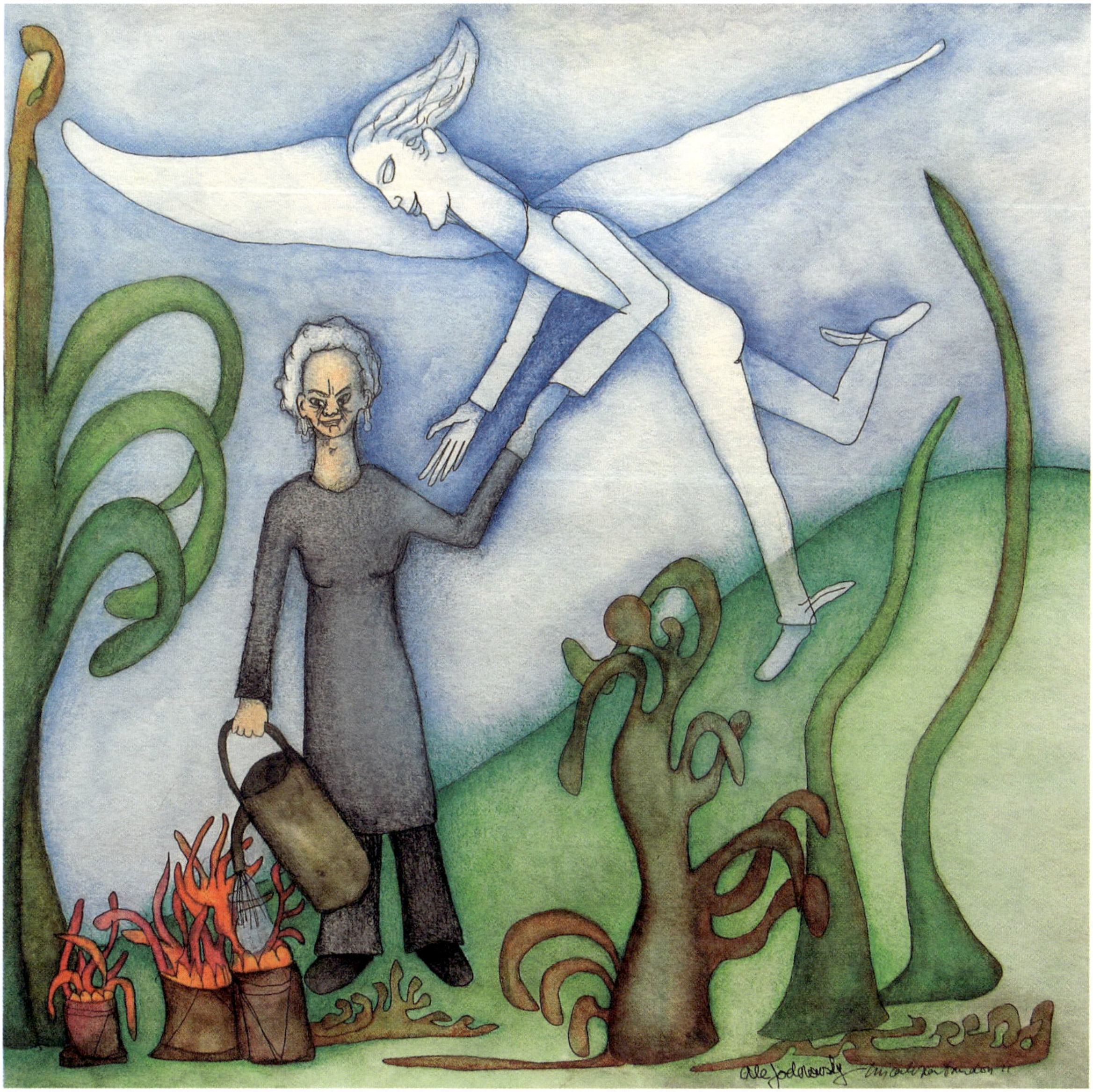

*Eternal Love*, 2011
40 × 40 cm

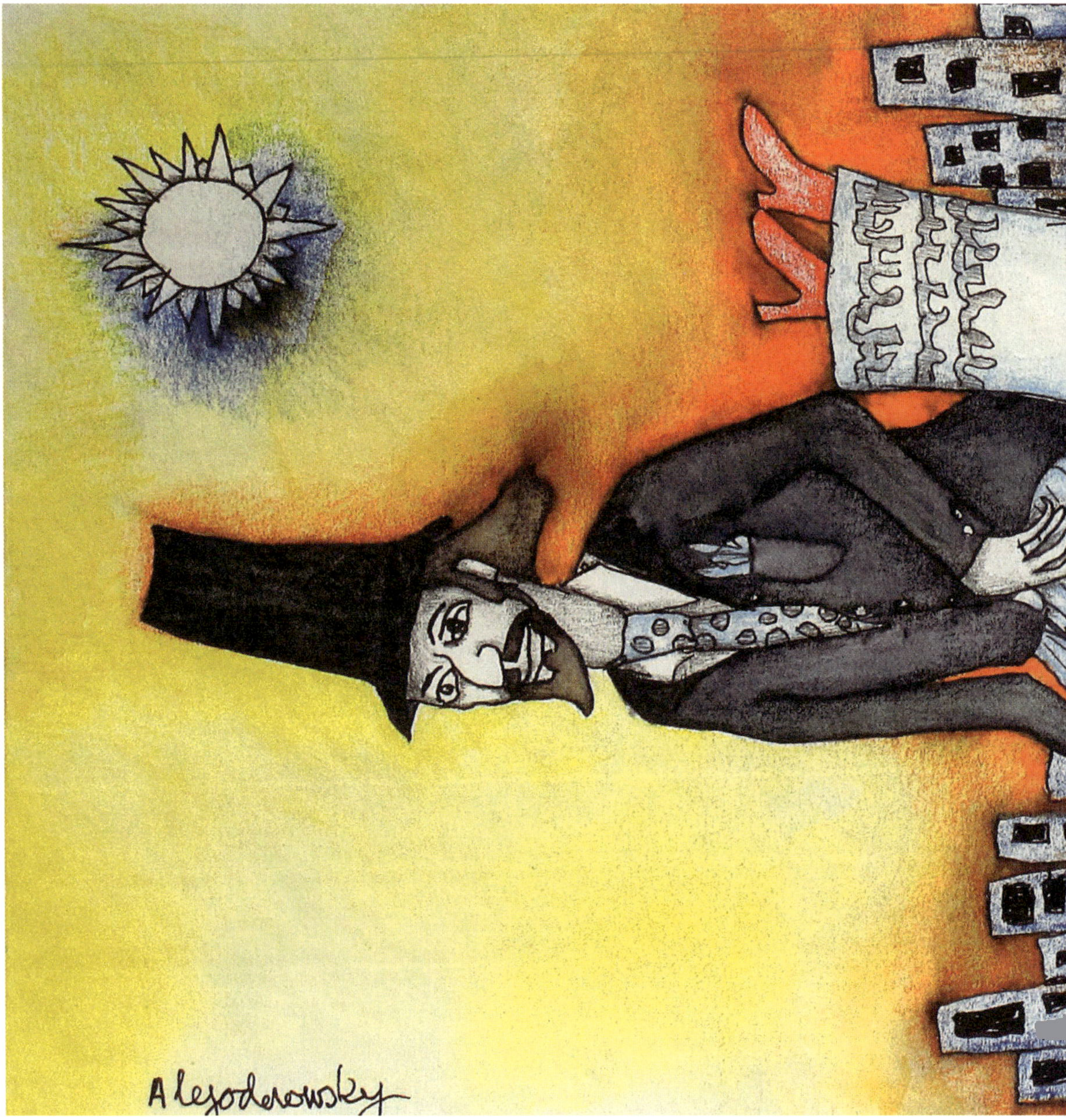

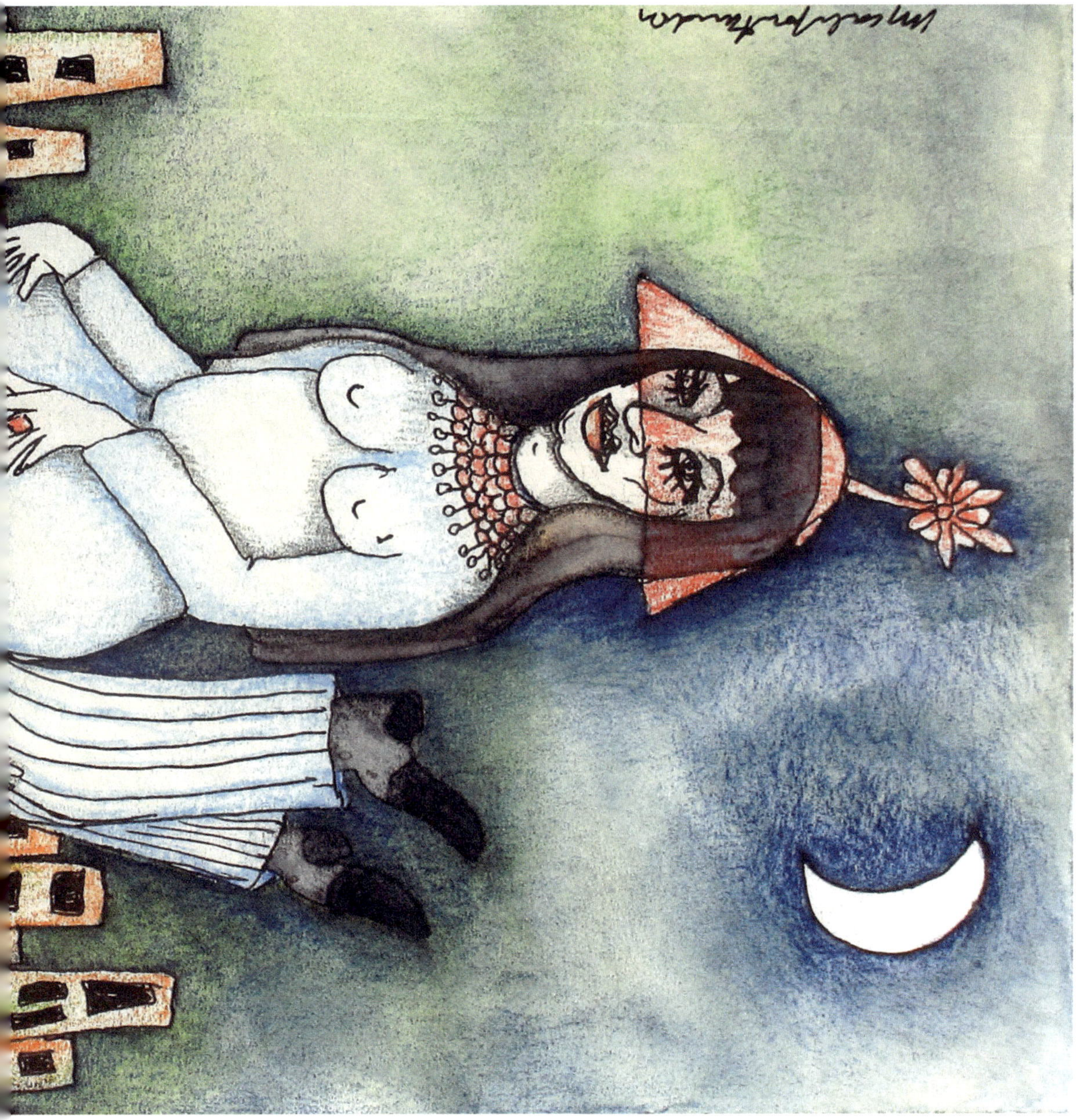

*The Wedding*, 2010
15 × 30 cm

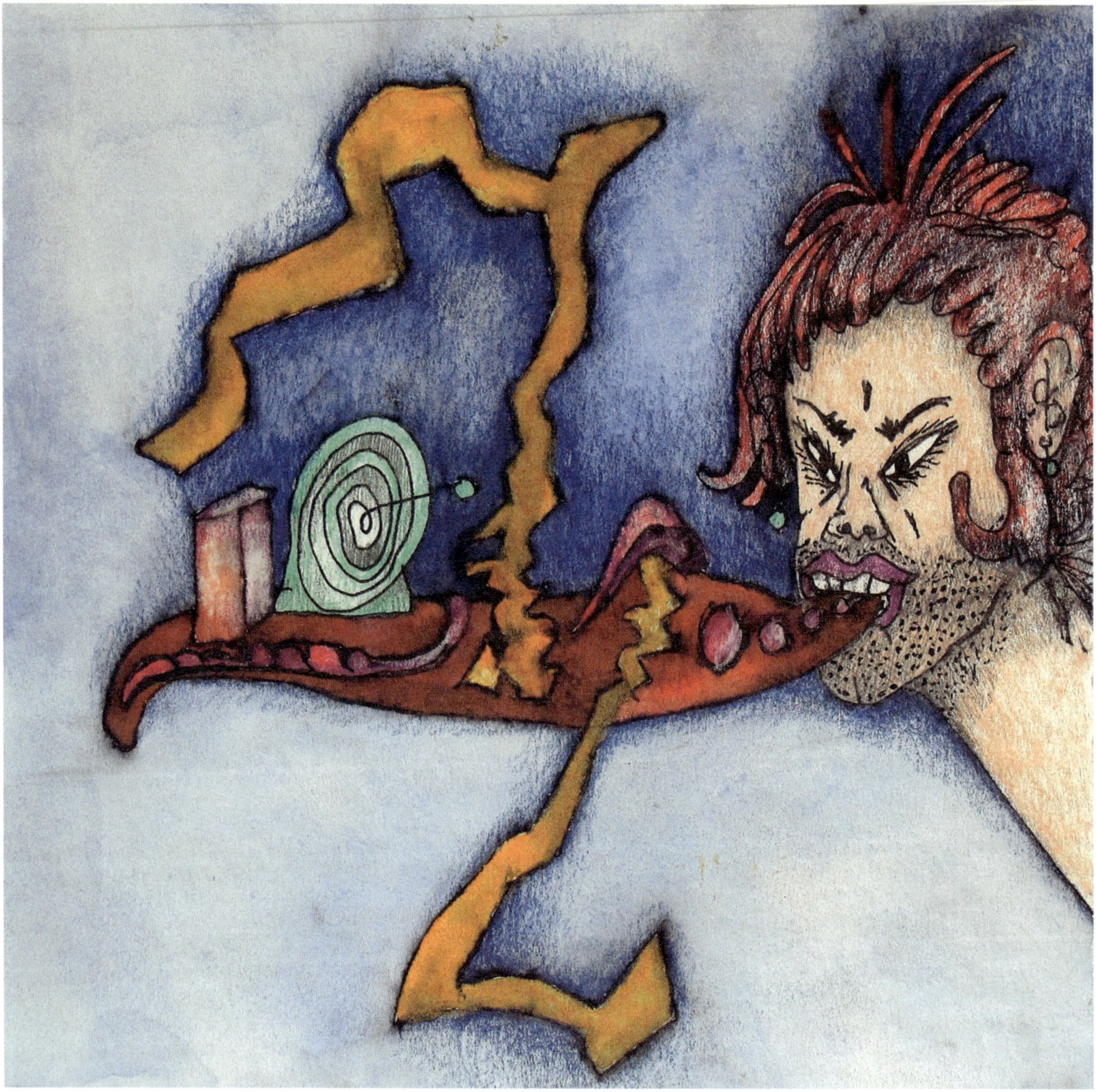

*Ill Tongued*, 2010
15 × 15 cm

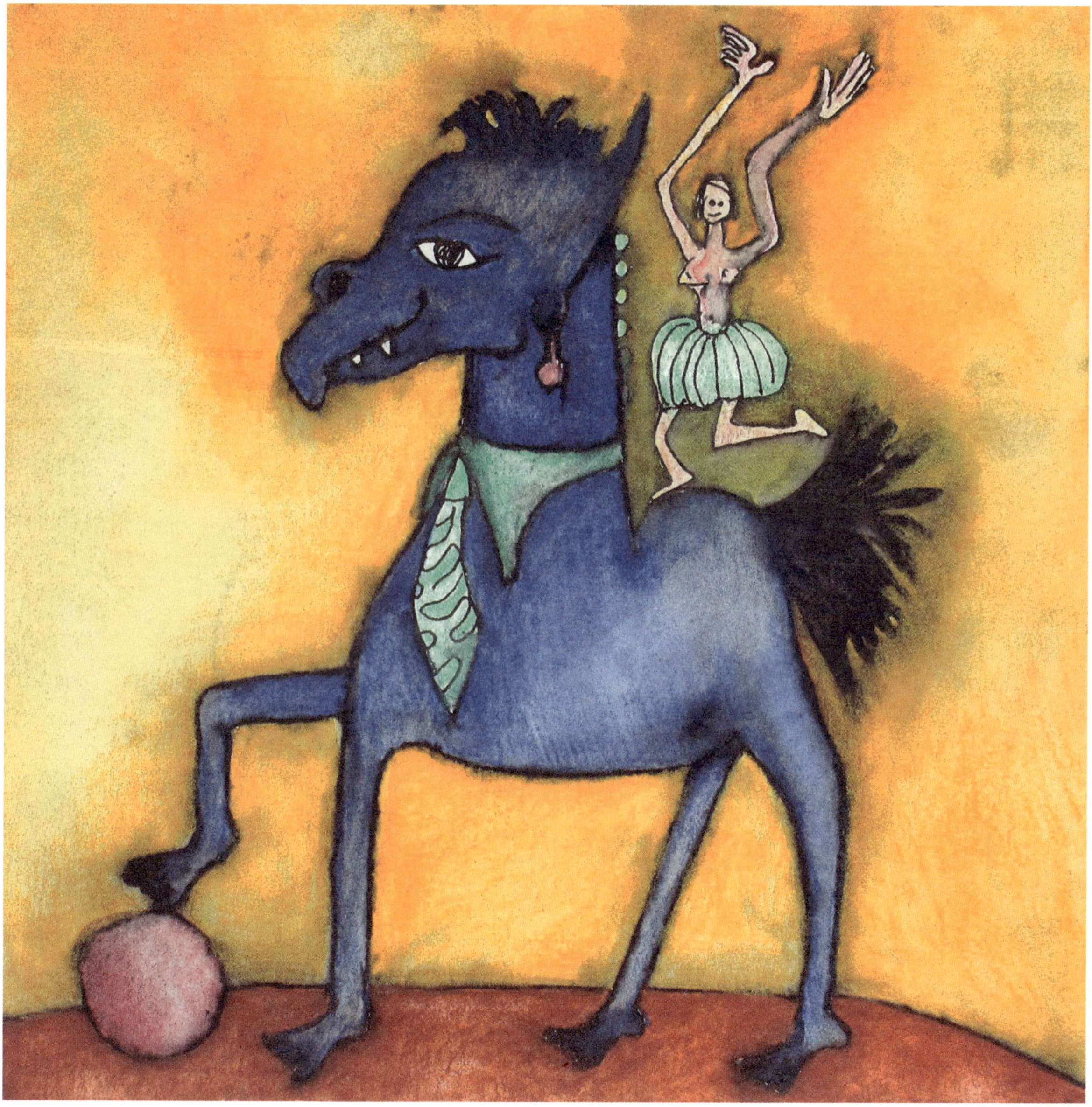

*The Joy of Circuses*, 2010
15 × 15 cm

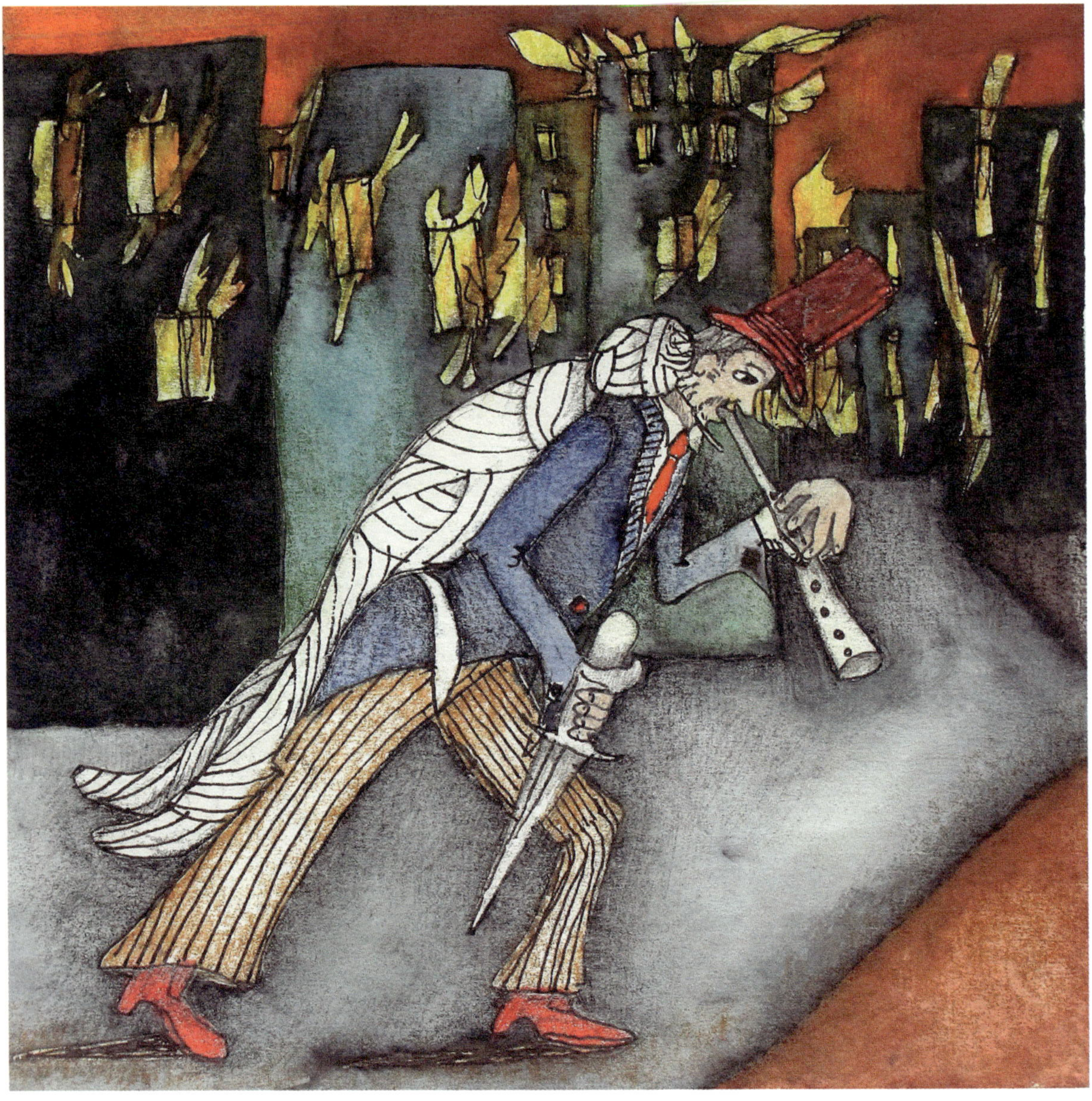

*The Parricide*, 2010
15 × 15 cm

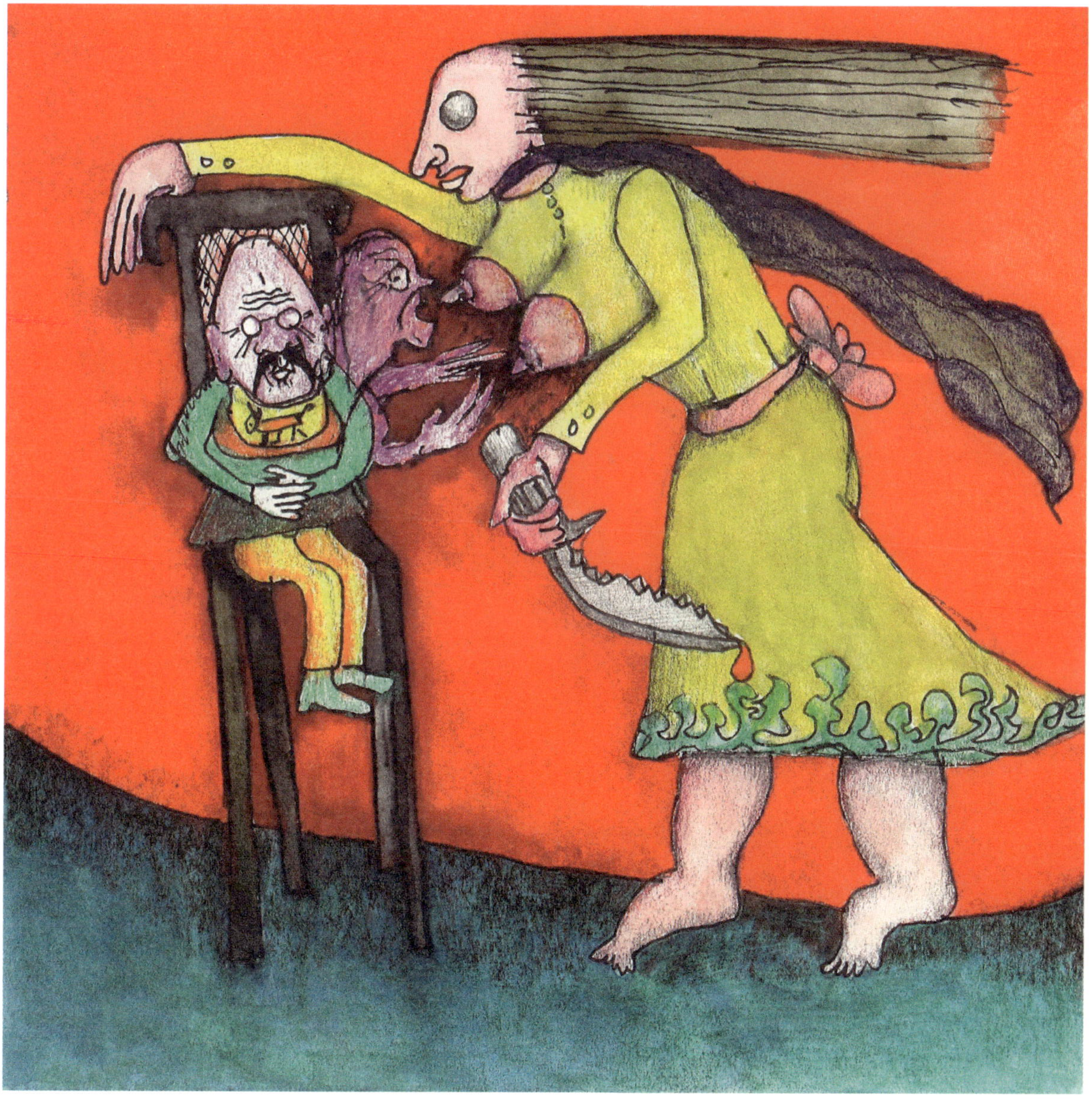

*The Grandfather's Breakfast*, 2010
15 × 15 cm

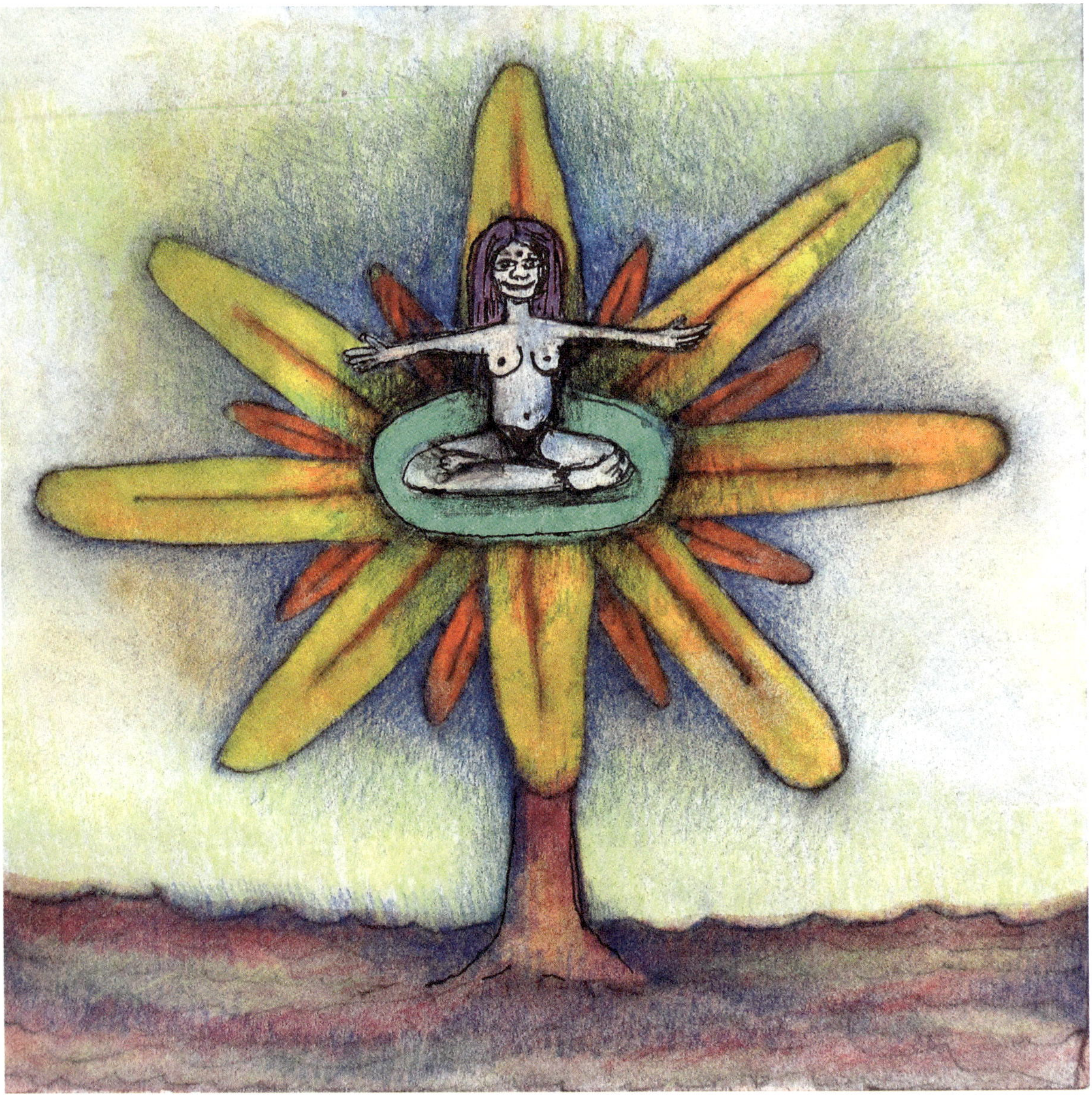

*Lotus Pearl*, 2010
15 × 15 cm

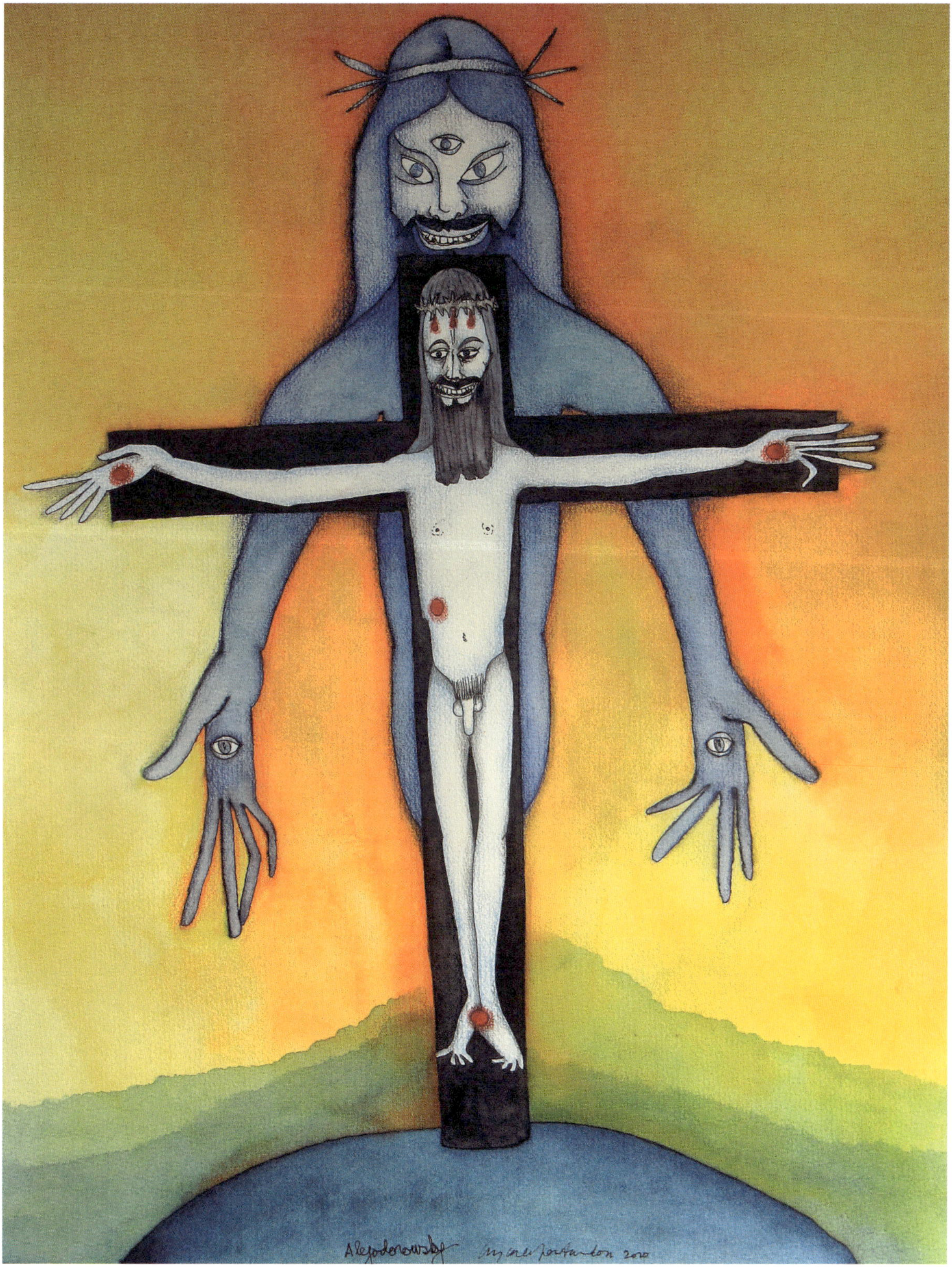

*Father and Son*, 2010
56 × 42 cm

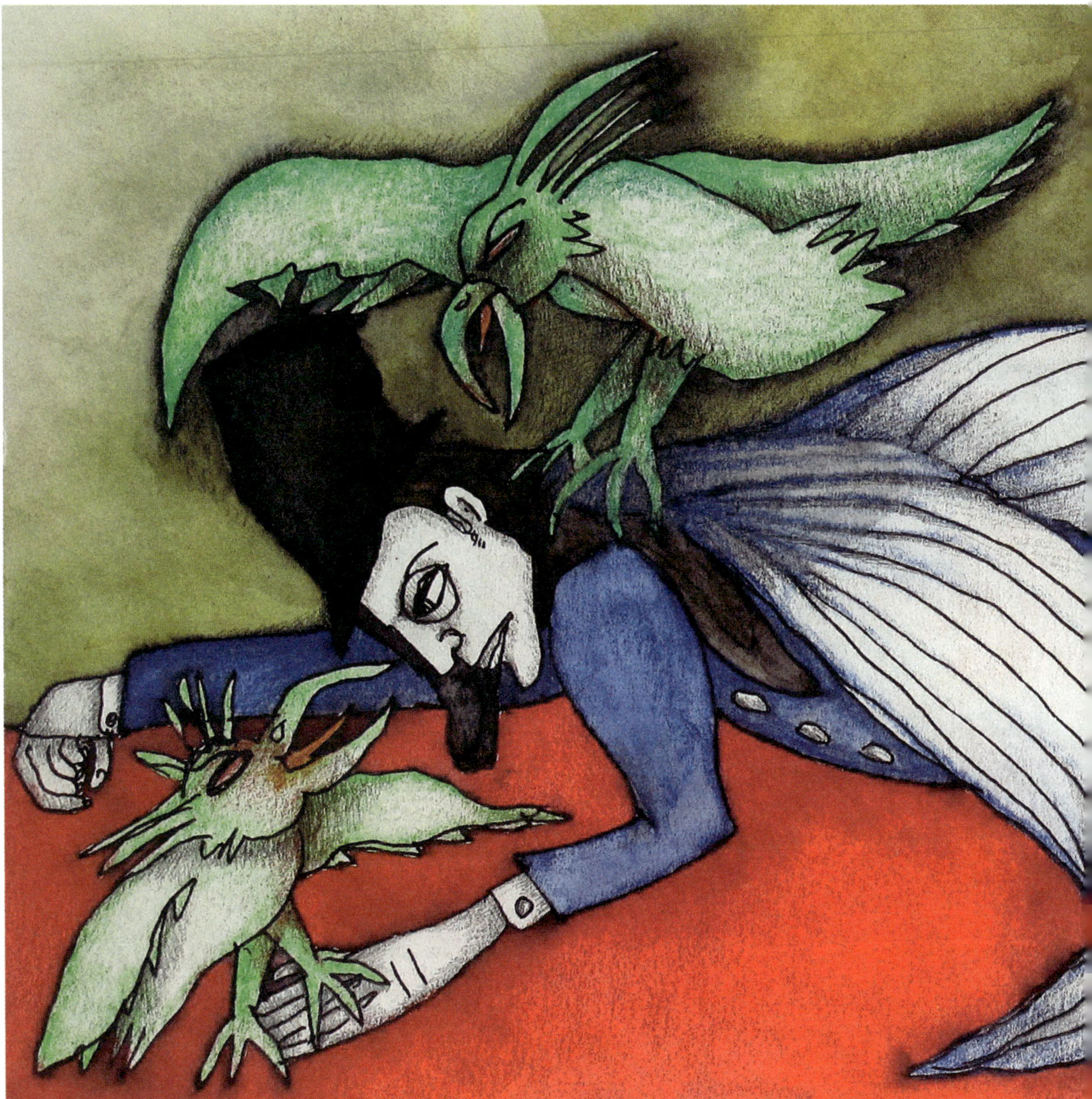

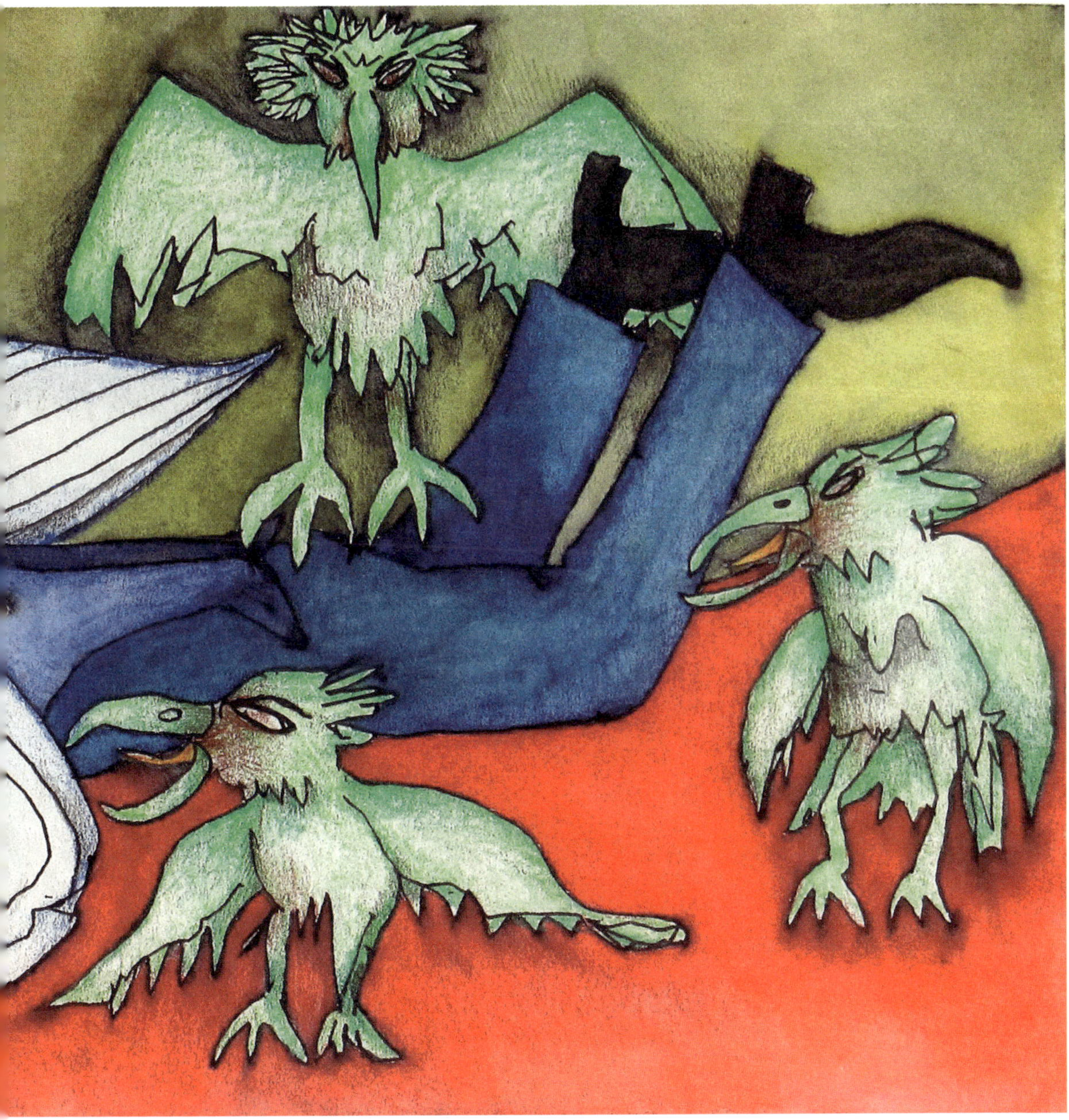

*Angelivorous Birds*, 2010
15 × 30 cm

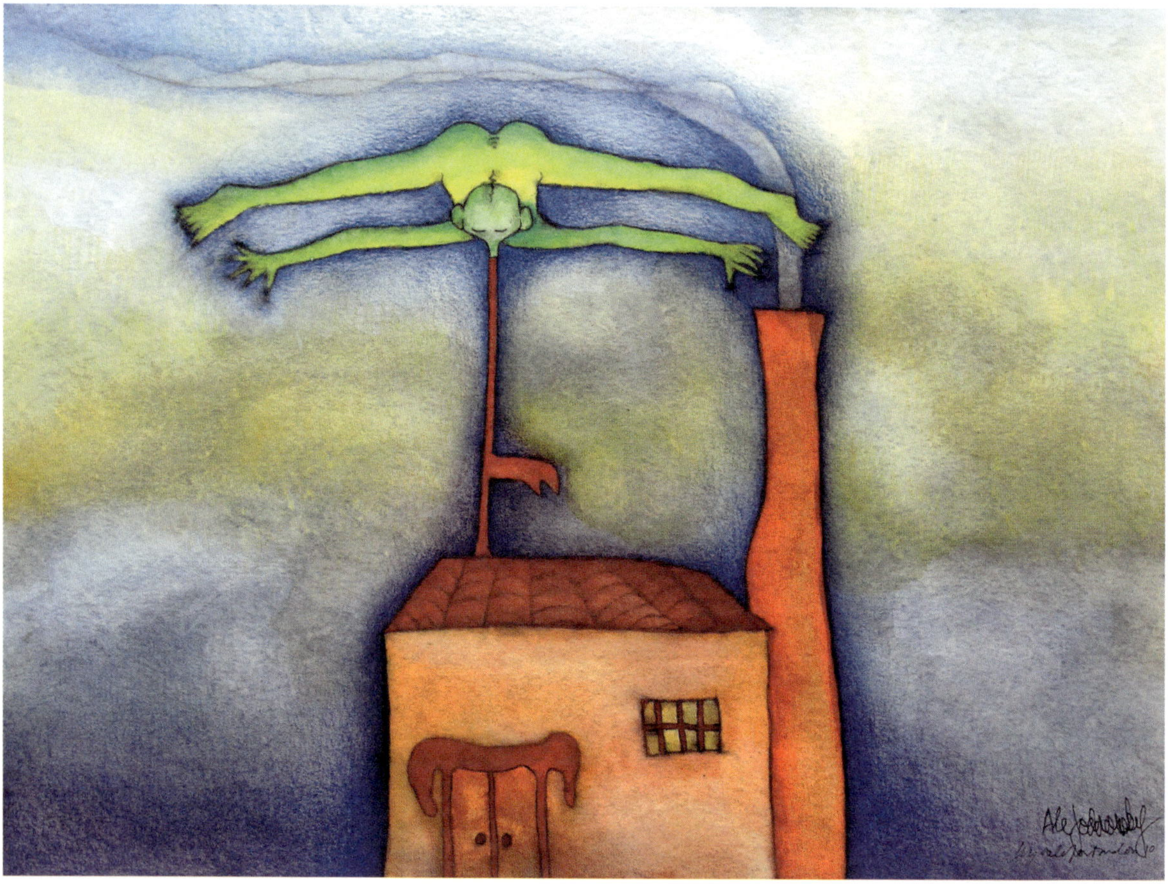

*Balancing on the Roof*, 2010
32 × 41 cm

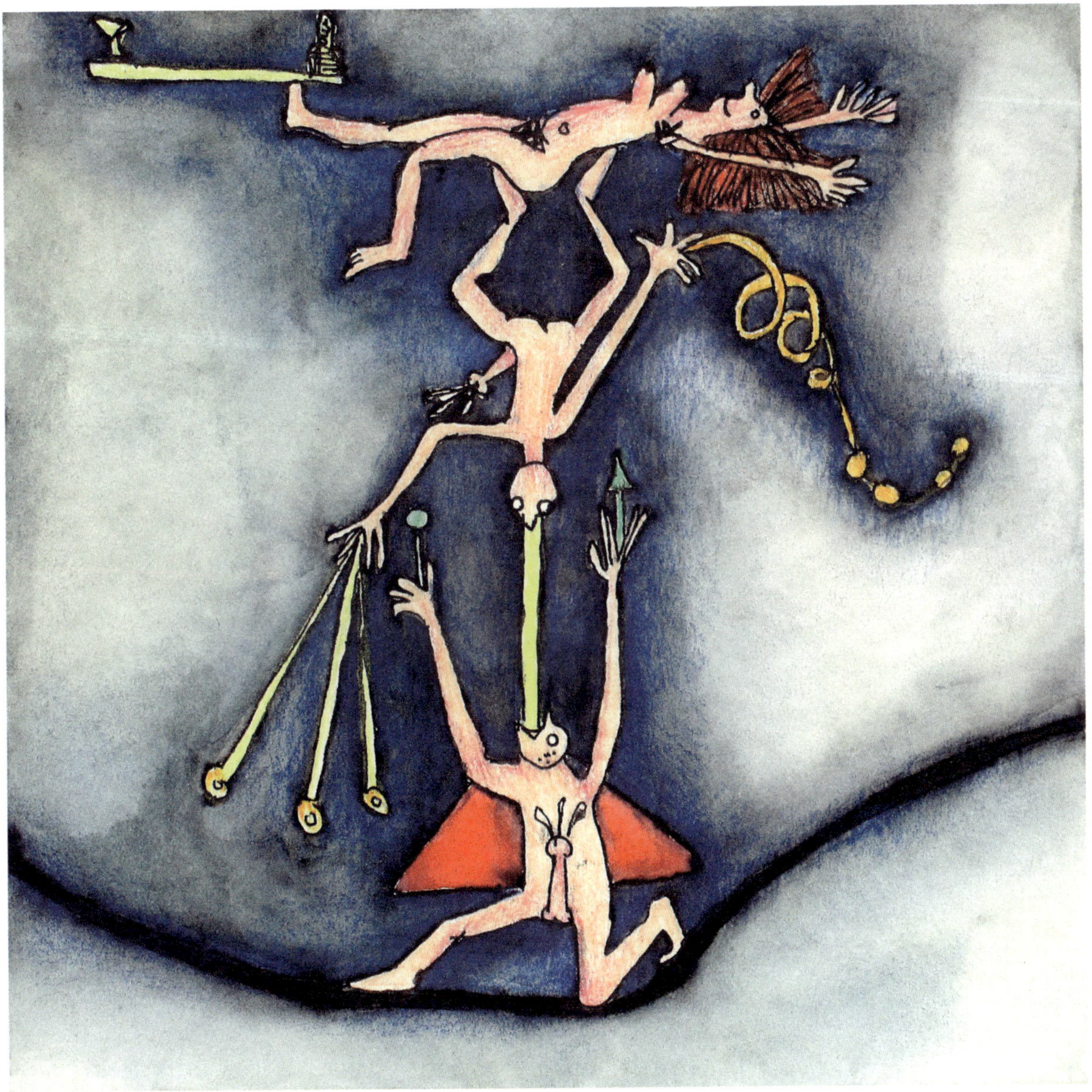

*Tightrope Porno*, 2010
15 × 15 cm

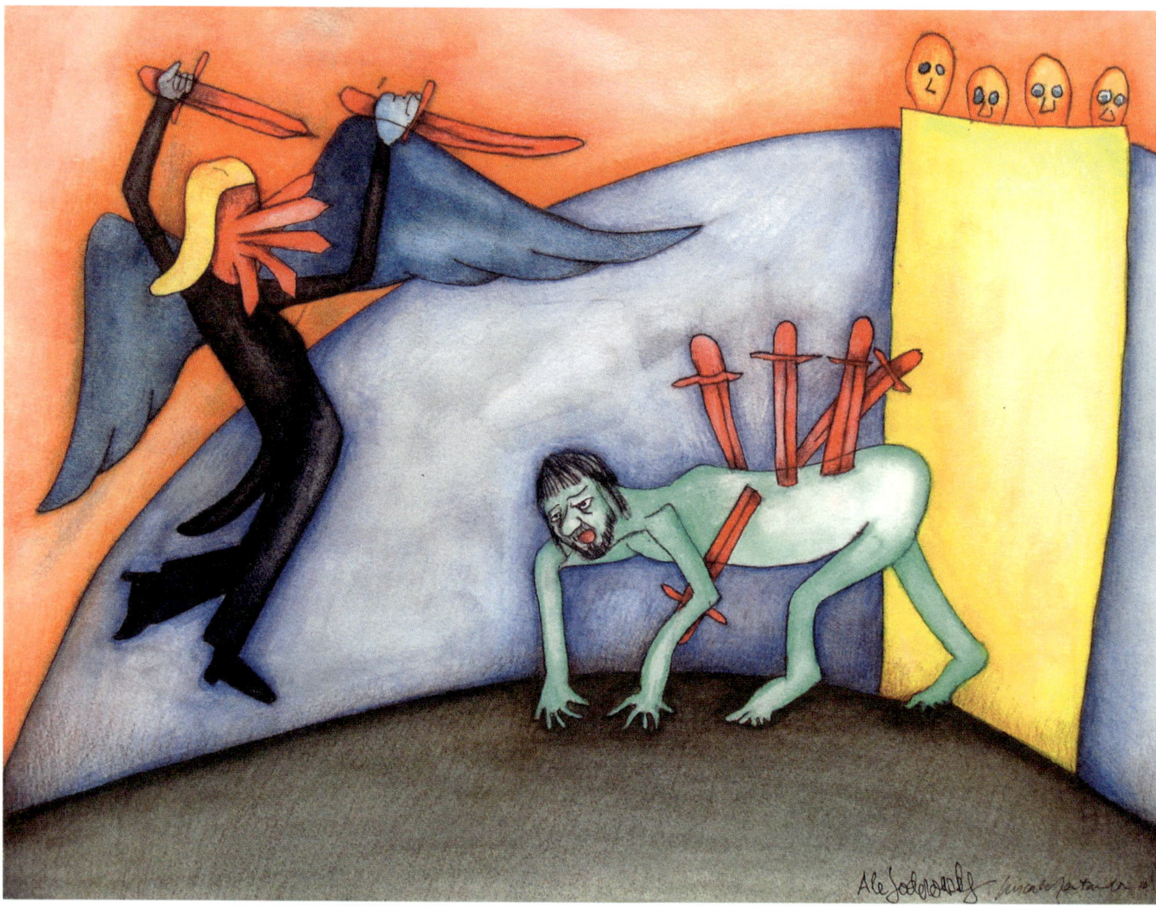

*Andro Corrida 1*, 2010
32 × 41 cm

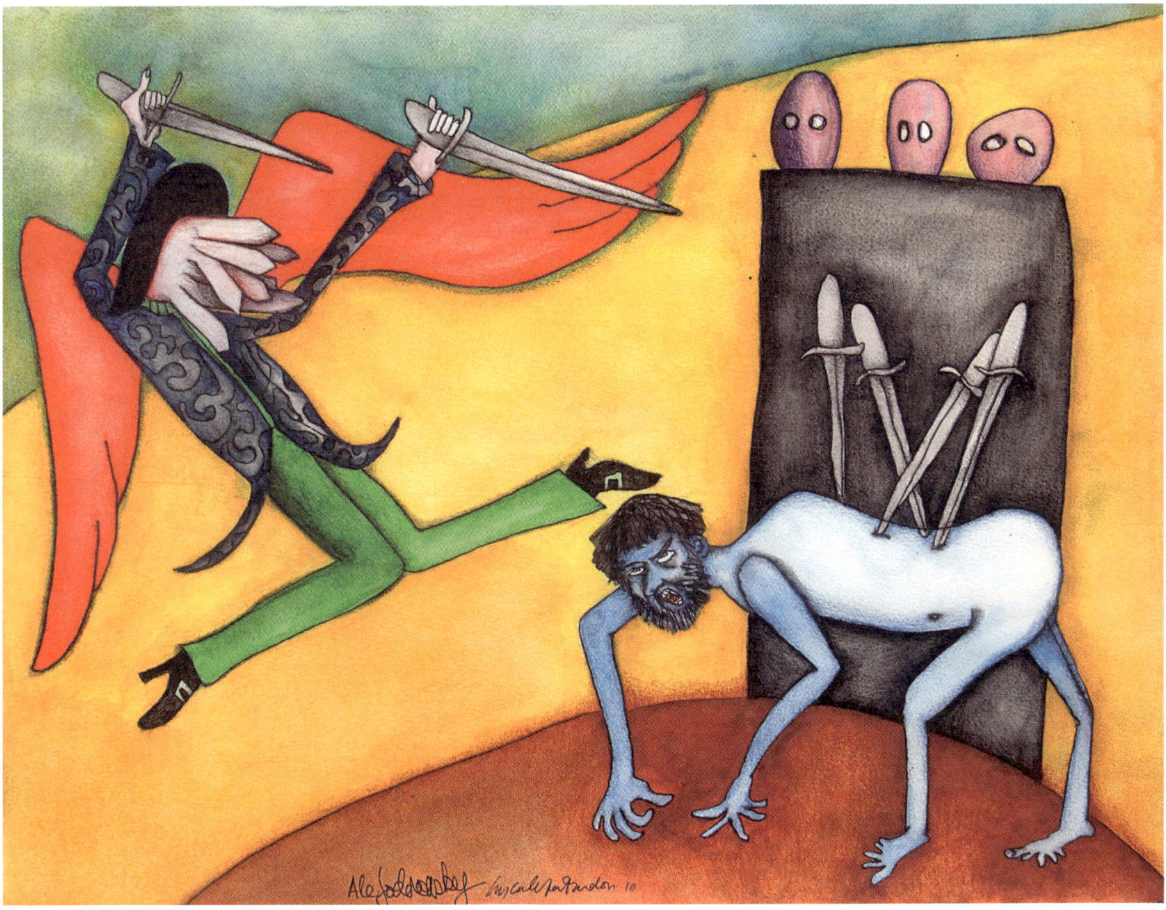

*Andro Corrida 2*, 2010
32 × 41 cm

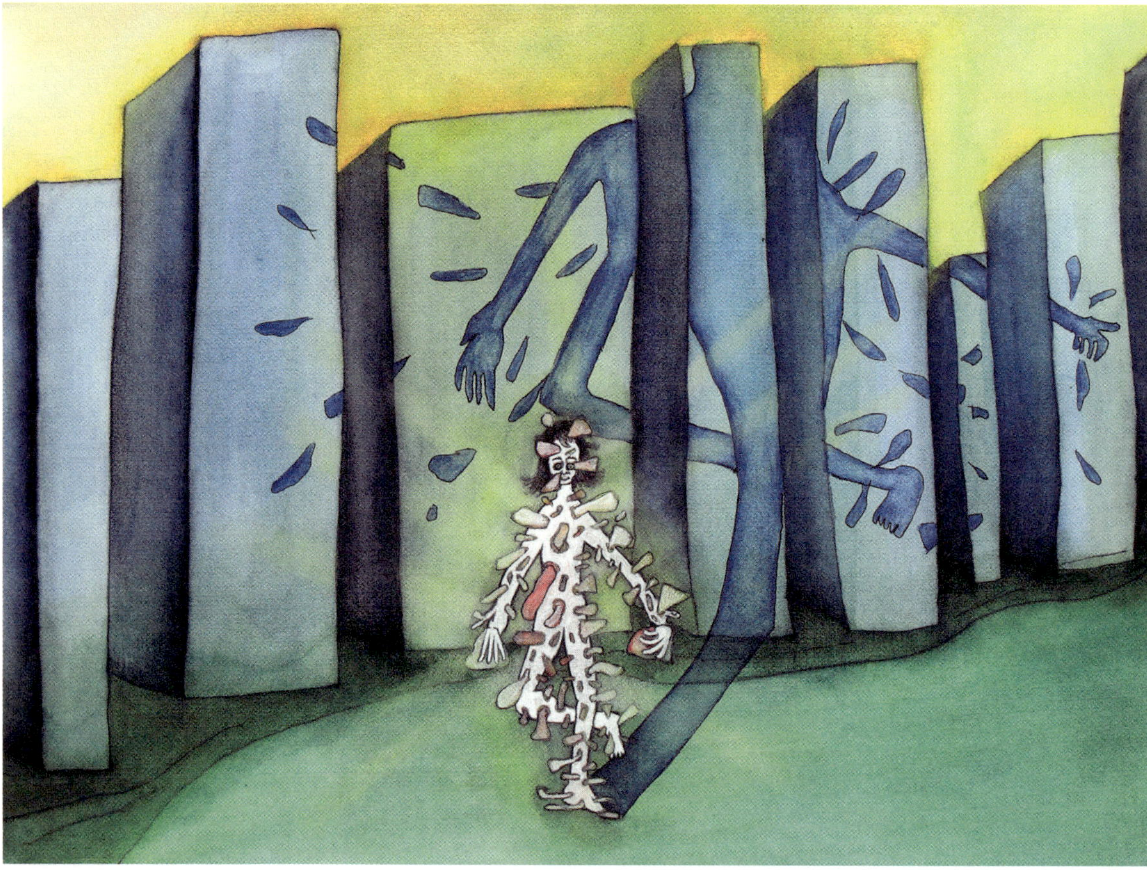

*The City Dweller*, 2010
42 × 56 cm

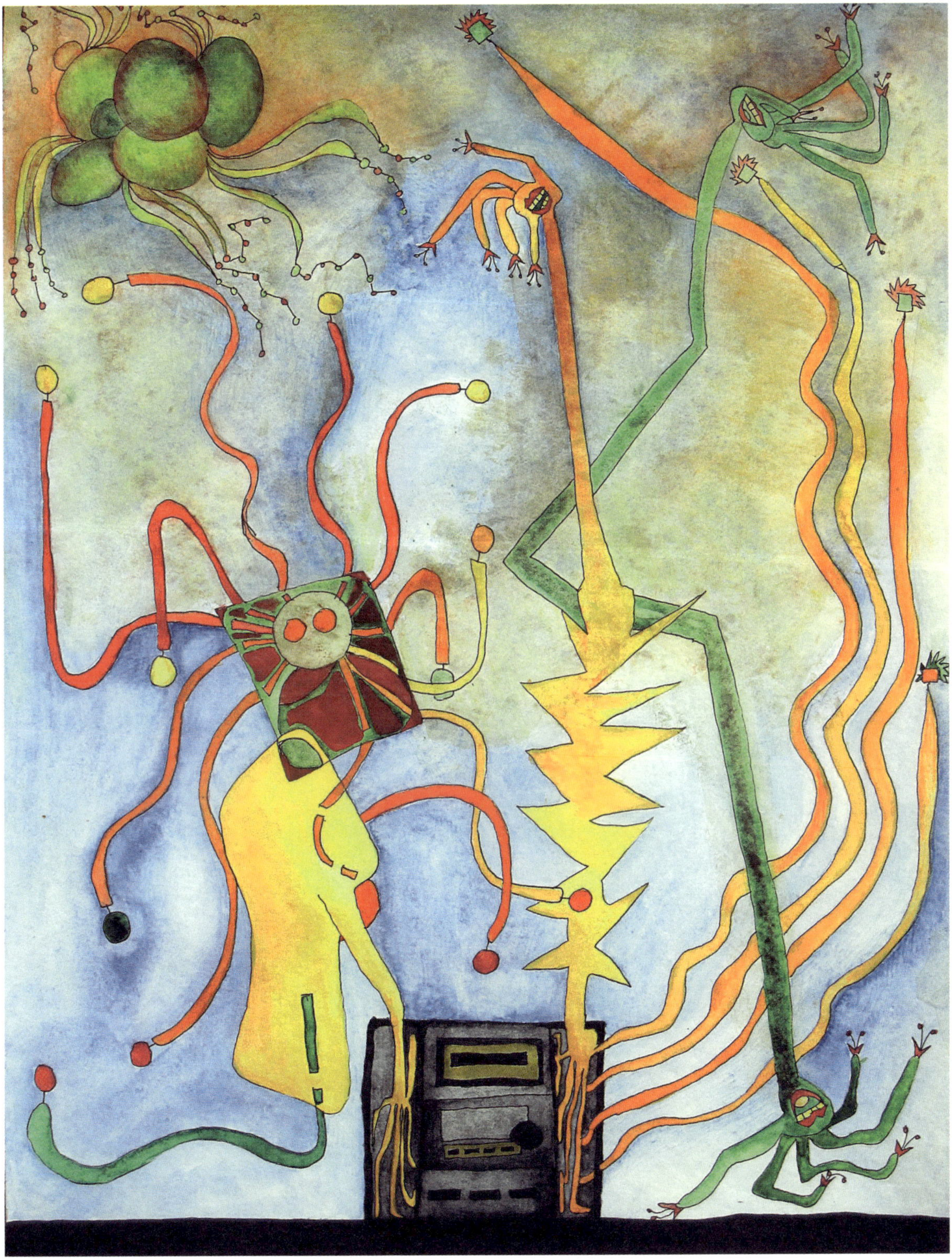

*Crazy Radio*, 2009
48 × 36 cm

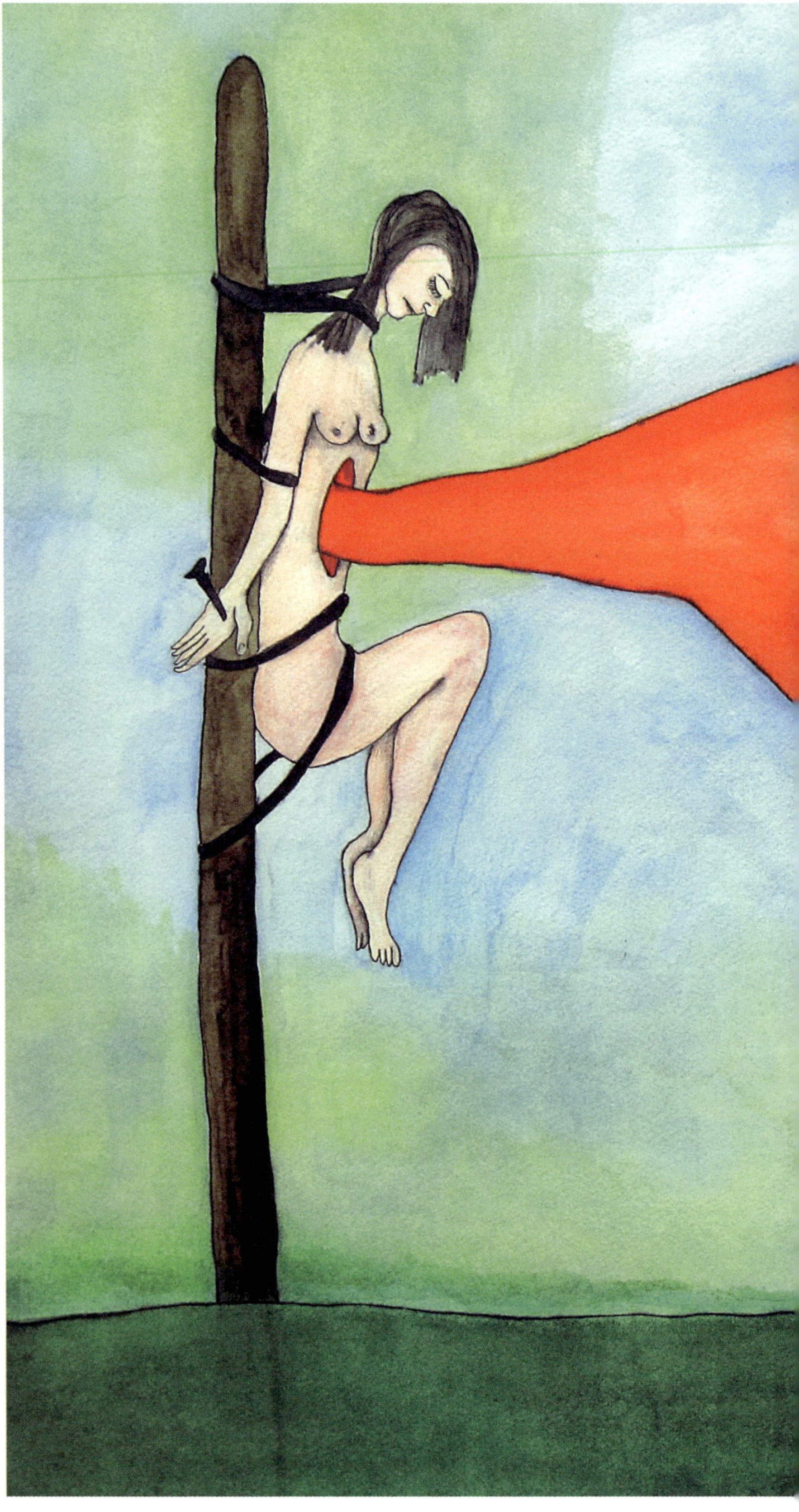

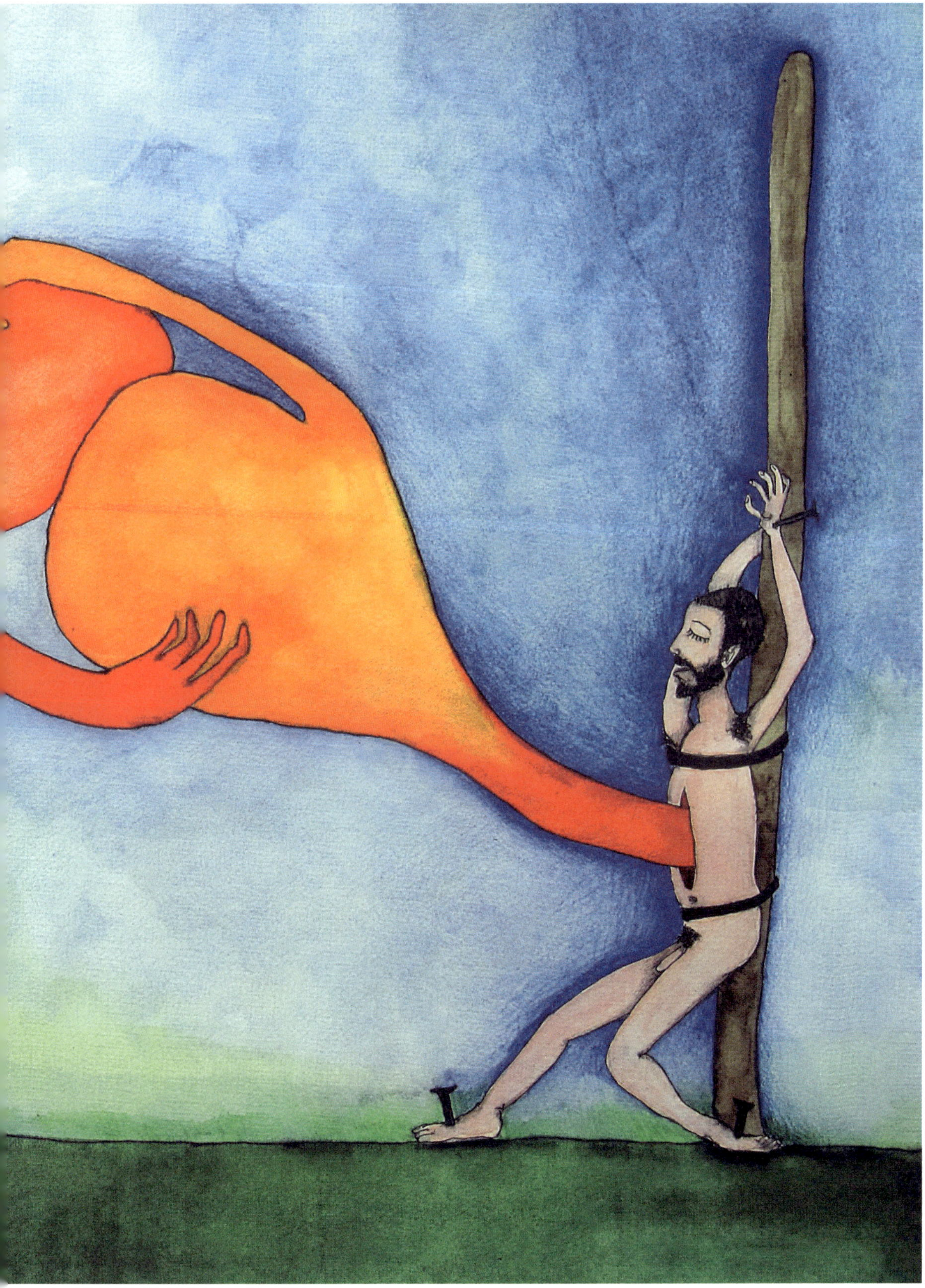

*Love Which Is Stronger Than Death*, 2009
50 × 65 cm

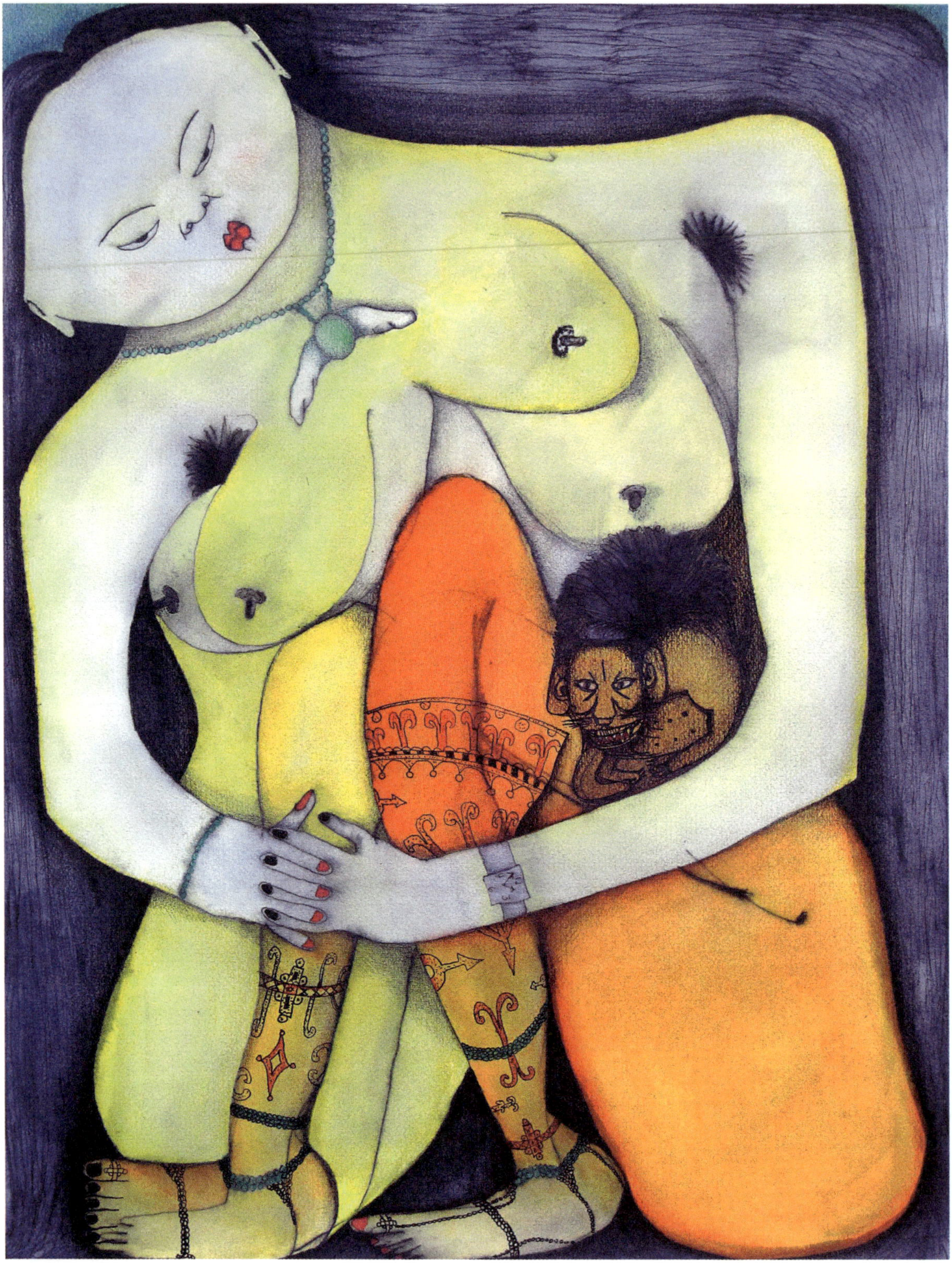

*Courtesan and Little Monster*, 2009
56 × 42 cm

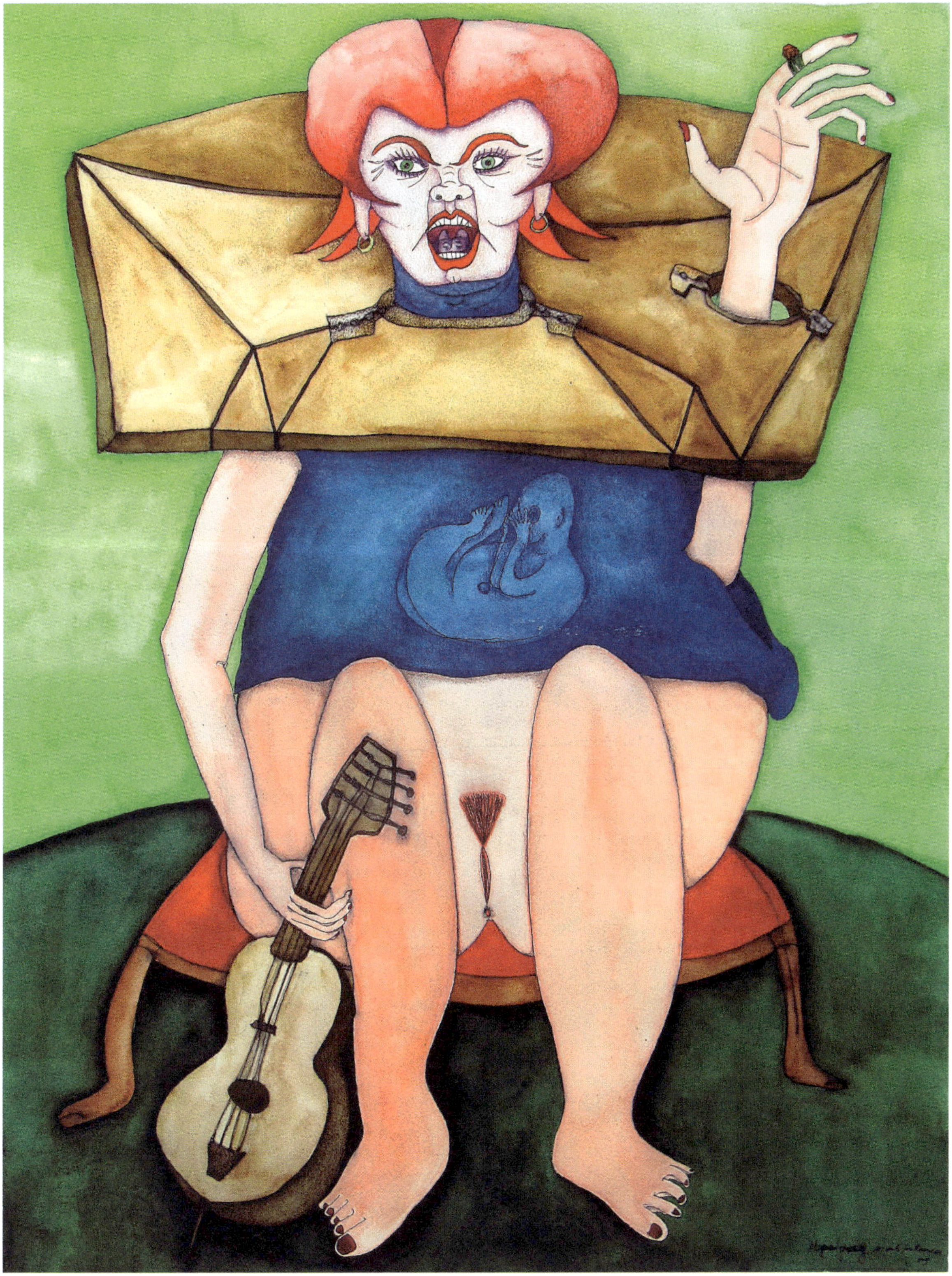

*The Scream*, 2009
76 × 56 cm

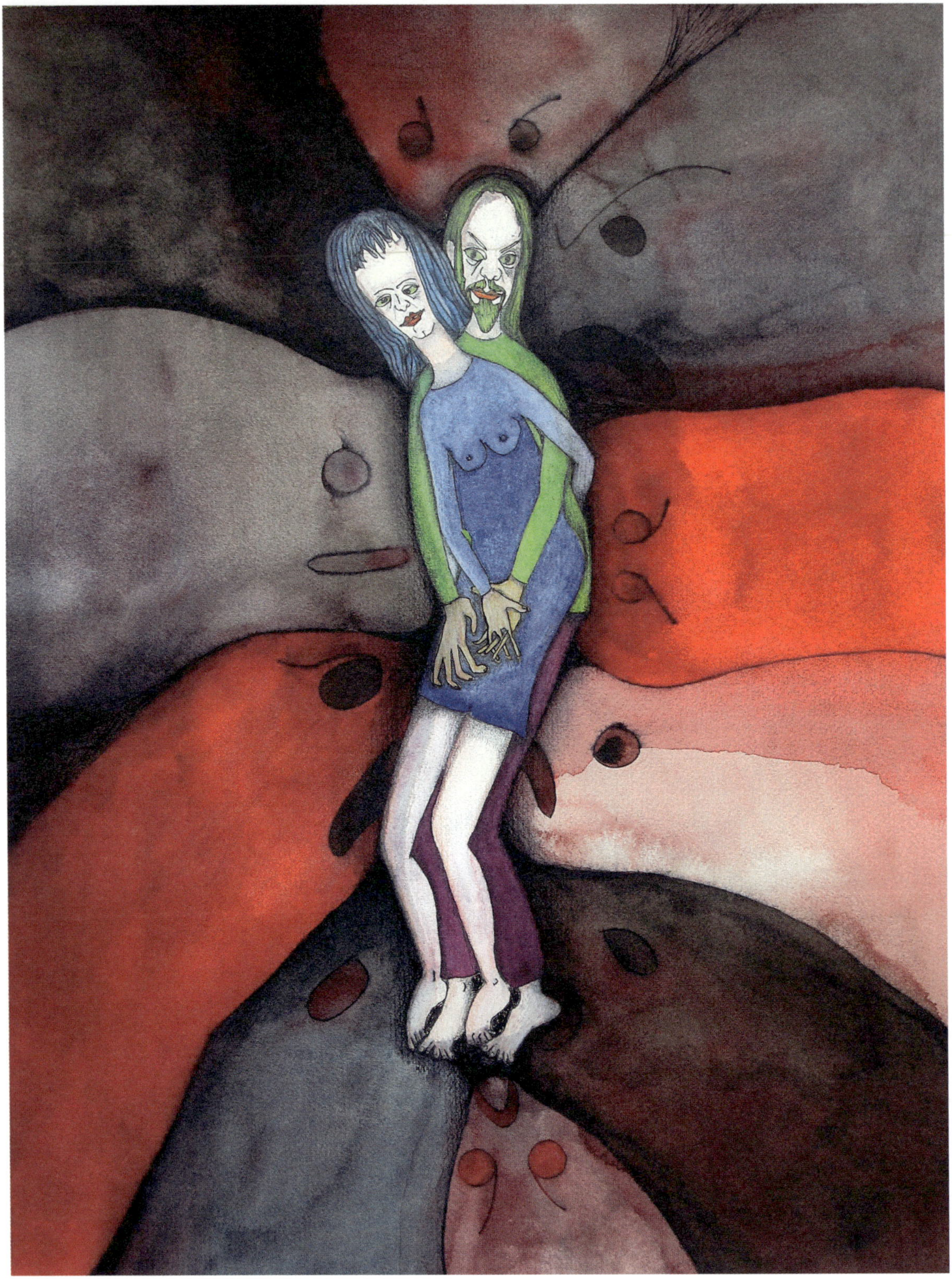

*Two against All*, 2009
56 × 42 cm

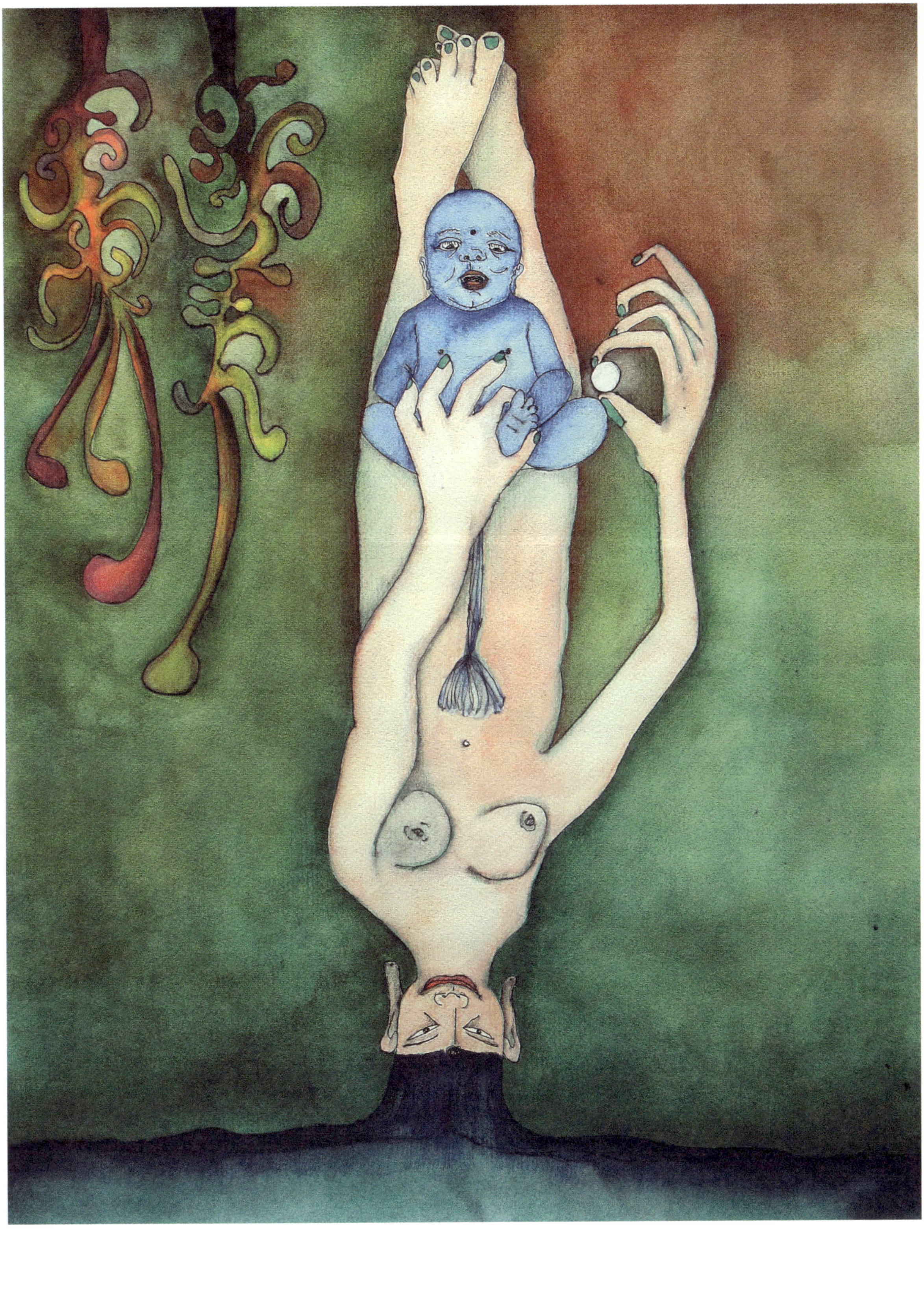

*Sacred Mother*, 2009
56 × 42 cm

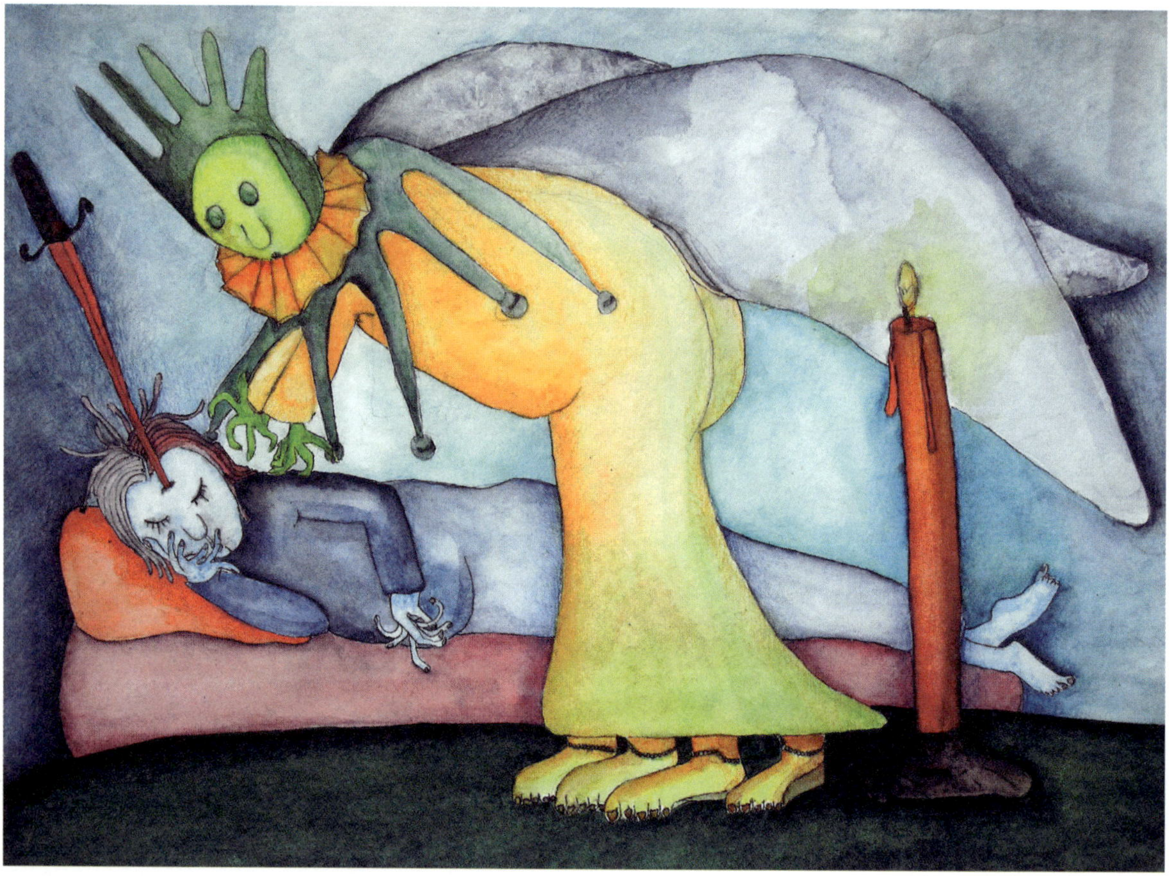

*Annunciation*, 2009
36 × 48 cm

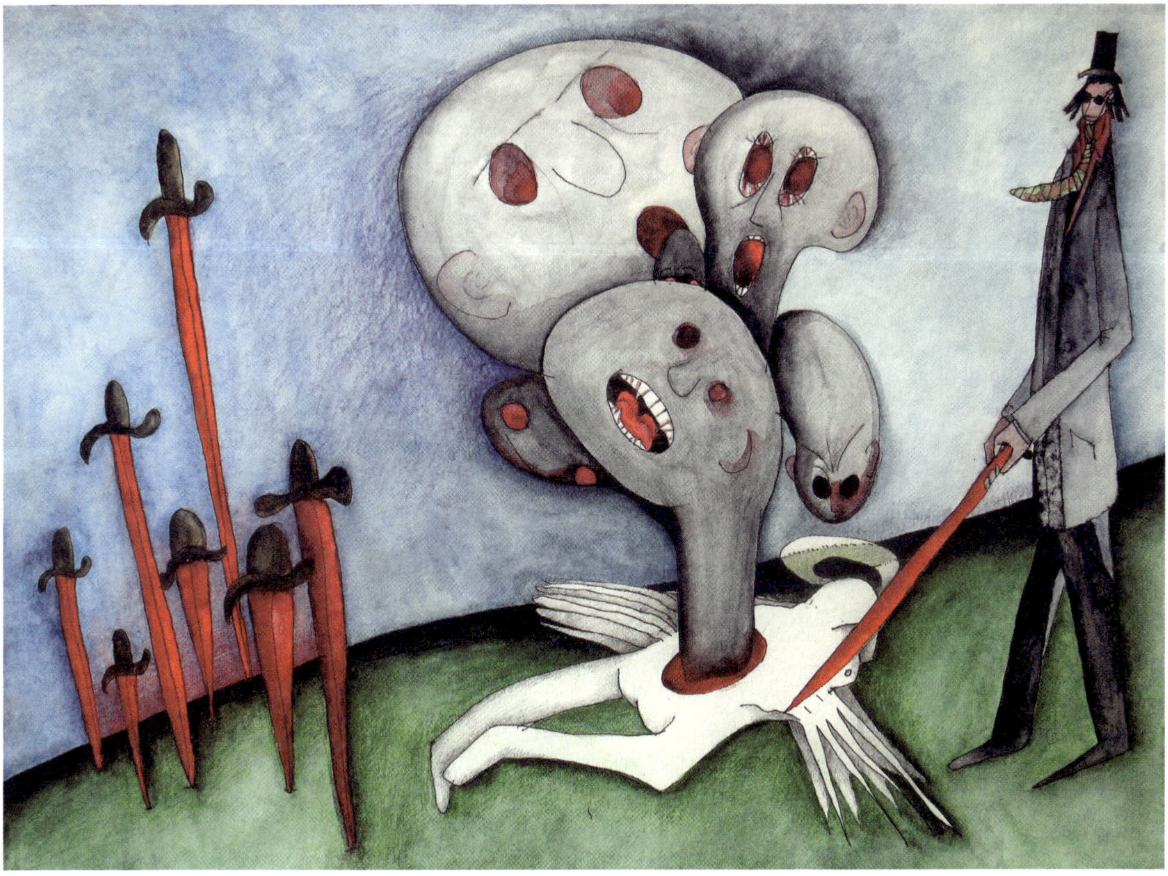

*Falling Angel*, 2009
36 × 48 cm

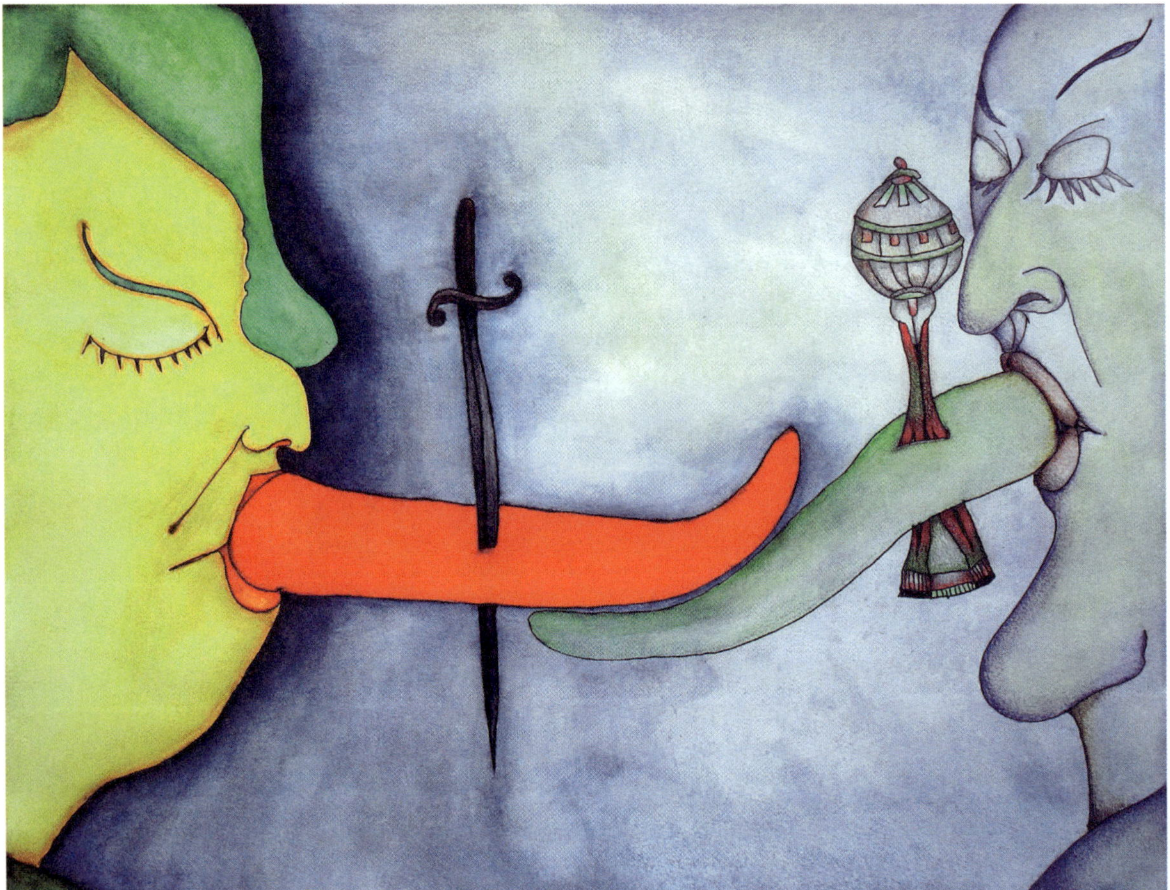

*Wise Tongues*, 2009
32 × 41 cm

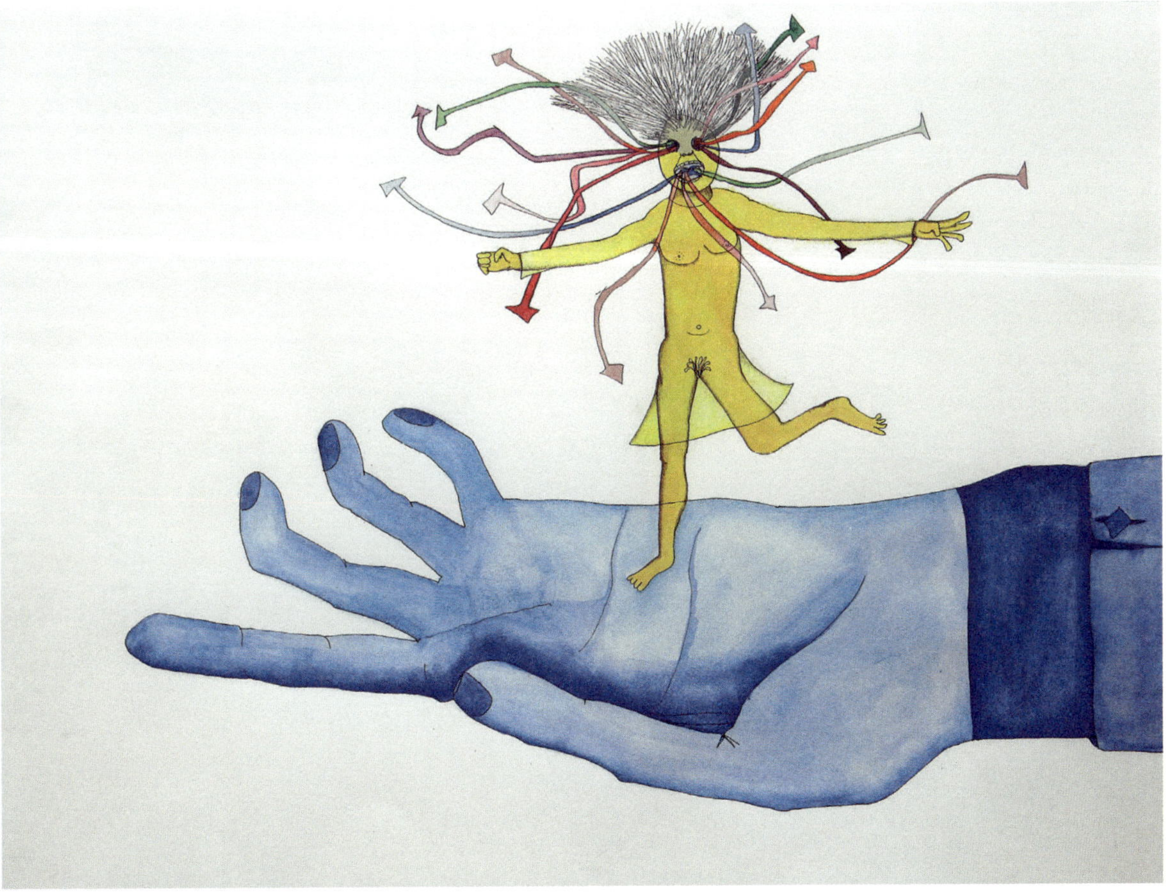

*In God's Hands*, 2009
50 × 65 cm

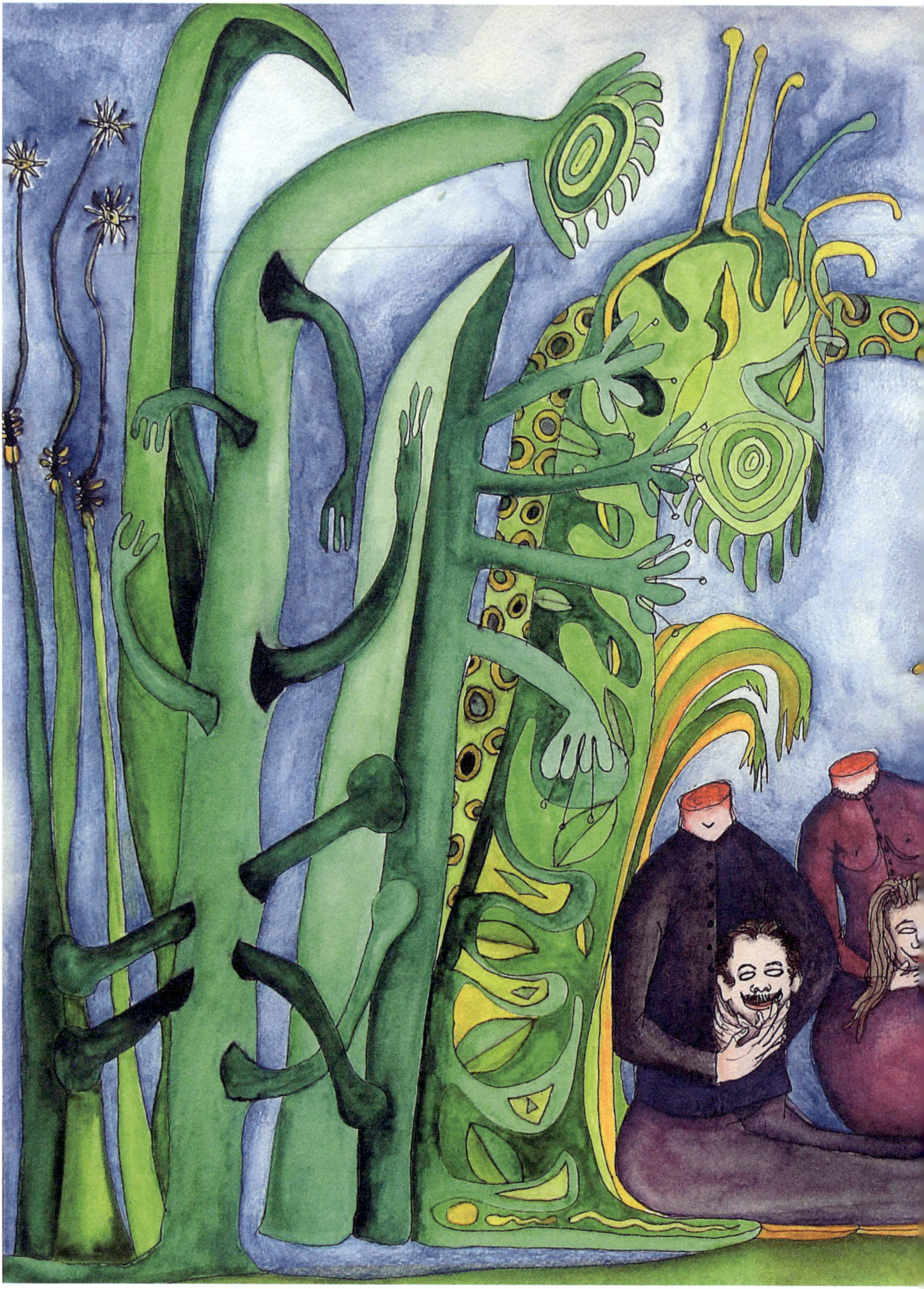

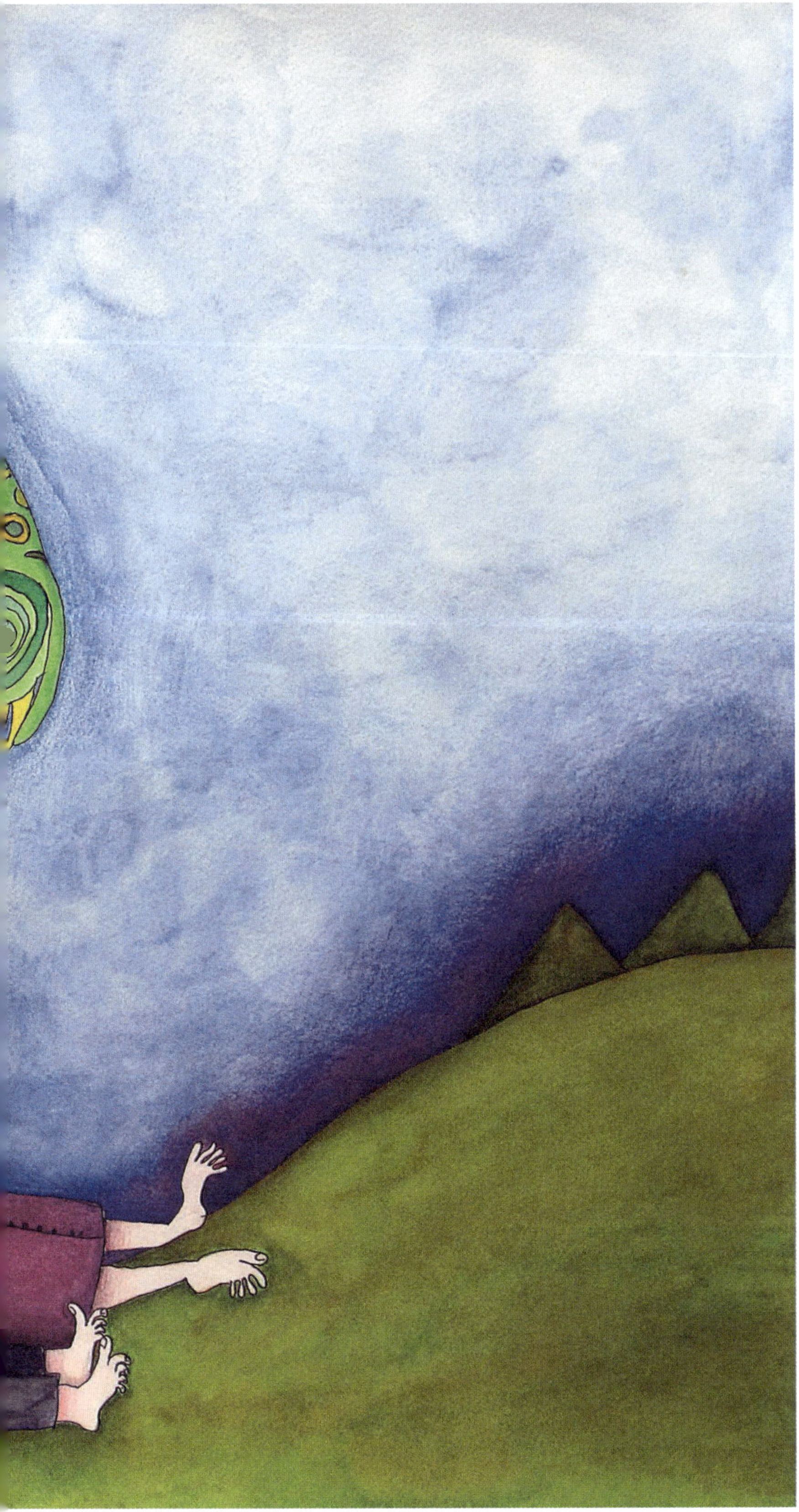

*Happy Corpses*, 2009
50 × 65 cm

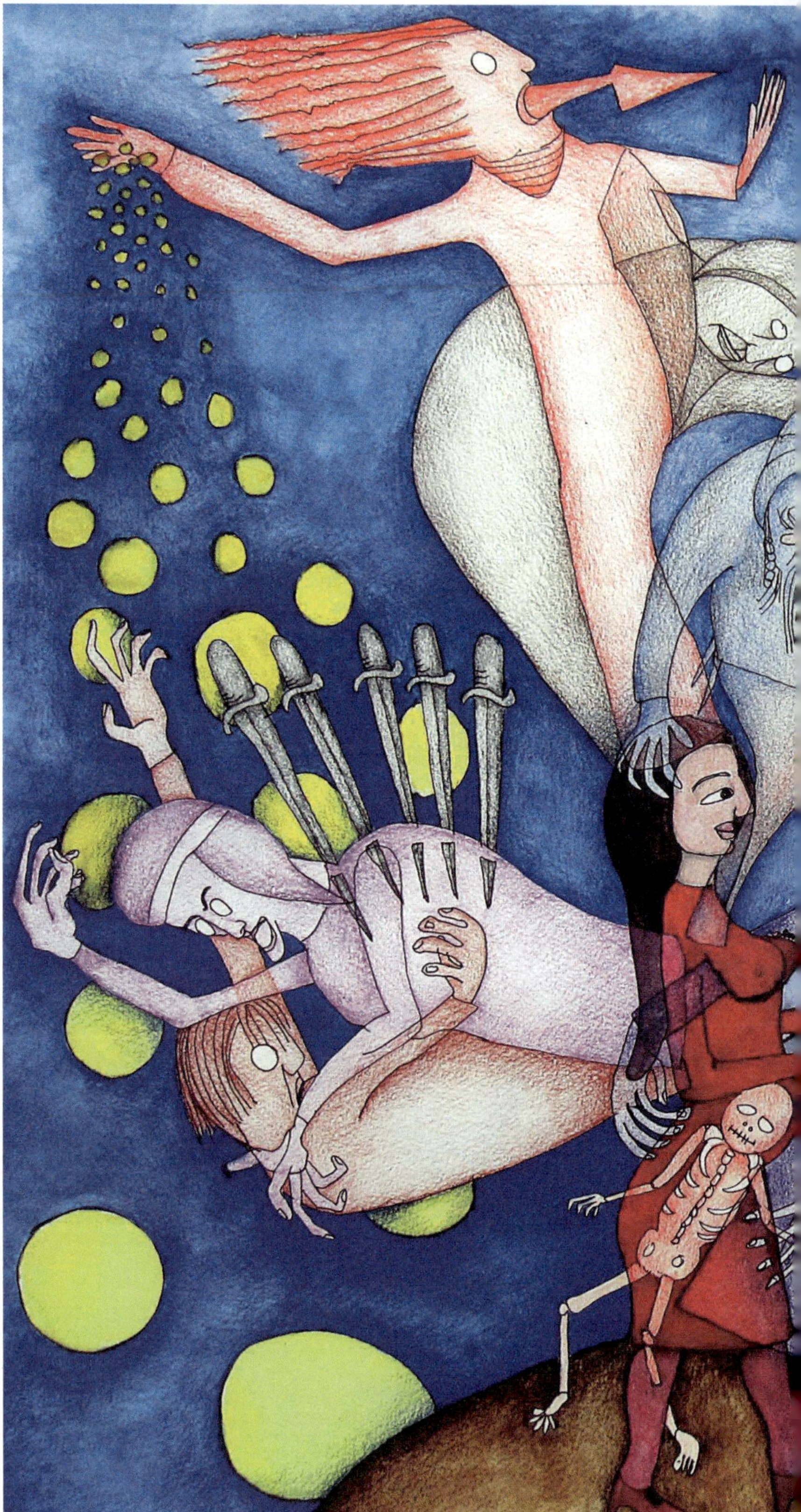

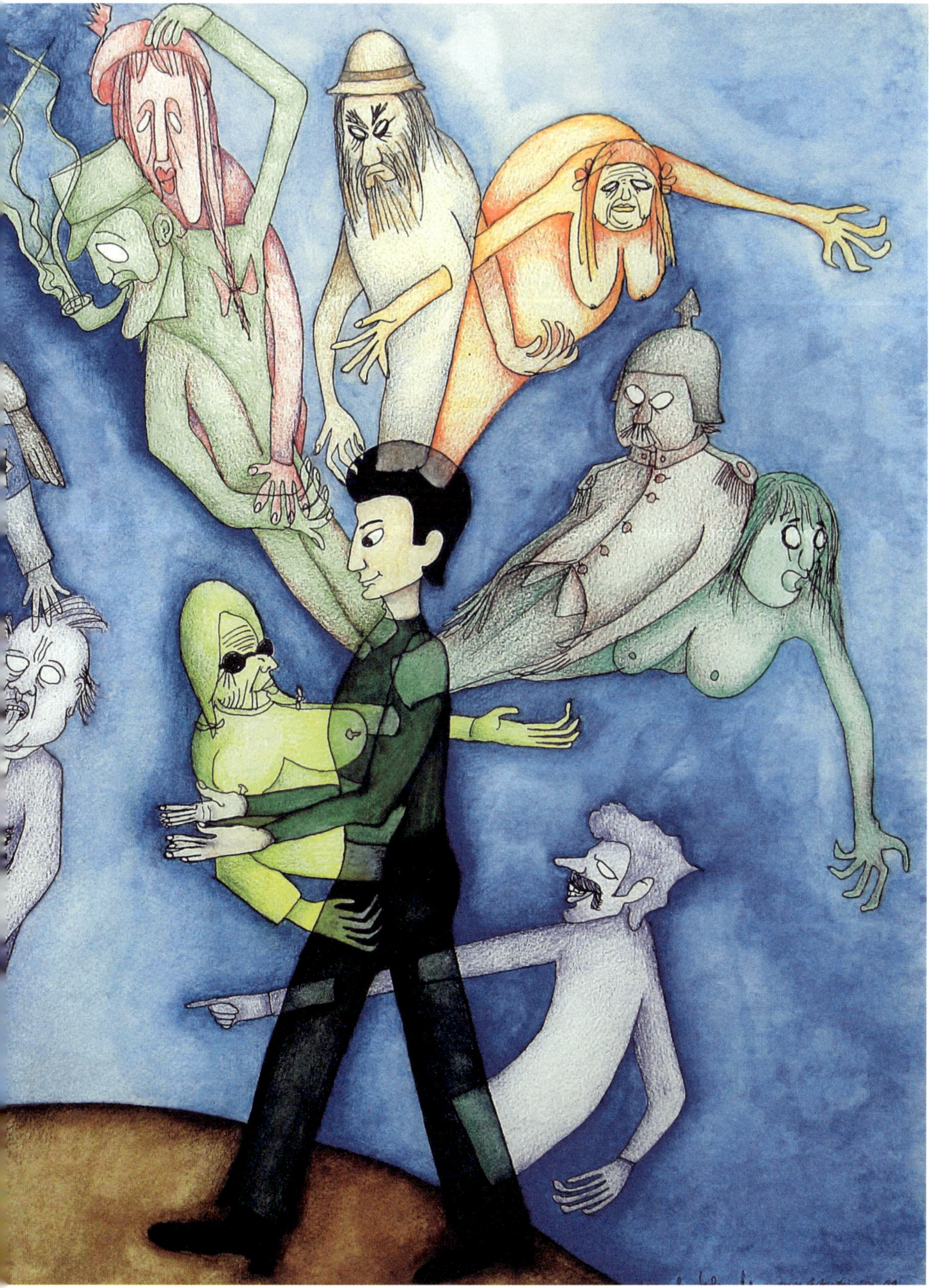

*Love at First Sight*, 2009
50 × 65 cm

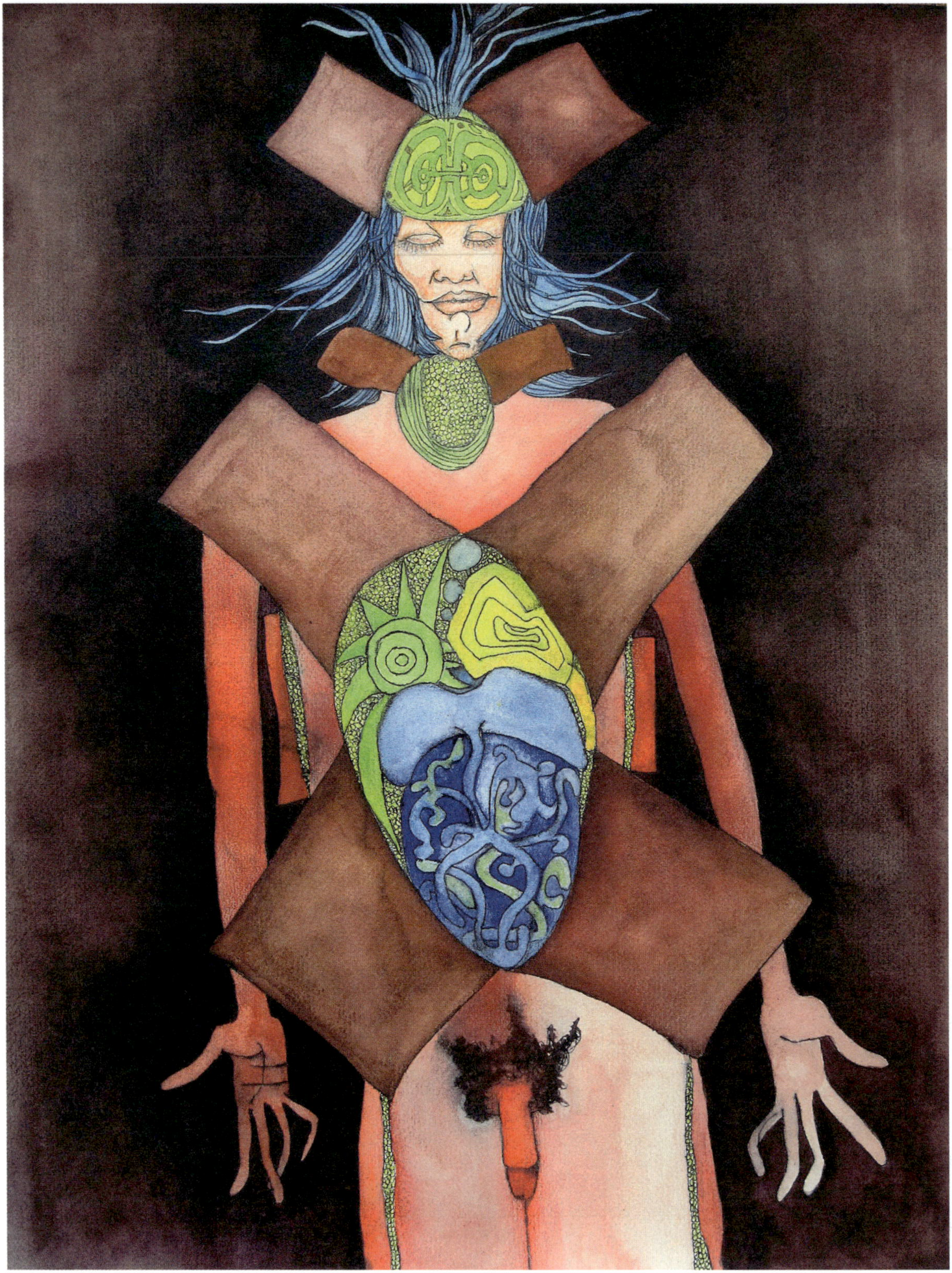

*Autopsy*, 2009
56 × 42 cm

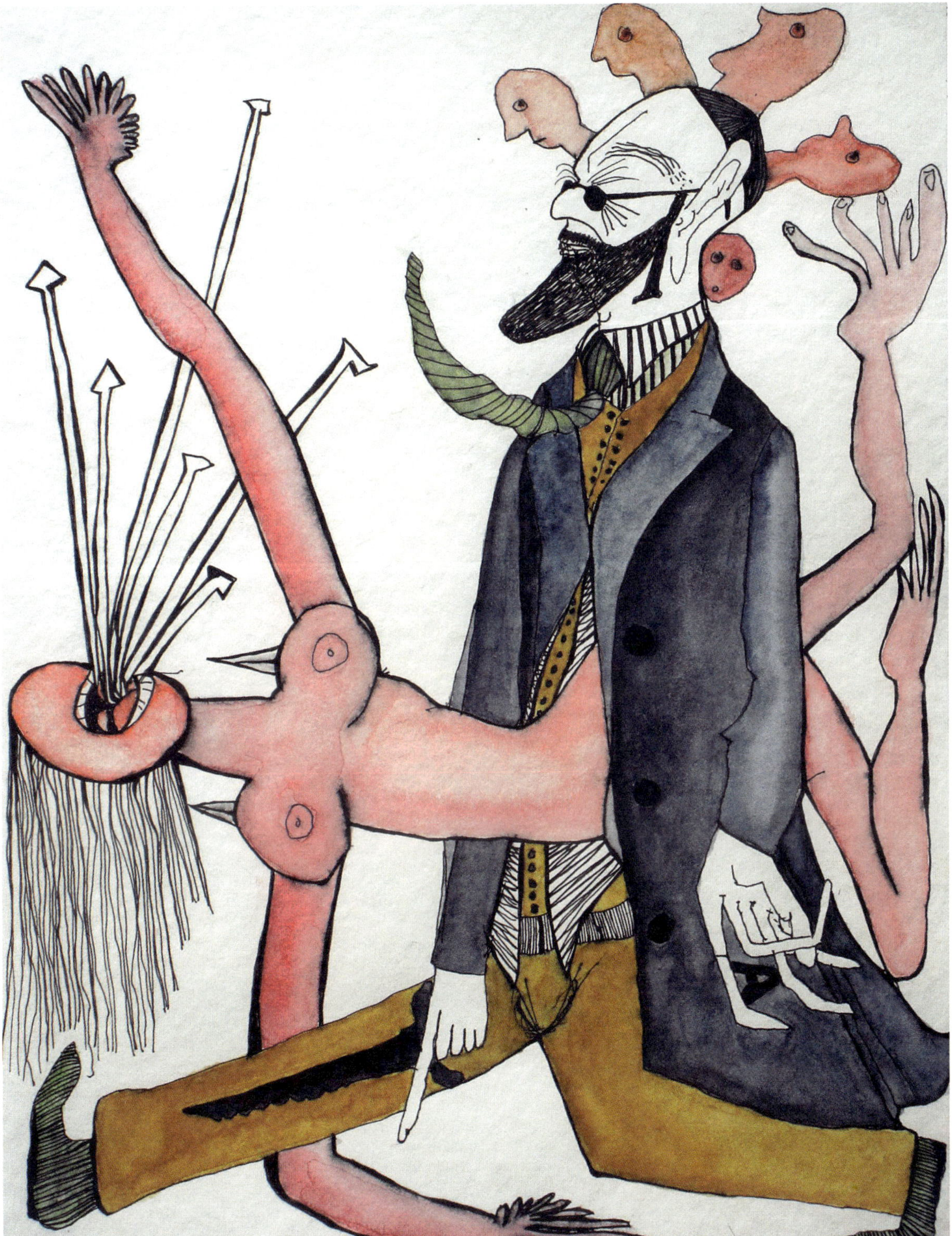

*Rutting Rabbi*, 2009
32 × 24 cm

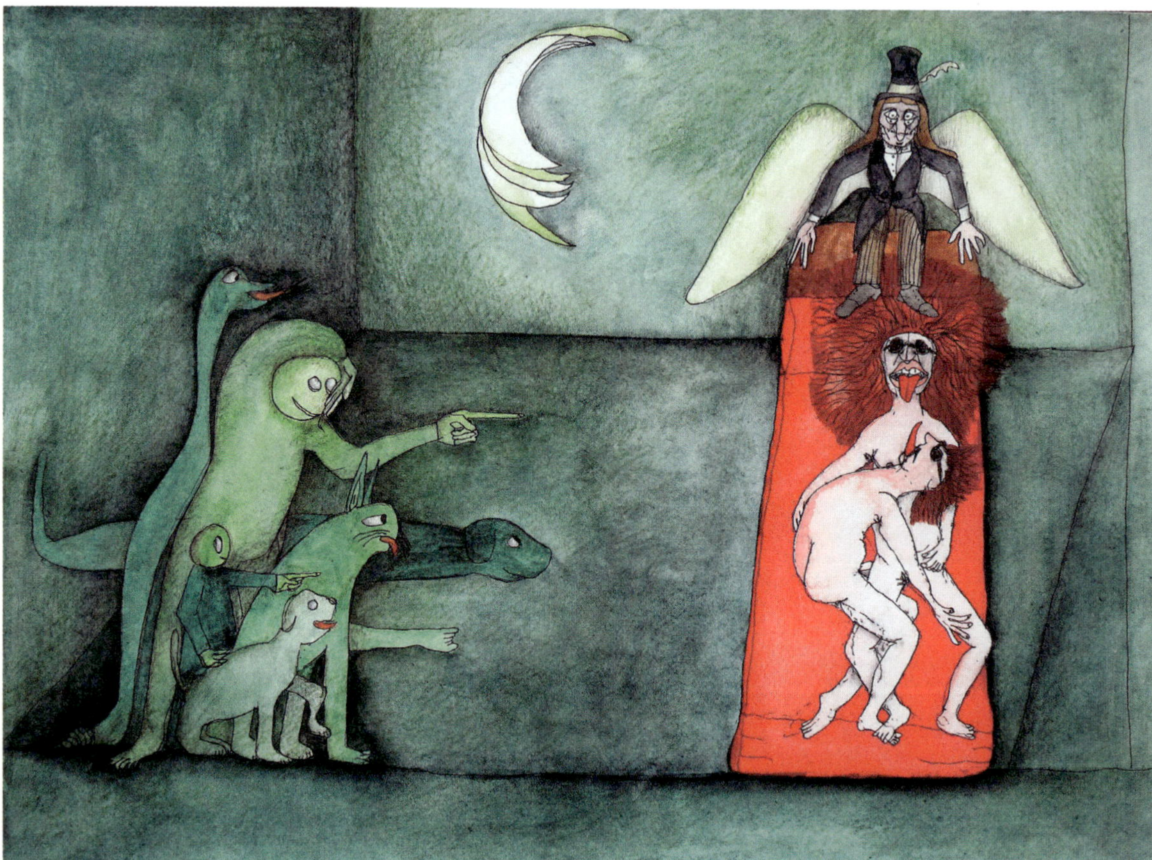

*The Voyeurs*, 2009
36 × 48 cm

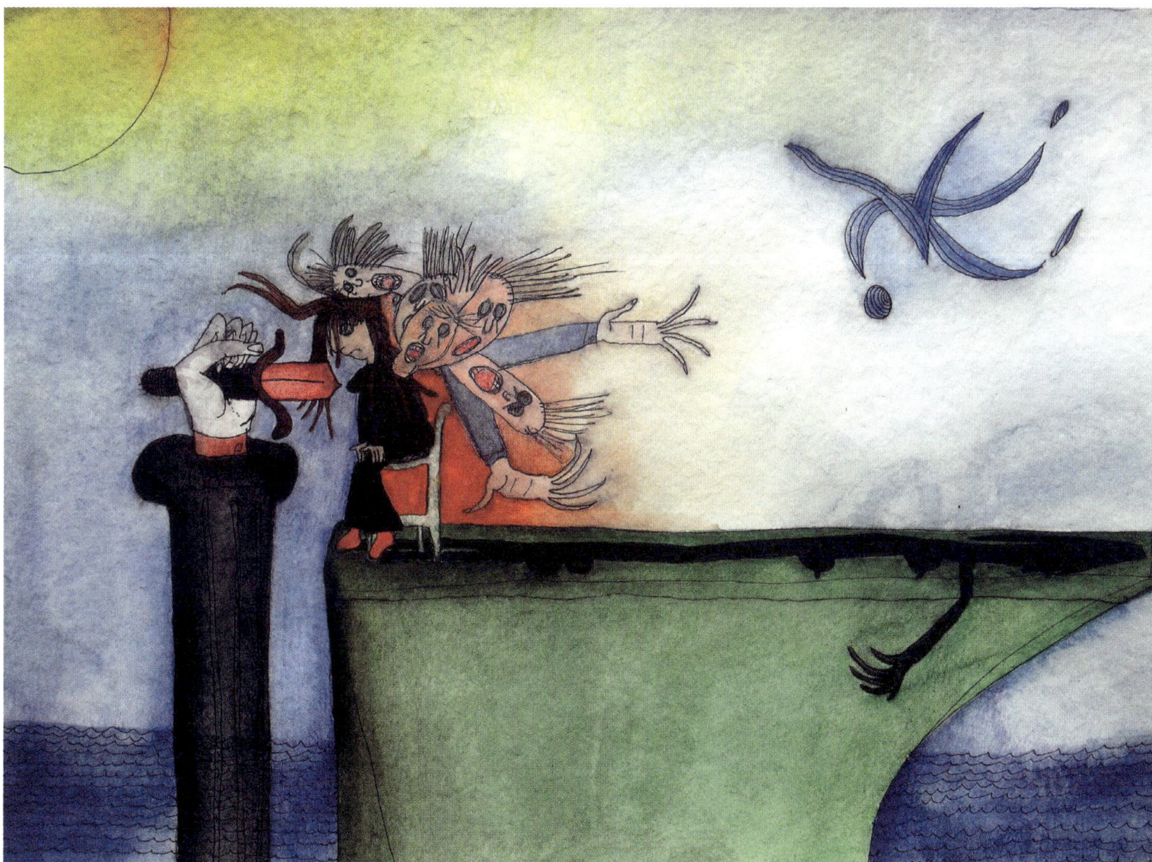

*Old Guilt*, 2009
36 × 48 cm

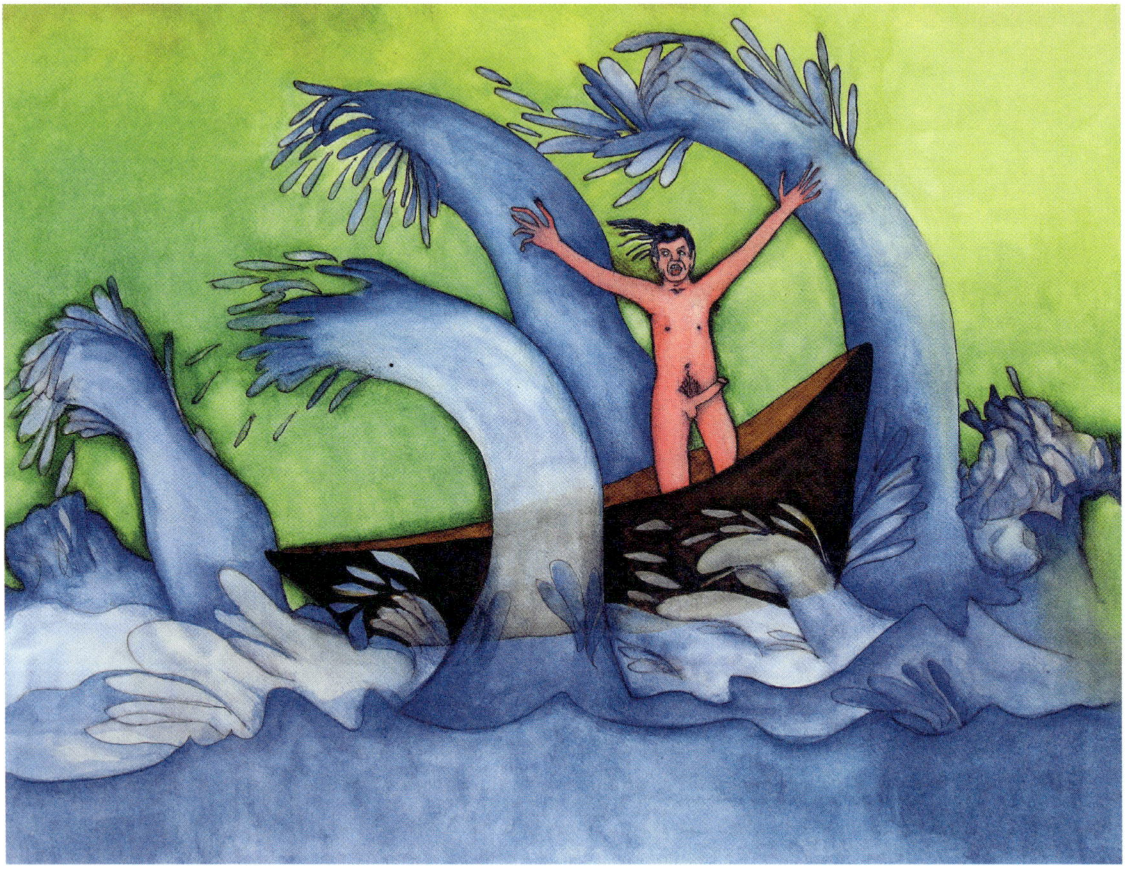

*The Waves*, 2009
50 × 65 cm

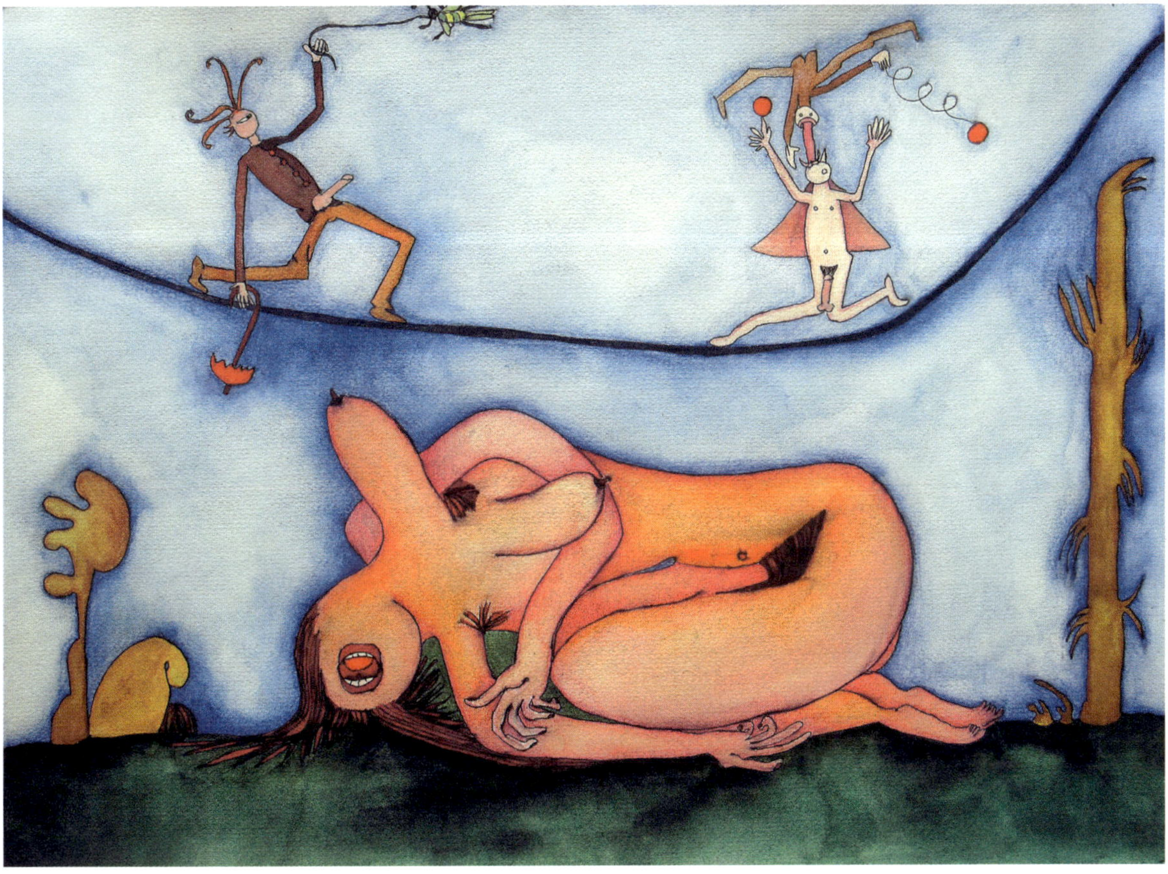

*The Weight of Flesh*, 2009
42 × 56 cm

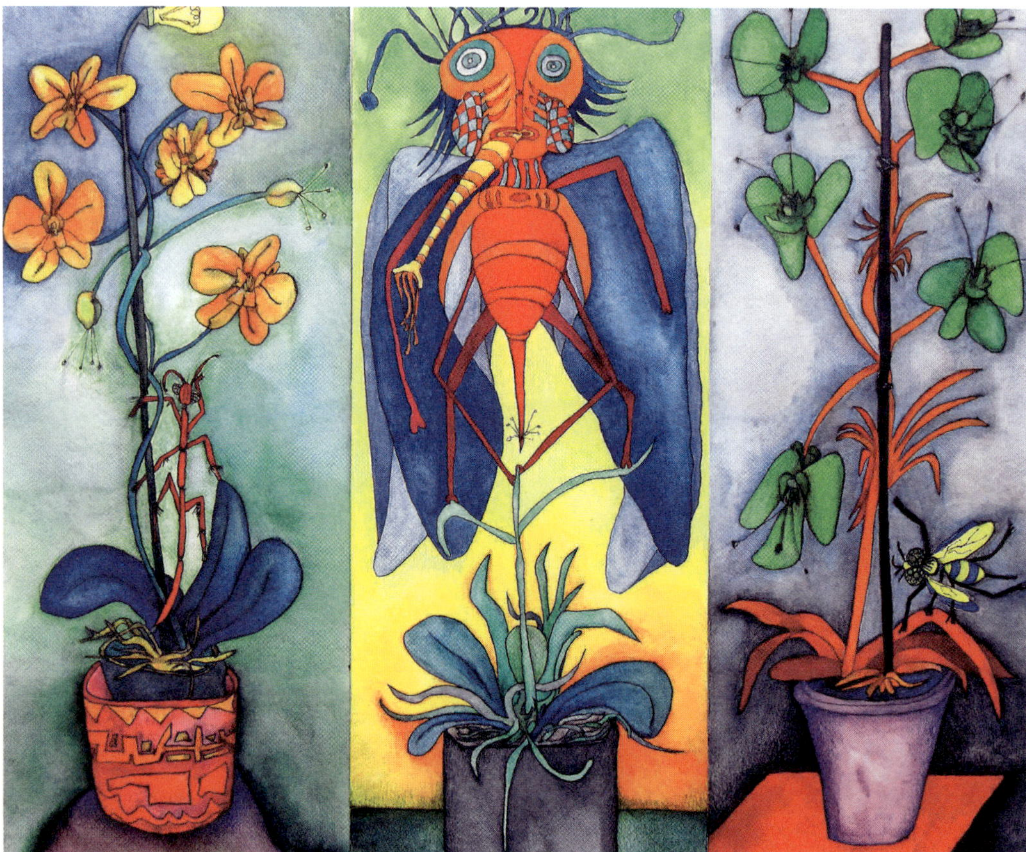

*Flowers and Insects*, 2009
3 × (50 × 20 cm)

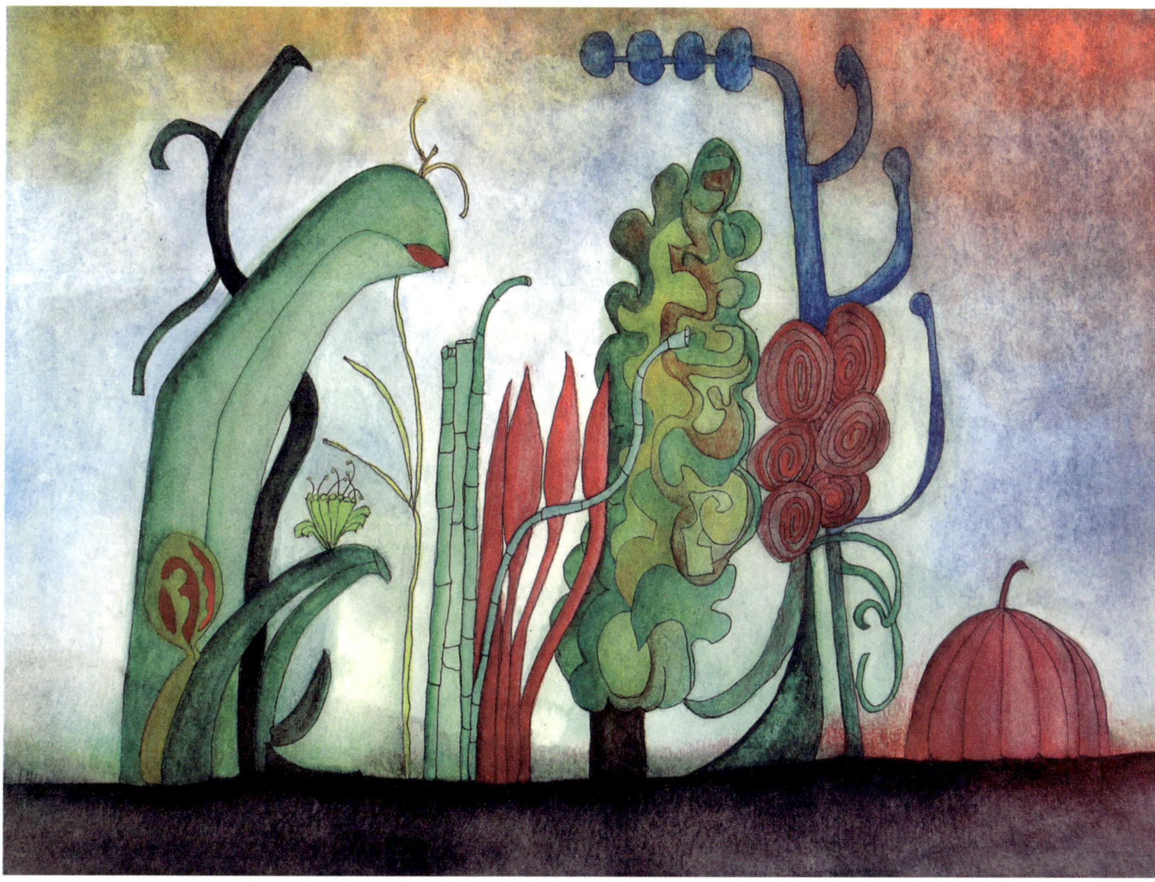

*Unstill Life*, 2009
36 × 48 cm

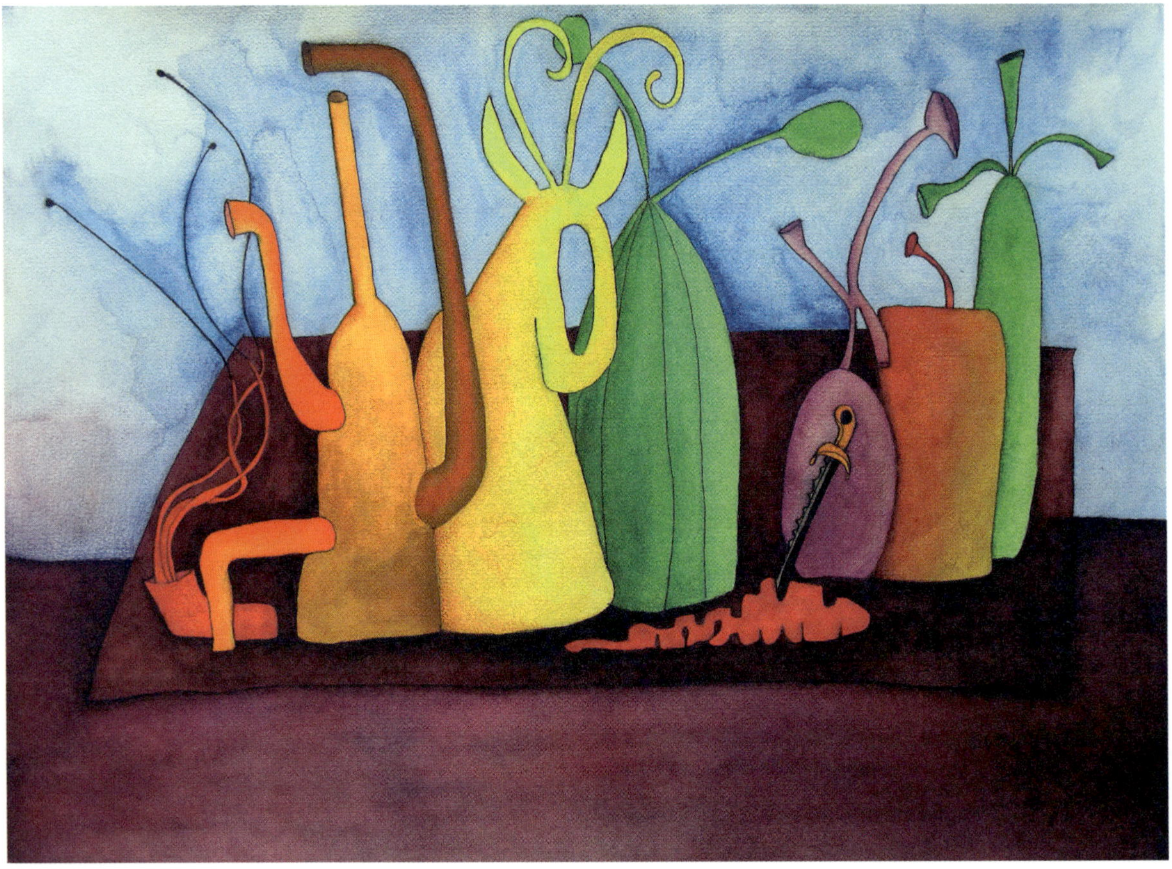

*On the Table*, 2009
42 × 56 cm

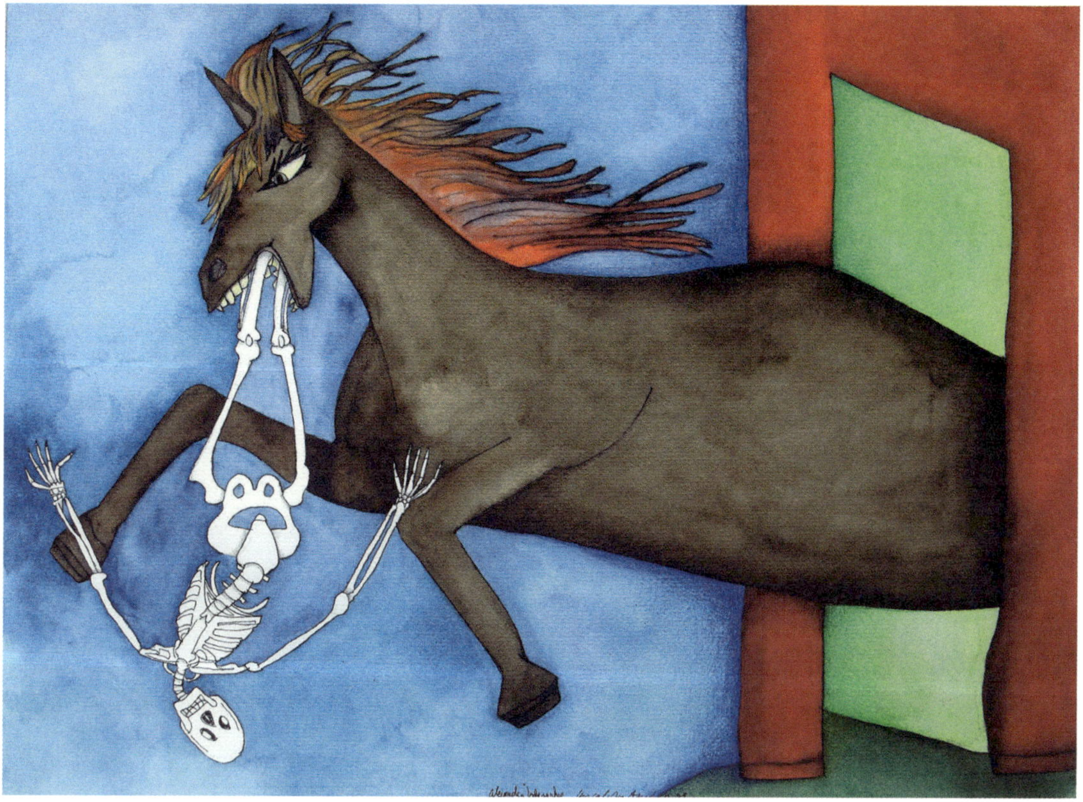

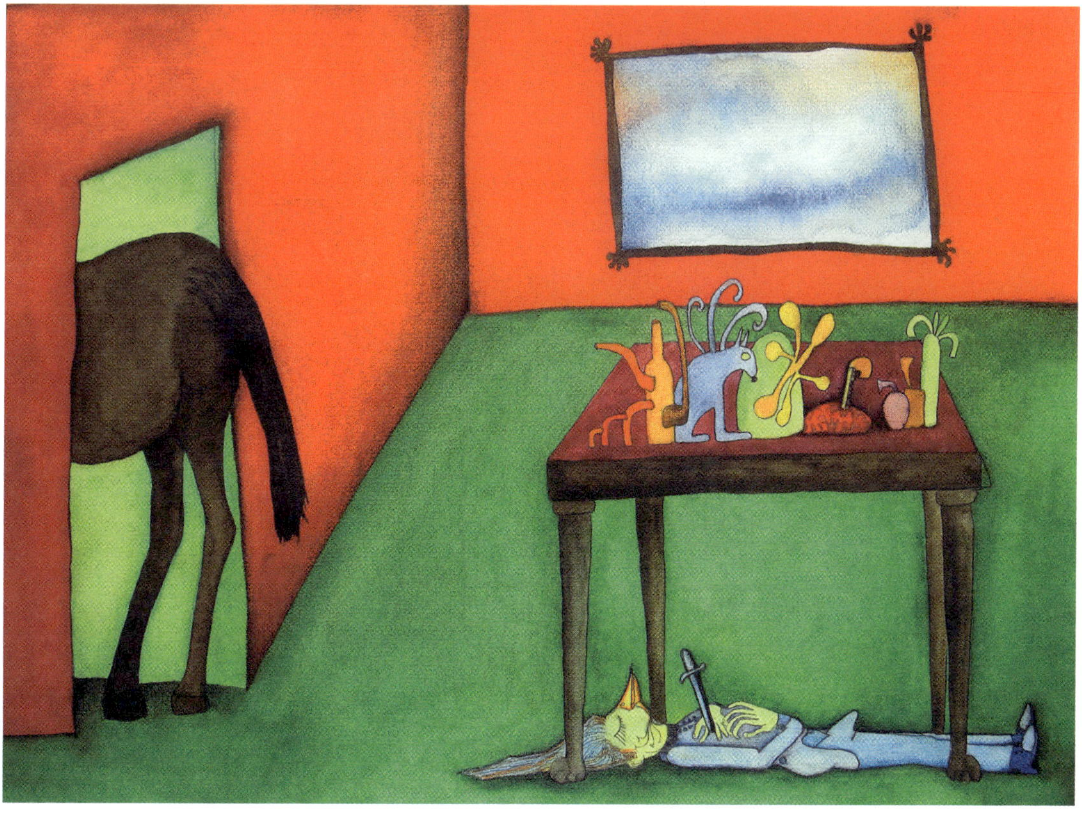



Top: *Outdoor Dream*, 20099, 42 × 56 cm / Bottom: *Under the Table*, 2009, 42 × 56 cm

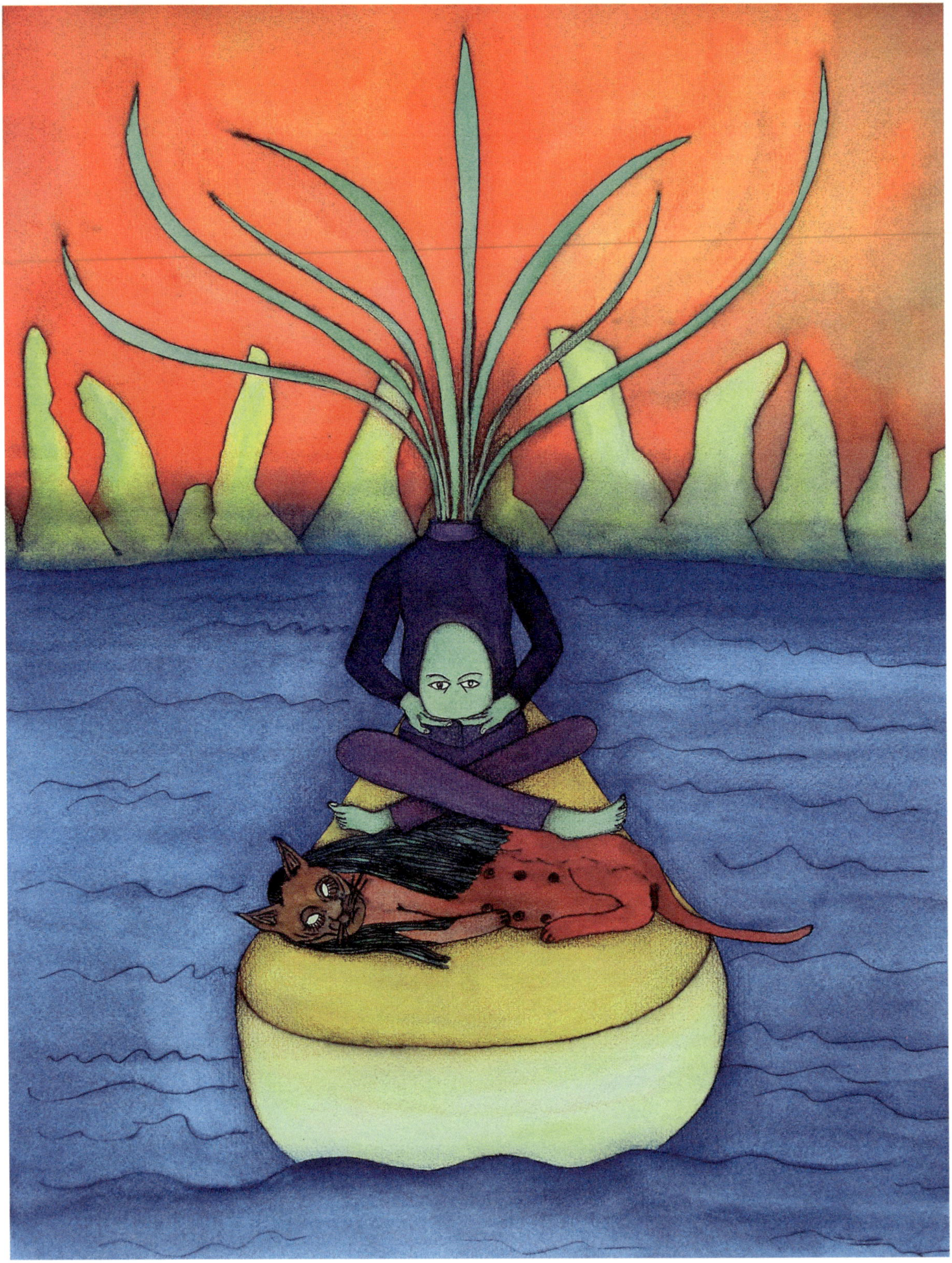

*Miraculous Journey*, 2009
56 × 42 cm

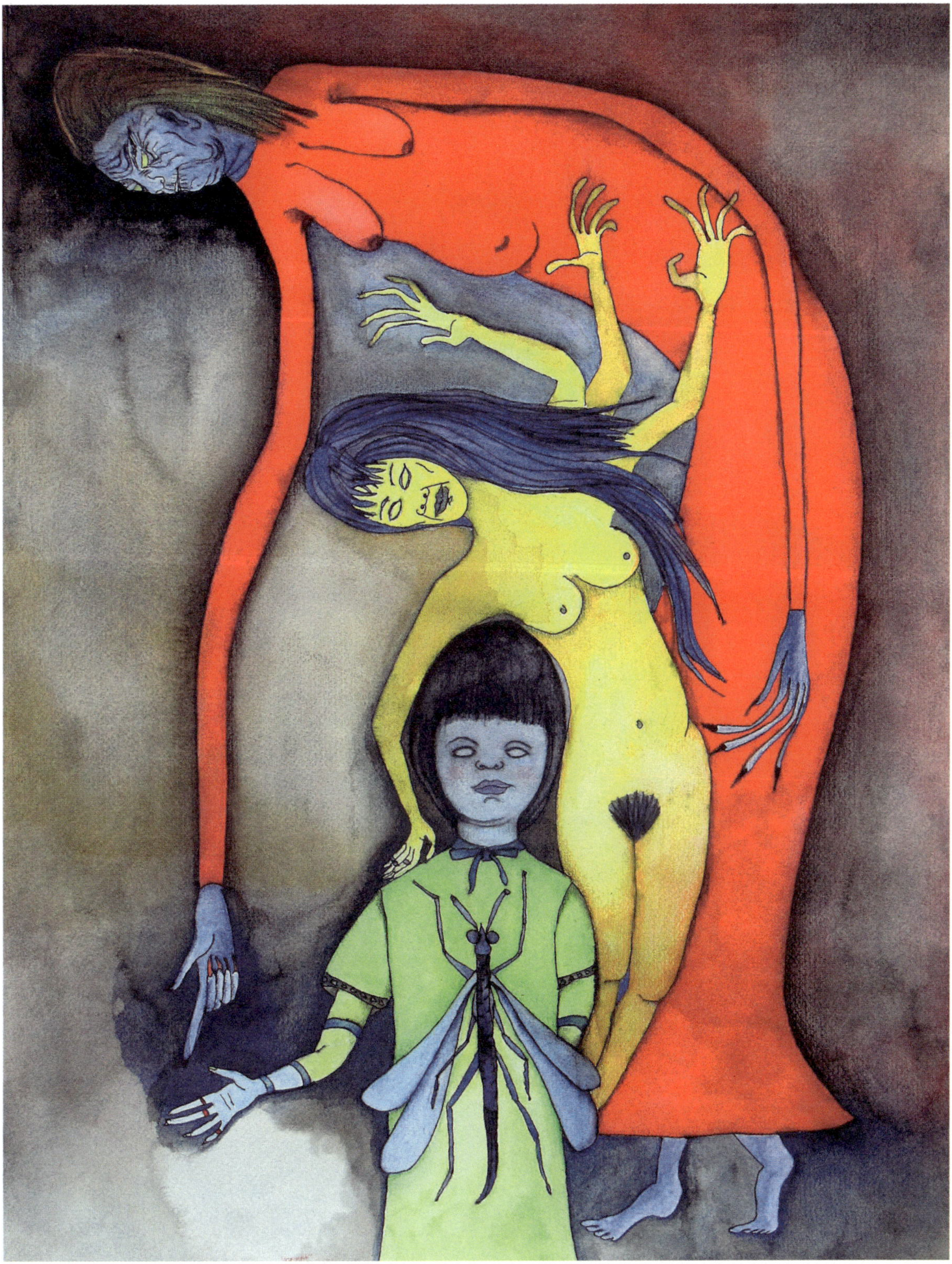

*Three Generations*, 2009
56 × 42 cm

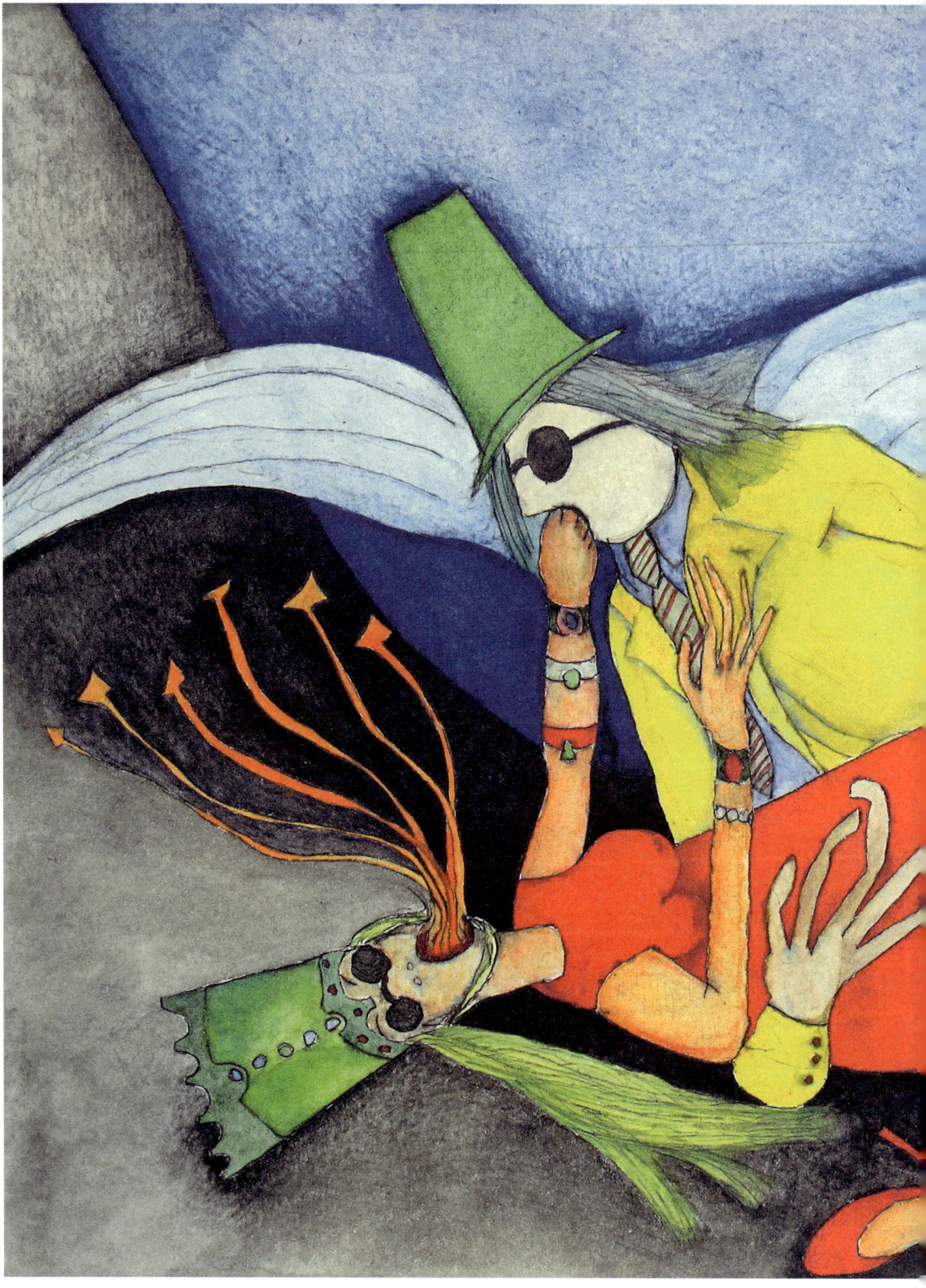

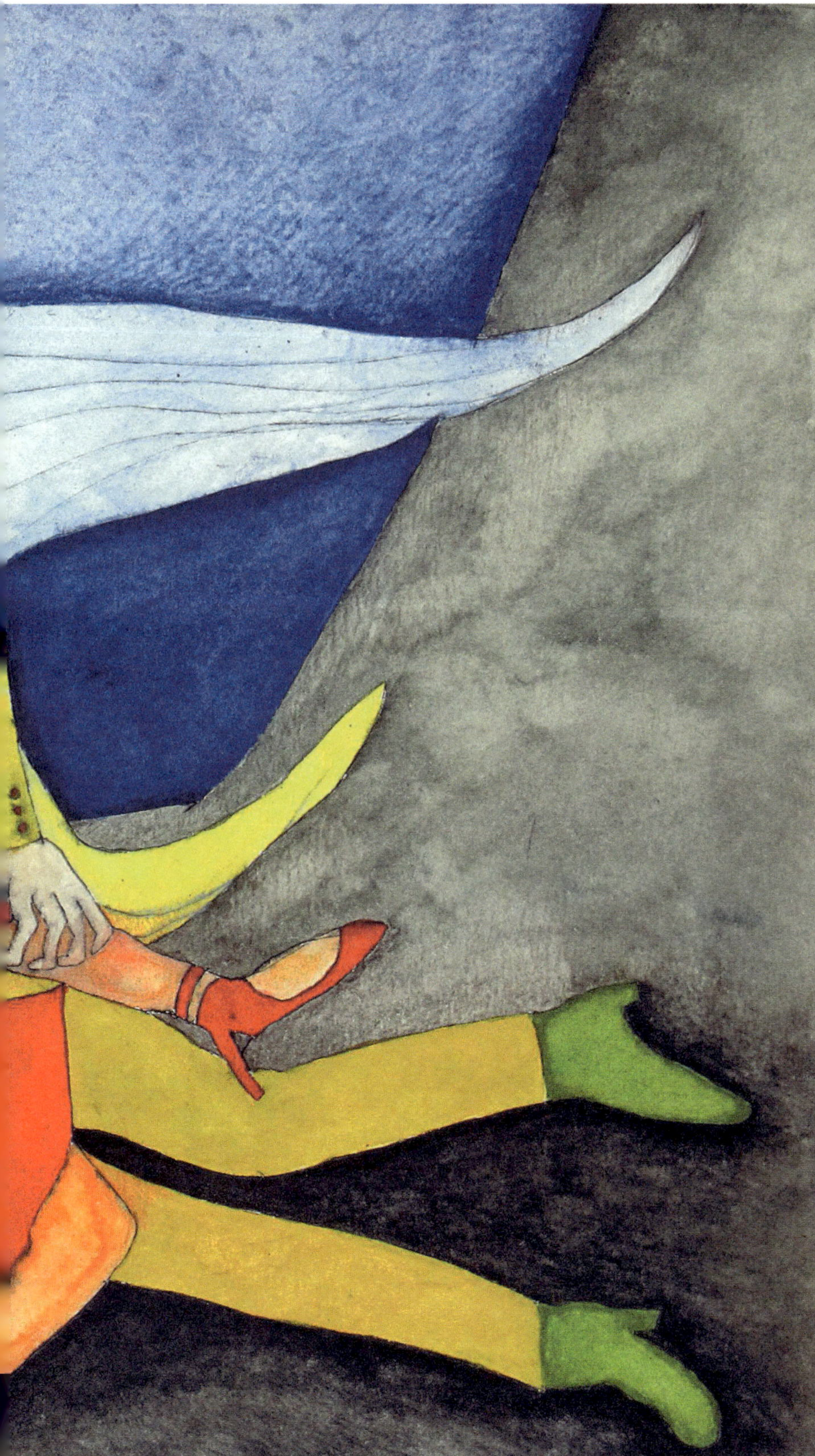

*For Each Other*, 2009
42 × 56 cm

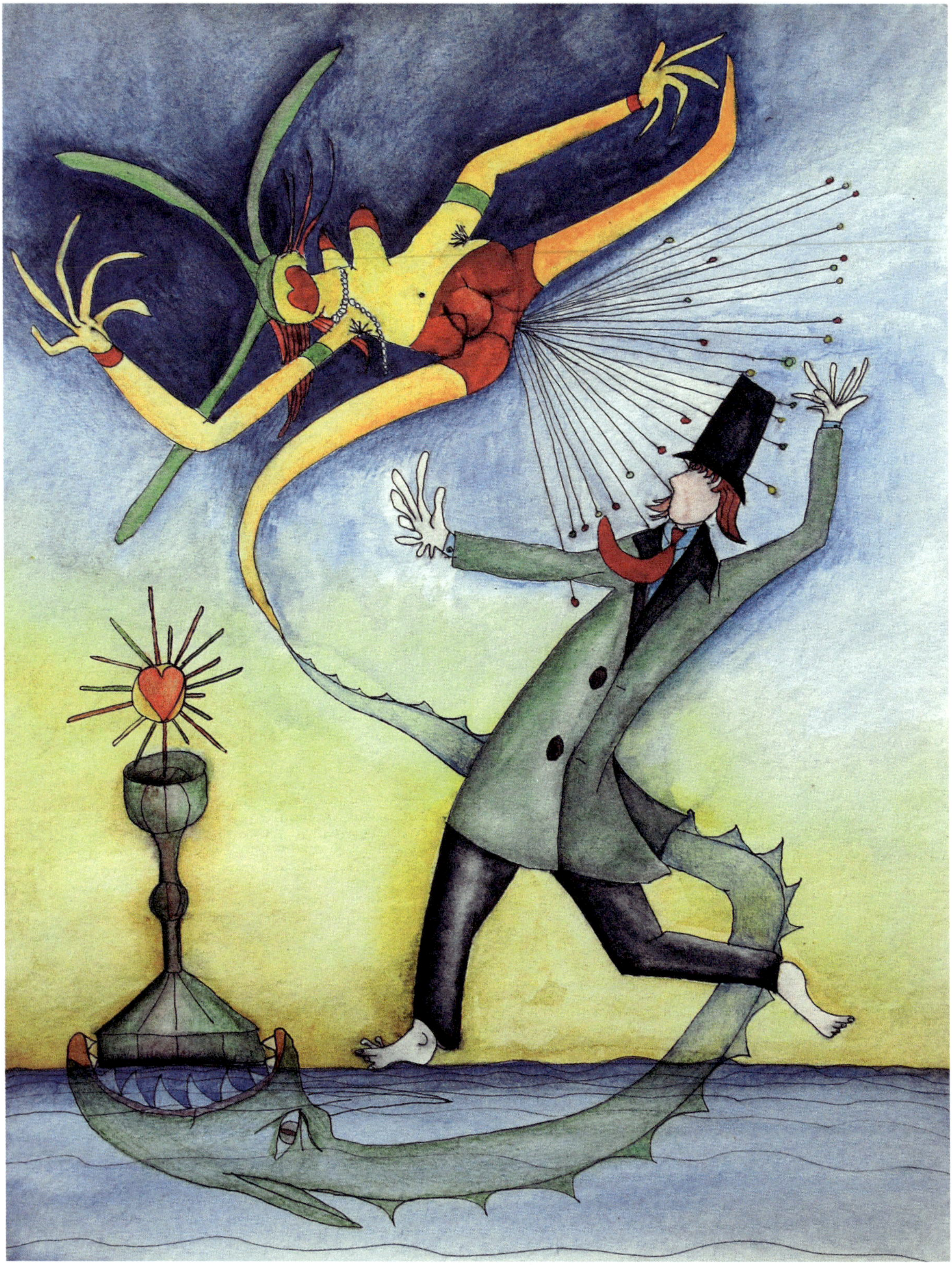

*Wild Love*, 2009
48 × 36 cm

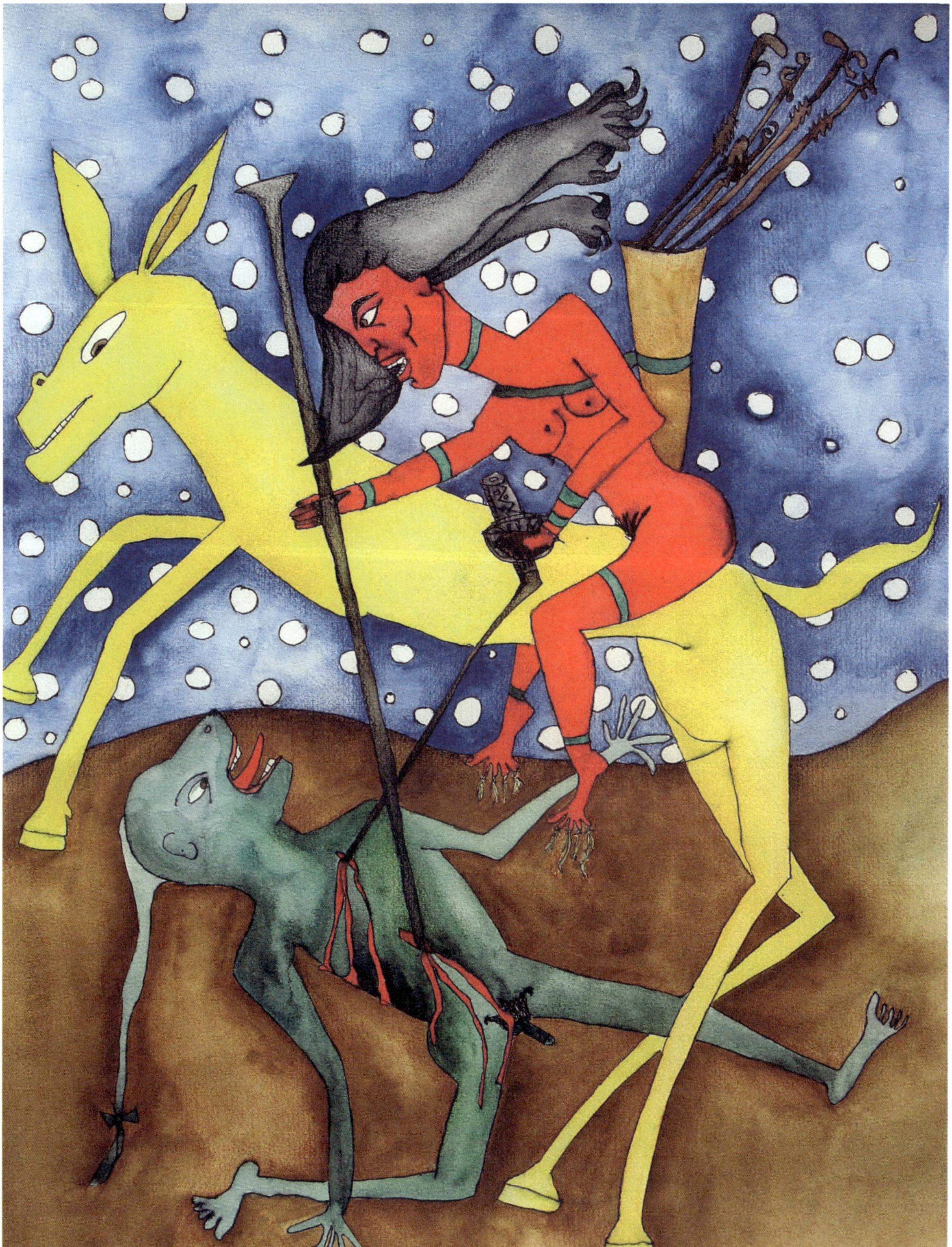

*Mythic Battle*, 2009
56 × 42 cm

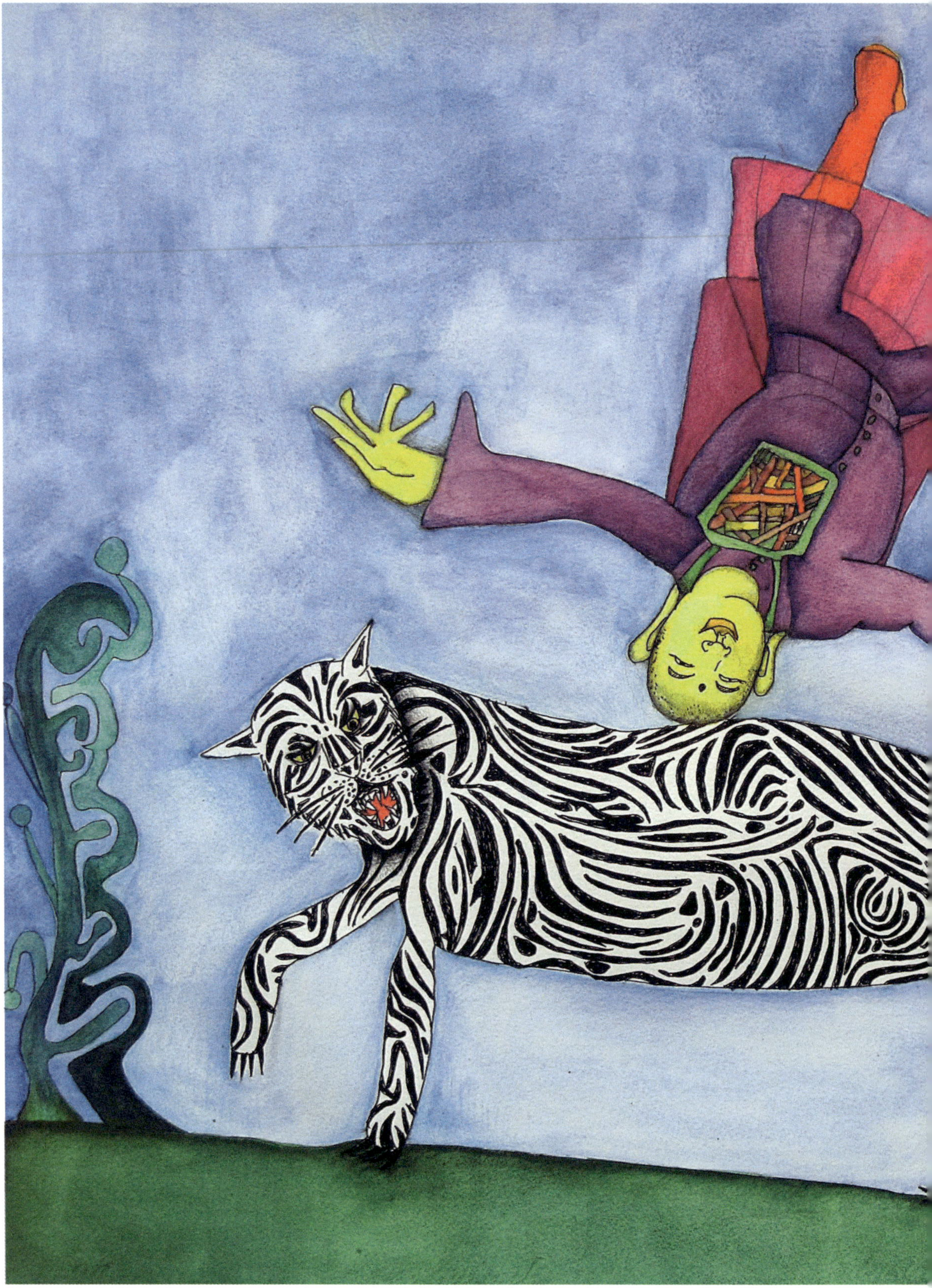

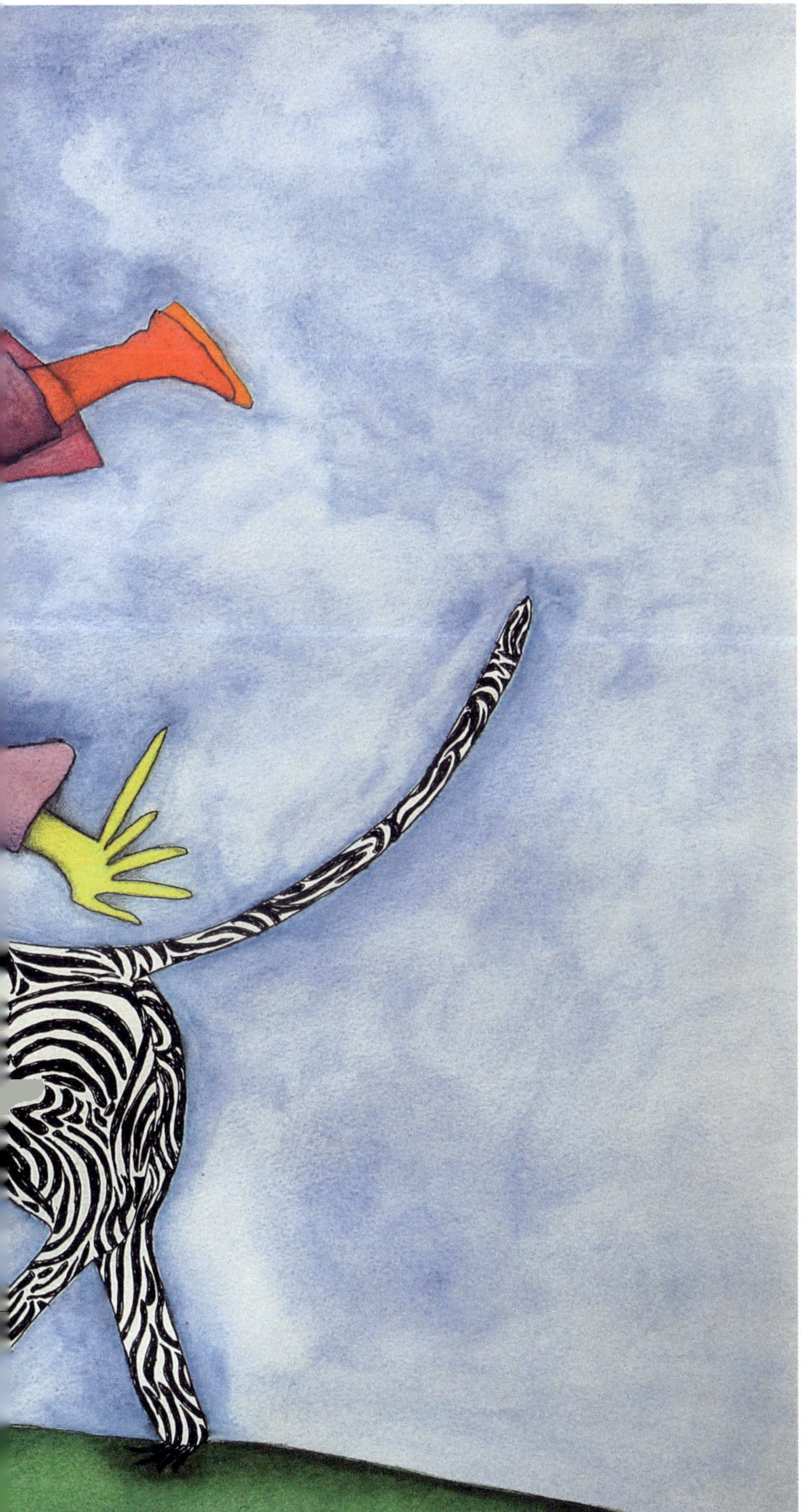

*Alegría! Alegría!* 2009
50 × 65 cm

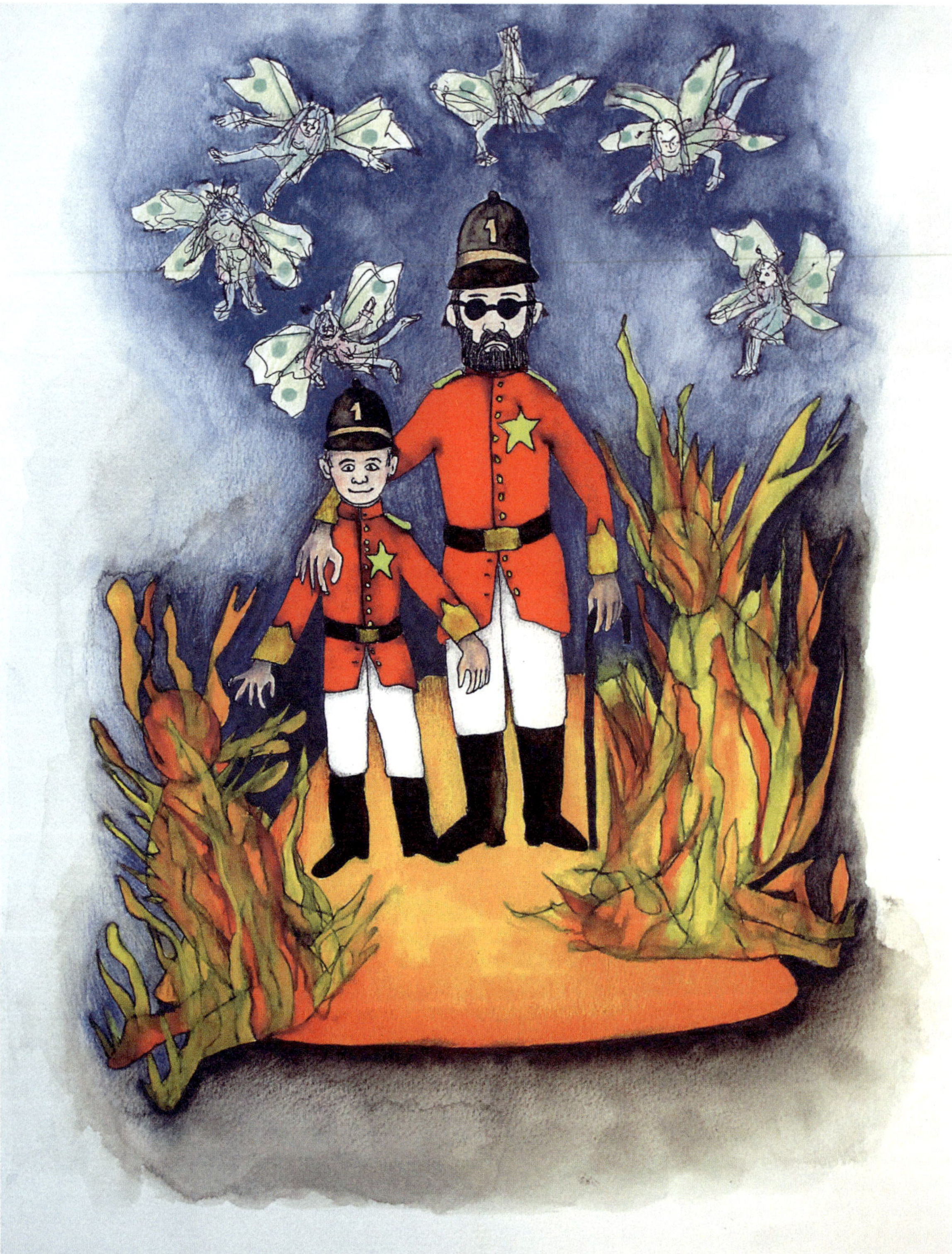

*The Child Fireman*, 2009
48 × 36 cm

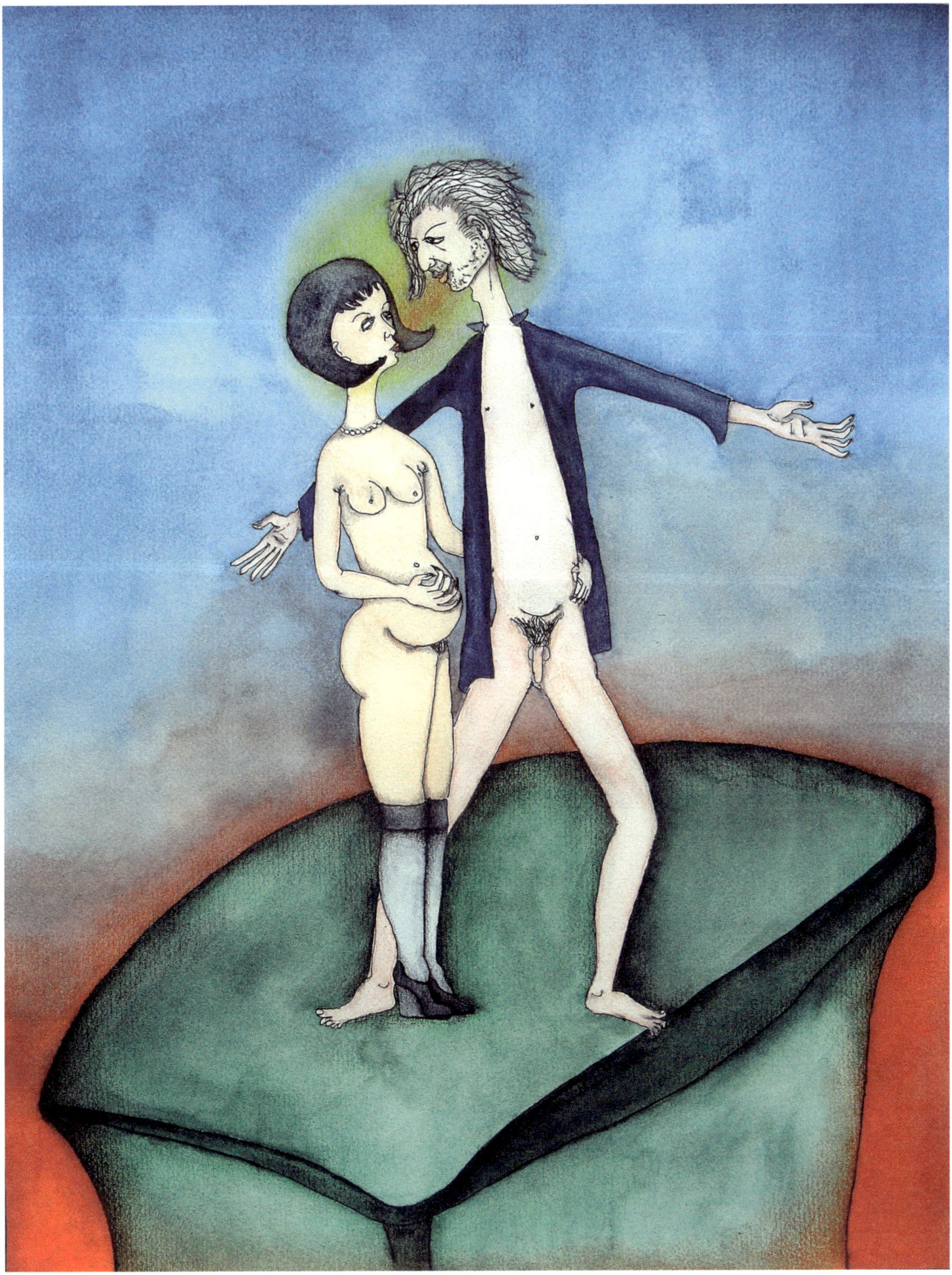

*The Two of Us*, 2009
56 × 42 cm

# The whole is greater than the sum of its parts…

**Maria-Inés Rodriguez**

To speak of pascalejandro is to enter a complex universe in which spirit and space-time intermingle. I close my eyes and can picture four hands and an unbroken line meandering inquisitively, endlessly across the page, leaving in its wake characters from a thousand and one stories in which the real and the imaginary travel side by side. Wherever the line pauses, color appears, quietly, peacefully, gradually taking each character over, one by one.

Solitary, long-necked, hungry or sated, terrified or sheltered men; thinking, dancing, suffering women, sometimes accompanied and sometimes not. Couples united or divided by an assortment of yokes, fastenings, and knots. They swim, fly, run, sleep, die, live together or apart in an imaginary world that, in the end, reflects our desires and frustrations.

In contrast to the Panic Fables—a comic strip published by Alejandro Jodorowsky in the Mexican newspaper *El Heraldo* from the late '60s to early '70s, whose characters discuss mystical and spiritual matters—the characters in pascalejandro's drawings coexist in relative silence. This silence is occasionally interrupted by whispers or stifled screams that materialize as words invading the surface of the page: YES, HOPE, STOP, INFINITE … hazard signs for a horrifying world that needs to go in a different direction.

Each of pascalejandro's works is charged with a tremendous creative energy that sparks the imagination and captures the power generated in the encounter between two individuals who radiate loving, visionary wisdom.

# pascALEjandro: exhibiting intimacy, exhibiting cruelty

**Olivier Zahm**

Which is foremost? Is it the drawing, with its tale of love's passion and violence? Or could it be the colors, applied second, which intensify this exhibition of intimacy and cruel hunger (for the Other)? Does the symbolic narration of love hold pride of place? Or is it these transformations of rose, red, yellow, orange and violet from a spectrum of cannibal passions that deserve the tiger's share? Admittedly, the drawing (Alejandro, the man) is technically made first; while the color (Pascale, the woman) comes afterward, after the fact (of love), in the end (love stories generally end badly). Unless there's no order at all—for in fact both emerge together: lines and colors explode, fuse, devour each other.

The color's violence lies precisely in that it eats the line, incorporates it—to the point that lines and colors compose a single whole in the "drawings" or "paintings" of pascALEjandro. Note the three fused letters, a pillar of cloud or flame, a wound shared between two lovers who love and officially agree to kill each other: between "I" and "thou." Between "you and "me," there's mutual intimacy and cruelty here, transfigured, sublimated, hallucinated and amusing (the humor of it). In these drawings made by four hands and two genders—male and female, Pascale and Alejandro—lines and colors unite and harmonize, fuse and embrace, interpenetrate and transpierce each other like all those who love each other, laughing. . . This union isn't uniform; on the contrary, it's an expression of love: separation that seeks its opposite in the great collision of existence.

pascALEjandro's drawings stand in open revolt against the pessimism of the French moralists who portrayed love as merely a hypocritical and fanciful coloring for irrepressible sexual desire. These drawings dance on the back of existence (the tiger): they are joyful creations, though cruel. Two beings meet and throw themselves at each other so they'll never have to part, while parting all the time (the separating without separation that composes the daily life of lovers). They celebrate love, without naiveté, in their firm innocence: this chance gift of life that lasts in its merriment, spontaneity, fragility and darkness, in its wrathful and chimerical beauty somehow inseparable from desire. For desire is not simply an act of devouring the Other; it is also the intertwining of bodies by which the Other in its possible persistence leads toward something higher, something still more spiritual or diabolical. . . All of this is in God's hands: desire and feeling mix and drag each other toward the grave (without end, forever).

In each drawing, their vision of love is dazzling, bloody, effervescent, and above all not serious, for the greatest profundity lies no thicker than paper, runs along the surface of a retina, of a mouth, of lips, spread legs and sky. pascALEjandro's collaborative works are, as we've come to understand, a strange theatre of love: "the scene of two" (Alain Badiou) in which each lover tries still and always to seduce the Other—to surprise, carry off, gut, assassinate, or resurrect the Other. The scene of two, according to pascALEjandro, becomes a dream rape committed by one against the other, by which the dance of life goes ever on as the encounter repeats itself—with the fear of losing the Other, with the joy of finding each other again. In these communicating vessels, love finally becomes the refined cruelty of life itself (or a return to infancy, back where the fears, traumas and dreams began, where love seeks the source of things it wants to resolve). All of this comes into play in these drawings, not merely in their representation, but in their secret process. For, at root, what we have here is an (impossible) exhibition of intimacy.

Certainly, if love had its way, we'd love each other forever. But much more than an attempt to keep at bay the end of love (the ever-feared attrition of feeling and desire) these drawings compose a trial of love in which each being comes face to face with a new temporality: life as a couple. That's the key to these drawings: the eternal promise of a life reinvented by love. Their outcry addresses itself to skeptics: to those who doubt the force and innocence of the great ecstasy of love. In order to last, or hoping to last, lovers generally have children. But what would happiness be without the transfigured violence of this life with paper lungs painted in the colors of madness? If having a child is a part of love, surely the fact of not having a child is as well. And all that makes love last is indeed here in this erotic and existential to-and-fro which slips into these drawings—between the line and the colors, in a life remade for two and a temporal frame transformed together, at full speed. For time is precious to lovers.

# pascALEjandro or the third artist

**Diana Widmaier Picasso**

pascALEjandro—a duo, pair, couple, or team: Who's hiding behind this signature for four hands? Born of a magical encounter between two individuals on different paths but driven by the same desire to create, the name came plain as day to the two lovers, Pascale Montandon-Jodorowsky and Alejandro Jodorowsky. Unlike Gilbert and George who declare, "We are one artist,"[1]Pascale and Alejandro keep their own specificities: she as a sculptor, designer, costumer maker and photographer; he as a mime, filmmaker, graphic novelist, poet, philosopher, alchemist and psychomagician. They fuse on paper. Firmly convinced of the importance of the collective unconscious, they consider that "the individual artist no longer exists."[2] They say this collaboration began as a game, but they soon noticed a coherence to their gestures: "As if it were really neither he nor I, but the fusion of both—as if it were the creation, the intervention of a third artist," says Pascale.[3] Without this artistic communion, this third person would never have seen the light

1. Martin Gayford, "Entretien avec Gilbert & George / Interview with Gilbert & George," in exh. cat. *Gilbert et George*, Musée d'art moderne de la ville de Paris, Paris, 4 October 1997-4 January 1998, Paris-musées, Paris, 1997, pp. 37-97, p. 55.
2. In "Yo no creo en la revolución política, creo en la re-evolución poetica / Not revolution, but poetic re-evolution," Alejandro Jodorowsky and Bayro Jimenez interview, in exh. cat. *Resisting the Present: Mexico, 2000-2012*, Musée d'art moderne-ARC, Paris, 9 March-8 July 2012 – Museo Amparo, Puebla, 15 October 2011-15 January 2012, Paris-musées, Paris, 2011, pp. 239-249, p. 247.
3. Pascale Montandon-Jodorowsky during the author's interview with Pascale Montandon-Jodorowsky and Alejandro Jodorowsky, Paris, 15 September 2016.

of day. A synthesis of art, life and love, this double represents their relationship's sublimation, their symbolic child.[4]

This spiritual fertility—an alliance of the male and the female principles—is common among artist couples.[5] In the works of Jean Tinguely and Niki de Saint Phalle, for instance, it bears witness to a harmony between the sexes, a constant celebration of ying and yang;[6] for Pascale and Alejandro, meanwhile, the very "nature of existence"[7] consists in coming to know yourself through the other. While the second half of the twentieth century saw the rise of many artist duos—each revealing a symbiotic relationship between two creative minds—the practice itself is attested in Europe as early as the XVII$^{th}$ century. Since the individualization of the figure of the artist during the Renaissance, single signatures have often been used in a dissembling way when work has actually been made collectively in a studio. Rubens used to call on collaborators, apprentices or famous artists such as Van Dyck, Snyders or Jan Brueghel, to whom he entrusted certain details of his paintings.[8] And yet the practice of working

4. Ibid.: "On the other hand, the fact of creating something together came about in a self-evident way, and so this work really became like a symbolic child, because it's a part of us and at the same time it's on its own and we feel responsible, we have to raise it, it has its own life, it has to develop, it really shares in the same kind of energy," explains Pascale.

5. see Nancy Huston, "Couples créateurs," in exh. cat. *Des duos et des couples*, Galerie d'art du conseil général des Bouches-du-Rhône, Aix-en-Provence 16 January-30 March 2003, Actes Sud, Arles, 2003, pp. 9-14, p. 14.

6. Erika Billeter, "Utopia Becomes Reality. Collaboration-Lived Harmony," in exh. cat. *Collaborations: Warhol. Basquiat. Clemente*, Museum Fridericanum, Kassel, 4 February-5 May 1996 – Museum Villa Stuck, Munich, 25 July-29 September 1996 – Museo d'Arte contemporanea, Castello di Rivoli, 17 October 1996-19 January 1997, Cantz, Stuttgart, 1996, pp. 28-32, p. 31.

7. Sophie Pinchetti, "Alejandro Jodorowsky & Pascale Montandon's Art for Mutation: The Latest Works from Their Collaborative Art on View in Paris," *The Third Eye*, 6 July 2014 (reprint of their interview from the review's first issue in 2012), www.thethird-eye.co.uk.

8. see Arnout Balis, "Rubens et son atelier: une problématique complexe," in exh. cat. *Rubens: l'atelier du génie. Autour des œuvres du maître aux musées royaux des Beaux-Arts de Belgique*, Musées royaux des Beaux-Arts de Belgique, Bruxelles, 14 September 2007-27 January 2008, Lannoo, Tielt, 2007, pp. 30-51.

collaboratively only truly took off at the turn of the XX$^{th}$ century, as experimentation became an essential component of such avant-garde movements as Dada or Der Blaue Reiter. During the same period, Pablo Picasso and Georges Braque's simultaneous studies in destructuring pictorial space arose from a close collaboration that led to the invention of Cubism. These two artists, working side by side from 1907 to 1911, went so far as to cultivate anonymity by refusing to sign their works, consciously playing on public confusion regarding the authorship of their paintings. In the 1950s and 1960s, collaborative experiments proliferated as the counterculture movement encouraged an expansion of artistic boundaries. These experiments took various forms and gave rise to original structures. *Erased de Kooning Drawing*, made by Jasper Johns and Robert Rauschenberg in 1953, calls into question artistic identity and the value of a signature. Today, the work is attributed to Rauschenberg, even though both he and Johns assert that the inscription "Erased de Kooning Drawing Robert Rauschenberg 1953" was written by Johns. Artists such as Christo and Jeanne-Claude, who started working together as soon as they met in 1958, would jointly sign their installations, and yet this didn't keep Christo's name from long being the only one recognized—a symptom of the masculinization of genius. In the case of Bernd and Hilla Becher, an emblematic couple in the history of photography, the artistic union culminated in an "authorless photograph," in which each of their signatures has vanished.[9] Still further, Andy Warhol and Jean-Michel Basquiat made more than one hundred and thirty works together in strictest secrecy, the harvest of a privileged artistic and personal relationship. These were unveiled to the public at large on the

9. They claimed there was no division of labor within their duo. Michael Schwarz, "Becher/Becher," *Kunstforum International*, t. XXVIII, n° 4, 1978, p. 102; quoted in Armin Zweite, "Bernd et Hilla Becher: 'Proposition pour une façon de voir,' 10 perspectives," in exh. cat. *Berndt et Hilla Becher*, Centre Pompidou, Paris, 20 October 2004-3 January 2005, pp. 7-33, p. 12.

occasion of the exhibition *Warhol and Basquiat: Paintings*, presented at the Tony Shafrazi Gallery in New York in 1985. Other duos like Marina Abramovic and Ulay or Gilbert & George have developed relationships of an intense and radical kind. The latter even reject the very idea of collaboration, playing instead on the neutrality of their appearance and taking twinship as their model. The negation of the ego thus reaches its climax, culminating in photomontages and performances that take no account of the spectator. Like these couples, pascALEjandro functions as its own entity, a union of two individualities whose artistic identities tend to vanish in favor of a third person. Indeed, both Pascale and Alejandro consider their work to be the child they never had.[10] The visionary power of this collaborative work unveils what Brion Gysin and William Burroughs, cult artists and authors of the Beat Generation, called the "unseen collaborator"[11]or *The Third Mind*, after their 1977 volume of the same name, conceived according to the methods of cut-up. Marina Abramovic and Ulay have styled this third power the "super-Self,"[12]an independently created double that suggests an ungraspable meta-identity. In the case of pascALEjandro, this phantom identity[13]crystallizes in their chosen name, which forms a single whole. In the words of the Bulgarian-born French essayist Tzvetan Todorov, "Two does not equal one plus one."[14]

10.Author's interview with Pascale Montandon-Jodorowsky and Alejandro Jodorowsky, Paris, 15 September 2016.

11. "It says that when you put two minds together… there is always a third mind… a third and superior mind… as an unseen collaborator," Brion Gysin and William Burroughs, interview conducted by Robert Palmer, *Rolling Stone*, 11 May 1972, p. 53.

12.Charles Green, *The Third Hand: Collaboration in Art from Conceptualism to Postmodernism*, University of Minnesota Press, Minneapolis-London, 2001, p. 180.

13.Nicolas Abraham and Nicholas Rand, "Notes on the Phantom: A Complement to Freud's Metapsychology," in *Critical Inquiry*, vol. 13, n° 2, *The Trial(s) of Psychoanalysis*, winter 1987, pp. 287-292.

14.Tzvetan Todorov, in exh. cat. *Des duos et des couples*, *op. cit.*, pp. 15-17, p. 17.

Pascale and Alejandro met under the sway of Tarot[15][16]: "I'm Pascale's first man, and she's my last woman: that's the truth of it."[16]He began drawing to seduce her. In setting down the lines, Alejandro unconsciously gives his partner the drawing's theme. Then it's Pascale's turn, entirely intuitively, to interpret in color what Alejandro sought to express. The colors "arrive as in a dream,"[17] in a natural way. The line becomes the stable principle, masculine; the color, the feminine principle, fluid. Equality and reciprocity are their work's watchwords. Hence they avoid the master-pupil dynamic, even though Pascale has always had the impression of being guided ever since her childhood,[18] and she claims to thrive on Alejandro who, for his part, sees himself as her artistic disciple.[19] This mechanism of transference and counter-transference is essential to their work, the goal of which is ultimately therapeutic. Alejandro makes art in order to heal, otherwise art loses all interest in his eyes and boils down to an affirmation of individuality: "I want to link healing and art, because human health is beauty. If I care about beauty, I have to care about human beauty, and the beauty of the human being is principally his or her health: mental, emotional, sexual and financial."[20] He claims moreover to have directed *La Danza de la realidad* (2013) not in order to make

15.In 2005, Jodorowsky was giving successful public Tarot readings in a Parisian café. As Pascale awaited her turn, he looked at her differently from how he looked at the others. It was "not a seductive gaze, it was a gaze which was more than a gaze, as if it were superhuman, like an apparition, as if it came from his unconscious." Pascale Montandon-Jodorowsky during the interview with Pascale Montandon-Jodorowsky and Alejandro Jodorowsky conducted by the author, Paris, 15 September 2016.
16.Alejandro Jodorowsky during the author's interview with Pascale Montandon-Jodorowsky and Alejandro Jodorowsky, Paris, 15 September 2016.
17. Quoted in Sophie Pinchetti, "Poetic Re-Evolution: An Interview with Alejandro Jodorowsky and Pascale Montandon," *Reality Sandwich*, 2013, http://realitysandwich.com.
18. Ibid.
19. Ibid.
20. Quoted in "Yo no creo en la revolución política, creo en la re-evolución poetica / Not revolution, but poetic re-evolution," *op. cit.*, pp. 240-241.

a film, but to heal his soul.[21] Though certain drawings allude to traumatic events in Pascale's childhood, for instance, or difficult periods in Alejandro's life, they never do so explicitly. The scenes are poetic, sublimated, transfigured. Each work leads to a kind of catharsis that allows both of them to face things: "What happens to Pascale happens to me, so if I heal something in Pascale, I restore my own health as well. Because if Pascale has a problem, I'll suffer from that problem."[22]

However, for art to possess therapeutic qualities, the connection between the therapeutic practice and the artistic practice has to be rooted in a human encounter. Therefore, it is necessarily a "reciprocal act."[23] Alejandro himself emphasizes his ties to psychoanalysis, but he also points to the significance of his study of shamans and healers.[24]It was in Mexico that he created the concept of psychomagic, a form of therapy that proposes to treat all kinds of ills through symbolic acts directly connected to the unconscious. When Pascale and Alejandro work together, they perform an act of psychomagic. Through a self-fulfilling prophecy, they escape death and enter eternity. Pascale and Alejandro arrange for their anxieties to burst so they can live in the present moment. As in the case of alchemy, the magnum opus cannot

21. Alejandro Jodorowsky during the author's interview with Pascale Montandon-Jodorowsky and Alejandro Jodorowsky, Paris, 15 September 2016.

22. Ibid.

23. Pierre Fédid repudiates autocratism (the claim of being able to heal oneself alone) on these grounds in "Discussion," in *L'Art médecine: actes du colloque*, musée Picasso, Antibes, 24-25 September 1999, RMN, Paris, 2000, p. 61.

24. On the role of his experiences in Mexico, he says: "I didn't know where I was headed, but I wanted to do it as an artist, according to my own conception of art. I've always accepted the right side of my brain, the intuitive side, as long as it works in a coordinated way with the left side, the rational. In the beginning, I worked on abstract art, the art of Ionesco, of Beckett, with this kind of intellectuality. Then I started to study the shamans, the healers. With them, I learned many things that I later applied to art: that's how I created psychomagic, from my experiences of happenings, of the ephemeral, of the theatre that I staged in Mexico," in "Yo no creo en la revolución política, creo en la re-evolución poetica / Not revolution, but poetic re-evolution", *op. cit.*, pp. 240-241.

take place without the encounter of true love. Thus, the work of art as active creation stakes a therapeutic claim, as the work of art "acts in order to reach the very being of the spectator, even to the point of fundamentally transforming him or her from within."[25] Moreover, if one attends to the parallels between shamanism and psychoanalysis suggested by Claude Lévi-Strauss in his reflections on the efficacy of certain magical practices, one finds a system in which the patient's experiences are of little importance, with "the essential relation being that between the shaman and the group."[26] Thus, "the efficacy of magic is inextricable from the belief in magic," which presupposes unanimity since "the magical situation is a consensual phenomenon."[27]

Where art and spirituality meet, pascALEjandro's works lead the spectator on an inner quest in which going beyond oneself is generally expected. These works are genuine acts of love. According to Alejandro, an artist should be at the service of his work like a lover at the service of his mistress. This inner blossoming can only happen if one's desire is turned toward another person, physical and mental energy being one and the same. Desire is empty when it confines itself to an external projection or a need to be wanted. Pascale and Alejandro banish the ego in order to be receptive to their unconscious, to those chance occurrences in life which Jung termed "synchronicities" but which they prefer to call "psychomiracles."[28] Their drawings immerse the spectator in a colorful dream world, where volcanic lava, symbolic of inner energy, summons an in-depth transformation of the self. Pascale and Alejandro engage in mutual introspection, even though, according to their principles, the true meaning of love necessarily comes through personal accomplishment. Indeed, their sexual and

25.Maurice Fréchuret, Thierry Davila, "Introduction," in *L'Art médecine: actes du colloque*, *op. cit.*, pp. 8-11, p. 9.
26.Claude Lévi-Strauss, *Anthropologie structurale*, Plon, Paris, 1958 (éd. 2003), p. 208.
27.Ibid., p. 193.
28.Quoted in Erik Pigani, "Alejandro Jodorowski: guérir, c'est être soi," *Psychologies*, January 2012, http://www.psychologies.com.

artistic symbiosis does not keep them from working individually: "When I was making my film *La Danza de la realidad*, I invited Pascale to accompany me. I started giving her sketches, and in the end she transformed the whole style of my film! She enriched it. She designed all the costumes; we worked on the colors together . . . She influenced me. In a collaboration, you influence each other's individual work. It's possible."[29] When Pascale contributes to a film, she places her creativity at the service of Alejandro's vision of the world. For *Poesia sin fin* (2016), she also conceived and designed the costumes, while pascALEjandro handled the colors: "It even became a second mise-en-scène for Alejandro because there's no limit to what you can do during the color grading, you can work on the color, the details, the lighting, like a painter's palette in fact. The image was completely altered."[30]

pascALEjandro's works stand as a manifesto. The two artists share a single imaginative space and a similar conception of artistic creation. Working together is a salutary exercise in which each of them holds a clearly defined role, without which this vital experience would lose its meaning.[31] Their bond is fundamental, though each of them holds back to highlight this new—surreal—entity. It stretches from the mythological to the cosmic, from the absurd to the tragic, with humor and psychomagic in between. Sacred since the beginning, their work is a strange and marvelous world in which mysticism and symbolism meet.

29. Quoted in Alexandra Profizi, "Entretien croisé avec Alejandro Jodorowsky et Pascale Montandon-Jodorowsky," *La Règle du jeu*, 10 June 2014, http://laregledujeu.org.
30. Pascale Montandon-Jodorowsky during the author's interview with Pascale Montandon-Jodorowsky and Alejandro Jodorowsky, Paris, 15 September 2016.
31. Alejandro is behind the drawings, a fundamental role which recalls a remark by the artist Lygia Clark, who stresses that therapists lose their function as such if they lose the perceptive imagination of their own dreams. Quoted in Pierre Fédida, *op. cit.*, p. 57.

# The Dance of the Sublime

**Donatien Grau**

In the treatise traditionally attributed to Longinus which would come to establish modern Western aesthetics, the sublime is defined as "loftiness and excellence in language." In his great foundational texts of American modernism, which would come to govern the interpretation of the works of Pollock and Rothko, Barnett Newman shows the immediate and radical power of a transcendental, sublime abstraction. Pascale Montandon-Jodorowsky and Alejandro Jodorowsky, in their individual works, have never ceased to confront the challenge implicit in these two definitions of the sublime: she tending more toward Newman's vision, and he toward that of Pseudo-Longinus.

Alejandro Jodorowsky's work confronts the sublime in three ways: by the dissemination of words, from tales to commentary, to philosophical writing, to theatre, to poetry which is the key to all; by the dissemination of images, whether moving on film, moving in fact, or fixed in drawings; and, above all, by the incessant combination of both, of words and images, images and words—and here we find his strong affinity for composite forms: graphic novels, films, calligrams, and tweets. We recognize in this approach a Pseudo-Longinian conception of the sublime: if there is loftiness and excellence here—and there most certainly is—it resides in the multiplicity of discourses, in a discursive order that wholly embraces the fact of not being unitary but rather of flowing into a great many channels from a single human source, to which it returns at last.

Pascale Montandon-Jodorowsky is also an artist of the sublime, heir to the Newmanian conception—that of the abstract expressionists and their motto, "Sublime is now"—according to which an abstraction, as a transcription of the inner strength of a human being, reveals his or her metaphysical grandeur. Playing with the application of pigment, imperceptible hues at first, then bright colors, she permanently creates a kind of ethereal music at once imperceptible to impure ears and marvelous to those who grasp its ineffable harmony. Her work is, in the strongest sense of the word, atmospheric. It gives rise to a connection between the mere placement of colors on canvas and the entire cosmos (the two meet in her work). This creates a simultaneously peaceful and alert sensation of the cosmological reality of our lives: a transcendental and therefore terrifying reality which exists beyond us and tips our lives into a metaphysical elsewhere as soon as we become aware of it.

**The Birth of pascALEjandro**

These two visions of the sublime unite in pascALEjandro, a creation which harbors both Newmanian abstraction and Pseudo-Longinian narrative even as it transcends them. For what is truly at issue here is also the age-old tension between the philosophically oriented story—syntagmatic narrative—and the extraordinary force of the paradigmatic miracle-moment: the syntagm and the paradigm; the tale and the poem, a pair which modernity, in all its savage power of negation, has first and foremost tried to separate. pascALEjandro isn't simply a collaborative enterprise: it is a metaphysical, personal, redemptive, and artistic—which is to say micro-political—response to the separation of the two sublimes, to the disconnection of our lives, to our existence.

One need hardly say more of pascALEjandro's origin, except perhaps to note that it is an act of love—that it is the creative actualization of the marriage of two beings, Pascale Montandon-Jodorowsky and Alejandro Jodorowsky. And it is significant that a creation with such exquisitely high artistic and human stakes began as a private endeavor between two beings who love each other, who wanted to make something with each other that would remain, beyond themselves, beyond their lives and yet at the heart of each.

And this creation bears a name of its own, which is not simply the cohabitation of two presences in a single finished object—not a mere achievement—but rather an achievement that holds a new beginning. pascALEjandro begins where Pascale and Alejandro leave off. The name is telling: it isn't pascALEALEjandro, which is to say one name added to another, but rather a new name entirely, which is to say a new entity created through the act of naming—an act in which a piece of the original names seems to have been lost (we don't know whose) and the two names and two souls, as in an act of infinite love, have come to overlap with each other, to exist in a new form. This other person doesn't exist in the world of passports, apart from its name. And yet this very name emphatically establishes its existence, with a commanding necessity many a person with a passport could only dream of. Pascale Montandon-Jodorowsky, in marrying Alejandro Jodorowsky, added her name, Montandon—in accordance with the civil norms of society—to that of Jodorowsky: she is at once herself and joined to him. But pascALEjandro bears the name neither of Montandon, nor of Jodorowsky, nor even of Montandon-Jodorowsky. This creation belongs to another order of reality, metaphysical, poetic. It comes from the extraordinary laboratory of private life: pascALEjandro issues from the fusion of two first names, the private parts of two individuals now united. This takes place outside of social conventions and yet also at their core: it is the duty of parents to name their child; this one happens to be born of the miraculous fusion of two beings united by themselves alone.

pascALEjandro is born of both of them, of their acts, of their lives, but also and principally of that other life which we could characterize as deeper since it reaches higher: their art, which is to say their true life, their shared intimacy—art in life, life as art. Certainly, one can interpret the choice of line as the masculine element—Alejandro—and the choice of colors as the more expansive element, and therefore feminine: Pascale. But to stop there wouldn't be enough. Alejandro's line is narrative: it establishes the motif, the work's apparent "subject"—one recognizes this as the element of a personal narrative, a narrative of civilization, which here finds voice.

**The Mystical Portrait**

One finds a synecdoche of pascALEjandro's creative process in a metaphorical portrait of the two lovers—naked side by side, upright in the perfection of their eternal childhood, with their ages hinted at and yet effaced by the vision brought to bear on them by the artists themselves, by the lines and the color: the bodies are without blemish, perfectly smooth, as if fixed at a single moment for all eternity. Of course, this metaphorical portrait is also a mystical portrait and a symbol.

Let us consider the decisions at work here: Alejandro himself has chosen to depict himself and Pascale thus in the drawing. He's the one who has drawn her pregnant with the child they will never have, but which is also precisely this body of work of which this image is a manifestation. Pascale has slipped one of her hands around Alejandro's waist and the other holds her pregnant belly, filled with this child who, biologically, will never be born and yet metaphysically will forever keep this perfection of high childhood: their age will never vary on this image; the child will always be about to be born and will always be perfectly realized in the fact that he is about to be born. Pascale wears only a necklace, a pearl necklace, as if the materials to clothe her could only be precious, could only be ornament: as if this ornament had come to tell us something about her nature, this ornament whose constituent parts—its pearls—are often perfect, but can also be baroque, which is to say naturally irregular, endowed with another kind of perfection, sublime in the eyes of those who understand the irregular truth of things. Alejandro, for his part, wears a shirt, wide open, and he holds his arms open wide for Pascale in a gesture of offering himself and welcoming her into his world. This shirt, as simple as can be, is like a remnant of the traveler he has been for more than sixty years and who has finally arrived at the house he was longing for and which was, no doubt, longing for him too; a gesture of relief, of enthusiasm, of entering into a new existence—the metaphysical child whose birth awaits. Both of them, in their ornamented nudity of two very different kinds—pearl; shirt—become in this work a synecdoche of love, standing on this ground whose substance is obscure: given its round surface, we might ask ourselves if it isn't the earth seen from above; and if this is the earth, then these are two giants, of superhuman size, or at least deliberately magnified, since what they are about to accomplish is like a enlarged model in the eyes of humanity.

Pascale's choices in the creative process are just as essential: she has decided that, in contrast to the other drawings, the skin tone of each of them here will be close to its natural shade; she has transformed the background into one of those cosmological spaces only she knows how to make, which she herself developed in her atmospheric works: these are the background to her world, which is to say a cosmological and atmospheric conception of existence—we stand on earth in a relationship with all things, with the stars, and each thing that exists around us is as important to the development of our sensibility as other human beings are: each thing comes to form the background of the shared world of human beings, and therefore of our own. The ground is green, which might seem an undoing of the tangible facts of this world—ground, green?—thereby tending towards a metaphorical transfiguration of this personal image, a kind of slipping into dream; or it might rather constitute a clear view of the essence of things: the ground, no doubt about it, and grass, in this world of which we have lost sight in cities, is green as can be. In the image, both Pascale and Alejandro have their heads encircled by a single golden halo, with red between their faces. We might interpret these colors as the gold of holiness, of going beyond existence, and the red of passion. The same red rests in a kind of halo around the earth itself, as if to suggest a continuity between the love of these two beings and the love for the Earth and for our world as a whole. These decisions are not only iconographic: they are artistic; they are experienced at the heart of the two artists themselves.

**The Human Species**

pascALEjandro is, of course, a biographical experience, the result of a love story between two passionate individuals—a creation story. Their personal situation is relevant to this body of work in so far as their work opens itself to the world and creates a space for everyone to come and get their bearings, to gather their thoughts and replenish their being. To understand this artistic and human work requires an act of synthesis: the very particularity of these creative individualities is what allows us to envision a new universality—to connect with the totality of men and women and thereby recapture that higher humanity buried beneath our boot-soles or drifting above our heads.

The motifs used by Alejandro Jodorowsky are diverse: all of them belong to the vocabulary of civilizations—of these manifold civilizations which he has embraced for decades, Chinese, Latin American, European. One finds traces of narratives here, especially from European folklore: in an image of a widow, an old man, deceased, has sprouted wings in accordance with Christian folk traditions; a dance on a tiger revisits an Asian custom, which indeed consists in dancing on a tiger; wrestling with the angel presents a Biblical iconographic motif. The revenge of the beast inevitably recalls Western medieval iconography. The Duke of

Marmelade is the name of one of Aimé Césaire's characters. Not to mention a whole stock of common folktale characters who arrive and pay their respects to the viewer before sulking back to their world of dreams. Together, these motifs compose a portrait of universality: a world with the human species at its center, structuring the whole—not a single drawing lacks a human figure appearing one way or another—but also a world in which the human species is permanently summoned to action, called into question, displaced, to keep it from being reduced to that rigidity which utterly destroys the transformative material of humanity: one might recall here Giordano Bruno, who placed the human hand halfway between an animal paw and the spiritual hand of god. In pascALEjandro's secular world, humanity appears as such, but constantly awaits redefinition: be it a pair of mystical lovers, all in gold, prey to djinns doing their best to devour them and incapable of recognizing the purity of creation which keeps them at bay and thwarts their evil ends; or be it a person pierced through with letters. At the uttermost limits, one finds hybrid forms: an anthropomorphic plant. For these works are based on the presupposition of a necessary transformation—still to come, but already prefigured in the space of these artworks—of all that we are as humans. The work *Poetic Re-evolution* seems to signal this process: a crowd of people at once bears aloft and lynches a rooster pierced through the heart—a rooster, symbol of morning, of awakening, of the new world, an image of this "poetic re-evolution" which is pascALEjandro's mission.

It is in view of this "poetic re-evolution" that pascALEjandro's colors acquire their full significance: they are the first step to derealizing the image, to launching it fully into the space of poetry, which is not our world as such, but acts as its symbol and vice versa: for there is always the paradoxical and yet nevertheless very strong sensation that this is a real world as well, a real purchase on our world, that these allegorical images, of mythic proportions, have much to reveal about our own existence in its current state. Let the colors be vibrant; let yellow and red confer with turquoise and azure; pascALEjandro isn't afraid of colors, nor of intensity—nor of letting the iconography itself be vibrant and powerful, so that it touches us to the quick. The satire contained in *Joined at the Tie* is overacted, transfigured into myth by the red face and violet hair: the color reveals to what extent this is not a subject but a motif—to what extent this dream image functions primarily as a means of plunging us into human introspection. These colors have a symbolic system all their own, just as each figure constitutes a portion of a symbol. Above all, the colors are arranged in a kind of visual dance, of meetings and partings, obvious facts and paradoxes, in which all of our senses are marshaled to create a synaesthetic experience of total intensity. These associations of color set our perception spinning, so we become conscious of it again as such: faced with these colors, we feel ourselves perceiving. Nothing is simply given. Horizons of meaning open, but also, alongside these meanings, all the imperceptible elements of our own perception.

**Reading and Creating: Of Men and Letters**

Letters have a strong presence in pascALEjandro's drawings: they form words and also stand as forms in themselves—abstract calligrams. *BASTA!* depicts this word issuing from a mouth with an exclamation mark. The letters stand all in red, and their outward expansion dramatizes the word's intensity, in opposition to the density of the face, almost Brutalist in structure. *YO* pierces the heart of an individual who seems to carry it both as a burden and wound. The letters are in red, as is also the case in *PATRIA*. In *NADA*, however, the letters, all in blue, seem to fall from the eyes of a face. *ILUSIóN* is grafted onto a woman's body, with a malignant visage gazing down on it from the clouds. In each instance, the image dramatizes a concept, and in each instance this takes place in a situation that surpasses common orders of representation: the power of the imagination—hand in hand with the great vigor of the allegories and metaphors each work presents—makes you think. Each of these works offers a piece of life advice to those spectators ready to receive it: the beauty of sexualized femininity can indeed be an illusion, flashed to lost bodies by a universal malignity which toys with each alike. "Nothing" is a corollary of our incapacity to see: we see nothing, because we don't see at all. Each of these works creates an image that invites the spectator to avoid a trap of contemporary existence.

pascALEjandro's dynamization of humanity reveals the supreme duality of creation, pitched between philology and divine agency. Philology constitutes our capacity to read the world, to understand its motions, its possibilities, its inflections, to resist its seductions in order better to grasp its terrifying simplicity and fascinating complexity—or the inverse. Philology is a discipline, whereas divine agency begets an act: the creation of the world. On the one hand, we find an excessive modesty, that of the reader plunging into the text of books—of beings and things—until, understanding the impossibility of his aims, he attempts to plumb the depths of hearts and monuments. On the other hand, we find a divine madness—to create a world as God once did—nevertheless touched with a paradoxical levity: to create a world, by the act of a human mind whose limits are unknown. These two penchants of the creative human soul find themselves reunited and reassembled in pascALEjandro—and it would be impossible to ascribe one or the other to Pascale or to Alejandro alone. pascALEjandro bodies forth the shared community of these two beings: Pascale reads the life of forms; Alejandro discovers the essences of existence.

### Like a Child

pascALEjandro's ultimate invitation is to rediscover the child inside of us, the child that we still are, like the initial point of the only archeology fully able to establish us. The world that these drawings present is filled with children and the creatures of childhood. We find the soldiers we used to play with as boys, the dolls that amused us as girls, the fears of all children, the parents who sometimes seemed too tall, distant, who could scare us; the world of our clowns and chimeras, this marvelous world where nothing is set in stone, where everything is in motion, where everything is possible; this world which could be ours, ours as adults, today, now, if we were mad enough or wise enough or terrified enough to go back to it, dive into it, discover ourselves there just as we were, and so see ourselves as we are, without fear, without pity, without sympathy for ourselves, and thus we could become not merely adults separated from childhood—a bleak ideology—but true beings graced with eternal life, who will die someday no doubt, but whose life will have been lived in the sublime conception of eternal childhood and certain immortality: which is to say in the awareness that we have grown up and that we will soon, on the scale of human time or indeed of any time, die.

And finally, through this work we rediscover the taste of the colors of childhood: these colors like candy which often made us discover for the very first time these tastes which are also a metaphysics—sweet, sour—and which made us understand that things are less cut and dry than we might have thought in our earliest days: that sour can be pleasant; that sweetness can also be unpleasant; that we have to mix and combine, in order to live better. The colors of childhood thoroughly understood, rethought, experienced fully, by their honesty, by their presence, invite us to get back in touch with this child that we still are, and to be ourselves, and be well. The mission of these drawings coincides with that of pascALEjandro: it is metaphysical, psychological—anagogical. pascALEjandro, this child unborn in the flesh but so present in spirit by the power of creation, has been given to us so that we can live better, so that we, who were born as children, can know that we are children still, and live that way.

These drawings, with their more than artistic—which is to say, fully artistic—mission, accomplish the synthetic union of the two sublimes, that of Pseudo-Longinus and that of Newman. They provoke the astonishment of abstraction and the fascination of the great narratives whose meaning comes word by word and makes us think. They are at once works of great simplicity—of line and color—and of great complexity: their framework is human, biographical, universal and artistic; it combines life, performance, tales and films—one drawing served as the poster of *La Danza de la realidad*—and why not also graphic novels, costume design and abstract painting. This is the complete fulfillment of the complete union of Pascale Montandon-Jodorowsky and Alejandro Jodorowsky—and a complete fulfillment of our own lives, of the potentialities of our lives, if we are ready, at last, to think, to feel, and to love, which are all the same; and therefore to exist.

# Our Encounter

### pascALEjandro

pascALEjandro is not an esthetic creation, but something given. This miracle we call chance united us during a Tarot reading. Alejandro read it, Pascale consulted it. The first moment our eyes met was enough for us to be united until death, and beyond, if that is at all possible. Each of us bore in our respective names pascALE and ALEjandro. The alchemical androgynous being, sought after for so long, was created in a fashion in which our own will did not intervene, but divine will: the harmonious union of the best of the feminine and the best of the masculine. Effortless, natural, just, balances, non-competitive union, full of love. From left to right we encounter the Hebraic syllable AL, which signifies « powerful, supreme ». From right to left, we encounter the Hebraic syllable EL, which also signifies "powerful, supreme". But ALE unites those two syllables, as if it were the union of two divine principles. And EL in plural is ELOHIM, GODS. Which, usually, instead of the plural GODS, is translated as a singular, GOD. ALE is therefore the union of two gods which form an androgynous being, the ideal as much of alchemy as of the Taoist doctrine with its Yin and its Yang.

## The Authors

Adonis is a poet. His recent publications include: *Sufism and Surrealism* (Saqi, 2016) and *Selected Poems* (Columbia University Press, 2012)." pour Philippe Rouyer, it should say "an editor of the magazine", plutôt que "editor in chief of the magazine.

Klaus Biesenbach is Director of MOMA PS1 and Chief Curator at Large at The Museum of Modern Art, New York. He was the founding director of the Kunste-Werke Berlin and of The Berlin Biennale.

Diego Moldes (Pontevedra, 1977) is a writer, professor, and historian of film. He has written and co-written a total of twenty-eight books, including Alejandro Jodorowsky (Cátedra, Madrid, 2012), based on his doctoral dissertation La imaginación simbólica en la obra cinematográfica de Alejandro Jodorowsky (2010), which was directed by José Luis Sánchez Noriega, and was awarded summa cum laude by an examining committee chaired by Darío Villanueva (director of the Real Academia Española – RAE). Since 2006 he has been a close friend of Jodorowsky. Moldes presented Jodorowsky's complete poetry, Poesía sin fin (Huacanamo, Barcelona, 2009), and organized the first complete series of all of Jodorowsky's films at the Filmoteca Española (2011), which they presented together at the Cine Doré with a screening of The Holy Mountain. In 2014 they presented La Danza de la Realidad in Spain at the Palafox cinema in Madrid, and held a lively discussion after the screening. Moldes has interviewed Alejandro a number of times; his Jodorowsky: A Retrospective Interview, conducted in November 2013, is considered one of the most comprehensive, and has been viewed over 158,000 times on Youtube.

Edgar Morin is a philosopher. Amongst his publications: *On Complexity* (Hampton Press, 2008); *The Stars* (University of Minnesota Press, 2005); *Homeland Earth: A Manifesto for the New Millenium* (1999).

Hans Ulrich Obrist is Artistic Director of the Serpentine Galleries, London. He is the author of *Ways of Curating* (Allen Lane, 2014).

María Inés Rodriguez has been Director of the CAPC—the Centre of Contemporary Visual Arts, Bordeaux—since February 2014. Previously, she was Chief Curator at the Museo universitario Arte contemporáneo (MUAC), Mexico City, and at the Museo de Arte contemporáneo de Castilla y Léon (MUSAC).

Philippe Rouyer is a film critic and film historian. Editor in Chief of the magazine *Positif* since 1985, he helms the cinema pages of the magazine *Psychologies*. A regular contributor to the programs *Mauvais Genres* (France-Culture) and *Le Cercle* (Canal+ Cinéma), he has also authored books and DVD extras.

Diana Widmaier Picasso is an art historian and expert on Picasso's sculptures. She co-curated, with John Richardson, *Picasso and Marie-Thérèse: L'amour fou* (Gagosian, New York, 2011) and, with Didier Ottinger and Émilie Bouvard, *Picassomania* (Grand Palais, Paris, 2015). She is the author of the book *Picasso: Art Can Only Be Erotic* (Prestel, 2005) and of numerous essays on Picasso, as well as on Bob Dylan's drawings, Michel Houellebecq, and Rodin.

Olivier Zahm is Editor in Chief of *Purple Fashion Magazine*. He has curated numerous exhibitions, including *L'Hiver de l'amour* (arc, Musée d'Art moderne de la Ville de Paris, 1994) and *Elysian Fields* (Musée national d'Art moderne – Centre Georges-Pompidou, 2000). He is the author of *Une avant-garde sans avant-garde* (Presses du réel, 2017).

P. 40-53: film by Alejandro Jodorowsky; photographs by Pascale Montandon-Jodorowsky
P. 82-125: works by pascALEjandro; photographs by Dennis Bouchard
P. 126-241: works by pascALEjandro; photography by Pascale Montandon-Jodorowsky

Contributions by Azzedine Alaïa, Edgar Morin, Adonis, Olivier Zahm, Diana Widmaier Picasso, Philippe Rouyer and Donatien Grau, as well as the conversations with pascALEjandro by Klaus Biesenbach and Hans Ulrich Obrist were translated from the French by Peter Behrman de Sinéty; Diego Moldes' contribution was translated from Spanish by Charlotte Whittle; María Inés Rodriguez's contribution was translated from Spanish by Heather Cleary; and pascALEjandro's contribution was translated from the French by Donatien Grau.

Graphic design : Actes Sud
Proof-reading : Peter Behrman de Sinéty
Fabrication : Karima Chabaud
Photogravure : Terre Neuve

The book was printed in March 2017 at the printer Printer Portuguesa for the éditions Actes Sud, Le Méjan, place Nina-Berberova, 13200 Arles.

1st edition : April 2017
(Printed in Portugal)